Melanie Goergmaier

The Transatlantic Agreement

Challenges and Opportunities for Economy, Health Care and Society

Nomos

Co-funded by the
Erasmus+ Programme
of the European Union

The Deutsche Nationalbibliothek lists this publication in the Deutsche Nationalbibliografie; detailed bibliographic data are available on the Internet at http://dnb.d-nb.de

a.t.: Miami, Univ., Diss., 2020
Original title: "Trade between the European Union and the United States: Transatlantic Opportunities for Business, Economy and Public Health Policy"

ISBN 978-3-7560-1347-0 (Print)
978-3-7489-1876-9 (ePDF)

British Library Cataloguing-in-Publication Data
A catalogue record for this book is available from the British Library.

ISBN 978-3-7560-1347-0 (Print)
978-3-7489-1876-9 (ePDF)

Library of Congress Cataloging-in-Publication Data
Goergmaier, Melanie
The Transatlantic Agreement
Challenges and Opportunities for Economy, Health Care and Society
Melanie Goergmaier
329 pp.
Includes bibliographic references.

ISBN 978-3-7560-1347-0 (Print)
978-3-7489-1876-9 (ePDF)

Online Version
Nomos eLibrary

1st Edition 2024

Abstract

While some believe and argue that TTIP is "dead", this book demonstrates why much of the TTIP negotiation content is more relevant today than ever before in connection with the ongoing EU-US trade negotiations that have been picking up new speed. From the Transatlantic Trade and Investment Partnership (TTIP) to the Trump administration trade war, this book examines the transatlantic trade relationship between the European Union and the United States as well as the policy impact on both sides of the Atlantic. This book also provides policy recommendations for both sides on how to move forward based on the analysis. A future outlook for trade in the 21st century is provided drawing on trade history between the two entities over the years up until the current 2023 trends. Case studies examining the automotive industry as well as the pharmaceutical sector demonstrate opportunities for business in the transatlantic economy. Overall, (public) health policy as well as environmental challenges including climate and energy policy must be tackled together on both sides of the Atlantic in order to also solve trade obstacles regarding pharmaceutical and medical equipment markets supply chain issues.

Dedication

To my family who has always been supportive of higher education and studying abroad. Instead of holding me back, my parents and my brother have always encouraged me to set goals, go after them, achieve them, and finish whatever I started. Growing up in the European Union has also taught me how to be a natural leader in the world every day in every situation: to always speak up, stand up for what is right and overcome every obstacle. Studying, working and teaching in the United States has allowed me to open up my horizon and always look at, learn and understand the other side of the story.

Acknowledgement

Thank you to all my dissertation committee members for their constant patience, support and guidance. This book would not have been possible without them. Professor Joaquin Roy, Jean Monnet Chair and Director of the European Union Center at the University of Miami in Florida has provided outstanding guidance and support as my dissertation Committee Chair. In addition, he has introduced me to the Jean Monnet Network, the European Union Delegations and to the European Union Studies Association conferences, which have all equally allowed me to network, learn and grow further in regard to teaching and research; Thank you to Professor Ambler Moss, Department of International Studies at University of Miami and former US Ambassador, for his patience, support and guidance. His positive outlook was very refreshing and has always inspired me over the years. Professor Dauer, Department of Biomedical Engineering at University of Miami, has provided valuable expertise regarding medical devices, pharmaceuticals, biomedical engineering and (global) public health issues for specific chapters. Francisco Acosta Soto, EU Fellow in Residence at the University of Miami 2016-2017, has provided hands-on expertise as an EU official from the European Union External Action Service and as a current European Union Deputy Ambassador for the EU Delegation.

In addition, I am grateful for the help and guidance of Peter Vavrik, EU Fellow in Residence at the University of Miami 2015-2016, European Parliament.

I would also like to thank all professors at the University of Miami who helped me along the way, particularly within the Department of International Studies. Thank you to Professor Richard Weisskoff for fostering interdisciplinary approaches to learning and for being supportive during my Ph.D.

Thank you to Dr. Douglas Fuller, Senior Associate Dean for Faculty Affairs and College Diversity, for awarding me the scholarship funding for my research. I also want to thank Dean Guillermo "Willy" Prado, Dean of the Graduate School at University of Miami for his invaluable advice and support throughout my graduate studies.

This research project would also have not been possible without the support of my colleagues: Dr. Hanna Kassab, Dr. Beverly Barrett, Dr.

Maxime Larive, Dr. Markus Thiel, Dr. Dina Moulioukova, Dr. Maria Lorca-Susino, Dr. Johann Besserer, Dr. Samantha Chaitram, and Dr. Natalie Ghosn. Thank you for making me feel welcome from the beginning at University of Miami and for encouraging and inspiring me throughout the Ph.D. program academically.

Preface

My first exposure to the European Union's exchange programs was in 1997, when my German high school sent me on a student exchange program to Lycée Marie Curie in Grenoble, France. One year later, I was able to participate in the Euroscola Program at the European Parliament in Strasbourg on December 6, 1998. After these experiences, I ended up participating in numerous additional exchange programs and study abroad experiences all over the world in Australia (Carey Baptist Grammar School), Jamaica (Hofstra University), Costa Rica (Centro PanAmericano de Idiomas), Chile (Elon University), Argentina (Elon University), Spain (University of Barcelona) and the United States (Catawba College and University of Miami). Working, teaching and researching in higher education has in turn led to this book project enabling me not only to teach but also conduct research both in the European Union as well as in the United States. This included conducting interviews and attending numerous conferences as well as events about TTIP and transatlantic trade in the US and in the EU from 2014 to present.

Table of Contents

List of Figures

List of Abbreviations

AEC	ASEAN Economic Community
AFTA	ASEAN Free Trade Area
AHK	Aussenhandelskammer (German Chambers of Commerce Abroad)
APTA	Automotive Products Trade Agreement
ASEAN	Association of Southeast Asian Nations
BDI	Bundesverband der Deutschen Industrie e.V. (Federation of German Industries)
BMWi	Bundesministerium für Wirtschaft und Energie (German Federal Ministry for Economic Affairs and Energy)
BPI	Bundesverband der Pharmazeutischen Industrie e.V.
BRICS	Brazil, Russia, India, China, South Africa (major emerging national economies)
CCCTB	Common Consolidated Corporate Tax Base
CEPR	Center of Economic Policy Research
CETA	Comprehensive Economic and Trade Agreement (between Canada and the European Union)
CGE	Computable General Equilibrium
CO2	Carbon Dioxide (chemical formula CO2)
CUSFTA	Canadian-United States Free Trade Agreement
DIHK	Association of German Chambers of Commerce and Industry (Deutsche Industrie- und Handelskammer)
EC	European Community
ECB	European Central Bank
ECSC	European Coal and Steel Community
EEC	European Economic Community
EMA	European Medicines Agency
EMU	Economic and Monetary Union of the European Union
ERDF	European Regional Development Fund
ESDP	European Security and Defense Policy
EU	European Union
EUR	Euro (currency)
Europol	European Union Agency for Law Enforcement Cooperation

FBI	Federal Bureau of Investigation (USA)
FDA	Food and Drug Administration (USA)
FDI	Foreign Direct Investment
FRONTEX	European Agency for the Management of Operational Cooperation at the External Borders of the Member States of the European Union
FTA	Free Trade Agreement
g	Gram
GATT	General Agreement on Trade and Tariffs
GDP	Gross Domestic Product
GMO	Genetically Modified Organism
GMP	Good Manufacturing Practice
HWLG	High Level Working Group on Jobs and Growth
ICSID	International Center for Settlement of Investment Dispute
IFO	Leibniz Institute for Economic Research at University of Munich, Germany
ILO	International Labor Organization
IMF	International Monetary Fund
IMK	Institut fuer Makrooekonomie und Konjunkturforschung (Macroeconomic Policy Institute)
IPE	International Political Economy
IPR	Intellectual Property Rights
IR	International Relations (theory)
ISDS	Investor-State Dispute Settlement
ISIS	Islamic State of Iraq and Syria
ISO	International Organization for Standardization
IT	Information Technology
ITO	International Trade Organization
JEFTA	Japan-European Free Trade Agreement
JHA	Justice and Home Affairs
KFZ	Kraftfahrzeug (common German abbreviation for motor vehicle)
MERCOSUR	Mercado Común del Sur (South Americas)
MFN	Most Favored Nation clause
MNC	Multi National Corporation
NAFTA	North American Free Trade Agreement
NATO	North Atlantic Treaty Organization
NGO	Non-Governmental Organization
NSA	National Security Agency (USA)

OECD TAD	Organization for Economic Co-operation and Development Trade and Agriculture Directorate
OEM	Original Equipment Manufacturer
OTC	Over the counter (drugs)
PTAs	Preferential Trade Agreements
PWC	Price Waterhouse Coopers (Corporation)
R&D	Research and Development
RCB	Regulatory Cooperation Body
RTA	Regional Trade Agreement
SME	Small and Medium-Size Enterprise
SWOT	Strengths, Weaknesses, Opportunities, Threats model
TAFTA	Trans-Atlantic Free Trade Area
TEP	Transatlantic Economic Partnership
TFEU	Treaty on the Functioning of the European Union
TIFA	Trade and Investment Framework Agreement
TNC	Trans-National Corporation
TOT	Terms of Trade
TPP	Trans-Pacific Partnership
TRIPS	Agreement on Trade Related Aspects of Intellectual Property Rights
TTIP	Transatlantic Trade and Investment Partnership
UN	United Nations
UNICE	Union of Industrial and Employers' Confederations of Europe
UNCTAD	United Nations Conference on Trade and Development
UNECE	United Nations Economic Commission for Europe
URL	Uniform Resource Locator
US(A)	United States (of America)
USCMA	United States-Mexico-Canada Agreement
USTR	United States Trade Representative
VDA	Verband der Automobilindustrie (German Association of the Automotive Industry)
WHO	World Health Organization
WMD	Weapon of Mass Destruction
WTO	World Trade Organization
WWI	World War I
WWII	World War II

Chapter 1: Introduction

1.1 Introductory Remarks and Statement of the Research Problem

After the disasters of two world wars, the main priority for Europe in the 20th century was the creation of an area of freedom, security, peace, and human rights. The general integration intention was to create an economic and political union, a free trade area, a customs union, as well as a common market including the free movement of goods, services, capital and people. Consequently, the original European Economic Community, cemented on the base of the European Coal and Steel Community, developed into the European Union (EU). The Maastricht Treaty enacted in 1993 led to the official creation of the European Union and Economic Policy Integration.

It is essential to understand the institutions of the European Union when looking at the recent events of the latest world financial crisis. Due to globalization, new economic great powers are developing in Asia and Latin America creating a potential risk of displacement of the United States and Europe in the global competition. Given this shift of global power, what role will the United States and the European Union play in facilitating cooperation in this new global environment? A Transatlantic Trade and Investment Partnership (TTIP) between the U.S. and the EU would create new opportunities for both sides of the Atlantic Ocean. This book assesses the reasons for TTIP's failure and provides recommendations as well as solutions for moving forward with Transatlantic trade negotiations.

1.2 Background of Trade Relations between the U.S. and the EU

High-level working group analysts from both the European Commission as well as from the White House have contended that the proposed Transatlantic Trade and Investment Partnership would contribute significantly to the economic competitiveness for both the United States as well as the European Union. The United States and the European Union "account for nearly half of the world GDP and 30 percent of world trade"[1]. However, some social scientists and policy analysts such as De Ville and Siles-Bruegge argue that the asymmetrical benefits would produce major distributive consequences, creating winners and losers[2]. In addition, many Europeans are afraid of TTIP, due to hormone-treated meat and genetically manipulated food from the United States supposedly threatening European Union consumer and data protection laws, eroding workers' rights, contributing to raising health care costs, etc. Therefore, this book seeks to examine whether these fears are actually fact or fiction. In addition, this book seeks to point out the important role the US and the EU play in facilitating cooperation in this new global environment of power shifting. Furthermore, this book will point out the opportunities a transatlantic agreement would present by focusing on facts and data-based examples such as pharmaceuticals and the automobile industry. Finally, the potential consequences and impact of a US-EU trade agreement will be discussed including the negative impacts for the US and the EU of such a deal not being implemented.

1.2.1 Advantages and Need for an FTA between the U.S. and the EU

In June 2013, President Obama as well as European Commission President Barroso and European Council President Van Rompuy announced that mutual trade negotiations would commence the following month[3]. TTIP negotiations between the European Union and the United States did in fact begin in Washington, D.C., on July 8, 2013, with an assessment of current trade relations[4]. Karel De Gucht, EU Commissioner for Trade, and

---

1 Office of the United States Trade Representative. *Final Report: High Level Working Group on Jobs and Growth.* Executive Office of the President. February 11, 2013. https://ustr.gov/sites/default/files/02132013%20FINAL%20HLWG%20REPORT.pdf

2 De Ville, Ferdi and Gabriel Siles-Bruegge. *TTIP: The Truth about the Transatlantic Trade and Investment Partnership.* Cambridge/ Malden, MA: Polity Press, 2016, page 2.

3 Office of the United States Trade Representative. "White House Fact Sheet: Transatlantic Trade and Investment Partnership (T-TIP)". *Executive Office of the President,* June 2013. https://ustr.gov/about-us/policy-offices/press-office/fact-sheets/2013/june/wh-ttip

4 Office of the United States Trade Representative. "Fact Sheet: United States to Negotiate Transatlantic Trade and Investment Partnership with the European Union". *Executive Office of the President.* February 13, 2013. https://ustr.gov/about-us/policy-offices/press-office/fact-sheets/2013/february/US-EU-TTIP

Michael Froman, the U.S. Trade Representative (USTR)[5], were the initial key negotiators and leaders in charge of the TTIP negotiations. After De Gucht's term ended, Commissioner Malstroem (2014-2019) had taken over with Ignacio García Bercero as the Lead Negotiator for the EU and Dan Mullaney as the Chief Negotiator for the US[6]. With the formation of a huge trade area, not only nearly all custom duties were supposed to be eliminated, but also the opportunities and support for private investments in almost all trading areas were supposed to be sealed by the TTIP creation. In addition, the number of laws, rules and regulations were supposed to be minimized, since they currently prevent economic relations from transatlantic trade. The agreement was supposed to generate €120 billion per year for the economy of the European Union and $150 billion for the US economy. Two million new jobs would be expected on both sides of the Atlantic[7]. In Germany alone, around 181,000 jobs were expected to be created for the heart of Europe[8]. Besides, the agreement is supposed to serve as a blueprint for future agreement negotiations with other countries.

Serving as the European Union's negotiation leader in 2013, Karel De Gucht questioned why such a free trade agreement has not already been in existence for a long time, since goods, services and investments flow between the European Union and the United States every single day in the value of nearly two billion euros[9]. According to De Gucht, each relief, even if very small, of the exchange of goods, and each dismantling of trade barriers has an enormous economic effect and leads to a clear growth spurt. The former EU Commissioner for Trade further stated that the potential annual growth spurt is estimated at €119 billion for the European

---

5 Office of the United States Trade Representative. "United States Trade Representative Michael Froman". *Executive Office of the President.* Accessed May 2, 2016. http://www.ustr.gov/about-us/biographies-key-officials/united-states-trade-representative-michael-froman

6 Office of the United States Trade Representative. "List of Lead Negotiators for the Transatlantic Trade and Investment Partnership (TTIP)". *Executive Office of the President.* Accessed May 3, 2016. http://www.ustr.gov/sites/default/files/lead%20negotiators%20list%20TTIP.pdf

7 Frankfurter Allgemeine Zeitung. "Die Handelsgespräche mit Amerika", Nr. 38, February 14, 2014, page 13.

8 Felbermayr, Gabriel. "TTIP, Macroeconomic Effects", *GED-Studie.* Gütersloh: Bertelsmann-Stiftung, June 17, 2013, page 40. Accessed May 4, 2016. http://www.bfna.org/sites/default/files/TTIP-GED%20study%2017June%202013.pdf

9 De Gucht, Karel. "Der richtige Anstoß", *Süddeutsche Zeitung,* Nr. 184, August 10/ 11, 2013, page 12.

Union alone, which corresponds to an annual income increase of €500 per family in the European Union. These numbers provided by the EU Commissioner for Trade seem quite realistic and accurate when compared with the information provided by the Executive Office of US President Obama, according to which goods and private services in the amount of $458 trillion were exported from the US to the EU in 2012 alone, resulting in the world's largest investment relations with a value of $3.7 trillion[10]. The Federal Association of the German commerce industry, for example, estimates an annual growth of 1.5% as well as a surplus of German exports into the U.S. of €3 to 5 billion per year for Germany alone[11]. According to the Florida House of Representative Resolution designated on May 1, 2014, "the transatlantic economy is the largest in the world, encompassing nearly 36 percent of the $88 trillion global gross domestic product (GDP)" resulting in negotiations for TTIP in order to create economic growth and jobs by "creating the world's largest free trade zone between the world's two largest economies with combined GDPs of more than $31 trillion"[12].

As already established, TTIP has the potential to create yields, jobs, growth and prosperity on both sides of the Atlantic. However, how would TTIP differ in comparison to all other mutual trade agreements and trade associations so far such as the Trans-Atlantic Free Trade Area (TAFTA), the OECD Trade and Agriculture Directorate (TAD), or the Transatlantic Economic Partnership (TEP)? Do they all just represent abbreviations for failed approaches to deepen relations between the US and the EU? Even other trade agreements, associations and organizations around the world such as the "Eurasian Union"[13] or "MERCOSUR"[14] have been in a crisis. Why is TTIP needed, when the World Trade Organization (WTO) in

10 Office of the United States Trade Representative. "White House Fact Sheet: Transatlantic Trade and Investment Partnership (T-TIP)". *Executive Office of the President.* June 2013. https://ustr.gov/about-us/policy-offices/press-office/fact-sheets/2013/june/wh-ttip

11 Federation of German Industries (BDI). "BDI-Konferenz zur transatlantischen Handels- und Investitionspartnerschaft (TTIP)". *Conference Statement (BDI News).* November 12, 2013. Accessed May 5, 2016. http://bdi.eu/artikel/news/bdi-konferenz-zur-transatlantischen-handels-und-investitionspartnerschaft-ttip-imagegallery/

12 Florida House of Representatives. *House Resolution* HR 9093. May 1, 2014.

13 Atilgan, Canan et al. "The Eurasian Union", *Foreign Information of the Konrad Adenauer Foundation.* February 2014. pp. 8-10. http://www.kas.de/wf/doc/kas_36785-544-2-30.pdf?140207134233

14 Wesemann, Kristin. "South American Alliances Mercosur and Unasur face crisis". *Konrad-Adenauer-Stiftung International Reports.* February 2014, p. 71. https://www.ka

Geneva has been in existence as a world trade construct for rules and procedures including a comparatively well-designed arbitration of arguments system? The WTO has managed to achieve some successes such as considerable lowering of custom duties and non-tariff trade barriers since 1995 and again in January 2014. Nevertheless, TTIP is necessary for the following reasons:

Despite some previous successes of the WTO, protectionist tendencies have been increasing worldwide. Approximately 425 active trade barrier restrictions obstruct trade around the world[15], for example hygiene regulations, regulatory requirements for certification procedures, restricted access to public tenders, new import duties since Donald Trump became President in the U.S., unnecessary licensing procedures "behind the border"[16]. Most of these barriers originate in China, India, the U.S. and Algeria[17]. These trade barrier issues will be discussed in detail in a later chapter in regard to growing protectionism and counterstrategy of the EU through further free trade agreements.

Multilateral trade agreements and trade organizations have reached some barriers in recent times demonstrated by the failure of the WTO Doha Round. Therefore, the protectionist subsidies and barriers within the agrarian sector are still very high, especially between the U.S. and the European Union. At the same time, Chinese trade has been increasing heavily worldwide. Consequently, a common European-American market area becomes important, since it would unite one third of the world's trade and therefore create important opposition and competition for China[18]. Especially since doubts have been on the rise as to whether the latest WTO agreement negotiated in January 2014 is sustainable and will hold, the vision for TTIP is to create more than just a free trade agreement, according to the lead negotiators. The following goals have been established by Karel De Gucht/ Cecilia Malstroem and Michael Froman:

s.de/documents/252038/253252/7_dokument_dok_pdf_36787_2.pdf/f6d81e46-4d24-0923-4ba1-788f12ddbdb2?version=1.0&t=1539654628782

15 Beise, Marc. "Handel für alle", *Süddeutsche Zeitung*, Nr. 136, June 15/16, 2013, p. 12a.

16 European Commission. "2018 Annual Activity Report". *Directorate-General for Trade. Annual Report on Trade and Obstacles to investment.* June 14, 2019 http://ec.europa.eu/trade/trade-policy-and-you

17 Handelsblatt. "Behind the border". Nr. 114, June 17, 2019, p. 48.

18 Rosecrance, Richard. *The Resurgence of the west. How a Transatlantic Union can prevent war and restore the United States and Europe.* New Haven: Yale University Press, 2013, p. 202.

- Elimination of all tariff trade barriers
- Eventual abolishment of all hidden "non-tariff barriers" behind borders which obstruct the flow of goods including agricultural goods
- Strengthened access and fewer barriers of entrance for service enterprises to trade and markets
- Reduction of differing regulations and standards by creating larger compatibility, transparency and cooperation, while maintaining high levels of standards within health, security and environmental protection sectors
- Development of rules, principles and new possibilities of cooperation concerning productivity, tasks and intellectual property for globally operating companies, including state-owned enterprises in market-focused industries
- Proscription of commercial barriers on a local and/ or regional level as well as increase of ability to compete globally for small and medium-sized enterprises[19].

1.2.2 TTIP and Civil Society

After two rounds of negotiations, European Union Commissioner Karel de Gucht decided to request a delay from his official negotiation partner Michael Froman due to increasing criticism by consumer protection federations in the European Union in 2013. The delay had allowed time in order to mediate a discussion in Brussels regarding the raised issues and fears[20]. These fears mainly developed based upon the original vaguely expressed status by negotiators García Bercero (EU) and Dan Mullaney (US) on November 15, 2013, in Brussels[21]. Therefore, EU consumer federations stressed wanting to interrupt negotiations regarding investor protection for three months[22]. This topic has created fears for non-governmental organi-

19 Office of the United States Trade Representative. "White House Fact Sheet: Transatlantic Trade and Investment Partnership (T-TIP)". *Executive Office of the President.* June 2013. https://ustr.gov/about-us/policy-offices/press-office/fact-sheets/2013/june/wh-ttip

20 De Gucht, Karel. "Der richtige Anstoß", *Süddeutsche Zeitung*, Nr. 184, August 10/11, 2013, page 12.

21 Süddeutsche Zeitung. "Es gibt keinen Grund, Angst zu haben", Nr. 13, January 17, 2014, page 7.

22 Handelsblatt. "EU legt Verhandlungspause ein", Nr. 15, January 22, 2014, page 11.

zations (NGOs), lobbies as well as for citizens[23]. Some of them are afraid that TTIP would enable enterprises to fight laws for the protection of health or the environment with proceedings in front of non-transparent arbitral tribunals. Even some parties within the EU Parliament fear that the Investor-State Dispute Settlement (ISDS) could potentially expand into a new Act[24], according to Marietje Schaake, a member of the European Parliament for the Dutch liberal left-wing party "Democrat 66". She was also a member of the "US-Monitoring Group", a committee of the European Parliament, which is to observe the TTIP negotiations. Based on these concerns, De Gucht and García Bercero had been enabling federations as well as any other interested parties since April 2012 with the opportunity to express feedback regarding ISDS until October 2014. The opportunity for feedback also existed for all other topics as they were scheduled to be negotiated with respective deadlines published on the website for all the negotiation years 2014 -2016[25]. The official European Parliament position, reflected in the texts adopted, requested that ISDS should be replaced with a new system "to ensure that foreign investors are treated in a non-discriminatory fashion, while benefiting from no greater rights than domestic investors, and to replace the ISDS system with a new system for resolving disputes between investors and states which is subject to democratic principles and scrutiny, where potential cases are treated in a transparent manner by publicly appointed, independent professional judges in public hearings and which includes an appellate mechanism, where consistency of judicial decisions is ensured, the jurisdiction of courts of the EU and of the Member States is respected, and where private interests cannot undermine public policy objectives"[26].

European Commission representatives had stressed that the goal is not to arm enterprises against governments. Therefore, the European Union

23 Frankfurter Allgemeine Zeitung. "Handelsgespräche mit Amerika stocken", Nr. 38, February 14, 2014, page 13.

24 Süddeutsche Zeitung. "Befürchtungen von Marietje Schaake, Mitglied des Europäischen Parlaments", in *Blackbox Freihandel*, Nr. 286, December 11, 2013, page. 19.

25 European Commission Public Consultations. "Feedback Questionnaires ", accessed May 1, 2016. http://trade.ec.europa.eu/consultations/index.cfm?cons

26 European Parliament resolution of July 8, 2015, containing the European Parliament's recommendation to the European Commission on the negotiations for the Transatlantic Trade and Investment Partnership (TTIP). Texts adopted in Strasbourg, 2(d) (xv). http://www.europarl.europa.eu/sides/getDoc.do?pubRef=-//EP//TEXT+TA+P8-TA-2015-0252+0+DOC+XML+V0//EN&language=EN

member states had assigned Brussels with the task to negotiate investment protection clauses in order to close those legal loopholes in the approximately 1400 existing bilaterally finalized investment protection agreements of the European Union member states[27]. During the three months of the negotiation break in 2013, the European Commission wanted to accomplish a uniform EU-position about the topic of investment protection. According to the 2014 American negotiation model for investment agreements, measures for the protection of public interest do not represent an indirect expropriation of the investor. The outcome of the European Commission initiative on a uniform EU position regarding these issues resulted in publishing several fact sheets on a new ISDS proposal that was very different from the US position. The first Fact sheet published in November 2013 focuses on clarifying and improving investment protection rules as well as "improving how the dispute settlement system operates"[28]. In January 2015, the European Commission published a report about the online public consultation on ISDS concluding that "there are in particular four areas where further improvements should be explored: the protection of the right to regulate; the establishment and functioning of arbitral tribunals; the relationship between domestic judicial systems and ISDS; the review of ISDS decision through an appellate mechanism"[29]. A summary of this very lengthy report was also made available in a comprehensible manner on the European Commission website including a decision timeline and a reference to whether "other trade agreements include an ISDS clause"[30]. During the same month (January 2015), the European Commission also published an additional Fact Sheet on the creation of more investment opportunities in the US and in the EU including "Sensitive or controversial issues" in regard to ISDS outlining the concerns as well as the EU response to each respective issues (Governments' right to regulate, Lack

27 Süddeutsche Zeitung. "Das Grundrecht auf ungestörte Investitionen "., Nr. 92, April 22, 2014, page 4.

28 European Commission. "Investment Protection and Investor-to-State Dispute Settlement in EU agreements". *DG Trade Fact Sheet.* November 26, 2013, page 2. Accessed May 7, 2016. http://trade.ec.europa.eu/doclib/docs/2013/november/tradoc_151916.pdf

29 European Commission. "Online public consultation on investment protection and investor-to-state-dispute settlement (ISDS) in the Transatlantic Trade and Investment Partnership Agreement ". *Commission Staff Working Report.* Brussels, January 13, 2015, page 4. http://trade.ec.europa.eu/doclib/docs/2015/january/tradoc_153044.pdf

30 European Commission. "Question and Answers on the results of the public consultation on investment protection in EU-US trade talks". *DG Trade Policy,* January 12, 2015. http://trade.ec.europa.eu/doclib/press/index.cfm?id=1233

of transparency and legitimacy of ISDS, Lack of consistency in ISDS decisions)[31]. If an agreement cannot be reached on the ISDS issue between the EU and the US, there is a possibility that "controversial Investor-State Dispute Settlement provisions could be taken out of" TTIP[32], according to European Commission First Vice President Frans Timmermans. This sort of exclusion strategy can also potentially apply to some other aspects of TTIP, if a compromise cannot be found regarding a controversial issue. In November 2015, the EU published a new detailed "proposal for Investment Protection and Resolution of Investment Disputes"[33] which "is more transparent and safeguards the EU and its Member States' regulatory freedom"[34].

After dealing with this major hold-up obstacle, negotiations continued regarding all other ranges of topics. The dismantling of custom duties and regulations alone is to trigger large growth impulses in the US as well as in the EU. In any case, there were bright outlooks for TTIP based upon the fact that transparency was correctly created by keeping the communication and input open with NGOs as well as with federations. The more secretive and confidential negotiations ran, the higher the risk that not only stakeholders would be upset, but also negotiation results might fall through in the EU Parliament at the end. Contrary to public opinions, TTIP talks were fairly transparent when compared to other trade agreement negotiations. There is a lot of publicly accessible information available for free on the European Commission website in every EU language. Free EU paper publication booklets such as "Inside TTIP" (an overview and chapter-by-chapter guide in plain English) or "The top 10 myths about TTIP: Separating fact from fiction" provide a very comprehensible summary for the general public and can be ordered by any individual online free of charge in

31 European Commission. "Investment ". *DG Trade*. January 2015, page 3. Accessed May 8, 2016. http://trade.ec.europa.eu/doclib/docs/2015/january/tradoc_153018.5%20Investment.pdf

32 European Parliament Research Service Blog. "TTIP & ISDS". *EU-documents*. February 4, 2015. https://epthinktank.eu/2015/02/10/ttip-isds/

33 European Union. "TTIP – Trade in Services, Investment and E-Commerce: Chapter II – Investment". *European Commission*, November 12, 2015. http://trade.ec.europa.eu/doclib/docs/2015/november/tradoc_153955.pdf

34 European Commission. "Fact Sheet: Why the new EU proposal for an Investment Court System in TTIP is beneficial to both States and investors". *Press Release*. Brussels, November 12, 2015. http://europa.eu/rapid/press-release_MEMO-15-6060_en.htm

every EU language[35]. Alternatively, these booklets can be picked up free of charge at any European Union Center, from the EU's representations in each country[36] or by contacting the Europe Direct Service online or via a toll-free phone number from anywhere in the EU[37]. In fact, the TTIP "talks are the most open ever for a trade deal"[38]. The European Commission further stated, "We want to do all we can to make the TTIP negotiations transparent. That's why we've now gone further than ever in talks on earlier trade deals – by publishing EU negotiating texts for chapters where we've already drafted them"[39] available and accessible on the European Commission website. However, besides ISDS, criticism has also been occurring in other topic areas such as climate, environmental and consumer protection. The "Green" Party in the European Parliament even used such topics as climate protection, energy policy, privacy, animal welfare and sustainable rural economy in the European election in May 2014 to fight against TTIP [40]. In addition, the differing regulatory frameworks and treatments of Genetically Modified Organisms (GMOs) "in the US and EU have led to a serious trade dispute, which continues to be a contentious issue in TTIP discussions".[41]

---

35 European Union Publications Office. "Inside TTIP". *Directorate-General for Trade.* February 22, 2016. Accessed May 10, 2016, page 51. http://bookshop.europa.eu/en/inside-ttip-pbNG0215971/?CatalogCategoryID=m0sKABstN9AAAAEjuJAY4e5L

36 European Commission. "Local offices in EU member countries." *Representations of the European Commission.* Accessed May 9, 2016. http://ec.europa.eu/represent_en.htm

37 European Union. "Contact: Questions about the EU – Telephone, Email, Contact points in your country". Accessed May 5, 2016. http://europa.eu/contact/index_en.htm

38 European Commission. "A balanced EU-US Free Trade Agreement: Freer trade – without sacrificing Europe's standards ". Accessed May 10, 2016. http://ec.europa.eu/priorities/balanced-eu-us-free-trade-agreement_en

39 European Commission. "Inside TTIP: An overview and chapter-by-chapter guide in plain English". Luxembourg: Publications Office of the European Union, 2015, page 10. http://trade.ec.europa.eu/doclib/docs/2015/july/tradoc_153635.pdf

40 Frankfurter Allgemeine Zeitung. "Auftakt zum ‚knallgrünen' Europawahlkampf", Nr. 32. February 7, 2014 page 16.

41 Dudek, Carolyn M. "Genetically Modified Foods and Trade Controversy", in Joaquín Roy and Roberto Domínguez (editors). *The TTIP: The Transatlantic Trade and Investment Partnership between the European Union and the United States.* Miami-Florida European Union Center/ Jean Monnet Chair, 2014, page 111. https://eucenter.as.miami.edu/_assets/pdf/ttip.pdf

1.2.3 TTIP Overview[42]

TTIP consists of 24 chapters that are being negotiated grouped into the following three parts[43]:

1. Market Access (export, import, investments)
1.1 Trade in goods and customs duties
1.2 Services
1.3 Public procurement
1.4 Rules of origin
2. Regulatory Cooperation (safety, quality, technical rules and procedures, protection)
2.1 Regulatory cooperation
2.2 Technical barriers to trade
2.3 Food safety; animal and plant health
2.4 Chemicals
2.5 Cosmetics
2.6 Engineering products
2.7 Information and communication technologies (ICT)
2.8 Medical devices
2.9 Pesticides
2.10 Pharmaceuticals
2.11 Textiles
2.12 Vehicles
3. Rules (intellectual property rights, access to energy and raw materials for companies, save time and money on customs paperwork, sustainable development, government disputes)
3.1 Sustainable development
3.2 Energy and raw materials
3.3 Customs and trade facilitation
3.4 Small and medium-sized enterprises
3.5 Investment protection and, investor-state dispute settlement (ISDS)

42 Council of the European Union. *Directives for the negotiation on the Transatlantic Trade and Investment Partnership between the European Union and the United States of America.* Nr. 11103/13, Brussels, June 17, 2013, pp. 5-14. http://data.consilium.europa.eu/doc/document/ST-11103-2013-DCL-1/en/pdf

43 European Commission. *Inside TTIP: An overview and chapter-by-chapter guide in plain English.* Luxembourg: Publications Office of the European Union, 2015, p. 8-9. http://trade.ec.europa.eu/doclib/docs/2015/july/tradoc_153635.pdf

3.6 State-state dispute settlement
3.7 Competition policy
3.8 Intellectual property and geographical indications

In summary, the main goal of TTIP is to ease trade between the European Union and the United States. One of the primary goals is the elimination of currently existing market access restrictions, for example, the elimination or reduction of unnecessary custom duties and tariff barriers which also includes reducing delivery times producing more incentives for entrepreneurs to engage in transatlantic trade. This includes either the mutual recognition of each other's standards (EU and US) or the harmonization of rules, easing of investment transfer regulations (mutual certification and norm recognition) as well as equal opportunities and standardized treatments for investors in order to prevent and reduce potential discrimination. For example, this also includes health and hygiene laws for food, chemicals, automobile industry, finance etc. Moreover, the protection of intellectual property rights is essential not only within TTIP, but also for being able to set international standards for other nations, for instance China. This includes underlining the importance of conducting trade within a social and sustainable development framework pertaining to raw materials and energy (transparency and competition), (public) health, public services and education.

These different contents had been negotiated in 15 different negotiation rounds so far since July 2013. Each negotiation round focuses on different topics and allows input from the public during the stakeholder parts of the meetings (Stakeholder Presentations by Topics; Press Conference with Chief Negotiators for Stakeholders; Question and Answer Session with Chief Negotiators and Stakeholders). Negotiation round meetings so far have been taking place either in Europe (Brussels) or at various locations in the US (Washington, DC; Arlington; Chevy Chase; Miami and New York). The 13th round of negotiations took place in New York from April 25-29, 2016. The EU and the US negotiation parties hoped "to agree on consolidated texts by the 14th round of TTIP negotiations to take place in Brussels in July 2016"[44]. EU and U.S. negotiators hoped to finalize negotiations in October 2016 by holding regular intercessional discussions between formal rounds. However, at the end of the last round in New York, it was

44 McKeon, Michael. 2016. "Latest round of TTIP talks boost momentum". *EurActiv*, March 10. http://www.euractiv.com/section/trade-society/opinion/latest-round-of-ttip-talks-a-momentum-boost/

announced that the EU and the US could not agree on issues such as ISDS and agriculture and therefore, TTIP negotiations were put on hold.

1.3 Literature Review and Theoretical Framework

This book includes a literature review on the topic of trade debates within the International Political Economy field discussing the pros and cons of trade in general as well as the historical development of (transatlantic) trade starting from centuries ago until the present.

Even if a proposed transatlantic agreement never comes to fruition, this book contributes to examining whether the proposed TTIP would have been more beneficial for the US and the EU than no agreement at all. Therefore, this book is an important contribution to the broader trade debate and trade agreement literature within International Relations (IR), International Political Economy (IPE) and European Union (EU) Studies, as it also focuses on sustainable trade agreement contents for all (future) EU and US trade agreements such as CETA (Trade Agreement between Canada and the EU implemented in 2018).

The purpose of this book is to use a SWOT analysis to present how a transatlantic agreement would be affecting the US and the EU by studying the weaknesses and threats that TTIP faces, as well as which opportunities and strengths TTIP could bring to society and markets in the EU and the US.

1.4 Hypothesis, Discussion of Research Design, Methods, Data Collection

The consequences and opportunities of a transatlantic agreement for the EU and the US are discussed in detail within various chapters in this book. Besides tariff abolishment and increased legal security, particularly for small and medium-sized enterprises, transfer of technology in the automobile economy and in the information and communication technology (ICT) industry would improve, which would in turn lead to cost advantages created by common service management including fixed exchange rates for euro and dollar.

In view of the carbon dioxide (CO_2) increase and the dramatically increasing climate change, energy supply with renewable energy sources combined with a better climate and environmental protection presents a further challenge, which can only be mastered jointly by the U.S. and Europe. On both sides of the Atlantic, more than 200,000 jobs and economic impulses of up to 200 billion euros are expected to be created by a transatlantic agreement. Likewise, public health policy needs to be mastered on both sides in solidarity in view of aging societies.

This research compares the strength and weaknesses of TTIP as well as the opportunities and threats. Specifically, it also focuses on what major aspects of a potential transatlantic agreement are interesting and puzzling to think about in light of International Political Economy/ International Relations theory. Even if the agreement never comes to fruition or changes in shape, this book examines those aspects, which contribute to a broader trade agreement literature applicable in other cases. Most importantly, this research will point out why a transatlantic agreement presents more advantages than disadvantages for the US and the EU and if it does not happen now, why it may be unavoidable to implement some sort of trade agreement between the US and the EU in the future regardless based on International Relations theories.

A second part of this research also focuses on the opportunities "after TTIP". Because of their mutual occidental origin as well as their long-term peaceful partnership for 70 years now, the European Union and the US are well suited to move closer together than ever with a transatlantic agreement even beyond the character of a pure free trade agreement. As an Atlantic "community of values", the proposed policy recommendation is to expand the transatlantic agreement. TTIP should first serve as an inspiration for NAFTA as well as its subsequent transformations, and then eventually, TTIP rules should gradually be applied to EU and NAFTA states in order to create an even bigger trade area, but also a community of shared values. This research demonstrates how a transatlantic agreement could become a true Atlantic bridge based on several areas, which go beyond TTIP. The following chapter topics develop and outline how a closer "Atlantic Union" could develop beyond TTIP:

1. Ethics in economics and society; security of state, economy and society - joining forces (Europol and FBI) to fight against organized crime, falsification of money, drug & human trafficking, child pornography, brand and patent robbery;
2. Common currency, fiscal and stability union for the US and the EU;
3. Stronger combination of EU and US energy and climate policy based on more scarce resources such as fossil combustibles;

4. Partnership between the EU and US in the areas of public health (policy), prevention and healthy standards of living (diabetes, gastro-intestinal diseases, cancer, heart cycle mass damage) in order to combine public as well as private research and development
5. Both sides of the Atlantic have major automotive industries that have the potential to be developed jointly.

Since the BRICS states are growing at a much faster rate than the EU and the US regarding population and competences, forces have to be joined not only economically in the form of a trade agreement, but in other areas as well (environmental, health, climate policy etc.). The geographic situation of the EU and the US close to each other divided "only" by the Atlantic Ocean, also favors a transatlantic agreement as well as a future Atlantic Union with close neighbors such as Canada and Mexico.

The methodology consists of a multi-method research design using qualitative as well as quantitative data such as growth models, case studies of other trade agreements around the world, and regional integration examples. In addition, a SWOT analysis will outline weaknesses and threats as well as strengths and opportunities. Using data from both, the EU and the US, a simulation of a potential economic trade model will be created outlining how the combined numbers would look like after TTIP implementation. At the same time, those models provide an outlook in regard to the alternative outcome in case a transatlantic agreement will not take place and how the EU and the US will be becoming smaller and smaller in all aspects of rankings when compared to the BRICS states. These models will be based on sources such as Statista, World Bank, IMF, Google Scholar, etc., and will include a measurement of the consequences of trade deals in general (regression analysis). Important actors such as institutions, companies, interest groups, policy advocates, lobbyists, etc., will also qualitatively contribute to the analysis.

Qualitative aspects will first focus on the historical background. The European Coal and Steel Community (ECSC) was created as a tool for Europe's reconstruction. In addition, the US was present at the European Union's creation and has frequently been using Germany in particular as well as Europe in general as an (economic) shield during the Cold War. According to former European Commission President Barroso, "the relationship between the US and Europe constitutes the world's strongest, most comprehensive and strategically most important partnership"[45]. Even before modern times, the US originates from Europe and due to this long mutually beneficial history based on shared strong fundamental beliefs in democratic government, human rights and market economies, the relationship between the US and the EU is central and irreplaceable in the world. "America's strong ties to Europe are reflected in the largest two-way trading and investment relationship in the world...more than a fifth of all US exports go to the EU, and millions of Americans depend for their paychecks on the local affiliates of European parent companies.... Today, security, justice and prosperity for our world depend on America and Europe working in common purpose. That makes our transatlantic ties as vital as they have ever been"[46], as summarized in President George W. Bush's speech.

1.4.1 The Automotive Industry on both Sides of the Atlantic

Since 1970, the automotive industry has developed into a growth and innovation driver for a number of sectors and services in the United States and in the European Union, above all in Germany, France, Italy, the UK, Poland, Spain, Slovakia, the Czech Republic, Sweden and Austria. It has thus become a real source of impetus for the added value of economies on both sides of the Atlantic. The automotive industry in particular is burdened with massive trade restrictions, protectionism, state aid distortions and subsidies in the US and Europe. Consequently, it seems logical to develop the current success factors of the automotive industry starting from 2014 and to create alternative scenarios for the future, which should be either included in a EU-US trade deal or implemented after a transatlantic trade agreement as an addition.

1.4.2 Health and Pharmaceutical Industry as a Sector with a High Added Value Share on both Sides of the Atlantic

The health care industry and the pharmaceutical industry, which understand the commercial, industrial and ethical benefits of the highest assets of

45 European Commission President Barroso, Jose Manuel. *Press Release.* Brussels, February 9, 2005.

46 White House Office of the Press Secretary. *US President Bush Press Release*, February 19, 2005. https://georgewbush-whitehouse.archives.gov/news/releases/2005/02/text/20050219.html

customer groups such as health, life expectancy, quality of life and future-oriented research, are oriented towards the added-value share of balancing one of the most profitable industries and service providers on both sides of the Atlantic. At the same time, they are increasingly meeting the requirements of lifestyle, life expectancy and quality of life for people. It also seems logical in the field of health care and the pharmaceutical industry to investigate whether it would benefit from a EU-US trade agreement in its essential orientation, similar to the approach adopted by the automotive industry. Since the quality of training and further education of personnel as well as standards, testing and approval procedures are developed on a similar high level on both sides of the Atlantic, especially in the health industry and pharmaceutical industry, a high degree of harmonization through a future EU-US trade deal is to be expected in the future, as the TTIP negotiations have previously demonstrated. Also, the high expectations of this industry after the elimination of double certifications and approval procedure have already become clear during the TTIP negotiations regarding business cooperation between the US and Europe, company takeovers or research alliances.

1.5 Significance and Scholarly Contribution

This research will not only contribute to the International Relations and the International Political Economy field of International Studies, but it also intends to provide significant policy recommendations to advance trade related environmental standards, consequently also positively affecting trade related global public health policies. Most scholars view all those areas separately. However, my contribution will be to demonstrate how all those areas are interconnected and influence each other in important ways. The goal of this research is to demonstrate and prove the huge economic, social, environmental and public health impact for US and EU consumers and population. Therefore, this research is to point out ways and possibilities for the arranging political participants. In addition to trade, climate and global public health policies will be keys for the future strength of both, the US and the EU and will be part of the impact of TTIP on the global competition. As experts point out, "there are major priority aims in the energy sector (given Europe's dependence on Russian gas), and in securing access to raw materials where combined pressure on other countries may be vital"[47]. Consequently, this research will point out steps and policies that need to be implemented in order to strengthen both, the US and EU economies. In addition, costs and benefits of alternative policies will be outlined as well as possible winners/ losers in alternative scenarios. While economic, climate and global public health policy all influence each other, most scholars have treated them as separate entities, even though they are intertwined and affect each other. Consequences of TTIP as well as additional suggested trade-related aspects for the EU and US will be outlined in this research. Moreover, this research will also point out the fascinating fact that TTIP, similar to the notion of the EU, is "bound together by will.... not forced by conquest, war or political pressure"[48]. Whether TTIP will be resumed or given a different name under the current ongoing EU-US trade negotiations will be determined by the current negotiators in charge.

Different chapters in this book will not only apply (transatlantic) trade history and tie trade theories to the current EU-US trade relations, but case studies of potential strategic changes specifically for the automotive and pharmaceutical sectors will be cross-examined. The basis for these possible changes is a transatlantic free trade agreement between the EU and the US. Since an agreement to ensure and facilitate free trade between the world's largest economic blocs is a central component of the analysis, one section of this dissertation outlines the effects of free trade and existing free trade areas. The goal is to identify important features and developments of the past for both industries and their markets. Another section of this dissertation is directly related to the TTIP negotiation and its predicted economic consequences for the current ongoing EU-US trade negotiations. This dissertation also contains an environmental analysis and the creation of scenarios for both the automotive as well as the health and pharmaceutical sectors, including the results of the TTIP effects. Finally, a comparison of current strategies of these industries with the created scenarios will be showcased[49].

---

47 Abbott, Roderick. "A close look at the Transatlantic Trade and Investment Partnership". *Europe's World,* March 28, 2014. https://www.friendsofeurope.org/global-europe/a-close-look-at-the-transatlantic-trade-and-investment-partnership

48 Roy, Joaquin and Roberto Domínguez (eds.) *The Transatlantic Trade and Investment Partnership between the European Union and the United States.* Miami-Florida European Union Center/ Jean Monnet Chair, 2014, page 8.

49 Das Parliament. "Das Transatlantik Handels und Investitions - Partnerschaftsabkommen (TTIP)" in: *TTIP im Kontext anderer Freihandelsabkommen.* 64.Jg. 50-51/2014. December 8, 2014 p. 20-23.

1.6 Definition of Case Studies in the Automotive and Pharmaceutical Industry

The term "automotive industry" subsumes final manufacturers and suppliers who contribute to the added value of an automobile[50]. The pharmaceutical industry is understood to be that part of the chemical industry that commercially produces and markets human pharmaceuticals, including all types of medicinal substances[51]. The term patient refers to the end user, who uses the produced human pharmaceuticals. This dissertation confines itself to defining what can basically be understood by a strategy. Definitive subtleties such as those existing between famous representatives of strategic management are not included in this dissertation. Thus, the strategy describes the long-term focus and responsibilities of organizations within the automotive and pharmaceutical industries. The aim of the organizations is to use the strategy in a changing environment to gain competitive advantage using resources and competences and to serve the expectations of stakeholders[52]. The question of strategic change thus aims at the just mentioned macro environment of the organizations and at their potential modification by an EU-US trade agreement.

50 Stratmann (2010), page 109
51 Schmidt (2000), page 21
52 Johnson, Scholes and Whittington (2011), page 22, 4

Chapter 2: History and Literature Review on (Transatlantic) Trade

In order to analyze the current transatlantic trade relationship, this chapter will draw from (recent) history regarding proliferation of Regional Trade Agreements (RTAs) in the international trading system.

Mercantilism was dominating states from the 16th until the 18th century with protectionist and nationalistic trade policies based on the infant industry argument[53], which was focused on domestic politics and domestic trade in order to protect the local state economies. International trade was only desirable in this period for imports and as long as there was a positive trade balance. Exporting gold and silver was avoided in order to keep the national domestic economies stable[54].

During the enlightenment period, however, Adam Smith came up with the "absolute advantage" theory[55]. Smith emphasized the role of individuals to pursue wealth and trade freely. In his mind, trade should be allowed to be conducted internationally without any country border restrictions or barriers. The theory of "comparative advantage"[56] was added to this notion referring to open trade as well, specifically to whoever produces most efficiently shall gain an advantage. For example, if a company can produce and sell cars more efficiently than other companies, they could have a competitive advantage. During this enlightenment period, Great Britain took the lead and created the period known as Pax Britannica. Due to the industrial revolution, a period of economic growth occurred, and this also triggered 100 years of peace between 1814 and 1914 until World War I. This economic growth and peace period was based on liberalism occurring after the mercantilist period ended. These liberalism notions also

53 Hamilton, Alexander. *Report of the Secretary of the Treasury of the United States, on the Subject of Manufactures: Presented to the House of Representatives*, December 5, 1791.

54 Gilpin, Robert., and Gilpin, Jean M. *The Political Economy of International Relations.* Princeton, N.J.: Princeton University Press, 1987.

55 Smith, Adam. *An Inquiry into the Nature and Causes of the Wealth of Nations.* London: Electric Book, 2001.

56 Ricardo, David. *On the Principles of Political Economy and Taxation.* London: Electric Book, 2001.

led to capitalism in combination with the industrial revolution as well as international trade.

Marx and Engels criticize capitalism, as it (in some instances) results in overproduction and therefore unemployment for some laborers and could consequently lead to the proletariat (workers/ laborers) overthrowing the bourgeoisie (elite)[57]. Lenin took Marxism a step further and applied it to the Imperialism period in which the European states exploited their colonies in order to enrich their domestic economies[58]. Some of these Marxist notions are still relevant in regard to domestic trade policies today. Unemployment and low wage jobs are affecting domestic support for potential trade agreements in the United States as well as in the European Union. Thousands of demonstrators went into the streets on a regular basis to oppose mega-regional agreements in Europe and in the United States such as TPP and TTIP, because they fear job losses and economic losses. Demonstrators believe that they may lose their current jobs, as some jobs may be transferred overseas once these trade agreements go into effect. These phenomena are referred to as domestic society-centered pressures against these regional trade agreements.

In trade politics, a society-centered approach is one in which a government's trade policy objective is designed by politicians in response to interest groups' demands. The society-centered approach emphasizes the relationship between organized societal interests and political institutions. These distributional pressures generate political competition as the interested parties (winners and losers) from trade turn to the political field to advance and defend their economic interests. With respect to trade policy preferences, followers of a society-centered approach argue that trade policy reflects the demands of the people, and this approach devotes considerable attention to the sources, the content, and organization of such demands.

In many cases, groups cannot organize because they confront a collective action problem[59]. Collective action problems arise from a phenomenon called "free riding". The free riding concept describes the situations in

57 Marx, Karl, Friedrich Engels, and Gareth Stedman Jones. *The Communist Manifesto.* London: Penguin, 2002.

58 Lenin, Nikolai. *Imperialism, the Highest Stage of Capitalism.* 2017.

59 Olson, Mancur. *The Logic of Collective Action: Public Goods and the Theory of Groups.* Harvard Economic Studies; v. 124. Cambridge, Mass.: Harvard University Press, 1971.

which individuals depend on others to bear the costs of a program from which they derive benefits[60].

Even in the case where consumers share a common goal, the collective action problem prevents them from putting some pressure on politicians to achieve this goal. The incentive to free ride makes collective action in search of a common goal very difficult. The magnitude of the collective action problem depends in part upon the size of the group. In large groups, the incentive to free ride faced by each individual is very strong and large groups face very severe collective action problems. In small groups, each individual contribution is large relative to the total contribution and therefore each contribution has a greater impact on the group's ability to achieve its common goal. As a result, the incentive to free ride is weaker in small groups. The logic of collective action helps us understand why the interests of producers (organized in small groups) dominate trade politics, while the interests of consumers (organized in large groups) are often neglected. The large and heterogeneous group that bears the cost of the tariff finds it much more difficult to organize for collective action. Given these differing abilities to organize, trade politics is dominated by import-competing industries demanding protection.

In a society-centered approach, trade politics are driven by competition between organized interest groups[61]. This competition sometimes revolves around class conflict, which confronts workers against business owners, and sometimes revolves around industry conflict, which confronts import-competing industries against export-oriented industries. The American electoral system is based on single-member districts. The nation is divided into mutually exclusive electoral districts with one person elected to represent each district. To win elections in this electoral system, politicians must satisfy the demands of the residents of their districts. Such an electoral system creates an incentive for groups to organize around narrow industry lines and creates incentives for elected officials to represent and defend the narrow interests of the industries in their districts. Industries needing protection will be most likely to organize. Consequently, American electoral institutions create strong incentives for elected officials to bring the narrow, industry-specific interests of import-competing industries into Congress. In Congress, legislative dynamics practically guarantee that any effort to

60 Sandler, Todd. *Collective Action: Theory and Applications.* Ann Arbor: University of Michigan Press, 1992.

61 Baldwin, Richard E. *A Domino Theory of Regionalism.* 1993

protect a single industry will be transformed into legislation that protects many industries.

The state-centered approach suggests that one looks at the political influence of the industries concerned, and its supporters argue that national policymakers should intervene in the economy in pursuit of objectives that are determined to be independent from the domestic interest groups narrow self-interest. This approach suggests that such intervention may raise aggregate social welfare. Proponents of the state-centered approach, with its specific focus on government intervention, feel it is designed to promote the development of specific national industries. The society-centered approach is based on the belief that protectionism reduces social welfare by depriving society of the gains from trade and by employing society's resources in comparatively disadvantaged industries, but proponents of the state-centered approach argue that, under certain circumstances, trade protection can raise social welfare. From the perspective of the society-centered approach, national policy reflects the balance of power among competing interest groups, but under specific circumstances governments are relatively unconstrained by interest-group demands. Therefore, a government's trade and economic policies represent the goals of national policymakers rather than the demands of interest groups.

Citizens during the last several decades have faced collective action problems. While there were some demonstrations, it was not enough to prevent NAFTA from being implemented, for instance. However, in the case of TTIP and TPP, the society-centered pressures have actually succeeded so far in preventing these trade agreements from being approved. The migration crisis in Europe has led to disapproval of the current administration of the European Union. Regional elections have turned out right-wing in Europe or far left either way back-lashing against the traditional parties in power. Demonstrators in Europe including interest groups (farmers, lobbyists, environmentalists) managed to take collective action as far as to demand from the European Commission to publish all documents related to TTIP on the internet. After so many pressures and demonstrations, the Commission actually started to comply with the pressure of the people and politicians. In the United States, demonstrators against TPP also succeeded, because the US election outcome on November 8, 2016 produced a new right-wing president (Donald Trump) who was generally opposed towards any type of Trade-Agreement during his campaign. Whether he can actually succeed with his Neo-mercantilist and protectionist nationalistic proposals remains to be seen. Some economic analysts do not believe that his policies will work, because a lot of great opportunities and economic boosts could be lost by not implementing TPP and TTIP.

International Trade Regime negotiations between the United States and Europe began in the 1940s. The goal of the conference held at Bretton Woods, New Hampshire in July 1944 was to agree on a set of institutions to regulate international trade and monetary relations. U.S. and UK policy makers drew important lessons from the previous century: international economic integration in the pre-1914 eras was worth emulating and a more open international economy requires cooperation only sustainable with strong domestic political support for governments. Therefore, bilateral talks extended into multilateral negotiations in 1945. By 1947, negotiations had created an agreement on the postwar trade system. The International Monetary System was implemented with a fixed exchange rate system, the International Monetary Fund (IMF) and the World Bank. The implementation of an International Trade Organization failed which led to a General Agreement on Tariffs and Trade (GATT) for the international trading system embodying liberal ideas about the benefits of free trade. In addition, it may have also been of economic interest to the United States. The goal of the General Agreement on Tariffs and Trade (GATT) was to promote freer and fairer trade through negotiated reductions of formal tariffs according to two main principles: reciprocity (mutual balanced concessions) and multilateralism (trade rules extended without discrimination to all members). Unilateralism, bilateralism and trading blocs were prohibited except in certain circumstances (human rights violations, war etc.). The Bretton Woods Monetary System had fixed exchange rates. All currencies at the time of establishment were pegged to the dollar, which was pegged to gold. The International Monetary Fund was created to monitor national economic policies and to extend balance of payments financing to countries at risk using contributions from members to offer reserve credits to states with international payment problems. The World Bank provided financing for reconstruction of Europe after World War II. The goal was to achieve both national autonomy and international stability created by the fixed or pegged exchange rates, while still allowing sufficient flexibility to enable individual states to deal with extraordinary situations. The basic principle was to create multilateral surveillance through international institutions and institutional specialization at the international rather than the regional level. In addition, the non-discrimination policy goal was to create transparency for tariffs according to the GATT/ IMF. The GATT was emphasized on border controls and did not restrict domestic regulatory intervention. The Bretton Woods System allowed capital controls and national autonomy over exchange rate pegs – a product of postwar Keynesian views in the UK. Postwar regimes were characterized by very liberal formal principles (multilateralism and non-discrimination) at the international level with considerable scope for domestic interventionism (informal norms), particularly in macroeconomic management and social insurance policies. Therefore, the Bretton Woods compromise consisted of embedded liberalism including the following: economic middle ground between globalism, national economic management, free markets and government intervention; political class compromise among big businesses, labor and the middle class, ideological between the center left and the center right against extremes of fascism and communism, gradualism and exceptions for politically controversial measures.

Old Regionalism started shortly after the end of World War II with the European Integration from the late 1950s until the 1970s imposed from the outside by the superpowers. It was characterized by Cold War logic including the following: introverted and protectionist, specific and narrow objectives, exclusive in terms of membership, state-centric and state-dominated (Neofunctionalism, Intergovernmentalism). The resurgence of regionalism in the 1980s and 1990s was considered Post-Cold War Regionalism from a Mainstream International Relations Approach (Neorealism, Neoliberal Institutionalism). New Regionalism is based on post-Cold War logic as well. However, the approach is based on Constructivism and post-positivist theories, as it is often developed from within the region. It is inclusive, open, and linked with globalization guided by comprehensive and multidimensional objectives such as economics, politics and security involving the state, the market and civil society actors worldwide. Institutionalism places emphasis on the functions that regimes perform for states and view regional institutions as a joint attempt by states to manage the problems generated by increased interdependence (e.g. NAFTA). Realists explain the resurgence of regionalism with external balancing arguments (regional blocs are formed as a response to external or extra-regional threats or challenges). Constructivists argue that regional cooperation creates "shared identity" (of regional elites) leading to the emergence of self-sustaining integration (regional identity/ sense of community). At the domestic level, regional cooperation can also be driven by the preferences and goals of governments (Statist argument) or driven by the preferences of business groups (Interest Group Explanations).[62] Tariffs reflect a balance of supply and demand for protection (political economy explanation). The formation of RTAs re-aligns political economy forces in non-members (due to discrimination) resulting in a pressure for either joining or creating a new RTA. If a new member joins an existing RTA, forces for inclusion get stronger in non-member nations (Domino Effect). The original trade of goods turned into international investment in production facilities, training, technology and long-term business relationships utilizing infrastructure services such as telecoms, internet, express parcel delivery, air cargo, trade-related finance, etc. in order to coordinate the production process. As a result of these changes, the demand for deeper integration rules arose resulting in 21st century regionalism[63]. New international risks and threats to property occurred as firms began doing business abroad (behind the border barriers). In addition, obstacles arose to flows of goods, people, ideas and investment required to coordinate international production facilities (cross-border barriers). Incentives to remove these 21st century barriers are the source of demand for more complex trade disciplines. Since the WTO was otherwise occupied, this demand was filled by deeper RTAs and unilateral reforms. There are four deeper disciplines that appear in these RTAs, but not in the WTO: competition policy, movement of capital, intellectual property rights and investment assurances.

The formation of regional trade agreements has been, by far the most popular form of reciprocal trade liberalization in recent decades. The discriminatory character of these agreements has raised three main concerns: first, that trade diversion would increase, because special interest groups would induce governments to form the most distortionary agreements; second, that broader external trade liberalization would reverse and third, that multilateralism could be undermined.

Various scholars have debated throughout the 20th century whether RTAs are "trade creating or "trade diverting"[64]. Trade creation is the increase in intra-regional trade by shifting resources from inefficient domestic suppliers to more efficient producers in the region. Trade diversion is the increase in intra-regional trade by shifting resources from efficient external produc-

62 Baldwin, Richard E. *A Domino Theory of Regionalism.* 1993

63 Baldwin, Richard E. *21st Century Regionalism Filling the Gap between 21st Century Trade and 20th Century Trade Rules.* 2010.

64 Viner, Jacob. "Power Versus Plenty as Objectives of Foreign Policy in the Seventeenth and Eighteenth Centuries." *World Politics* 1, no. 1. October 1948: 1-29.

ers to inefficient producers in the region. Some scholars argue that RTAs should be referred to as Preferential Trading Agreements (PTAs) and are trade diverting and not creating. Bhagwati argues that RTAs are "Termites in the Trading System"[65] and therefore should be viewed as "stumbling blocks" and a form of protectionism as opposed to "building blocks."[66]

On the one hand, scholars view RTAs as Building Blocs due to less actors involved leading to easier and faster negotiations, because RTAs tend to go further than tariff reductions and are "open", hence compatible with multilateralism. On the other hands, scholars argue that RTAs are stumbling blocks, as they are inward-looking and protectionist, discriminatory (against WTO goals). Bhagwati argues that the surge of RTAs has led to a "spaghetti bowl effect" of trade agreements. This "spaghetti bowl" does not just exist between the US and Europe, for example, but it exists in Africa as well. In addition, an "East Asian noodle bowl" exists.

In "A Domino Theory of Regionalism," Baldwin argues that RTAs discriminate against third parties[67]. In terms of economic laws, David Ricardo developed the concept of comparative advantage[68]. It is important to note that the Ricardo-Viner model assumes that factors (labor and capital) are immobile and do not move[69]. A brief example will help explain this concept. A country produces two goods: shirts and cars. This country, however, might have a comparative advantage for various reasons in shirts and, therefore, should focus on producing shirts instead of both shirts and cars. This will enable a country to optimize efficiency and produce more shirts. The country can import cars from another country that is more efficient in building them. RTAs — or PTAs —could technically violate the laws of comparative advantage. Three countries, for example, might join a RTA for political reason and forgo including another country for political reasons. However, perhaps the fourth country is more efficient and has a comparative advantage in a very useful product. For example, country X might produce cars much better than country Y, but country Y is accepted

---

65 Bhagwati, Jagdish. *Termites in the Trading System: How Preferential Agreements Undermine Free Trade.* Oxford University Press, 2008.

66 Bhagwati, Jagdish. "Regionalism versus Multilateralism." *World Economy* 15, no. 5, 1992: 535-56

67 Baldwin, Richard. "A Domino Theory of Regionalism." *NBER Working Paper Series,* 1993, 4465.

68 Ricardo, David. *The Principles of Political Economy & Taxation.* Everyman's Library. Science, No. 590. Dent: Dutton, 1911.

69 Ishikawa, Jota. "The Ricardo-Viner Trade Model with an Intermediate Good." *Hitotsubashi Journal of Economics 41,* no. 1, 2000: 65-75.

into the RTA, because it is a political ally with the other two countries in the agreement. This is an example of how politics can play a role in RTAs and hinder what — at least economically — would be a better arrangement for all parties in the RTA.

Bhagwati also is very critical of "natural trading partners."[70] A country might appear to be a natural trading partner because it is close in proximity. How one perceives a country is a constructivist issue[71].

Regionalism refers to the negotiation and construction of interstate or intergovernmental agreements or regimes, involving specific and conscious policy decisions by governments to coordinate economic and political activities within a region.[72] Regionalism can be defined as a regional inter-state cooperation and is a special case of international or global cooperation. Different sectors and areas of regionalism include security/politics, economic (preferential trade agreements) and environmental issues. Regionalism is a "political process of cooperation and coordination on economic policy among states"[73]. Multilateralism on the other hand is the idea that "Most Favored Nation", should be applied to all states, and avoid discriminatory practices at all costs. PTA's or Preferential Trade Agreements are agreements in which states cooperate on economic policy as it pertains to trade. There are two types of PTA's: Customs Union and Free Trade Agreements. CU's are agreements that have no internal barriers to trade and impose a common external tariff to outside states. Free trade agreements on the other hand also have no internal barriers to trade, but do not impose a common external tariff on outside states.

Regional trade agreements are complimentary to the objectives of the General Agreement on Tariffs and Trade (GATT). Article XXIV of the GATT allows Free Trade Areas (FTAs) and Custom Unions (CUs) to exist as long as trade barriers do not rise on average after integration, agreements eliminate all tariffs and other trade restrictions on intra-regional exchange

---

70 Bhagwati, Jagdish Natwarlal. 1992. "Regionalism Versus Multilateralism". *World Economy.* 155: 535-555.

71 Wendt, Alexander. *Social Theory of International Politics.* New York: Cambridge University Press, 2014.

72 Fawcett, Louise L'Estrange., and Andrew Hurrell. *Regionalism in World Politics: Regional Organization and International Order.* Oxford [England]; New York: Oxford University Press, 1995.

73 Mansfield, Edward D., and Helen V. Milner. "The New Wave of Regionalism." *International Organization* 53, no. 3 (1999): 589-627.

of goods and agreements are notified to the GATT, which may decide to establish whether these conditions are satisfied.

The last several decades have witnessed a proliferation of RTAs in the international trading system. As of 2006, 214 Regional Trade Agreements (RTAs) were active and in force[74]. In 2010, the World Trade Organization (WTO) estimated that 271 RTAs existed around the world. Since the WTO came into being, the number of Regional Trade Agreements (RTA) in existence rose from 100 to over 300. According to the WTO, already 379 RTAs were in force as of 2013. Almost every country in the world has membership in at least one RTA. They have become a major international regime that demands attention. RTAs are fundamentally trade agreements, which discriminate between members and nonmembers. Nations who participate in these blocs eliminate tariffs on goods entering their markets from their FTA partners, but each member retains independent tariffs on goods entering from non-FTA members. In a world economy governed by the WTO and the reduction of tariffs barriers to trade, in which 164 countries are members[75], how is this possible? Why are RTAs so popular? Does the existence of RTAs destroy multilateral economic relationships around the world? Do RTAs discourage or promote free trade? What are the ramifications for the future?

The major principle of the General Agreement on Trade and Tariffs (GATT) was the Most Favored Nation clause (MFN), which requires the same rights to be given to every country in a trade agreement. The MFN is designed to avoid discrimination and preferential treatment. Article 24 of the GATT, however, allows Regional Trading Agreements. Based on this, some economists argue that RTAs are a "building block" and should be viewed as a positive, because they promote trade and exchanges between countries. In other words, RTAs are positive because they promote trade, and trade is better than protectionism.

Many have raised concerns about the rapid increase of RTAs (Regional Trade Agreements) and assert that their complex frameworks have created an overlap in policies and have stunted the progress of multilateralism. Others attest that RTAs enhance the multilateral system by providing neces-

---

74 Fiorentino, Roberto V., Christelle Toqueboeuf, and Luis Verdeja. *The Changing Landscape of Regional Trade Agreements: 2006 Update.* Geneva, Switzerland: World Trade Organization, 2007.

75 World Trade Organization. *Members and Observers.* Accessed May 1, 2019. https://www.wto.org/english/thewto_e/whatis_e/tif_e/org6_e.htm

sary reform to countries who seek to become more integrated. Bhagwati asserts that PTAs (Preferential Trade Agreements) are here to stay and are not going to disappear. He argues that RTAs have occurred in different waves. The "first wave of regionalism"[76] occurred during the 1960s. Functionalism theory[77] in connection with the European Integration Theories explains the development of the European Coal and Steel Community (see Treaty of Paris 1952) and the attempts to promote integration with the foundation of the European Economic Community (see Treaty of Rome 1957). Neofunctionalism refers to the positive spillover effect democracy and institutions can have on other states triggering more and more states to cooperate based on benefits such as peace, trans-national trade, and economic prosperity[78]. Intergovernmentalism, initially proposed by Stanley Hoffmann, was refined into Liberal intergovernmentalism by Andrew Moravcsik as an explanation for the foundation of the European Union in 1992.[79] In "the first wave of Regionalism," the US, contrary to Europe, promoted multilateral trade. However, Bhagwati coins the term standing on "Two feet.", because today, the U.S. tends to focus more on FTAs as a form of trade.

In the most recent wave of regionalism today, the US is a major player in RTAs. One could use Hegemonic Stability Theory (HST) to explain the current situation in connection with the U.S. being considered the most powerful country in the world. However, such an argument can be countered. It could be argued that the reason that RTAs have proliferated in recent years is because the US has not assumed the leadership role and has not provided the public good of trade openness. As previously mentioned, Kindleberger[80] discussed the importance of having a country assume a leadership role and promote trade openness. The failure of the US, which is considered the world hegemon by some, to promote trade openness is one argument for why we have witnessed a proliferation in RTAs.

---

76 Bhagwati, Jagdish. "Regionalism versus Multilateralism." *World Economy* 15, no. 5, 1992: 535-56

77 Mitrany, David. *The Prospect of Integration: Federation or Functional?* in International Regionalism: Readings, ed. Joseph S. Nye Jr. (Boston: Little, Brown and Company, 1968), p. 52

78 Haas, Ernst B., *ed. (2004) [1958]. The uniting of Europe: political, social, and economic forces, 1950–1957 (3rd ed.).* Notre Dame, Indiana: University of Notre Dame Press.

79 Moravcsik, Andrew. "Preferences and Power in the European Community: A Liberal Intergovernmental Approach". *Journal of Common Market Studies,* December 1993.

80 Kindleberger, Charles. *The World in Depression 1929-1939.* London: Allen Lane, 1973.

It is important to note that not all scholars believe that the US is the world's hegemon. Offensive realists argue that a country can only aspire to dominate its region and that geography and the seas prevent a country from dominating the entire world[81]. However, the US has lost a tremendous amount of "soft power,"[82] but in terms of "hard power"[83] and economics, the US is the most powerful country in the world; the current US GDP is approximately $14 trillion dollars.

Ann Krueger examines the role of NAFTA, in particular, and believes that RTAs are a step in the right direction and help facilitate trade.[84] In addition, Mansfield and Milner support RTAs and view them as trading creating[85]. It could be argued that RTAs are a form of trade, which is ultimately better than high tariffs and limited trade occurring among the international community.

2.1 Politics

This section will examine several other political aspects that could lead to the promotion of RTAs. As previously mentioned, a state might form an RTA due to natural inclinations of affinities for another state based on culture, history, language, etc. For example, Canada and the US are natural trading partners due to sharing a large border and because both countries are democracies. In addition, both countries have historical, cultural, and linguistic connections. However, other political reasons exist for RTAs. Rogowski discussed the political aspects that can occur in society between urban and rural sectors, for example[86]. Also, certain groups can lobby the government and advocate for certain policies, such as protectionism

81 Mearsheimer, John J. *The Tragedy of Great Power Politics*. Updated ed. New York, NY: W.W. Norton, 2014.

82 Nye, Joseph S. *Soft Power: The Means to Success in World Politics*. New York: Public Affairs, 2009. <http://public.eblib.com/choice/publicfullrecord.aspx?p=903654>.

83 Campbell, Kurt, and Michael O'Hanlon. *Hard Power: The New Politics of National Security*. New York: Basic Books, 2007. <http://public.eblib.com/choice/publicfullrecord.aspx?p=952693>.

84 Krueger, Anne O. *Trade Creation and Trade Diversion under NAFTA* (December 1999). NBER Working Paper No. w7429. Available at SSRN: https://ssrn.com/abstract=203157

85 Mansfield, Edward D., and Helen V. Milner. "The New Wave of Regionalism." *International Organization* 53, no. 3 (1999): 589-627.

86 Rogowski, Ronald. "Political Cleavages and Changing Exposure to Trade." *The American Political Science Review* 81, no. 4 (1987): 1121-137.

or RTAs, for example. The farmer lobby in the US is very powerful, for instance, and tends to lobby for protectionism.

2.2 Security

Various other security reasons exist and could help explain why a country would join an RTA with other countries. A group of countries might want to join in order to "balance against" other countries, according to realist logic[87]. States might want to strengthen ties and linkages with potential patterns in order to balance against other threats and potential issues[88]. The Cold War, which lasted from 1945 until 1989, could be a perfect example when states formed trading blocks in order to increase linkages and balance. It is possible, for instance, that during the first wave of regionalism, which occurred in the 1960s, the US sought to increase ties with potential adversaries and participated in RTAs with allies, as opposed to adversaries, for security reasons.

2.3 International Relations Theory Explanations

One can invoke the use of International Relations theory in order to examine RTAs. Neo-Liberal Institutionalism would view RTAs as a positive aspect because they promote cooperation. Keohane argued that institutions help promote cooperation, decrease transaction costs, and increase efficiency[89]. As previously mentioned, Neo-Liberal Institutionalists argue that institutions can help mitigate anarchy. Constructivists challenge this argument. Wendt fundamentally challenges the realist notion that anarchy is the main structural element and is a given. Wendt argues that anarchy is a social construction.[90] Constructivism could be used to explain why countries join an RTA. A country might have a trade agreement in order to "socialize other

87 Layne, Christopher. *The Peace of Illusions: American Grand Strategy from 1940 to the Present.* Cornell Studies in Security Affairs. Ithaca: Cornell University Press, 2006.

88 Layne, Christopher. "Offshore Balancing Revisited." *The Washington Quarterly* 25, no. 2 (2002): 233-48.

89 Keohane, Robert O. *After Hegemony*. Princeton University Press, 2005. <http://www.myilibrary.com?id=275144>.

90 Wendt, Alexander. 2008. "Anarchy Is What States Make of It: The Social Construction of Power Politics". *Theories of International Relations.* 301-335.

countries" and promote certain norms, values, etc. Also, countries might join an RTA because they have common norms, values, etc. In addition, it depends on how a country views another state (enemy or friend).[91]

Despite their peculiarities and incremental nature, free-trade agreements can serve the cause of freedom and development by breaking down barriers to trade between nations. RTAs get free trade moving along in five fundamental ways and make up for the flaws of the WTO. Moreover, RTAs act as a launching pad, or a stepping-stone, to further multilateral free trade rather than hinder it.

RTAs are possible, because they are legally allowed by the rules of the WTO (the General Agreement on Tariffs and Trade amended by the Uruguay round) as an exception to the principle of nondiscrimination. Nondiscrimination demands that all WTO members grant any advantage, favor, privilege or immunity granted by any contracting party to any product originating in or destined for any other country shall be accorded immediately and unconditionally to the like product originating in or destined for the territories of all other contracting parties. This means that if one country reduces a tariff to one nation, it must be done for all. The exception to this rule is found in Article XXIV of the WTO charter. It appreciates the desirability of increasing freedom of trade by the development, through voluntary agreements, of a closer integration between the economies of the countries [party] to such agreements. Thus, a member nation has the right to form RTA if they so desire for the purpose of closer integration. This forwards liberalization. There are of course limitations. Most important of these limitations are: RTA member countries cannot hike additional barriers to the other WTO member countries and, RTAs must eliminate duties and other restrictive regulations of commerce on substantially all trade between the constituent countries and do so within a reasonable length of time. The WTO places constrains on RTAs, so they do not engage in illiberal practices against others. Interestingly, Article XXIV, and therefore RTAs, can be waived entirely by a two-thirds vote of WTO members. States choose not to do so because they have much to gain from these arrangements. RTAs get free trade moving along in five ways. This makes up for the flaws of the WTO and thus, simultaneously encourages multilateralism and RTA proliferation.

91 Jervis, Robert. *Perception and Misperception in International Politics*. 2017.

In order to describe the advantages of RTAs and its proliferation, the institutionalist perspective highlights the necessary functions of the RTA in order to judge its beneficial use. Firstly, since the WTO contains many members in contrast to a RTA, the WTO's system of governance can prove to be quite inefficient, expensive and drawn out. It takes up to nine months to a year to settle a dispute. WTO negotiation rounds last years and sometimes, with no result. The need to gain consensus with all the members is a long arduous task and this is the root of the problem. The RTA system of governance provides a remedy to this because of its small membership. It would not take very long to settle a dispute and negotiate regulations. Not only that, RTAs are also flexible to the changing environment, their choice of partners and their policy scope[92].

Secondly, RTAs make it easy for countries that have been excluded from other RTAs to compete more fiercely and this would attribute to its proliferation. For example, if the United States was locked out of an RTA, American exporters would suffer unfairly. To get around that, the United States must create its own RTA, or join an existing one in order to compete on an equal footing. Since RTAs are an existing part of the world economic system, one would be foolish not to "go with the flow". Thus, the benefits of joining an RTA system are obvious. It is an instrument used to remedy regional ties in order to create and maintain markets regardless of geographical location.

Thirdly, an RTA functions as an indication to the wider world that a country, most likely a developing nation, is preparing itself to join the global market. These indications assist the developing nation by attracting foreign investment as well as grants access to markets and, as a result, spur economic growth. RTAs give developing countries the confidence they need to enter the global market. More developing countries are joining RTAs. North-South RTAs make up for 27% of total RTAs and South-South 25% percent. Through RTAs, the nature of North-South trade relations appears to be evolving to a framework of reciprocity and ambitious trade policy scope. RTAs, in this case, serve as water wings for the infant country that is ready to swim in the waters of the free market. This would further explain its spread.

---

92 Fiorentino, Roberto V., Christelle Toqueboeuf, and Luis Verdeja. *The Changing Landscape of Regional Trade Agreements: 2006 Update*. Geneva, Switzerland: World Trade Organization, 2007.

This leads to the fourth reason RTAs are so widely proliferated: they serve as the launching pad for further trade negotiations. As stated, because of its large membership, the WTO takes a very long time to initiate, negotiate and establish trade rules and regulations. The RTA, with its small amount of likeminded nations, would allow negotiations to be less painful and productive and therefore, more efficient in ensuring trade liberalization. These negotiations can serve as a springboard for additional multilateral discussions. Thus, RTAs prove more practical than WTO multilateralism. RTAs are seen as spaces for future multilateral trade developments. Connected to the fourth is the fifth factor: RTAs help nations cement ties to one another in order to continue their economic relationship. This is very attractive to nations and would again help explain its wide popularity.

RTAs spread ideas of free trade just like the WTO. Since both facilitate the idea of free trade, it can be concluded that RTAs assist multilateral trade. However, some scholars do not think this is exactly the case. Bhagwati, for example, believes that RTAs will lead the world down the path of solidified trading blocs and illiberal trade practices[93]. He argues that RTAs are not helpful to multilateralism. Rather, RTAs are a danger to trade liberalization. First, he argues that RTAs could divert trade from the cost-efficient non-member countries to the relatively inefficient member countries. He further points out that this would damage world welfare. This argument does have some weight, but as mentioned earlier, if a country is not a member of an RTA, that country can simply join or create one and that would allow for a more efficient allocation of resources and production methods.

Second, Bhagwati cites the "Spaghetti bowl" systemic concern. He states that when a country is a member of two or more RTAs, rules and regulations may crisscross and contradict one another. According to Bhagwati, with PTAs proliferating, the trading system can then be expected to become chaotic and interferes with the rules of origin. These distortions and ensuing confusion would ultimately raise prices and discourage trade. On the surface, all this red-tape and disorganization makes one large organization like the WTO a dream. However, one could argue that there is a trade-off between the WTO's long drawn out court-like process and the Spaghetti bowl. Would one rather take the case to the WTO, spend lots of time and resources (not to mention the bad publicity), or go to the RTA of

93 Bhagwati, Jagdish. "Why PTAs Are a Pox on the World Trading System." In *Termites in the Trading System*, Termites in the Trading System, Chapter 3. Oxford University Press, 2008.

choice and resolve it through a relatively quicker, flexible and inexpensive negotiation? It would be more efficient to resolve disputes through an RTA. This encourages trade liberalization and explains RTA popularity. However, Bhagwati fails to see the benefits of RTAs in this case.

Third, Bhagwati maintains when poor countries enter into PTAs with... the United State and often the European Union, the lobbies in the hegemon countries insist on inserting into agreements a number of 'trade-unrelated' demands on the poor countries. As said, North-South RTAs make up for 27% of the world's total RTAs. They are formed mutually through contracts. If Southern nations did not want to agree to these 'trade-unrelated' demands, they would not enter into these agreements. It would be in the interest of Southern nations to enter into RTAs with Northern nations because of their access to markets. Bhagwati's argument does not hold much water here.

A large part of Bhagwati's entails the fear of the world going back to the 1930's. However, the world's current level of integration and economic interdependence has changed quite a bit since then. Again, the exception to the WTO's nondiscrimination clause contains limitations, most importantly: RTA member countries cannot hike additional barriers to the other WTO member countries. Thus, the WTO places constrains on RTAs, so they do not engage in illiberal practices, especially the type Bhagwati fears. From this, the argument can be made that RTAs speed up the process of trade liberalization and multilateralism through decentralized blocs. This would explain why they have proliferated to the extent they did. As discussed, RTAs correct the deficiencies of the slow-moving WTO. They facilitate and encourage developing countries to enter trade relations with other nations to boost economic growth and development. RTAs are defended by the WTO and with the two-thirds waiving mechanism, this exception to reciprocity can be deleted if needed. Therefore, RTAs are not a threat to multilateralism, rather they encourage it.

Trade regimes can be multilateral, bilateral or regional in their nature. Different theoretical approaches can be applied to explain trade regimes creation, existence and success. The multilateral trade regimes have been introduced with GATT (General Agreement on Trade and Tariff) and later replaced by a formal organization – the World Trade Organization (WTO). Regime theory of IPE attributes stability of international economic system to be associated with the regime itself, its norms and principles. Moreover, regime theory provides a set of tangible recommendations that can assist in making regimes more operational. Some of them have availability of information on the regime itself, clarity of its rules, and flexibility of the regime: possibility to adjust the rules according to the needs, how malleable regimes are, escape clauses, etc. From the regime theory point of view, multilateral trade regime's rules are codified by GATT and made operational by the WTO. Multilateral trade regimes are governed by two major principles shared by its members such as trade liberalization and non-discrimination. This makes regime attractive to its members. The principles are reflected in two major provisions codified in GATT as Most Favored Nation and National Treatment.

However, despite its advantages, the multilateral trade regime also has its disadvantages. From the point of view of regime theory, the non-binding and ineffective dispute resolution procedure does not put the WTO as a viable option for trade related disputes. This is the shortcoming of the regime making the states try to resolve their trade disputes under a different forum. HST attributes stability of the system to the overwhelming power of a hegemon that can either be benign or coercive but in either case provides the common good enjoyed by others. In case of the WTO, despite the obvious US hegemony as economic power, the presence of other powerful players such as Japan and the EU makes reaching decisions on particular issues quite difficult. There are still some issues pending and unresolved since the Doha round, which arguably demonstrate weaknesses of the regime overall.

Therefore, it can be argued that both Regime Theory and HST can find multilateral trade regime to be a suboptimal choice for the states in their trade policies. This can explain recent proliferation of a new wave of trade agreements. The first wave of trade agreements was mostly attributed to political integration and fostering of peace (the case of the European Union). The second wave of regionalism was mostly of economic nature. Moreover, the provisions of the GATT itself, as stipulated in article XXIV make Regional Trade Agreements (RTAs) possible.

Arguably, according to Art XXIV, RTAs are not to hamper but rather further advance the proliferation of international trade. Since they are possible only in the case of complete elimination of trade barriers, they should further provide liberation of trade flows. From the theoretical perspectives as well, both RTA and CUs (Customs Unions) make sense, since they enable members to address the issues that multilateral regimes are not capable of addressing (in case of RTAs, issues that are sensitive to the region). Moreover, the establishment of new regimes under RTAs and CUs allow member states to further advance their agenda by establishing the norms, rules and principles that are better tailored to their needs. Therefore, RTAs can be argued are optimal choice for many states in advancement of their trade agenda. Both multilateral and Regional Trade Agreements provide an important tool for states to advance their policy.

Many scholars have expressed several reasons why RTAs have seen a surge over the last several decades, but two authors in particular make a clear point as to why they have become so prevalent. The rapid spread of RTAs can be connected to change in American economic policy. For quite some time, the US had been the "champion"[94] of multilateralism and inspired other countries to become more open with their trading policy. It was not until the conclusion of the Uruguay Round and the implementation of Article XXIV of the GATT (General Agreement on Tariffs and Trade), that persuaded the US to engage in more regional trade. Since then, the US has promoted RTA's and other less developed countries have followed suit and adopted RTA's as an alternative to multilateralism. There are 6 reasons why countries have engaged in RTA's and have contributed to the increase in RTA's. The 6 reasons are: security concerns, hegemons attract LDC's, credibility among states, avoid divergence of trade, tit-for-tat among countries to join RTA's and lastly, RTA's allow powerful countries to advance un-related trade policies on weaker countries, in hopes of reform. It is also important to mention that many nations have become increasingly tired of dealing with the WTO and the difficulties that have been shown to come to agreements.

Some scholars have advocated for the spread of RTA's and believe that they can positively contribute to the multilateral system. They understand that the current multilateral system, based on the structure of the WTO, is slow in advancing open trade policy. States are more inclined to strike agreements with each other, especially if they have similar characteristics and are of economy of scale[95]. If RTA's are struck among several less developed countries, it can spark economic reform and persuade governments in these countries to become more open. RTAs will help the multilateral system by reforming those nations that otherwise would not through the current multilateral paradigm.

94 Mansfield, Edward D., and Helen V. Milner. "The New Wave of Regionalism." *International Organization* 53, no. 3 (1999): 589-627.

95 Griswold, Daniel. "Bilateral Deals Are No Threat to Global Trade: DANIEL GRISWOLD." *The Financial Times*, 2003.

On the other side of this debate, RTAs can be viewed as damaging to the multilateral system. Bhagwati believes that the fast spread of RTA's has caused contradictions to occur, while allowing more powerful nations to impose "un-related" trade policies onto its weakest members[96]. He uses the term "Spaghetti Bowl", in order to imply the crisscrossing of overlapping policies and the confusion imposed on nations when trading with one another. In this sense, it is clear to see why RTA's are stumbling blocks to multilateral trade. If countries are continually imposing different tariffs and policies on member and non-member states, this can eventually increase tensions among states and create a hostile environment. States, especially powerful states, can side step the bureaucracy of the WTO, in favor of striking agreements with other countries in order to expand their influence. Some scholars have assessed the second wave of regionalism has distinctive features that make it benign[97]. First, there is a GATT/WTO framework to work under and have as a guide. The next distinctive feature is that liberal democratic reforms are being locked-in legally when signing an RTA. Another distinctive feature is that gains from trade are not being used to bolster political military power. This wave has the US as the hegemon leading the way at signing RTAs under high levels of interdependence. It is easier to get more done with less actors and it is possible to include more things like democracy and human rights in these agreements.

NAFTA and the EU are proof that RTAs can be beneficial and act as nice compliments to the WTO[98]. Regional agreements are monitored by WTO member states and guided by those rules. However, RTAs act with much autonomy as it relates to the WTO. Member states fail to check their activities, and this can hurt trade[99]. The US approach can be defined as

---

96 Bhagwati, Jagdish N. *Termites in the Trading System: How Preferential Agreements Undermine Free Trade.* Oxford; New York: Oxford University Press, 2008.

97 Mansfield, Edward D., and Helen V. Milner. "The New Wave of Regionalism." *International Organization* 53, no. 3 (1999): 589-627.

98 Abbott, Frederick M. "The North American Integration Regime and Its Implications for the World Trading System." In *The EU, the WTO, and the NAFTA*, The EU, the WTO, and the NAFTA, Chapter 6. Oxford University Press, 2001.

99 Fabbricotti, Alberta, Joost Pauwelyn, and Gabrielle Marceau. "Multilateralizing Regionalism and the Future Architecture of International Trade Law as a System of Law." *American Society of International Law. Proceedings of the Annual Meeting*, 2009, 119-28.

competitive liberalization, because the US pursues free trade in all possible ways - "walking on two legs."[100]

Bhagwati refers to RTAs as PTAs, because they are inherently preferential and discriminatory[101]. He argues their vast proliferation came about during the Uruguay Round, because the US feared EU voting in unison at GATT, was tired of waiting for stalled multilateral talks and had poor leadership. He further argues that PTAs are proliferating and have become systemic. The "spaghetti bowl" model is a complex set of PTAs crisscrossing the globe from so many states signing so many different PTAs. He argues it is too complex for logistics and distorts international trade. It is impossible to reduce it all into a single integration model. Tariffs have to be reduced to negligible levels and make preferences worthless[102].

There are many different positions when it comes to benefits and consequences of regionalism. Overall, RTAs act as compliments to the international trading system based on realist terms. States trade more within alliances than across alliances, because it is easier to monitor allies than non-allies[103]. States are always concerned with externalities and watching to see, if others are gaining relatively more than them. Fulfilling this is much easier in a small RTA than it is in the large WTO.

On top of this, states know what they are doing when they sign an agreement. States fail to monitor, if RTAs are WTO consistent[104]. As an example, Obama created a team to monitor China and has won small disputes at the WTO, which eventually adds up. If a state thought it would experience consistent trade divergence, then it will not sign an agreement. The state does what is best for the state and if it does not feel it will receive benefits, it will not sign an agreement in self-help analysis.

---

100 Zoellick, Robert. "US Trade Strategy and European Interests." *CESifo Forum* 4, no. 3 (2003): 18-23.

101 Bhagwati, Jagdish Natwarlal. 2008. *Termites in the trading system: how preferential agreements undermine free trade.* Oxford: Oxford University Press.

102 Fabbricotti, Alberta, Joost Pauwelyn, and Gabrielle Marceau. "Multilateralizing Regionalism and the Future Architecture of International Trade Law as a System of Law." *American Society of International Law. Proceedings of the Annual Meeting,* 2009, 119-28.

103 Gowa, Joanne. 1995. *Allies, adversaries, and international trade.* Princeton, N.J.: Princeton University Press.

104 Fabbricotti, Alberta, Joost Pauwelyn, and Gabrielle Marceau. "Multilateralizing Regionalisma and the Future Architecture of International Trade Law as a System of Law." *American Society of International Law. Proceedings of the Annual Meeting,* 2009, 119-28.

If a transatlantic trade agreement between the US and the EU was to become reality, this could mean that a major hegemon (the US) is able to remain a hegemon by joining with another powerful entity (the European Union) in order to become the largest economy in the world overpowering China, which is threatening the US as a hegemon, according to Realists. In addition, other BRICS states such as Brazil, Russia, India and South Africa could potentially pose a future threat as well, which would then require a further extension of the US-EU trade agreement in include other entities such as Canada, for example.

Contrary to realist notions that state power shapes the international anarchic system, Keohane and Nye developed the complex interdependence theory in 1977. While acknowledging that the international system is anarchic, Keohane and Nye added that institutions play an important role to facilitate cooperation and trade among states[105].

The theory of interdependence also applies to an EU-US trade agreement as an example of how democracy can create other democracies due to the spillover effect. Contrary to Realists, Neo-Liberal Institutionalists believe that cooperation and peace is possible due to institutions. Realists tend to have a more pessimistic outlook arguing that if one nation wins, another one loses. Neoliberal Institutionalists such as Keohane argue that institutions can be a win-win situation for everyone. This certainly applies to an EU-US trade agreement. Democratic Peace Theory[106] applies as well in this case, since one democratic nation applies a positive spillover effect to others[107]. An EU-US trade agreement would also be based on soft power[108] principles as opposed to (military) hard power.

Targeted government intervention in particular sectors, can increase aggregate social welfare. In the standard model, society does best by removing all forms of trade protection and by specializing in its comparatively advantaged industry. Factors of production will move into relatively advantaged industries because it is profitable to do so.

---

105 Keohane, Nye, and Nye, Joseph S. *Power and Interdependence: World Politics in Transition.* Boston: Little, Brown, 1977.

106 Doyle, M. "The Democratic Peace." *International Security* 19, no. 4 (1995): 180-84.

107 Kant, Immanuel, and Ted Humphrey. *Perpetual Peace and Other Essays on Politics, History, and Morals: A Philosophical Essay.* Indianapolis: Hackett Pub. Co, 1983. <http://public.eblib.com/choice/publicfullrecord.aspx?p=775229>.

108 Nye, Joseph S. *Soft Power: The Means to Success in World Politics.* New York: Public Affairs, 2009. <http://public.eblib.com/choice/publicfullrecord.aspx?p=903654>.

The infant-industry case for protection argues that there are cases in which newly created firms will not be efficient initially but could be efficient in the long run if they are given time to mature. A short period of tariff protection is advocated to enable these infant industries to become efficient and begin to export. Once this point has been reached, the tariff should be removed. There are two reasons why an industry may not be efficient in the short run, but could be efficient in the long run, one is economies of scale and the other economies of experience[109].

The formation of regional trade agreements has been, by far the most popular form of reciprocal trade liberalization in the past decades. The discriminatory character of these agreements has raised three main concerns: first, that trade diversion would increase, because special interest groups would induce governments to form the most distortionary agreements, second, that broader external trade liberalization would reverse and third, that multilateralism could be undermined.

In case of the WTO, the presence of multiple powerful players makes reaching decisions on particular issues quite difficult. Therefore, it can be argued that both Regime Theory and HST can find multilateral trade regimes to be suboptimal choices for states in their trade policies. This can explain recent proliferation of a new wave of trade agreements. While the first wave of trade agreements was mostly attributed to political integration and fostering of peace (the case of the European Union), the second wave of regionalism is mostly of economic nature. Moreover, the provisions of the GATT itself, as stipulated in the article XXIV make Regional Trade Agreements (RTAs) possible.

To follow a constructivist approach, RTAs as well provide more stable regimes as they tend to be present in states with cultural proximity (as in case of the European Union) that as well can facilitate success[110]. In the case of the European Union, cultural proximity is reflected in need for new member states to adopt all legal body of the Union and play according to the Union's rules.

Both, multilateral and Regional Trade Agreements provide an important tool for states to advance their policy. As both Regime and HST theory

109 Kenen, Peter B. *Managing the World Economy: Fifty Years after Bretton Woods.* Washington, DC: Institute for International Economics, 1994.

110 Katzenstein, Peter J. "International Interdependence: Some Long-term Trends and Recent Changes." *International Organization* 29, no. 4 (1975): 1021-034.

demonstrate, the attractiveness and flexibility of RTAs can explain their proliferation in recent years.

Today's trade politics serve as a reminder of what could potentially repeat itself in history. During the inter-war years (between World War I and World War II), Great Britain was unable to resume its leadership role due to the destruction of the war. The United States could have assumed a leadership role, but instead decided to pursue protectionist economic policies. This neo-mercantilist behavior in combination with weakened European economies from World War I eventually resulted in the Great Depression from 1929-1939. In the realist view, a hegemon was needed to stabilize the international system in order to keep other nations in checks and balances, in order to provide peace and protection[111]. Similar to the US behavior back in the 1930s, the Trump Administration's protectionist trade policies could potentially trigger another depression. Therefore, it is highly recommended that the US continues trade talks with the EU in order to form an official trade agreement and possibly create a repetition of the "Great Transformation"[112] in order to combat economic instability based on liberalist principles. In contrast to the Great Depression, liberalism is a double movement. First, creating a stable system for trade and cooperation and second stabilizing this system based on Keynesian notions by institutions. After World War II, the different nations were fed up with the economic instability caused by wars and therefore decided to found the Bretton Woods Institutions: the International Monetary Fund and the World Bank in order to finance development for the European Nations to rebuild after the war as well as for developing nations. In addition, the GATT (General Agreement on Trade and Tariffs) set the foundation for a more liberalist period again. In contrast to the Great Depression, liberalism can be viewed as a double movement. First, creating a stable system for trade and cooperation and second stabilizing this system based on Keynesian notions by institutions. In addition, a stable exchange rate system was created by pegging the dollar to gold and all other (European) nations pegged their currencies to the dollar. This system worked well for trade and created economic growth for several decades until the United States experienced a deflation in the 1970s. In order to devalue its currency, the

111 Kindleberger, Charles. *The World in Depression 1929-1939.* London: Allen Lane, 1973.

112 Polanyi, Karl. *The Great Transformation.* First Beacon Paperback ed. Beacon Paperback No. 45. Boston: Beacon Press, 1957.

US decided to leave the gold standard and all other nations consequently followed after that. In addition, the OPEC oil crisis occurred in 1973 setting an end to this stable and reliable Bretton Woods system. Several economic and financial downturns all over the world followed in Asia and Europe. Therefore, the 1980s were characterized of a more neo-liberal capitalist Reagan-Thatcher economic trend in order to boost the economies and encourage international trade again.

These principles are still applicable today when it comes to EU-US trade policies.

Some scholars contend that both mega-regional trade agreements (TTIP and TPP) have been proposed in order to counter the emerging BRICS (Brazil, Russia, India, China, South Africa) which are threatening to overthrow the highly developed United States and the European Union, for example. Especially China should be a central focus of attention, according to Keohane[113]. Since the rise of China, the United States is no longer the hegemon, according to some realists such as Gilpin[114] and therefore, the United States sees it as a necessity to engage in trade-agreements in order to create a bigger economy with more opportunities. The United States economy alone can no longer compete with China. However, combining the European Union economy with the United States economy, would mean that through a joint trade agreement, both, the US and the EU, can overpower the Chinese economy. From a Liberalist point of view, these trade agreements are also attempts to prevent another economic crisis. The US economy is not growing as much as it used to be. Therefore, regional trade agreements are a way of boosting the economy and creating new opportunities on both sides of the Atlantic. From a Constructivist point of view, the United States and Europe share mutual (Western) values, cultures, norms, identities and ideas historically. Therefore, an EU-US regional trade agreement could also be viewed as a joint community of values from a Constructivist lens[115].

---

113 Keohane, Robert O. "The Old IPE and the New." *Review of International Political Economy* 16, no. 1 (2009): 34-46.

114 Gilpin, Robert., and Gilpin, Jean M. *Global Political Economy: Understanding the International Economic Order*. Princeton, N.J.: Princeton University Press, 2001.

115 Katzenstein, Peter J. "International Interdependence: Some Long-term Trends and Recent Changes." *International Organization* 29, no. 4 (1975): 1021-034.

The context and timing of an EU-US trade agreement could also be explained with the Domino Effect Theory[116]. When the GATT (General Agreement on Tariffs and Trade) was implemented after World War II, the US was more focused on multi-lateral trade up until the Uruguay Round in the 80s and 90s which eventually led to the creation of the World Trade Organization (WTO) in 1995. At this time, the United States was still committed to multi-lateral trade and international multi-lateral trade was viewed as beneficial[117]. However, when the Doha Round in 2001 stalled any further progress with the WTO rules, the United States decided to change the multi-lateral trade policy to a more regional trade-policy. The WTO has too many member states who cannot all agree on and decide on trade policy. Therefore, regional trade agreements started rising in popularity resulting in NAFTA, for example, in 1994 (North American Free Trade Agreement between the United States, Canada and Mexico). This created a "Domino Effect" leading other nations to engage in Regional Trade Agreements as well. NAFTA and regional trade agreements in general may have benefits and supporters, but they also have opponents.

116 Baldwin, Richard. "A Domino Theory of Regionalism." *NBER Working Paper Series,* 1993, 4465.

117 Mansfield, Edward D., and Helen V. Milner. "The New Wave of Regionalism." *International Organization* 53, no. 3 (1999): 589-627.

Figure 1: Tariffs and World Trade 1946-2001[118]

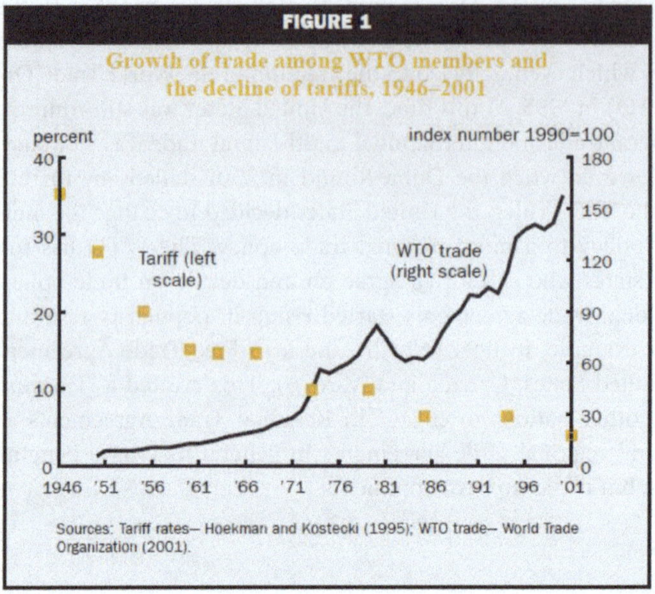

Sources: Tariff rates– Hoekman and Kostecki (1995); WTO trade– World Trade Organization (2001).

In the case of TTIP, the United States and the European Union were unable to agree on the final terms during the last negotiation round in 2016. Due to the agricultural lobby in the United States, the US did not want to establish higher agricultural food and safety standards compliant with EU laws and due to consumer and agricultural lobbies in the EU, the EU was unable to lower its standards in order to find a compromise with the United States[119]. At the center of this debate was genetically-manipulated food, hormone treated meat and chlorine bleached chicken – all commonly accepted standards in the US, but rejected by the EU. If the US were to increase these standards, the contents of TTIP could technically still be ratified. However, this seems quite unlikely under the current Trump administration which is neither very environmentally friendly nor very "green"/organic oriented. TTIP actually did not face too much opposition in the US. Most US citizens do not even know about TTIP, because the media did not focus on this

118 Sources: World Trade Organization (2001); Hoekman and Kostecki (1995)

119 Rogowski, Ronald. "Political Cleavages and Changing Exposure to Trade." *The American Political Science Review* 81, no. 4 (1987): 1121-137.

agreement during the elections, but TPP was the sole focus of public and media attention. In Europe, however, TTIP faced a lot of public and media opposition and would therefore probably not be able to pass unless it was to be re-negotiated under a different name and higher standards (from the US side compliant with EU norms). Since the Trump administration has signaled an intention to negotiate with single partners, it will be interesting to see how this will affect the outcome of a US-EU agreement.

Cultural influences on economic growth and trade with the example of locals versus cosmopolitans can have an impact[120]. "Regular" locals are US citizens living in rural areas, for example in the Mid-West, and they have not much understanding of international cultures. They are mainly concerned with their local employment and local domestic environment. Cosmopolitans, on the other hand, usually live in big cities such as New York, London, etc.; they travel a lot and are familiar with different cultures and languages. The difference in this lifestyle and education also shows how their viewpoints on trade can be affected. Domestic locals tend to be against trade agreements whereas cosmopolitans tend to be pro-trade. Urban versus rural lobbies can make a big difference when it comes to influencing the farmers lobby, for example.

In both, TPP and TTIP, domestic pressures have been the main cause for the failure of these agreements. The consequence for the economies on both sides of the US territory may be that trade agreements with China could be formed leaving the US out. The EU, for instance, is already starting trade negotiations with China. The same could be true for Australia and Japan for instance. The US might find itself left out in the end, if the Trump Administration does not manage to boost the US economy and satisfy unemployed workers. However, the question remains whether this can be done by pursing protectionist measures. Globalization cannot be halted, and jobs lost due to technological advances will not return. The only alternative remains to re-train those workers into other fields, which requires an investment in education. However, the Trump administration already made some budget cuts in the education sectors which is quite concerning given the unemployment dilemma connected to trade.

The more and more unequal distribution of wealth is not due to trade nor due to globalization, but due to domestic social welfare policies in

120 Friedman, Thomas L. *The Lexus and the Olive Tree.* First Anchor Books ed. New York: Anchor Books, 2000.

order to protect citizens of the impact of globalization and trade agreements[121]. The unequal distribution of wealth causes social and economic instability[122]. However, the Trump Administration removed many of the protective measures the Obama Administration had put in place in order to prevent another financial crisis, in order to prevent banks overpowering the markets etc. As history has demonstrated, most mercantilist and protectionist trade policies did not last, because they create power for the nation and wealth for the government while decreasing international competitiveness. The Great Depression in the 1930s was a result of US protectionist policies. On the other hand, too much liberal trade without government control and stability measurements are not good either as the Reagan, Nixon period has shown removing too many industry protection measurements. Therefore, a balanced approach is important supported by governing and regulating institutions for social (welfare) protection. Ruggie concurred that an "Embedded Liberalism" is necessary in order to keep capitalism and trade in check.[123]. He agrees with the Keynesian approach of stabilizing the liberal system with institutions and the state controlling the market up until a certain point, but not to the mercantilist extend. Krasner added Regime Theory[124] to this idea explaining how institutions such as the United Nations or the Bretton Woods institutions serve an important role in stabilizing the international system and facilitating trade. Keohane builds on Kindleburger's hegemonic stability theory[125] demonstrating that a hegemonic stabilizer was not necessarily needed due to international institutions[126].

The advantages of RTAs outweigh the disadvantages. However, every argument has validity. Most RTAs are, in fact, created for power and protectionist reasons (Realist argument). However, the cultural factors are even

121 Stiglitz, Joseph E. *The Price of Inequality*. First ed. New York: W.W. Norton &, 2012.

122 Piketty, Thomas, and Arthur Goldhammer. *Capital in the Twenty-First Century*. 2018. <https://doi.org/10.4159/9780674982918>.

123 Ruggie, John Gerard. 1982. "International Regimes, Transactions, and Change: Embedded Liberalism in the Postwar Economic Order". *International Organization*. 36, no. 2: 379-415.

124 Krasner, Stephen D. *International Regimes*. Cornell Studies in Political Economy. Ithaca: Cornell University Press, 1983.

125 Kindleberger, Charles. *The World in Depression 1929-1939*. London: Allen Lane, 1973.

126 Keohane, Robert O. *After Hegemony*. Princeton University Press, 2005. <http://www.myilibrary.com?id=275144>.

more influential. The fact that a sense of community is created weighs even more. Therefore, the constructivist argument is the strongest.

President Obama and Secretary of State John Kerry demanded a free trade area of the Atlantic-Initiative for Europe and the US in 2013. By 2016, the negotiations were supposed to be completed (degradation of e.g. subsidies for export of agricultural products, the removal of customs duty, elimination of demanded import restrictions, disappearance of visa requirements, etc.). A trade area of 800 million dollars and millions of new jobs was intended to arise. Mutual trade would have been greatly increased.

The economic crisis and migratory pressures in the world in general and most specifically in Europe and the Western Hemisphere, in addition to the rise of populism and the rebirth of renationalization, have presented challenges serious to trade and regional integration projects. The comparable context and timing of TPP and TTIP were no coincidence. The economy is not growing as it used to. Republicans in the US blocked Obama in almost every policy he proposed except for in trade. They actually granted him Trade Promotion Authority which demonstrates how important these trade agreements are. If Democrats, Republicans, Congress and the Senate can actually agree on something with a clear majority, it is definitely a strong indication on its validity and importance. While there are some losers with trade agreements, there are overall more winners than losers. If a joint EU-US trade agreement is not implemented, there will be more negative consequences for the United States and for Europe than positive. This is one of the reasons why China and Russia were so happy with the election outcome, because TPP and TTIP were both put on ice. Consequently, China might even create a bigger economy than it already has and surpass the US and the EU once and for all. Hopefully, the Trump administration will be smart enough to catch on to this quickly, as it has already been all over the scholarly news (of course not the popular one as usual).

Some of the US unemployment and economic problems which were the heart and center of the very recent November 8, 2016 US election outcome could be solved by copying other successful models such as a dual education and employment system that Germany offers for example. Therefore, I recommend for the US administration to copy these successful already existing models and apply them to the US system to come up with actual solutions for these ongoing problems. The key is to combine the best of each, the US and the EU, to come up with tangible and working policy recommendations that could actually be implemented by administration and governments domestically. A joint EU-US trade agreement is the first step in the right direction and will be ultimately be beneficial for both sides.

Chapter 3: Why a US-EU Free Trade Agreement?

Understanding the impact of TTIP on business strategy requires first of all understanding the meaning, purpose and impact of free trade agreements (FTAs) and clarifying why it is desirable for the United States (US) and the European Union (EU) to build the largest free trade area in the world. Since free trade in general is not the main component of this work, the advantages and disadvantages as well as the wider economic impact are shown below only in an overview.

3.1 Foreign Trade Theories

The best-known supply-oriented foreign trade theories are those of the comparative cost advantage according to Ricardo and those of the Heckscher-Ohlin model. The former attributes foreign trade and the emergence of foreign trade gains to differences in labor productivity, the latter adding to the model the different factor endowments of two countries[127]. Both theories can only be applied in a limited way for this particular topic due to implicit restrictive or outdated assumptions and the similarity of the productivity structure of both economic blocs. Recent statements seek to identify causes of external trade, particularly in domestic demand, with the approximation of capital intensity and per capita income and the product life cycle playing an important role. Other arguments relate to dynamic aspects which, in essence, constitute the variability of comparative advantages and involve the existence of multinational sum-up sum, i.e. intra-company trade[128]. The German automotive industry illustrates the latter reason, since 38.8% of exports to and 80% of imports from the U.S. are due to trade between related manufacturers[129]. It seems that in times of intra-industrial trade, a comprehensive explanation is only possible with the inclusion of several approaches. Reference should be made in this context to the theory of National Competitive Advantages of Porter, which is not new in its indi-

127 Krugman/ Obstfeld/ Melitz (2012), page 85, 156.
128 Frontzkowski (1994), pages 2019- 20; IFO-Institut (2013), page 10.
129 IFO-Institut (2013), p. 37, 5

vidual statements, but combines different explanatory approaches through modification and combination[130].

3.2 Free Trade Agreements

Neoclassical theories conclude that free trade leads to the maximization of the welfare of a single country and that of the world. The problem is that this statement is based on assumptions whose full compatibility with reality is not always present, so that in addition to the advantages of free trade, its disadvantages are also taken into account below[131].

3.2.1 Advantages of Free Trade

3.2.1.1 The Efficiency Argument

In line with the efficiency argument, free trade eliminates the distortions of consumption and production caused by a customs order, thereby increasing national welfare[132].

3.2.1.2 Dynamic Gains

Profits are generated by free trade due to a more complex process in the longer term. The elimination of tariff and non-tariff barriers and discriminatory measures requires the guarantee of free market access for foreign companies[133]. As a result, competition is increasing, companies are facing increased pressure stake in innovation and productivity, and the use of internal or external economies of scale is more extensive[134].

130 Frontzkowski *(1994)*, p. 20- 21.
131 Gerken (1999), page 29.
132 Krugman/ Obstfeld/ Melitz (2012), page 309.
133 Frontzkowski (1994), page 255.
134 Krugman/ Obstfeld/ Melitz (2012), page 310.

3.2.1.3 The Political Argument for Free Trade

According to this argument, trade policies are influenced in the way stakeholders work so that the macroeconomic benefits cannot be maximized. Advocacy of free trade deprives stakeholders of the basis, as trade policy measures are no longer necessary (such as enforcing U.S. government anti-dumping measures in favor of the solar industry in 2013)[135].

3.2.2 Disadvantages of Free Trade

The following presentation of the counterargument refers in particular to trade diversion effects. This is done for three reasons:

- The terms-of-trade argument (TOT) is more theoretical in nature, especially because it has potentially negative consequences for international multilateral coordination of trade policy[136].
- The argument of domestic market failure is not entirely convincing, as direct domestic policies appear to be possible, provided that they are appropriate in accordance with economic accuracy[137].
- Although trade diversion is not a classic counterargument, it needs to be given greater weight in this work, since not the economic impact on two countries alone but on two sectors must be analyzed. Thus, in addition to the consequences of changing framework conditions within the EU and the US, wider effects on current and future sales markets and production sites must also be considered.

3.2.2.1 Terms of Trade and Domestic Market Failure

A country that is able to influence foreign export prices due to its size and importance in world trade can reduce import prices by a relatively low optimal tariff and thus improve its real exchange ratio. Like the US, the EU would be able to increase welfare through the common external tariff, provided that TOT profits exceed the tariff losses.

135 Krugman/ Obstfeld/ Melitz (2012), page 312.
136 Krugman/ Obstfeld/ Melitz (2012), page 316.
137 Krugman/Obstfeld/Melitz (2012), pages 319-320.

In the event of domestic market failure, the costs and benefits of the consumer or producer's pension may not be correctly mapped. For example, it is not possible to grasp the social marginal benefits of a technology in the producer's pension if markets do not function optimally. In such a case, intervention may be justified by protectionist measures according to the Second-Best Theory. In this way, internal functional defects of a market are remedied by external economic interventions[138].

3.2.2.2 Trade Diversion Effects on Bilateral Agreements

The classic trade creation and diversion analysis can be traced back to Jacob Viner (1950). Thus, a far-reaching removal of tariff barriers between the EU and the US will lead to the creation of trade in substitutable goods, provided that there is sectoral redistribution in the area of production costs due to competition. As a result of the reallocation of factors towards more productive areas of use, real income increases in both economic regions. Trade diversionary effects now occur when a cheaper producer from a third country loses competitiveness with the EU or the US as a result of tariff disposal. This is the case where the production cost advantage is lower than the discrimination margin (customs) that continues to exist for this producer. As a result, world production is shifting to a country with higher production costs. Real income within the free trade area is falling. Whether the net size of trade creation and diversion is positive or negative depends on the extent of the differences in production costs and the level of duty. The greater the differences in production costs and the smaller the tariffs, the greater the welfare gain[139].

The reduction of non-tariff barriers can also have a negative effect on the framework conditions and competitiveness of third countries and their companies in such a way that their barriers to entry remain unchanged. The exception is exporters who export to both the US and the EU, as they benefit from the approximation of standards or the elimination of double authorization and audit expenditure[140]. Some theorists in the literature go so far as to say in their analysis of trade diversion effects that trade creation

138 Krugman/ Obstfeld/ Melitz (2012), pages 315-316.
139 Langhammer (2013), pages 75-76.
140 IFO Schnelldienst (2013), page 4.

at the expense of third countries reinforces regional protectionism and is therefore made more difficult for global free trade[141].

3.3 Classification of TTIP in the Current Development of Regional Trade Agreements and Trade Policy Considerations

According to the World Trade Organization (WTO), 387 regional trade agreements (RTAs) are currently in force worldwide. The bulk of this is accounted for by FTAs (223), Economic Integration Agreements (118) and Customs Union Treaties (18)[142]. In terms of current developments, TTIP is not an isolated case either. Many of the agreements currently under negotiation remain bilateral. Negotiations on multilateral trade agreements in the Asia-Pacific and South Pacific or within Africa are the exception[143]. The reasons for the sharp increase, especially between WTO Member States, since the mid-1990s are manifold and were already covered in Chapter 2 of this dissertation. Since taking into account all the motives for concluding regional or multilateral agreements goes far beyond the scope of this particular chapter, the following, especially with regard to the external developments of the United States, will only be limited to ensuring the competitiveness of a country.

The Canadian American Agreement (CUSFTA) understands the importance of FTAs to secure strategic market access and strategic political alliance as economic importance declines[144]. For example, the problems of the Canadian export industry between 1980 and 1990 are one reason for signing CUSFTA[145]. A losing economy should be guaranteed barrier-free access to the American market[146]. Canada's subsequent accession to the North American Free Trade Agreement (NAFTA) and negotiations on FTAs with states that also negotiated with the US served in turn to protect

141 De Melo/ Panagariya (1993), page 7.

142 World Trade Organization. *Regional Trade Agreements Database.* Accessed September 24, 2019. http://rtais.wto.org/UI/PublicMaintainRTAHome.aspx

143 World Trade Organization. *Regional Trade Agreements.* Accessed September 25, 2019. https://www.wto.org/english/tratop_e/region_e/region_e.htm

144 Fiorentiho/ Verdeja/ Toqueboeuf (2007), page 6; Bartels/ Ortino (2007), page 21.

145 Frontzkowski *(1994)*, pages 54 – 56.

146 Bartels/ Ortino (2007), page 21.

against trade diversionary effects[147]. This short example of Canada's motives at the time coincides with the impact that the Leibnitz Institute for Economic Research at the University of Munich e.V. (IFO Institute) predicted for TTIP. According to this study, those countries that already have an agreement with the US or the EU will be affected in particular by trade diversionary effects[148]. As briefly pointed out below, TTIP is also important for the US, in addition to the declining competitiveness of its own foreign trade.

Compared to the US, the EU currently has a much higher number of FTAs (35 to 14) and is currently in further negotiations on future agreements with 13 countries and one community (MERCOSUR)[149]. In addition to the parallels with the race for FTAs, these are also conceivable between the state of Canadian and US foreign trade for the period 1999-2012. Looking at American exports in nominal terms as measured by the world market share during this period, there is a decline of 6.5%. Although the price-adjusted loss of market share has been relatively constant since the mid-2000s, this means that it has not been possible to increase the share of the world market since then[150]. The pattern is also in line with the assessment of the Association of the Automotive Industry (VDA), but is extended by this to the European share of total world trade, according to which, due to the advancing globalization of third countries, in the long term, third countries will determine world trade[151].

In conclusion of these trade policy considerations, reference should be made to a study on TTIP by the Friedrich-Ebert Foundation, according to which the agreement is considered critical, taking into account the European internal market and current account balances. Thus, despite the free exchange of goods, services and capital over the last 15 years, the European internal market, which can serve as a model for transatlantic

147 "The TTIP, NAFTA and Mexico" in Roy, Joaquin and Dominguez Roberto. *The TTIP.* Miami-Florida European Union Center/ Jean Monnet Chair, 2014, pages 151-171. https://eucenter.as.miami.edu/_assets/pdf/ttip.pdf

148 IFO Summary (2013), page 7.

149 World Trade Organization. *RTAs in force, including accessions.* Accessed September 24, 2019. http://rtais.wto.org/UI/PublicAllRTAListAccession.aspx

150 IMK Report Nr. 85 (2013), pages 2-3.

151 Dominguez Roberto. "The Automotive Sector in light of the Free Trade Agreements between the EU and North America", in Roy, Joaquin and Roberto Dominguez. *The TTIP.* Miami-Florida European Union Center/ Jean Monnet Chair, 2014, pages 101-109.

trade, does not document any stronger trade dynamics than trade with the non-internal market country United States of America (measured by the single market of Germany). The second essential point concerns trade policy between countries and the implementation of TTIP. Taking into account the different evolution of the current account balances of Europe and the US and the fact that free trade is not a zero-sum game in the long run, the study points to the fact that the US will not accept future trade surpluses of the trading partner in the long term[152]. The author's further criticism of alternative studies using equilibrium models for calculating trade trends under TTIP is not addressed due to the lack of alternative calculations. Thus, from chapter 3.5.2 onwards, reference is made to the results of the equilibrium models.

3.4 Impact of Existing Free Trade Agreements (NAFTA, ASEAN, CETA, APTA, MERCOSUR)

Since the advantages and disadvantages of free trade have already been examined in previous chapters on the basis of theoretical foundations, and a classification of TTIP has already been carried out in this dissertation, the real impact on participating countries and sectors to be investigated is presented below. As TTIP would create the largest free trade area in the world, the effects on NAFTA, on the ASEAN Free Trade Area (AFTA) and the Common Market of South America (MERCOSUR) are shown to ensure comparability. The aim is to gain more precise indications of possible scenarios under TTIP from past developments and taking into account current trade trends.

3.4.1 Impact on the Participating Countries

If NAFTA and AFTA are considered the period before and after the agreement is closed, the theoretically predictable effect of an increase in intra- and extra-regional trade is confirmed. However, the exact assignment of the effect to the respective FTA is not without its problems. It is often the case that agreements only follow above-average trade relations. The increase

152 Friedrich-Ebert Stiftung (2014), pages 2-7.

in trade is therefore often visible well before an agreement is signed[153]. This trend is also evident in NAFTA and AFTA. Rather, the agreements concluded must be interpreted as confirmation of a long-standing trend of additional trade that reduces trade costs. MERCOSUR is an exception to developments within NAFTA and AFTA. Since the agreement was signed in 1991, significant trade diversionary effects have been observed, which, contrary to the preceding descriptions, have also been accorded to this agreement. A significant increase in intra-regional trade was also linked to an equally clear decrease in extra-regional trade. Estimates suggest that the previously described net size of trade creation and diversion was negative for the Southern market[154].

The examples presented show that the success of TTIP depends, among other things, on the long-term importance of trading partners for each other. In import demand, the US is the EU's third most important trading partner after China and Russia, with the share falling by almost half between 1999 and 2011.

A similar trend can be seen over the same period for the export of EU products. Although the US remains the most important market, the share fell by around 10% over the course of the year.

The sectoral relationship shows an opposite trend to the aggregated trend. Between 1999 and 2011, the share of imports and exports of pharmaceutical products increased by around 8% and remained relatively stable in the motor vehicle (automotive) sector[155].

From the US's point of view, the EU as a whole has lost relevance. Over the above period, there has been a decline in aggregate deliveries, but this is not quite as significant at 3% and 4% respectively. The share of imports of motor vehicles also followed this trend (-2.5%). Exports developed slightly positively in the run-up but are not significant at 4.4%. Only the import and export of pharmaceutical products shows an increase of 8%[156]. These are, after all, the largest sectors with the same standards and testing methods on both sides of the Atlantic.

---

153 World Bank (2005), page 58.

154 Malamud, Carlos. "The TTIP and Mercosur". In Joaquin Roy and Roberto Dominguez. *The TTIP.* Miami-Florida European Union Center/ Jean Monnet Chair, 2014, pages 173-183.

155 IMK Report Nr. 83 (2013), page 7-13.

156 IMK Report Nr. 85 (2013), page 6-14.

3.4.2 Impact on the Automotive Industry

The conditions under which the automotive industry can benefit from TTIP can be seen in the consideration of five agreements according to their chronological order. The Canada-US Agreement on the Free Trade of Automotive Products (APTA) negotiated in 1965 agreed to align local value-added requirements and other non-tariff barriers. As a result of the integration of both industries, there have been rationalizations within manufacturing, the expansion of intra-industrial trade and increased trade in intermediate products (e.g. largest Canadian supplier Magna International). The 1988 CUSFTA shows, as a second example, that a comprehensive FTA has little positive impact on an industry that has already been well integrated across countries[157]. From example two can thus be concluded that the determination of the already existing degree of integration of both industries is also important for the later scenario analysis.

NAFTA (1994) as a third example shows how a free trade area between two industrialized and emerging countries can be used to achieve a sustainable increase in the competitiveness of trade barriers and different framework conditions of the automotive industry[158].

The distribution of production and development activities within NAFTA shows that competitiveness can be achieved, on the one hand, through wage reductions and, on the other hand, by increasing productivity. End manufacturers (OEMs) and suppliers mainly use low personnel costs within Mexico for wage-intensive production depths, and conduct research and development in the United States and Canada[159]. A parallel with TTIP is appropriate in that there is also a clear pay gap within the EU[160].

The fourth example, which, as in the previous chapter, shows a contrary development, is MERCOSUR, which gives an advantage to only a certain part of the automotive industry. Due to tariffs and subsidies, inefficient Brazilian end manufacturers succeeded in pushing foreign imports out of

157 U.S. International Trade Commission (2003), pages 230-240.

158 AHK (2011), page 4, 25

159 Hübner, Kurt. "TTIP: Opportunities and Challenges for the EU" in Joaquin Roy and Roberto Dominguez. *The TTIP.* Miami-Florida European Union Center/ Jean Monnet Chair, 2014, pages 35-50.

160 Schröder (2012), page 6

the single market[161]. Recent FTAs with other producer countries, which have already been concluded or are still in negotiations, show that such a development is to be taken into account, but is unlikely in the long term for the American and European automotive market. Examples include US (2012) and EU (2011) FTAs with South Korea[162] and current EU negotiations with Japan.

The final example of AFTA confirms how dynamic profits are put into practice through free trade and the resulting tightening of competition. Since governments of the ASEAN states agreed in 1993 to establish a free trade area within 15 years, the share of investment by foreign car manufacturers has increased. Between 1995 and 1999 alone, EUR 1.6 billion euros were invested.

Originally in force in 2003, Malaysia intervened and secured a postponement of free trade in the automotive sector until 2005. Malaysia, the largest automotive market within ASEAN, deliberately protected domestic manufacturers, as Japanese imported vehicles were expected to be 30 to 50% cheaper[163].

The fact that developments for the automotive industry are sustainable within a developing free trade area is demonstrated not only by NAFTA but also by the growing importance of the Asian sales market. With the launch of the Economic Community of ASEAN (AEC) in 2015, it is estimated that the region will become the sixth largest car market in the world[164].

3.4.3 Impact on the Pharmaceutical Industry

Although the pharmaceutical industry benefited from reductions or the total abolition of tariffs decided in the Uruguay Round, in particular because of a generally high dependence on intermediates, pure trade liberalization, however, only had moderate consequences until 2001 within CUSFTA and

---

161 Steinmeier, Florian. "Pazifikallianz - die Bessermacher", in: *Markets* 5/2014, pages 10-15.

162 Office of the United States Trade Representative. "U.S. – Korea Free Trade Agreement". March 15, 2012. https://ustr.gov/trade-agreements/free-trade-agreements/korus-fta

163 European Commission. "The EU-South Korea free trade agreement". December 2015. https://ec.europa.eu/trade/policy/countries-and-regions/countries/south-korea/

164 German-Thai Chamber of Commerce (2013), pages 20 – 24.

NAFTA. Much more important was the extension of the patent period from 17 to 20 years, as initiated by the Agreement on Trade-Related Aspects of Intellectual Property Rights (TRIPS) consequently incorporated and clarified in NAFTA[165].

The precise structural consequences of TRIPS[166] for the pharmaceutical industry were illustrated by developments within MERCOSUR, to which the agreement applies within the framework of the WTO[167]. Contrary to the theory, the new market openness within MERCOSUR did not create a dynamic process of intensification of competition or strong integration processes[168]. This was due to a market tied to renowned brand names and a highly controlled quantity of imported precursors by producers. The main structural changes in the sector can only be explained by the amendment of patent law. Due to the extension of patent protection over time, the production of profitable copycat preparations, such as those which come onto the market after the expiry of a patent, has been significantly restricted. As a result, smaller local pharmaceutical companies sought a strategic alliance with transnational corporations. The aim was either to secure early production through licenses or to offer themselves as a sales partner. The market for generics has also undergone a transformation in that the importance of economies of scale to reduce production costs has increased. This development improved the positioning of transnational corporations, which, in the context of increasing specialization, expanded their own production activities through reconstruction or acquisition. Therefore, MERCOSUR also shows the trend towards the distribution of specific production lines between countries or country groups towards globalized strategy and intra-company trade[169].

---

165 U.S. International Trade Commission (2003), page 192-201.

166 World Trade Organization. "Trade-Related Aspects of Intellectual Property Rights". *Trade topics.* April 4, 2020. https://www.wto.org/english/tratop_e/trips_e/trips_e.htm

167 EU Commission. "EU-Mercosur Trade Agreement". July 2019. https://trade.ec.europa.eu/doclib/docs/2019/june/tradoc_157954.pdf

168 Malamud, Carlos. "The TTIP Negotiations and their Impact on the EU-MERCOSUR Accord" in Joaquin Roy and Roberto Dominguez. *The TTIP.* Miami-Florida European Union Center/ Jean Monnet Chair, 2014, pages 173-184.
Schröder (2012), page 6

169 Bekerman/ Sirlin (2001), pages 229 – 232; Vega Canovas, Gustavo. "The Mexico-European Union Free Trade Agreement, NAFTA and TTIP", in Joaquin Roy and Roberto Dominguez: *The TTIP*, 2014, pages 151-171.

Within AFTA, considerable efforts have been made to harmonize non-tariff barriers since 1992[170] with the first sustained successes achieved in 2008[171]. The approximation of barriers is equivalent to an average reduction in costs, as there is, among other things, no expenditure on double authorization procedures. Indonesia is the best example in order to demonstrate the resulting advantages of this. If significant negative effects on the domestic pharmaceutical industry were forecast in the run-up to the increase in competition, this did not actually materialize. It is of particular importance that, in the case of Indonesia, the improvement of a framework will meet strong demand in the future. In particular, the planned introduction of a statutory health insurance system and the increase in per capita income must be mentioned regarding this[172].

3.4.4 Interim Results and Conclusions

In addition to the conclusions already made, it can be said that for the vast majority of the free trade areas under consideration, there are positive welfare effects and that people's real income increases through trade creation. Thus, the increase in income can be used as added value for products and services of the automotive and pharmaceutical industries. The extent to which the welfare effects can be seen depends on the extent of reciprocal trade links and trade elasticity. The EU and the US have a high-level but long-term downward trend in this regard. In the sectoral view, only the pharmaceutical industry documents a significant increase in trade.

In the context of previous agreements, the removal of tariff and non-tariff barriers for the automotive industry has a lasting positive effect, provided that the degree of integration was previously low. The example of AFTA in particular illustrates how a free trade area encourages the industry to invest additionally with already high levels of investment.

Even though the pharmaceutical industry also welcomes classic trade liberalization, changes in patent law are of greater importance in this sector. In addition to the prolonged maintenance of a certain profit margin, significant structural changes can also be observed. It is undisputed that

170 World Bank (2005), page 58.

171 European Commission. "EU-Mexico Trade Agreement". April 2018. https://ec.europa.eu/trade/policy/in-focus/eu-mexico-trade-agreement/

172 ASEAN Roadmap 2015 (2013), pages 31 – 32.

TTIP would include intellectual property (IPR) rules in the area of trade-related aspects[173]. Furthermore, the example of MERCOSUR documents the importance of economies of scale for the industry and the need to classify the market created by TTIP as a tied or free market. As a final conclusion derived from the example of Indonesia, it is necessary to take account of an increase in demand and its impact on dampening the effects of competition. In addition to increasing incomes in the European Union, demographic change and the extension of life expectancy must be considered.

3.5 Role Model Effects in the Negotiation Process of Free Trade Agreements

This final sub-chapter on the meaning, purpose and operation of free trade agreements is intended to answer three questions:

- Do older agreements affect the design process of younger FTAs?
- Can the European-Canadian Free Trade Agreement (CETA) serve to limit the sectoral rules of TTIP and thus provide a tool for scenario analysis?
- Will technical standards and arbitration rules in TTIP also serve as an example in current and future negotiations with emerging economies such as India or China?[174]

In an interview on October 10, 2014, Karel de Gucht, then EU Trade Commissioner, answered the above questions himself, as he stated: "I hope that CETA will be the blueprint for the agreement with the US, because it is an excellent agreement for Europe."[175] He also stated that a waiver of investment protection clauses (ISDS) would have a serious impact on future negotiations, such as with China[176]. The Federal Association of German In-

173 European Commission. “EU trade policy and intellectual property”. September 26, 2019. https://ec.europa.eu/trade/policy/accessing-markets/intellectual-property/

174 World Trade Organization. “Regional Trade Agreements Database”. October 1, 2019. http://rtais.wto.org/UI/Publicsummarytable.aspx

175 Interview with Karel de Gucht. October 10, 2014 https://trade.ec.europa.eu/doclib/press/index.cfm?action=search

176 Neuerer, Dietmar. “EU-Handelskommissar provoziert die SPD”. *Handelsblatt,* page 1. October 10, 2014. https://www.handelsblatt.com/politik/deutschland/handelsabkommen-ceta-und-ttip-eu-handelskommissar-provoziert-die-spd/10823508.html

dustry (BDI) shares that fear[177]. Thus, the renunciation of ISDS clauses and other high standards would be a strategic mistake, as agreements between developed countries serve as a template for agreements with developing or emerging countries[178].

Having established that CETA is a blueprint for TTIP, the extent to which it can be used for direct sectoral reference must be answered. With CETA, Canada and the EU agreed to reduce customs duties and levies having an equivalent effect on all industrial goods[179]. The current text also contains provisions to remove technical and other non-tariff barriers to market access. In this way, the parties were able to agree on the mutual recognition of quality standards in the pharmaceutical sector within the framework of good manufacturing practice (GMP)[180]. As in the past, however, much higher effects for the industry can be expected from the agreements on IPR and patents. In addition to the objective of acting in accordance with the Geneva Patent Law Treaty, patent-like agreements of their own kind were incorporated under sui generis protection. As a result, after the expiry of the actual patent, a retrospective protection of two to five years can be granted for the specific active substance. More extensive information on these and other safeguards will follow in chapter 6.2.1.6.

For the automotive industry, the agreement reached so far seems to be of a smaller scale. In this way, only a few points have been able to achieve agreement with the standards of the Economic Commission for Europe (UNECE)[181]. It should be noted that CETA serves as a blueprint for TTIP, and that it will shape the standards for subsequent negotiations.

177 Neuerer, Dietmar. "EU-Handelskommissar provoziert die SPD". *Handelsblatt,* page 2. October 10, 2014. https://www.handelsblatt.com/politik/deutschland/handelsabkommen-ceta-und-ttip-mit-schiedsgerichten-gibt-es-keine-freihandelsabkommen/10823508-2.html

178 BDI (2014), page 20.

179 EU Commission. "Consolidated CETA Text". September 26, 2019, pages 344-347.

180 EU Commission. "Consolidated CETA Text". September 26, 2019, pages 428-440.

181 EU Commission. "Consolidated CETA Text". September 26, 2019, pages 91-98.

Chapter 4: TTIP (Transatlantic Trade and Investment Partnership)

After an EU-US summit in November 2011 decided to set up an expert group (HLWG) and the eulogy of a comprehensive trade and investment agreement some two years later, the mandate was given to the EU Commission by the Council of the EU on June 17, 2013. A few days later, the negotiations were proudly announced by US President Obama and the President of the European Commission Barroso[182]. After much hesitation by the EU Commission, the negotiating mandate (guidelines for TTIP negotiations) was officially published on October 9, 2014[183]. The following comments on the likely content of TTIP refer to this document. The presentation is limited due to reference to the industries to be investigated.

4.1 Nature, Content and Scope of EU-US Trade Agreement

The agreement will include rules on trade and trade-related areas, with the aim of complying with and exceeding WTO rules. Furthermore, all levels of government will be bound by TTIP for market access, regulatory issues, non-tariff barriers and rules. In order to ensure market access, all customs duties, with a few exceptions, should be eliminated, in compliance with rules of origin. If possible, the reduction should come into force and then take place in stages. The fact that goods from the automotive and pharmaceutical industries are covered by the few exceptions is also unlikely when considering CETA as a guiding document[184].

In addition to customs clearance, market access in public procurement is to be ensured at all levels of administration. The focus is on simplifying the respective procedures and reducing requirements for technical and local standards[185].

182 BMWi Brochure, April 2014, page 10.

183 Council of the European Union 11103/13 DCL 1, June 17, 2014. Published October 9, 2014.

184 Council of the European Union 11103/13 DCL 1 (2014), pages 2-5, 5 and 6.

185 Council of the European Union 11103/13 DCL 1 (2014), page 10, 24.

In the field of authorization and qualification procedures, the agreement includes binding obligations for transparency, impartiality and regulatory procedures. The aim is to strengthen the regulatory discipline of the authorities. In addition, equal treatment is required for companies, subsidiaries or branches regarding intra-company trade.

The parties are making particular efforts to achieve wide-ranging technical accessibility in both sectors. Efforts are focused on the past and the future. As previously mentioned, TTIP will also include the issue of Intellectual Property Rights. Based on TRIPS and extended by additions, the chapter is to be additionally covered by investment protection. The agreement aims to maintain industry standards and regulations implemented up to now as well as avoid a qualitative reduction in mutual recognition[186]. The extent to which the support for small and medium-sized enterprises (SMEs) promised by TTIP has a direct or indirect impact on both sectors through the subcontracting structure is not yet clearly defined at this stage[187].

4.1.1 European Union Negotiation Position: Automotive Industry

The abolition of discounted tariff barriers means a reduction of around 8% of European and 1.2% of US import duties[188]. In order to reduce non-tariff barriers, the approximation of technical standards is being pursued. Currently, technical standards within the EU are largely harmonized with UNECE, whereas in the US the Federal Motor Vehicle Safety Regulations are applicable[189]. The EU's current negotiating position emphasizes the mutual recognition of standards, the objective of implementing this as a priority within UNECE and that the process will be long-term and gradual due to the complexity[190].

186 European Commission. "Report - 7th Negotiation Round". September 29 – October 3, 2014 page 7.
187 European Commission. "Introduction to the EU legal text on Regulatory Cooperation in TTIP". February 10, 2015, pages. 8-10.
188 CEPR (2013), page 14.
189 Komnerskollegium (2012), page 15.
190 European Union Position on Motor Vehicles (2014).

4.1.2 European Union Negotiating Position: Pharmaceutical Industry

For the pharmaceutical industry, a tariff reduction due to a low initial level would not have a lasting impact. The EU import duty is currently 2.3%. Imports to the US are subject to duty at 1.2% of their import value[191]. The EU Commission's position paper shows that there is a certain degree of integration in the industry regarding non-tariff barriers. In addition to partial considerations in approval processes, priority is therefore given to further harmonization of technical requirements and the avoidance of unnecessary overlaps of controls. These aim to strengthen cooperation and exchange of information between the institutions on biosimilars, generics, pediatrics and the uniformity of terms.

The primary objective of the EU Commission of process efficiency improvements and cost reductions is to be achieved in each section[192]. According to the assessment of the Federal Association of Pharmaceutical Industries (BPI), the sections just listed are those in which a negotiation success seems realistic[193].

4.2 Projected Macroeconomic Impact on EU and US

In this section, it is important to clarify to what extent welfare effects of TTIP on the economic and sales area can be expected. Reference is made to studies by the IFO Institute, Bertelsmann Stiftung, Center of Economic Policy Research (CEPR), ECORYS and Komnerskollegium[194]. The presentation in this section is summarized based on these studies. This is also useful because the studies of the Bertelsmann Foundation and the IFO Institute have the same scientific background and most of the studies use an identical calculation model (CGE model)[195]. All studies have in common that they work with two scenarios. The first scenario includes the consequences of a tariff reduction with no or only marginal reductions in non-tariff barriers. Since the average tariff in transatlantic trade is low at 3.5%, the calculated impact on the welfare development of the member

191 CEPR (2013), page 14.
192 EU Position on Pharmaceutical Products (2014).
193 CEPR (2013), page 14.
194 IFO-Institute (2013); Bertelsmann Stiftung (2013); CEPR (2013), ECORYS (2012); Komnerskollegium (2012).
195 The exception is the IFO Institute (2013).

states is small. More interesting is the second scenario, which also assumes a reduction in non-tariff barriers between 25% and 50%. The interpretation of non-tariff barriers as fixed costs of market access shows that the effects must be greater in this case[196]. This is confirmed by all studies, as both scenarios have significant differences. The long-term effect on EU and US welfare is positive across all studies, with significant differences between the IFO Institute's calculations and the rest of the studies. For example, ECORYS, representing the lower limit, notes growth in gross domestic product (GDP) of 0.3% (US) and 0.5% (EU)[197]. In contrast, the IFO Institute forecasts an increase of 4.95% (EU) and 13.4% (USA)[198]. The figures given are long-term effects, hence a minimum implementation period of 10 years. If trade diversion effects occur for third countries, this can be explained by increased competitiveness.

EU and US companies are reducing production costs due to the favorable reciprocal supply of precursors, an increase in the productivity of the labor factor through reallocations and a stronger competitive situation as a result of the opening[199]. One aspect to be taken into account for the structure of the subcontracting industry in both sectors is the indirect ratio of productivity increase to the number of enterprises in the given employment sector. In the overall economy, the IFO Institute's calculation compensates for negative effects by increasing the number of jobs in the most productive enterprises[200].

4.3 Economic Impact on the Automotive Industry

4.3.1 Industry Assessment

The IFO Institute's survey on the weighting of tariffs, non-tariff barriers, exchange rate fluctuations and customer proximity for the competitive position in the US shows an important to very important significance of all four factors[201]. The fact that the low US import duty was rated as significant by the respondents can be explained by the volume of imports and the

196 IFO-Institute (2013), page 15.
197 ECORYS (2012), page 32.
198 Bertelsmann Stiftung (2013), page 42.
199 Bertelsmann Stiftung (2013), pages 16–19; IFO-Institute (2013), page 17.
200 IFO-Institute (2013), pages 95 - 96.
201 IFO-Institute (2013), page 56.

value of the import. According to this, a tariff reduction for the German automotive industry would mean a saving of EUR 650 million per year[202]. The estimation is also consistently high in the assessment of the US as a market, export market and production location[203]. The assessment is in line with the VDA's statement[204] that the US should be included in the future growth markets in the medium term alongside China (in the long term)[205]. Consequently, the future importance of the US is at odds with the general trade trend of both countries.

In line with the weighting of the above-mentioned market competitive factors, the CEPR assesses the impact of a comprehensive liberalization scenario on the market entry option. The automotive industry is given the highest index value by far in comparison to all other sectors[206]. However, the result is at odds with the IFO Institute's surveys, which show that only 5% of SMEs and 10% of large companies believe in new market opportunities[207].

In conclusion, this means that success factors beyond looking at the price elasticity of US import demand to the level of trade barriers must be decisive for market entry and the perception of new market opportunities.

4.3.2 Calculations by CEPR and the IFO Institute

In the absence of a reliable estimate of the exact scope of the arrangements contained in TTIP at this stage, a limited scenario of tariff reduction with little to no further impact is expected to be used in the presentation of the potential economic effects, approximations and one of the comprehensive liberalizations, thus taking into account the additional removal of non-tariff barriers.

Based on the high assumed price elasticity, the CEPR calculates in a limited scenario a development of EU exports to the USA of plus 13.7%. A truly extraordinary increase of 109.5% is forecast for the opposite direc-

---

202 European Commission. October 9, 2019. https://ec.europa.eu/germany/

203 IFO-Institute (2013), page 56.

204 Verband der Automobilindustrie. October 3, 2014. https://www.vda.de/en/press/press-releases.html

205 Handelsblatt Nr. 11. January 16/17/18, 2015, page 44.

206 CEPR (2013), page 32.

207 IFO-Institute (2013), page 55.

tion[208]. The latter calculation could be based in part on the current eight times larger European import duty. If the forecast is correct in its tendency, this will lead to a significant increase in the market shares of American producers on the European sales market in the long term as a manifestation of increased competition. A similar trend can be seen in the calculations of the total trade development of the sector, taking into account trade diversion and other external effects. EU exports are up by around 3% and EU imports by 9.21%. However, this trend would be surpassed by the gains in US exports (15%) especially in relation to the increase in imports (around 2%)[209]. Judging by the CEPR figures, the US automotive industry seems to be significantly becoming more competitive through tariff reductions. It should be noted that the results given are long-term effects and thus the change in the figures for 2027 to a state without TTIP.

The IFO Institute's calculations for 2025 are difficult to compare at sectoral level with those just presented, as both institutes use different computational models and regional references. Nevertheless, the results are represented, as the automotive industry is often of strategic macroeconomic importance, especially at national level. In addition, additional data shows a more consistent picture of the future. According to IFO calculations, German exports to the US are increasing by 11.45%. The discrepancy in the opposite direction is again striking, with an increase of 51.85%. If one breaks away from the regional view, German exports as a whole increase by 1.65% and those of the US by 6.33% [210]. Both calculations therefore agree on two points:

- There are significant positive effects for the automotive industry on the markets under consideration, which correspond to the dynamic gains of free trade.
- The positive effects for the US sector on the EU sales market are far more pronounced than vice versa.

Projected sectoral effects of a comprehensive scenario[211] with the removal of non-tariff barriers are only available from CEPR. As a result, EU exports to the US are up by 148% and those of the US by 346.8%. As in the first

208 CEPR (2013), pages 38-39.
209 CEPR (2013), pages 40-42.
210 IFO-Institute (2013), pages 115 - 117.
211 the CEPR divides the comprehensive scenario into ambitious and less ambitious, this presentation refers to the former.

scenario, the trend in the involvement of third countries is less pronounced, with EU exports/ imports developing by 41.75% and 43.75% respectively, and those of the US by 59.47% and 20.81% respectively[212]. Comprehensive liberalization therefore has the same effect on the automotive sector as tariff reductions mentioned above. Only the magnitude of the impact varies significantly.

4.4 Economic Impact on the Pharmaceutical Industry

4.4.1 Industry Assessment

Once again, starting with the assessment of the IFO Institute's respondents, it is characteristic that the US is regarded as an important sales market and production location. What is striking is a low valuation of the classic barriers to trade, only the proximity to the customer was considered very important[213]. The low assessment of non-tariff barriers is therefore in consistence with the EU's assessment[214]. With regard to the effect on market entry and market opportunities, there is a correlation with the result of the CEPR, with a moderate price elasticity being less decisive than the high share of import demand[215]. The discrepancy between large enterprises (5%) and SMEs (55%) is striking as it relates to assessment of new market opportunities[216]. This may indicate, on the one hand, a potential structural change in the market, but on the other hand, it may also be due to the fact that the IFO Institute's definition of the size class of SMEs used by the EU Commission does not refer to the sectoral specifics of the pharmaceutical industry[217]. For example, companies that are SMEs within the pharmaceutical industry would be assigned to large enterprises in the study. According to the BPI, large companies are currently operating globally, and SMEs are predominantly locally positioned within the pharmaceutical industry[218].

212 CEPR (2013), pages 64 -69.
213 IFO-Institute (2013), page 56.
214 EU-Position Paper on the TTIP negotiation: *Pharmaceutical Industry Chapter.* October 10, 2019.
215 CEPR (2013), page 31.
216 IFO-Institute (2013), page 55.
217 BPI (2014), page 27.
218 Interview 3 (see Appendix A)

4.4.2 Calculations by CEPR and the IFO Institute

In a scenario limited to CEPR, the pharmaceutical industry will see an increase of 5.46% and 12.45% respectively in EU exports/ imports to and from the US. For total trade, the long-term consequences for both countries are of little importance, as EU exports and imports are only 1.23% and 2.46% and those of the US by 4.05% and 1.06% respectively[219]. For Germany, exports and imports with the trading partner USA increased evenly by 16.28 % and 18.29 %. The IFO Institute also calculates marginal effects for the entire trading level. For example, the growth of German exports remains below one percent, while that of the United States increases by 3.5 percent[220]. The results thus reflect the respondents' assessment of which tariff barriers are of little importance. In a comprehensive scenario, EU exports and imports are very evenly developed with the US by 36.2% and 34.2% respectively. The comparison with the overall development of trade shows an equally positive but less pronounced development. The increase in EU exports and imports is about 9% each, and that of the US by around 11%[221]. This confirms two facts for the pharmaceutical industry. On the one hand, the forecast trade trend shows a much less asymmetric trend, and, on the other hand, the importance of non-tariff barriers is less important in terms of figures than in the automotive sector.

219 CEPR (2013), page 38-42.
220 IFO-Institute (2013), pages 115 - 117.
221 CEPR (2013), pages 64 -69.

Chapter 5: Environmental Analysis in the Automotive and Pharmaceutical Industries regarding Transatlantic Trade

In addition to the findings made up to this chapter, the basis for determining future strategic changes is the environmental analysis, which is compiled below for each industry and is divided into four process steps:

- determination of relevant influencing factors by using the PESTEL method taking into account respective future developments
- analysis of interdependencies between influencing factors
- creation of different scenarios based on possible developments in and by TTIP
- Assess the scenarios created with respect to the current strategy of the industry[222]

Building on the first two process steps, the third step in the process takes into account the economic forecasts for TTIP as well as the mechanisms and consequences of free trade presented. The most important factors with their respective consequences are identified in this chapter.

5.1 Automotive Industries

5.1.1 PESTEL Method

The English acronym PESTEL stands for the determination of political, economic, social, technological, environmental and legal factors of an undertaking or, as in the present case, an industry environment[223]. In order to avoid the mere accumulation of factors, the focus is on those which are and will be the cause of the important future developments of the industry.

222 Steinmann/ Schreyögg (1997), page 165.
223 Johnson/ Scholes/ Whittington (2011), pages 80 – 81.

5.1.1.1 Political Factors

Regulatory policies of states and communities of states concern the automotive industry in particular in the areas of carbon dioxide emissions (CO2 emissions), regional value added (local content), customs duties, non-tariff barriers, subsidization and tax law.

Since 2015, new vehicles placed on the European market are subject to a ceiling of 120g of CO2 emissions per kilometer. If the upper limit is exceeded, OEMs are obliged to pay heavy penalties in the form of a levy for exceeding emissions[224]. In 2020, therefore, €4,000 per vehicle would have to be paid in punitive duty[225]. Constant statements by the EU Commission, as well as the negotiating mandate, pointed out that TTIP would not reduce existing protection and environmental standards. However, a correction of CO2 values only seems to lead downwards, as 95g per kilometer are targeted for 2021. Particularly strong interactions with technological success factors result from the agreements of rebates, which are based on the fleets of premium manufacturers and include, for example, electric vehicles[226].

So-called "local content" requirements are designed to ensure that value creation is also provided by regional suppliers or on-site work.

NAFTA, which increased a mandatory and tax-deferred local content to 60%, is an example of this rule[227]. If Mexico's low wage costs, which were already foreseen at the time, are taken into account, these provisions are not the sole reason, but certainly an important part of the considerations at the time. Between 1994 and 1996, Japanese and German OEMs invested more than 5 billion US dollars in new production sites[228]. In order to meet the interests of OEMs, regional requirements are also reflected in the EU negotiating mandate under the concept of rules of origin[229]. CETA is used to assess the extent to which car manufacturers are taken into account. In order for the EU and Canada to trade a large proportion of motor vehicles (engine class greater than one liter) duty-free, the regional share of value added must be 50% to start out with and after 7 years 55%. If TTIP is signed, this figure will rise to 60% after a one-year transition period. In or-

---

224 Wüste (2010), page 3.
225 PWC (2013), page 94.
226 Handelsblatt, November 14.- 16., 2014, page 18.
227 Kilper/ Pries (1999), pages 99-100.
228 Dörre, Klaus. "Unternehmen in transnationalen Wertschöpfungsketten", in: *Aus Politik und Zeitgeschichte*, 64. Jg-, 1-3/2014. December 30, 2014, pages 28ff.
229 Council of the European Union 11103/13 DCL 1 (2014), page 5.

der to mitigate the asymmetric consequences for Canada (see distribution of subcontracting structures), an allowance and the inclusion of American value-added shares in CETA were included in this case[230].

Due to a lack of conflicting information, it can be assumed that similar levels of arrangements would be included in TTIP.

Will some OEMs expand their production and procurement in the EU and the US, as happened in NAFTA, if the agreement contains provisions of this kind? The author of this dissertation considers the probability of a significant increase in investments that can be placed in this causal context to be low. As already demonstrated in Chapter 3.4.2, the negotiators have already concluded FTAs with producer countries or are about to be concluded. On the other hand, due to the strategic development of the sales markets, many OEMs already manufacture and procure in Europe and/ or the Americas with capacities still open[231]. Furthermore, the decision to invest in production sites is characterized by customer proximity and presence in the growth markets. The more detailed explanation of the factors just mentioned follow in Chapter 5.1.1.2. On the other hand, it is conceivable that capacity would be shifted within existing production sites. As part of the possibility of setting standards worldwide through TTIP, it is necessary to take into account current local content requirements in current and future growth markets. Examples include Russia, India and China, each with very high standards on local value-added shares, in conjunction with high import duties[232]. In this respect, TTIP could help the automotive industry to achieve a uniform (lower) level.

In the final consideration of local content, consideration is needed to take into account the desired mutual opening of public procurement[233]. As early as the early 1990s, foreclosed public procurement was classified as an obstacle to market access[234]. The dismantling (in CETA from 60% to 25% for local transport vehicles) would facilitate market access for OEMs on both sides. However, it remains to be seen to what extent *local content* will be replaced by *local value* in this area. The result would be a broad

230 Canadian Centre for Policy Alternatives (2014), page 77.

231 PWC (2013), page 70.

232 Mueller, Franziska. "Zur Architektur des Welthandels". *Bundeszentrale fuer politische Bildung*, page 21. December 19, 2013. https://www.bpb.de/apuz/175488/zur-architektur-des-welthandels?p=all

233 Hans Böckler Stiftung (2014), page 18.

234 Pfändner (1992), page 230.

interpretation of the term, which gives advantages to domestic OEMs, as maintenance and further support are included[235].

If the standard setting option is included, the expected effect appears to be greater, as public procurement in developing and emerging countries, compared to the European (degree of openness 90%) and the American system (degree of openness 35%) is considered to be much more closed[236].

As mentioned in previous chapters, the reduction of tariffs and non-tariff barriers is the main component of TTIP. Both are classic trade policy instruments. The first scenario is of great importance due to high trading volumes and the second scenario due to a high fixed cost share. Within the political-time framework, the parties agreed in CETA for the essential engine class on a complete tariff reduction over a period of eight years. For electric vehicles, the process is two years faster. Immediate effects are agreed for the import of Canadian supplies. If similar agreements were included in TTIP, for some OEMS the immediate increase in competitiveness would be the more favorable purchase of precursors. In the section on non-tariff barriers, the parties agreed on the extensive acceptance of UNECE rules and the expression of regular further cooperation[237]. As far as the duration of the adjustment is concerned, there is a need to differentiate between recognition and future harmonization of rules, the first of which, in principle, can be achieved more quickly through extensive technical discussions during the negotiations than the latter[238]. However, due to the complexity of the issue, it is not yet possible to estimate the exact timing of TTIP[239].

Politically motivated subsidies essentially influence the automotive industry in the choice of production sites and the creation of framework conditions for drive technologies and reflect the political argument for free trade (Section 3.2.1.3). For example, the French group PSA has largely refrained from setting up foreign plants in favor of domestically subsidized production. Norway promotes the sale of electric vehicles, which results

235 Canadian Centre for Policy Alternatives (2014), pages 33 - 34.

236 Hans Böckler Stiftung (2014), pages 54 – 55.

237 Canadian Centre for Policy Alternatives (2014), pages 76 – 78.

238 Müller, Franziska. "Zur Architektur des Welthandels" in: *Aus Politik u. Zeitgeschichte*, 64 Jg. 1-3/2014. December 30, 2014, pages 16ff. https://www.bpb.de/apuz/175488/zur-architektur-des-welthandels?p=all

239 Müller, Franziska. "Zur Architektur des Welthandels" in: *Aus Politik u. Zeitgeschichte*, 64 Jg. 1-3/2014. December 30, 2014, page 19. https://www.bpb.de/apuz/175488/zur-architektur-des-welthandels?p=all

in higher sales for German OEMs compared to cars with conventional combustion engines[240].

While the European negotiating mandate on TTIP includes anti-dumping and countervailing measures, these will not include subsidizing production sites and motor vehicles[241]. For example, the US could impose an anti-dumping duty only if the comparable export price to the US was lower than the price set within the EU[242].

The last aspect regarding important political factors is differentiated tax legislation. Different VAT rates are opposed to free trade in such a way as to lead to country-specific vehicle prices. The differentiated taxation of mineral oils and the favoring of petrol or diesel result in a product and engine policy geared towards this[243]. The competences of the individual member states or the US in the field of tax legislation are not directly emphasized by negotiating mandate. However, this issue must nevertheless be considered. Both CETA, which already contains a large investment protection chapter, as well as TTIP, which is to contain it, show a new quality of contained or sought safeguard clauses in the field of indirect expropriation. This form of expropriation-like interference may have an impact on the tax policy of the state[244]. A more detailed analysis of the topic in connection with the importance of the clauses to date and potential future developments will be carried out when legal factors are defined in Chapter 4.1.1.6.

5.1.1.2 Economic Factors

This section highlights the economic effects on demand, trade diversion effects, tariffs, non-tariff barriers, suppliers and customer proximity.

As already demonstrated in Chapter 3.4.1, trade in automotive products between the EU and the US has remained stable over a long period, contrary to general progress. However, the markets differ significantly in their assessment of the future. Since 1992, the European market has already

240 Müller, Franziska. "Zur Architektur des Welthandels" in: *Aus Politik u. Zeitgeschichte,* 64 Jg. 1-3/2014. December 30, 2014, page 21.

241 Council of the European Union 11103/13 DCL 1 (2014), p. 6.

242 Gabler Wirtschaftslexikon. "Antidumping Provision". November 26, 2014. https://wirtschaftslexikon.gabler.de/definition/antidumping-verordnung-31388/version-254947

243 Pfändner (1992), pages 228 – 229.

244 Fischer-Lescano/ Horst (2014), page 40.

been forecasted to experience a decline in demand and is in fact still continuing to experience a decline in demand to this day, the medium-term importance of the US can be considered to be high[245].

Objective determinants that determine demand include purchasing power, population development and the number of households[246]. If purchasing power is reduced to the development of income, assuming relatively stable currencies, there is a positive trend for the European and American markets. Based on the CEPR and its calculated additional GDP growth, there are annual income increases of €545 (EU) and €655 (US) for families of four[247]. Previously mentioned studies show similar or even greater effects.

At the beginning of this work, trade diversion effects were presented as a disadvantage of free trade, as these can subsequently cause income losses in other markets. Direct markets as well as processes beyond are relevant for the global automotive industry. Considering the duration of implementation of a comprehensive agreement, the focus will only be on markets that are important for the future[248]. These include Brazil, Russia, India, China (BRIC countries), Mexico, Iran, Thailand and Indonesia[249]. In order to ensure a heterogeneous picture, as previously, the reference to CEPR and IFO Institute follows.

CEPR excludes negative effects for the rest of the world. In particular, the ASEAN countries (including Thailand and Indonesia) would benefit from TTIP to a level far above the actual welfare effect for the EU and the US[250]. The results are explained by taking into account direct and indirect spillover effects. This opens up a direct effect for third countries from the harmonization of non-tariff barriers between the EU and the US, when the reduction in trade costs (down to tariff levels) affects exporters serving both countries. The indirect effect is a result of the supremacy and thus the implicit example effect of both economic blocs. In this case, third countries adopt the standards set by TTIP.

245 Pfändner (1992), page 223 – in reference to demand development on the European market.

246 Nolte (1991), page 165.

247 CEPR (2013), page vii.

248 Berger, Roland and Lazard. "Global automotive suppliers achieve record profitability, but volatility and uncertainty are on the increase". December 10, 2014. https://www.rolandberger.com/en/Media/Global-automotive-suppliers-achieve-record-profitability-but-volatility-and-unce.html

249 Hein, Christoph. "ASEAN, der übersehene Riese, a.a.o., page 12.

250 CEPR (2013), page 82.

In addition to simplifying market access for US or EU companies, there will be a reduction in trade costs and additional trade creation between third countries[251].

The IFO Institute's study concludes contrary results. The authors fundamentally acknowledge the existence and theoretical comprehensibility of spillover effects just described. As already indicated in Chapter 4.3.2, however, the quantification of non-tariff barriers is problematic for them and consequently no assessment is possible. However, they take account of the fact that the results they give are to be understood as upper limits[252]. The study calculates negative trade diversion effects for all the future markets mentioned above[253]. However, when the results are classified as a long-term course, these are to be classified as maximum and neglected of any spillover effects for almost all countries as very low to non-existent in real terms. The only exception is Mexico for which TTIP would affect GDP by 0.724% per year.

After the future development of demand related to trade diversion effects is outlined, the effects of tariffs and non-tariff barriers follow. The main accounting consequences of a reduction in trade barriers were already mentioned in Chapter 4.3. The results have concluded that the positive effects for the US sector on the EU sales market are far more pronounced than vice versa. The observation of asymmetries requires enlargement and deepening. In the US market, which is considered unsaturated in the medium term, the current share of European OEMs is 10% and therefore has additional potential precisely because of the removal of trade barriers. Furthermore, partial detachment from the saturation phases of the markets is necessary. This means that US OEMs do not necessarily benefit less strongly from TTIP[254]. Moreover, the scale of the removal of non-tariff barriers must be mentioned. For example, a German OEM calculates this with a value equal to a 26 percent tariff[255]. A cost reduction of this magnitude has a noticeable impact on all OEMs, even or especially in saturated markets.

These considerations must be linked to the demand and price elasticity that has just been dealt with. Just like the CEPR, the literature assumes

251 CEPR (2013), pages 28 - 29.

252 IFO-Institute (2013), pages 120 - 122.

253 IFO-Institute (2013), pages 159 - 161.

254 Dörre, Klaus. "Unternehmen in transnationalen Wertschöpfungsketten", a.a.O., page 32.

255 Radtke, Phillip and Andreas Abele. "Die smarte Revolution in der Automobilindustrie". Frankfurt/ Vienna: Redline-Wirtschaft, 2014, pages 15-19.

a high price elasticity of demand[256]. By passing on the cost reductions, increased demand would help to increase economies of scale, in turn unlocking potential savings.

Due to the very high share of total value added, the role of subcontractors as an important economic factor for OEMs is discussed below. In the context of the interpretation of non-tariff barriers as fixed costs of market access, suppliers in particular will benefit as representatives of SMEs. Compared to OEMs, this cost block is even more significant in relation to the financial and earnings situation. For illustrative purposes, Kirchhoff Automotive can be mentioned. For this large medium-sized company, the duplicate construction according to two different directives means a burden of several hundred thousand euros. If the barrier were to be eliminated, Kirchhoff Automotive would enter the US market[257].

With the expansion of the sales market, it would at best lead to the realization of economies of scale, which are passed on along the value chain, according to their high importance for capital-intensive final production. Suppliers have a key role within the automotive industry because of their high share of total value added. The elimination of tariffs and non-tariff barriers increases concentration, competitiveness and globalization pressures. Concrete consequences are continued cost pressures, the expansion of the range of competences, an increase in the pressure to innovate and, to a final consequence, an increased need for investment and capital. The fact that, contrary to the above example, not every supplier is able to meet these requirements is shown by the sharp reduction in the number of companies in recent decades. While 30,000 suppliers were registered in 1988, the forecast for 2015 is only around 2750[258]. The listed consequences of competition in the subcontracting industry explain the low assessments of SMEs (5%) presented in Chapter 5.3.1. on new market opportunities through TTIP. For the end manufacturers, the process raises two questions:

- Is TTIP further decreasing the concentration of suppliers?
- Is the bargaining power shifting to the remaining suppliers?

In order to answer the first question in the following scenario analysis, the current subcontractor structure must be applied to this case. Extensive

256 Pfändner (1992), page 238.
257 Die Zeit. "TTIP Freihandelsabkommen". November 13, 2014, page 3. https://www.zeit.de/2014/27/ttip-freihandelsabkommen-us-konzerne/seite-3
258 Pries/ Hertwig (2005), pages 77 – 80.

outsourcing processes and the bundling of value-added activities have resulted in large capital-rich module suppliers in the EU and in the US. Consequently, distinctions are required between direct suppliers, some of which have an oligopolistic subcontracting structure, and the other suppliers of components and parts[259].

Regarding the second question, there is a need to separate negative effects of competition and shifts in bargaining power. At least in the short term, the distinction is necessary, taking into account the just-in-time delivery principle, which applies to the entire automotive industry and causes a high degree of dependence. Thus, it is possible that a supplier who is not a direct supplier and would disappear from the market in the long term can exercise a high bargaining power in Porter's sense, even in the event of impending insolvency. This would be the case if the company is active in an area where few producers dominate and there are high conversion costs[260]. The VDA's position must be compared with the considerations relating to the short-term[261]. The federation assumes that the best-positioned suppliers will prevail in the now larger market and that the development will be very beneficial for the end manufacturers[262]. Thus, the first question for component and parts suppliers must now be answered unequivocally with a yes, as the opening of the market with TTIP sets dynamic processes in motion. In question two, the answer in the medium and long term is in favor of OEMs, since they can subsequently expand their supplier pool to include suppliers in the other market.

The last economic factors to be listed are proximity to the customer and regional cyclicality on the sales markets. These are mainly expressed by a high proportion of respective foreign production/ investment by OEMs and suppliers[263]. The need for presence in growth markets and immediate customer proximity is an essential feature of a globalized strategy for the automotive industry[264]. As previously mentioned, TTIP could include a new quality of investment protection clauses. The extent to which these also affect investments in production facilities in direct markets and/ or

259 Stratmann (2010), pages 124 – 127.

260 Krugman/ Obstfeld/ Melitz (2012), page 89.

261 Interview 2 (see Appendix A)

262 Ziff. "Monopolistischer Wettbewerb im Aussenhandel", in Krugman/ Obstfeld/ Melitz (2012), pages 242/ 243.

263 Pries/ Hertwig (2005), page 41, 77.

264 Dörre, Klaus. "Unternehmen in transnationalen Wertschöpfungsketten", a.a.O., page 29.

developing and emerging countries through their provisions is clarified in Chapter 5.1.1.6.

5.1.1.3 Social Factors and Transatlantic Trade

The definition of important social factors takes place within a framework that is not limited to the EU or the United States, as a cross-market approach in this area seems appropriate. In principle, emerging economies have as much a need for mobility as developed countries[265]. However, a restrictive generalization for all emerging countries cannot be made, as social needs vary according to the level of development of the middle-class income, and as the size of cities and their consequential problems, such as mass transport and air pollution, vary within these countries[266]. Within the industrialized countries, social needs are shifting to the topics of environment, urbanization, differentiation and rising energy prices. Cars are perceived less as valuable possessions, but more as a means of transport, which increases competition with alternative means of transport, focusing on operating costs[267]. The need for mobility in emerging markets has a positive impact on demand in principle, provided that products from the automotive industry are predominantly required. In this context, TTIP is crucial, on the one hand, as a requirement of a global standard, which would be adopted by third countries in subsequent periods and which leads to a reduction in trade costs and offer price, and on the other hand, assuming positive Spillover effects and income increases, increasing purchasing power and economic performance (financing of operating costs) of the population. As previously mentioned, TTIP should not reduce environmental standards in the two economic regions[268]. Again, considering the radiance of the agreement, this cannot be assumed for third countries either. Other success factors that are potentially affected are energy and operating costs. For example, the negotiating mandate contains a section on trade-related aspects of energy and raw materials. The aim is to ensure

265 EU Commission (2009), page 14.

266 Coni-Zimmer/ Flor Annegret. "Transnationale Unternehmen, Problemverursacher und Lösungspartner?" in *Aus-Politik u-Zeitgeschichte*, -43- 64 Jg.1-3/2014. December 30, 2013, pages 35ff.

267 EU Commission (2009), page 14.

268 BMWi Brochure (2014), page 28.

an open and transparent business environment in energy matters as well as sustainable and unrestricted access to raw materials[269].

It is not yet possible to assess the impact of the measures called for in the EU position paper on the future development of energy and the price of raw materials in the EU, the US and third countries[270]. In view of the competitiveness of the operating costs of motor vehicles in comparison to different means of transport as well as air pollution in large cities, reference should be made to the development of alternative propulsion technologies. The EU position paper on the automotive industry expresses the will to cooperate on future settings of standards[271]. The idea is that a uniform standard for future technologies promotes faster development and series production, resulting in lower overall operating costs for vehicles as a whole.

5.1.1.4 Technological Factors

Future technological success factors will mainly include electronics and information/ communication technology, new composites and new drive technologies[272]. As outlined in the previous section, TTIP can have simplistic and supportive effects by setting a uniform standard in the various areas. As a result, the automotive industry could save costs worldwide and promote developments more quickly through a uniform framework. However, the desirable effect of a targeted favoritism for technological advances by TTIP must be considered as relative in terms of its amount, since, for example, the Volkswagen Group currently has the highest expenditure on global production research and development (13.5 billion U.S. dollars)[273]. The large size of the budget can be explained by the process of further and new development of technological factors according to the principle of "saving, supplementing and replacing". This approach is necessary due to ongoing

269 Council of the European Union 11103/13 DCL 1 (2014), p. 16.

270 EU Commission. "Raw materials and energy". *EU-US Transatlantic Trade and Investment Partnership.* July 16, 2013. https://trade.ec.europa.eu/doclib/docs/2013/july/tradoc_151624.pdf

271 EU Position on Motor Vehicles (2014), page 3.

272 EU Commission (2009), page 14.

273 Handelsblatt. "Diese Konzerne sind Forschungsweltmeister". October 28, 2014. https://www.handelsblatt.com/unternehmen/industrie/ausgaben-fuer-entwicklungen-diese-konzerne-sind-forschungsweltmeister/10898476.html?slp=

uncertainty about the future market penetration of technologies and the continued dependence on vehicle classes for certain types of propulsion[274].

5.1.1.5 Environmental Factors

One of the most important environmental factors that is determining the industry in the long term is climate change and the CO2 emissions as a deeming cause. The political upper limits were already mentioned in section 5.1.1.1. Overall, there is an increased awareness of environmental protection across the target groups, which is reflected in the result of social, political and legal success factors, for example in the EU's current deliberations on the End of Life Vehicles directive[275].

5.1.1.6 Legal Factors (ISDS Procedures)

The automotive industry is characterized by numerous standards, guidelines and laws of national and supranational organizations and/ or states. All important safeguards, technical regulations and distribution restrictions, which guarantee market approval and designate distribution according to antitrust or joint venture rules, go beyond this work.

The extent to which TTIP seeks and can indirectly go beyond the recognition and harmonization of technical regulations in the two economic areas has been addressed in previous sections. In this section, the investment protection procedure is presented as a legal success factor for the automotive industry. This is due to investment protection clauses currently having a high degree of uncertainty about future developments, especially in comparison with regulations, directives and laws.

In the past, ISDS procedures have played little or no role. Due to a lack of transparency, it is difficult to define them precisely. However, by the end of 2013, the institution that negotiates the vast majority of cases (ICSID)[276] did not clearly show representatives of the automotive industry as plaintiffs[277]. In clarifying how the use of legal means of OEMs towards EU member

274 Cori-Zimmer Melannie/ Flohr Annegret. "Transnationale Unternehmen", a.a.o., page 36.
275 EU Commission. "End of Life Vehicles". *Environment.* August 7, 2019. https://ec.europa.eu/environment/waste/elv/index.htm
276 UNCTAD (2013), page 4.
277 BDI (2014), page 14.

states, the US and third countries could change in the future, consideration is needed for the following aspects.

Developments in the customer structure show that in recent years, large commercial customers with a high volume of procurement have become increasingly important in Europe and this trend continues unabated.

An interesting feature compared to other customer groups is the conscious demand for automotive financial services such as financing, leasing and insurance. The expansion of the classic financing with additional service modules leads to the bundling into service modules, which lead to sales promotion and customer loyalty[278]. Financial services are, however, also used for retail customers, depending on the market saturation phase. On the European market, OEMs do not earn exclusively, but at least a high proportion of their revenues from the sale of services and aftercare. In growth markets, profits can be made mainly from the original business[279].

In addition to the internal development of the automotive industry in response to customer needs, the quality of CETA's investment protection clauses must be taken into account. The uncertainty that still exists about this illustrates the very different results of two legal brief reports. A report commissioned by the German Federal Government certifies which member of the ICSID's List of Arbitrators considers the chapter on investment protection to be of low relevance to Canadian and European investors. Accordingly, the provisions contained therein do not exceed European and German law[280]. The report by the Federal German government does not share the possible option of industry to influence state taxation sovereignty as set out in section 5.1.1.1. Thus, only in the event of excessive taxation an expropriation-like intervention under ISDS can be assumed. Otherwise, CETA would contain exceptions which give the state sufficient room for maneuver in the area of taxation. The same argument is used in the areas of financial services and regulation[281].

Fischer-Lescano and Horst present the opposite view in their expert opinion prepared for the Attac Organization. The starting point for their argument is the formal overstepping of powers of the EU Commission. In this respect, the very broad version of the concept of financial services in

---

278 Stratmann (2010), page 114, 129 – 130.

279 Treeck,Till. "Globale Ungleichgewichte im Außenhandel" in: *Aus Politik und Zeitgeschichte*, 64Jg-1-3/2014. December 30, 2014, pages 26/ 27.

280 Schill (2014), pages i –ii.

281 Schill (2014), pages 17 - 21.

CETA and the EU's competence in the field of transport, which the authors of that report consider to be critical, should be highlighted. In addition, there are direct contradictions where the payment obligations of an investor arising from environmental, tax and tax law requirements are evaded by the award of damages and, overall, the risk of liability for the parties involved states are rising sharply[282]. Another risk is seen in a possible circumvention of standards of the International Labor Organization (ILO) by unclear formulations/ wording. The problem is that European law is not directly linked to them, but in the course of European legal formation there have been many indirect links to which CETA makes no clear reference[283].

At present, it is not possible to reach a conclusion on the beneficiaries of the investment protection contained in CETA, as it is not possible to assess the opinions in the context of the present work and the application of the law has yet to take place. Similarly, a reference to the quality contained in TTIP is problematic. While the general link remains that CETA is the blueprint for TTIP, it does not apply to the final investment protection chapter[284]. Irrespective of the evaluations and the extent of the procedures in the past, however, the importance of the investment protection chapter should be emphasized. For example, German OEMs underline the support of ISDS from the point of view of additional planning security for the already existing US production site while respecting ILO standards and employee participation rights[285]. Furthermore, this part of the agreement is also necessary with a view to establishing a standard in investor protection against direct or indirect expropriation from third countries, with the hope of additional protection, inter alia, by standardizing the interpretation methodology.

5.1.2 Analysis of Interdependencies between Success Factors

In the PESTEL analysis carried out, the interdependencies of the success factors at the beginning of the presentation are already expressed in the

282 Fischer-Lescano/ Horst (2014), pages 6 – 14.
283 Fischer-Lescano/ Horst (2014), pages 19 – 20.
284 Habisch, Andre`/ Popal, Pia. "Ethik und Globaler Handel", in: *Politik u. Zeitgeschichte*,64. Jg. 1-3/2014. December 30, 2013, pages 5-7.
285 EU-Commission-Grünbuch. "Soziale Verantwortung der Unternehmen". KOM (2011-2014) 681

fact that individual success factors cannot be assigned exclusively to one of the six sub-areas. Starting with the political success factors, carbon dioxide regulation has a knock-on effect on the technological sector and in turn is motivated by the social needs of the customer group and the electorate. Similarly, politically motivated customs duties have an impact on IT-based calculations in the planning of final production and therefore on the utilization of a technological success factor, since only a complete and correct preference origin from the EU and US customs authorities, therefore duty-free is guaranteed[286].

In addition, the regulation puts pressure on suppliers who have previously been assigned to the economic success factors, as this group's contribution to the CO2 reduction is 10g per km[287]. The taxation of vehicles, which is also associated with the political sphere, has an impact on the economic and technological success factor, as costs and complexity are influenced in vehicle development and production[288]. Whether this aspect could be influenced by the OEM by new investment protection clauses or could be claimed as damage is not yet clear as previously presented.

The Hans Böckler Foundation, which relies on trade diversion calculated by the IFO Institute, recognizes an interdependence between the effect associated with the economic success factors and considerable foreign policy tensions[289]. If the study of trade diversion still includes the most oil-producing countries at present, the results of the IFO Institute, using the previous benchmark for future markets, do not show any significant reductions in GDP for the respective countries[290]. Foreign policy tensions caused by TTIP, which have indirect negative consequences for the automotive industry, therefore do not seem to exist.

The customer's desire for product differentiation, which is assigned to the social success factor, for product differentiation, for example in the form of a larger product range or several variants of interior design, leads to an individualization of demand. Based on a more comprehensive product range, the number of components to be procured and batch sizes decreases[291]. The result is an impairment of the full realization of economies of scale/

286 PWC (2013), page 78.
287 Wüste (2010), page 4.
288 Stratmann (2010), page 109.
289 Hans Böckler Foundation (2014), pages 48 - 49.
290 IFO-Institute (2013), pages 159 - 161.
291 PWC (2013), page 75.

savings potentials and learning effects. The expanded product range also leads to increased competition for suppliers. Paradoxically, the expansion of models per platform means that procurement is done in a consolidated form and is therefore more closely linked to the actual platform[292]. The result is the preponderance of a reduction in individual orders over the number of increasing large orders.

5.1.3 Scenario Analysis

The scenario analysis is a systematic and forward-looking consideration based on the process steps and the interdependencies identified. On the basis of a current situation, the process shows the situation and the framework of future situations on the basis of the temporal reference of the developments[293]. The following four scenarios serve the detailed and plausible presentation of alternative situations, the value of which is not in the relative probability of their fulfilment, but in consideration, thinking through and planning[294]. Usually, each situation is created on the basis of the success factor, which has the highest degree of future uncertainty. In the following analysis, this approach is departed from on the basis of the direct reference to the work at hand. The aim of the investigation is to identify future strategic challenges with and through the entry into force of the transatlantic FTA. The subjects of the investigation are the global OEMs and suppliers.

The situation concerning the abolition of tariffs between the EU and the US is the basic scenario which, on the basis of this classification, is the most comprehensive scenario and the development of most of the success factors and already made findings on free trade, impacts and specific TTIP modifications.

Due to the current uncertainty about the feasibility and the further course of negotiations (as of 2019), the timing of the scenario can only be set in general terms on the future date of the agreement's entry into force[295]. The presentations listed according to the customs scenario are complementary alternatives based on the basic scenario, which depend on the scope of the respective agreement of the parties.

292 PWC (2013), page 87.
293 Behr (1993), page 8.
294 Johnson/ Scholes/ Whittington (2011), pages 81 – 83.
295 Handelsblatt, January 5, 2015, page 8.

It should be noted that a scenario of a global standard is not in itself an alternative that directly depends on the scope of the agreement between the parties. Despite the considerable economic power of the two economic blocs, the US and the EU cannot decide on global standardization under international law.

The following scenario is based on the fact that the mutual recognition and harmonization of non-tariff barriers is shaped by the requirements of industrialized countries involved in international trade. Although an agreed tariff reduction also has such an effect, the general agreements on trade and tariffs, which have already been justified in history, are disregarded.

5.1.3.1 Abolition of Customs Duties

The elimination of tariffs in transatlantic trade has a direct cost-effective effect for manufacturers, suppliers and customer groups. This will be phased in or take effect immediately, taking into account local content requirements for the individual engine classes and product groups. The export duty for suppliers' precursors is eliminated with the effectiveness of the agreement and enables OEMs in the EU-US reference area to obtain precursors at a reduced price. For the essential engine class, the contracting parties agree, in accordance with CETA and for the temporary protection of OEMs, a gradual reduction of the duty, which prioritizes electric vehicles, taking into account future types of propulsion and a reduction in the price of electric vehicles in order to promote sales. The reduction in trading costs increases disposable income within the customer group, in line with neo-classical theories and the results of comparable free trade areas (excluding MERCOSUR).

The savings for pre- and final products are passed on to the customer group through the indirect effect on the market and competition side and there is an increase in aggregate demand, which in turn leads to a more extensive utilization of production and the realization of economies of scale and inherent cost savings. Compared to the liberalization scenario presented below, the dynamic gains of free trade described are not as significant in the customs scenario, but due to high price elasticity, high levels of intra-company trade, high import volumes, high import value and assuming that the customer group does not postpone the purchase decision until the next stage of tariff reduction, the noticeable cost-side effect for OEMs and customer group described above are visible. Similarly, the asymmetric distribution of trade and the resulting market share shifts will not be as high for the future as predicted in the studies cited above, since, in addition to the saturation phases of the markets, the considerations also include their potentials must be taken into account on the basis of previous shares. As a result, European OEMs will benefit from the tariff reduction to an extent at least equivalent. Furthermore, the conditions for realizing the cost-side effect for the duty-free trade in motor vehicles and the trade gains to be achieved alone, even against the background of future market developments, will have no influence on the location choice of internationally producing OEMs.

Outside the EU and the US, a trade diversionary effect from TTIP will not adversely affect markets in third countries and, in particular, the development of their respective GDP. What all the markets to be considered have in common is that, regardless of the agreement, the social expectations of customer groups change and, as a result, the political success factors adapt. An increasing need for mobility, which can be managed differently depending on the region, has a positive impact on demand development in developing and emerging countries, even excluding a trade diversion effect. As in the sales markets directly affected, the need for mobility remains at a consistently high level in the industrialized countries. In the future, the demands of the customer groups in terms of resource and environmental protection as well as product differentiation and individualization will increase in the course of an unbroken progress towards Industry 4.0[296].

For the automotive industry, the great challenge is to bring industrial evolution into line with the realization of economies of scale. A solution to the problem will lie in increasingly networked as well as flexible production and value chains[297]. Finally, on the issue of mobility needs, it remains to be noted that brand names are gaining in importance. For example, OEMs will respond to the trend of car use becoming less and less a valuable property within developed countries and increasing competition with alternative means of transport through brand promotion. This is increasingly true beyond premium manufacturers[298].

Furthermore, the agreement does not affect future political efforts to protect the climate, reduce CO2 emissions, politically subsidize sites and interdependence with technological success factors. This leaves R&D activi-

296 German Federal Ministry of Education and Research. “Industry 4.0”. *Digital World.* October 23, 2019. https://www.bmbf.de/de/zukunftsprojekt-industrie-4-0-848.html

297 PWC (2013), page 72.

298 PWC (2013), page 14.

ties, the efficient conversion of production and compliance with guidelines for OEMs and suppliers characterized by complexity. Due to the uncertainty surrounding the market penetration of new drive types in the coming years, OEMs will continue to follow the principle of "saving, supplementing and replacing" in the coming years.

In other areas of technological success factors such as electronics, information and communication technology, trends and customer wishes are becoming clearer and, above all, faster. Given the capital expenditures required for this process, the cost-side effect of the scenario makes a contribution.

5.1.3.2 Abolition of Tariffs and Reduction of Non-Tariff Barriers

In addition to the basic scenario just described, the parties agree to reduce non-tariff barriers. Similar to the gradual process of tariff reduction, technical regulations will be progressively aligned through recognition and harmonization, with mutual recognition being completed by the time the agreement enters into force, with a few exceptions. The removal of the most important trade barrier on both markets has a high cost-related effect, which is directly dependent on the level of recognition as well as the future progress of harmonization and goes beyond customs removal. As a general rule, suppliers, which until now have been associated with SMEs, whose location decision and profit margin are not exclusively characterized by customer proximity or by fluctuations in the exchange rate, will win along the value chain and which serve the EU and US markets. Furthermore, innovative suppliers will be attracted in connection with future drive types such as electric drive, as the share of value-added shifts by about 10% away from the OEM compared to the internal combustion engine[299]. The market opportunities created by the expansion of the sales market and future innovations will be offset in the long term, in particular, by the same market risks, especially for component and parts suppliers, over the increased number of market participants through alignment. In response to the increased risks, technical requirements and the largely platform-linked procurement, cost leaders, specialists and global program managers will emerge[300].

299 PWC (2013), page 14.
300 PWC (2013), page 97.

In addition to competitive suppliers, OEMs, which are present in both markets, can claim cost savings from the supplier and have potential in terms of market share, benefit to a large extent. In addition, the economies of scale and volume rebates already occurring by the most productive suppliers are multiplied at the level of the multinational OEM by the even higher procurement and production volumes, while in particular harmonization of the regulations, for example for composite materials, will strengthen the learning effects. However, the profit attributable to the effects just described will not be an absolute size for OEMs.

On the contrary, in view of the complexity costs caused by the expansion of the product range, the possibility of offsetting arises.

Unlike for suppliers, the agreement does not result in reductions due to the greater interdependence of OEMs with the various submarkets. However, those who have already relied on a modular principle before TTIP or have built up on platforms are favored by standardization in the largest economic area in the world, since the composition is now more cost-effective to expand. In addition, in the context of standardization and the reduction of local content requirements for the respective state procurement market, entry into the market is facilitated or more attractive for the individual OEM.

The cycle of cutting trade costs, car prices, increasing demand and increasing disposable income, as described in the first scenario, is now being fully realized by liberalization. Beyond the EU and US markets, there will be a negative trade diversion effect for Mexico, which is also reinforced by the country's background as an automotive location, provided that the competitiveness of individual Mexican suppliers is strongly determined by low wages. For success factors that have already developed independently of TTIP in the basic scenario, a change through the liberalization of non-tariff barriers is not conceivable.

5.1.3.3 Investment Protection in TTIP

The presentation of the legal success factor is based on the high degree of uncertainty about the quality and scope of investment protection contained in TTIP in a separate scenario, which can be understood as complementary, with two characteristics.

In its first form, the ISDS clauses contained in the agreement do not provide OEMs with additional legal certainty and/ or the possibility of legal action. If regulations are adopted for the European and American sales markets which, by way of example, make it more difficult to use or distribute financial services, which influence engine and production policies through targeted arbitrary taxation, which in 2021 would lead to high penalties for exceeding the CO2 ceiling, which do not recognize the ILO standards or impair the production site in an expropriation-like intervention, the only possibility of bringing an action is the respective national legal remedy.

In the second form, international arbitral tribunals shall ensure a second action, which can be taken by the OEM after the use of national legal remedics. As future developments within the EU and the US always show some uncertainty, granting an additional option to future investment decisions is not detrimental.

5.1.3.4 Setting a Global Standard with a Transatlantic Trade Agreement

Due to the economic political power described in the introduction of the scenario analysis and the position of both economic regions in world trade, the process of unification for the automotive industry develops with the entry into force of the agreement on the limits of contract law. The standardization of technical requirements initiated by TTIP leads to a reduction in the transaction costs of all market participants due to the high degree of openness of the standard[301]. For suppliers who have not yet served the American or European market, indirect spillover and cost-side effects are now being realized, as international trade in automobiles in particular has been reduced by intermediates of reduced barriers to entry in the form of uniform regulations[302]. The "enlargement" of the sales market to those regions which adopt the standard now entails market opportunities and market risks for subcontractors under the same conditions as the previous scenario of reducing non-tariff barriers. There are also visible parallels for OEMs in this respect. Once again, based on the development of suppliers and the reduction of transaction costs, economies of scale as well as learning effects and volume discounts are multiplying. Due to increased compatibility of value-added partners in many economic regions of the world, the coordination necessary for the development and series production of

---

301 Ehrhardt (2001), page 12, 31.

302 Hesser/ Feilzer/ De Vries (2006), page 85.

innovations is additionally facilitated and accelerated[303]. Even within the OEMs themselves, the process shown improves the exchange between the production sites or expands the intra-company trade as a whole.

The positive effects of a sharp price reduction on demand and disposable incomes within the EU and the US also occur in this scenario at least to the extent previously presented. In addition, however, the ASEAN countries and thus the future sales markets of Thailand and Indonesia will be affected by the agreement through indirect spillover effects, thereby resulting in people in this region responding more quickly to the need for individual mobility.

With regard to the other major markets, the level of local content requirements is also standardized at a maximum level of 60%. This fits in specifically with the future structures of the automotive industry in China, as the consideration of breaking up the de facto still existing joint venture regulation is implemented, as the signal effect on global suppliers and OEMs. The area of public procurement and the agreement reached in this area on the reduction of the share of added value in this respect will not only be of importance to the automotive industry as a general standard, but TTIP will specifically provide the blueprint for continuous efforts in the agreement on Government Procurement and to promote the opening up of procurement markets also in developing and emerging countries[304]. These countries will not be able to intervene to maintain the protection of domestic OEMs because of their relatively low voting weighting in WTO negotiations, such as for example in Malaysia.

The inclusion of an investment protection chapter will benefit OEMs and suppliers from direct investment in developing and emerging countries, regardless of the differentiated forms set out above. This has a protective effect on investment decisions, especially with the background of a strategy of location presence in growth markets and proximity to customers, as the most minimal form of the chapter, protection is afforded comparable Western standards. Investment protection is also gaining in importance in the automotive financial services sector, as the expansion of the range of services will increasingly take place over the saturation phases of the markets. In the near future, the focus will no longer only be on saturated markets, but also on China and comparable developing countries.

303 Hesser/ Feilzer/ De Vries (2006), page 86.
304 Hans Böckler Foundation (2014), page 55.

In the People's Republic, the VW Group, which serves as an example and has become the highest-selling OEM, will expand the Range of Services of the Group-owned bank faster than in other future sales markets[305]. The other success factors not mentioned in this scenario evolve as in the basic scenario.

5.1.4 Current Strategies of the Automotive Industry

This section describes the current strategy of the overall automotive industry in relation to the macro environment. In addition to the general adherence by OEMs and suppliers to the general conditions identified in the PESTEL analysis, the strategy is characterized by the fact that its presence is maintained in the markets, which are characterized by high economic growth. The aim is to be represented in growing markets, where the population is in demand for private use because of the increasing need for mobility, and where the state and industry are encouraged by growth to maintain the economy with infrastructural resources. If the OEMs are not bound to the production sites because of their political influence, a two-pillar strategy is derived from the example of the German automotive industry. The first pillar is production at the site in Germany, which is linked to the second pillar, foreign production. In this way, the processing of the foreign market is not carried out exclusively by the location there but is complemented by the respective domestic location[306]. This is a case of the so-called intra-company trade.

With regard to the technological success factors, OEMs proceed according to the aforementioned principle of "saving, supplementing, replacing" or reacting to developments in information and communication technology with novel concepts[307]. OEMs are already managing the wishes of the customer groups for increasing individualization through a strong expansion of the product portfolio[308]. The interdependence of the factors listed is that only innovations maintain the attractiveness of the different series in the long term.

305 Handelsblatt, January 13, 2015, pages 4 – 5.
306 Cori-Zimmer/ Flohr Annegret. “Transnationale Unternehmen”, a.a.O., pages 35/ 36.
307 Handelsblatt, January 13, 2015, pages 4 – 5.
308 PWC (2013), pages 13 – 14.

The strategy decisions of the suppliers are primarily characterized by the customer's wishes and are characterized by customer proximity in the choice of production location.

5.1.5 Strategic Change

The final step of the environmental analysis includes the evaluation of the scenarios created with regard to conspicuous and recurring characteristics, the comparison with the current strategy and the answer to the question to what extent the discrepancies occurring are due to TTIP and trigger strategic changes.

What all scenarios have in common is that TTIP has a not insignificant cost-side effect for OEMs, which depends primarily on the procurement and production strategy, more precisely, on the local content requirements, and this circumstance alone does not entail the establishment of new production sites or the closure of old production sites. The end customer, regardless of whether he or she is an OEM or a consumer, also benefits from the setting of the effect through the market and competition side. Furthermore, the scenarios have relevant similarities in those social success factors that are to be considered causal for later processes. Thus, the challenges arising from the increasing product differentiation run like a common thread through the alternatives. The decisive factor here is the tension between the feasible economies of scale as well as learning effects and volume discounts on the one hand and the increasing complexity costs on the other. In addition, an expanded range of models, also with additional links with the factors of customer proximity and regional fluctuations in demand, implies a flexible production and value chain based on platforms. In the context of the processes described, but also on its own, the standardization resulting from the EU and US economic areas must be emphasized. Compared to the global unification scenario, OEMs, which are already heavily integrated into both markets, are given a competitive advantage over time. In addition to the higher cost-side effects resulting from a worldwide standardization of technical requirements, the "indirect standard" of TTIP's role model effect should be noted. Thus, the amount of the agreed local content arrangements will influence the future negotiations of FTA. This will be very relevant for the automotive industry in countries with high requirements and high import duties. At subcontractor level and/ or at the level of suppliers, the agreement is to be classified as ambivalent. For example, the removal of non-tariff barriers offers new market opportunities for SMEs. In the long term, they face market risks due to increasing competition, which have an effect in addition to the existing requirements. The possibility of generating long-term competitive advantages due to future technological success factors should be noted.

In this way, suppliers will emerge stronger in the areas in which OEMs hand over their original core competencies.

The last striking aspect is the possible facilitation of market access in the area of public procurement, particularly in developing and emerging countries.

In answering to what extent the strategy of the automotive industry is influenced by the agreement, the necessary differentiation in change and support has been shown in the course of the scenario analysis. Strategic changes result from the competitive advantages gained by the cost-effective effect of tariff reduction. In view of the high level of intra-company trade, the respective import value and the volume of imports, the agreement will bring about a targeted strategic change. OEMs and suppliers who can import their products to the US or the EU duty-free will generate the advantage over competitors who have to pay the full duty rate[309]. The concrete change is not based on the relocation of production sites, but on the realignment of sourcing and production strategies. The full potential of this realignment will be realized, especially for precursors of module suppliers (including a high share of value added), provided that the immediate reduction of the duty for precursors is agreed, as in CETA. Furthermore, sourcing and production strategies are not limited to the 'transatlantic internal market' in their preparation. On the contrary, due to the bilateral fragmentation of world trade, as indicated in Chapter 4.3, TTIP is an agreement among many and favors a global strategic orientation. In this way, preferential treatment in customs law can be optimized by means of a targeted linking of FTAs[310]. An example would be a timely linking of strategies of three economies via NAFTA, TTIP and the EU-South Korea FTA. In cases where the interdependence of the strategies is not yet possible, the inclusion of the role model of TTIP on future negotiations is necessary. Thus, the strategic change in sourcing and production planning affects OEMs and suppliers alike. Depending on the positioning and market positioning of the company, this results in strategic changes for the individual

309 PWC (2013), page 78.
310 PWC (2013), page 81.

supplier. The aim of a possible realignment must be to increase international competitiveness. Thus, in the long term, targeted diversification into cost managers, specialists and global program managers takes place at the level of the suppliers.

In addition, the long term will result in strategic changes in access to the public procurement markets of developing and emerging countries. This favors internationally competitive OEMs. In the short term, opening up the US procurement market through the cost-side effect and reducing the market access barrier will create market opportunities for EU OEMs.

Although sourcing and production strategies will change, the two-pillar strategy remains unchanged. Thus, the abolition of customs increases the expression of intra-company trade and the linking of various FTAs to global trade in automotive precursors and intermediates.

This is also demonstrated by another effect of TTIP, which has a supportive effect: the standardization of technical requirements. In terms of the expansion of product portfolios, regional fluctuations in demand and the adaptable design of value-added and production chains, the standardization not only counteracts the increasing costs of complexity, but also increases the flexibility of production sites. Standardized production and assembly facilities, tools and over-the-top trained workers reduce production's need for adaptation to specific models and platforms. Overall, the individual production site becomes more independent of models and fluctuations in demand[311]. The resulting importance of networked planning across the individual sites has a supportive but not changing impact on the strategy, as recognition and harmonization will not be one hundred percent within the EU and the US. The increased compatibility of market participants with the technological success factors also shows the same supportive effect, since the phase from development to series production is easier to coordinate across the various suppliers.

The other success factors/ challenges identified in the PESTEL analysis and scenarios each have the potential to bring about a strategic change in their future development. However, this would not be triggered by the agreement. The extent to which ISDS clauses would bring about change cannot be foreseen. Unless the rules go beyond the standards of EU and US jurisprudence, there can be a supportive effect on the strategy of presence in the growth markets.

311 PWC (2013), S. 76 – 77.

5.2 Pharmaceutical Industry

5.2.1 PESTEL Method

During the relevant environmental factors for the pharmaceutical industry analyzed in the literature, the division into factors of Environment I and Environment II takes place. Patients, doctors, health insurance companies, pharmacies, hospitals and the pharmaceutical wholesaler are assigned to the first category[312]. The following approach is limited to the analysis of Environmental factors II, as TTIP influences the general framework. As with the previous PESTEL method, which has shown explanations of the influence of suppliers in the automotive industry, the clean separation between these environmental factors is not always possible. Reference is made where there are overlaps and important interdependencies.

5.2.1.1 Political Factors

The main policy success factors are a changing public health system and a high national or supranational regulatory density. The transition between the two criteria is fluid.

The increased perception of health as a fundamental human right is increasing the politicization of health systems, which causally favors a greater economization of the system. By taking into account increased costs, decision-makers intervene more frequently in the short term, which has an impact on the pharmaceutical industry, especially in the case of long-term strategic planning. In Germany, for instance, this was reflected in the introduction of a points system in which prescription drugs (including high profit margins for manufacturers) were contingent. Further examples include recent interventions by the Italian and Greek governments. Due to the economic crisis, stricter requirements for eligible medicines were adopted in 2012 and/ or the use of generic medicines was strengthened[313]. An intervention of a similar effect is the transfer of drugs to the prescription-free area. The latter leads to a shift in demand for over the counter (OTC) medicines, economic relief for the health system and an increased patient self-medication rate.

312 Crisand (1996), page 46 – 52; Hahn (2006), page 21.
313 PWC (2012), page 17.

To the extent that medicines continue to be classified as prescription-only, state institutions are increasingly encouraging the prescription of generics instead of patent-protected branded products[314]. For the US, in the context of politicization, reference must be made to the politically and socially controversial introduction of "ObamaCare"[315]. One estimate concludes that the Affordable Care Act will bring manufacturers an additional profit of between 10 and 35 billion U.S. dollars by expanding the target audience within 10 years, despite additional expenses for regulations and taxes[316]. Thus, state intervention can have a positive effect, provided that it promotes the general introduction of a system. TTIP does not affect the health systems of the negotiating partners. The EU side refers to the observance of Protocol No 26 TFEU in regard to this topic[317].

Overall, national and supranational influence is characterized by the regulation and control of raw materials, production processes, advertising practices and the extent of the studies[318]. In the political context, authorization procedures and the framework conditions for pricing should be highlighted. Before the new active substance is marketed, manufacturers must go through authorization procedures that are considered to be the most significant non-tariff barriers for the pharmaceutical industry. The European Medicines Agency (EMA) and the US approval by the Food and Drug Administration (FDA) determine safety and efficacy for the European market. With a few exceptions, manufacturers can also apply to a Member State for EU-wide mutual recognition authorization. The overall complexity of the approval requirements and the higher requirements of the FDA mean that the respective manufacturers pursue a strategy of local presence for the production process and trade in intermediates increases[319]. An agreement contained in TTIP on the far-reaching approximation of authorization procedures for prescription-only medicinal products seems unlikely, as, on the one hand, the EU Commission's position paper on

---

314 Schmidt (2000), pages 25 – 26.

315 ObamaCare Facts 2019. "Facts on the Affordable Care Act". October 22, 2019. https://obamacarefacts.com/obamacare-facts/

316 Japsen, Bruse. "ObamaCare will bring Drug Industry 35 Billion in Profits". *Forbes*, May 25, 2013. https://www.forbes.com/sites/brucejapsen/2013/05/25/obamacare-will-bring-drug-industry-35-billion-in-profits/#42758a334a59

317 Council of the European Union 11103/13 DCL 1 (2014), p. 7.

318 Fischer/ Breitenbach (2007), pages 11 – 12.

319 Fischer/ Breitenbach (2007), pages 37 – 38.

general harmonization is very vague, and, on the other hand, sets specific priorities.

For example, the agreement aims to improve the exchange of confidential information between the EMA and the FDA, as well as cooperation in the testing of generic substances[320]. It can be assumed that manufacturers of patent-protected original prescription preparations are critical of the latter point. The background is the general trend towards stricter authorization rules, which in turn require longer development times, while simplifying conditions for authorization of generic medicines[321].

The framework conditions for pricing on the European Union market are closely linked to the politicization and economization of health systems described above[322]. Notwithstanding various national regulations of EU Member States in the field of pricing and the breakdown into reimbursable and receptive medicines, the development of the systems is leading to a trend towards justifiable pricing. This means that the pricing of the drug must reflect its own value, the value of the drug for the health system and, ideally, the value of an economy. Patent-protected medicinal products are excluded from these considerations, except for special constellations[323]. On the other hand, the price setting for medicinal products is calculated on the US market, taking into account individual legal requirements in accordance with the mechanisms of supply and demand. For patent-protected active substances, the manufacturer has the option to charge the monopoly price. However, it is often necessary to take into account other patent-protected active substances of other manufacturers within the same therapeutic class, so that an oligopolistic pricing is subsequently available[324]. Just as TTIP does not affect the basic design of health systems, the agreement will not change the framework conditions for pricing. The removal of tariffs only stimulates competition in medicines that compete with each other even without TTIP.

---

320 EU Position on Pharmaceutical Products (2014), pages 1 – 2.

321 Schmidt (2000), page 26.

322 Pharma Zeitung. "GBI: Sparmassnahmen in Europa beeinflussen Preisbildung von Generika". June 22, 2012. http://www.pharma-zeitung.de/gbi-sparmasznahmen-in-europa-beeinflussen-preisbil.4548.php

323 Schöffski/ Fricke/ Guminski (2008), pages 155 – 157.

324 Comanor/ Schweitzer (2013), page 541.

5.2.1.2 Economic Factors and the Pharmaceutical Market

The key economic success factors are the performance of health systems or patients as well as marketing.

Public health systems depend on the economic development of the states and the demand for health care in the form of services and pharmaceuticals. The extent to which pharmaceutical innovation determines the performance of an economy is demonstrated by a study conducted by the Federal Ministry of Economics and Energy, which shows an increase in productivity due to the significant decline in premature mortality and the duration of the sick leave[325]. Referring to the economic development of the EU and the US, Chapter 4.2 determined that TTIP can act as a smaller stimulus package.

An increase in the employment rate would mean a greater number of contributors to health insurance funds, which promote pharmaceutical progress by increasing reimbursement for innovative medicines. A more detailed description of the correlation between innovation and the scope of reimbursement is given in Chapter 6.2.1.4. As of 2019, the most important pharmaceutical markets are the US, the EU and Japan. Although sales on the US market fell by 3.2% in 2013 and rose by 5.6% in the EU, the US remains by far the most important market[326].

When looking at the demand for healthcare, the pharmaceutical industry, compared to the other market participants, is to a large extent blamed for the increasing economic burden on the systems. This perception puts increasing pressure on the research manufacturers and their products. In the field of tension are original preparations for cheaper generics[327]. In 2010, pharmaceutical spending accounted for 10% of total U.S. health care spending. Expenditure rose to 12.5% in 2015 and is projected to rise to 14% in 2020[328]. In the absence of EU-wide data, Germany, which is the fourth largest pharmaceutical market, will be used as an example. Expenditure on statutory health insurance for medicines in 2013 was 15.58 % in relation to total expenditure, which fell slightly over the period 2009 to 2012[329].

325 BPI (2014), page 23.
326 BPI (2014), page 44.
327 Hahn (2006), page 2.
328 Daemmrich (2011), page 31.
329 BPI (2014), page 56, 61.

The final aspect of the burden on health systems is the increase in the demand for medicines by them themselves, as the cumulative duration of consumption of patients is extended. The importance of the use of medicines will continue to increase in the context of an ageing society, even in old age[330]. Therefore, in the future, the share of medicines in the total expenditure of the systems will increase.

The demand for over-the-counter medicines is determined, among other things, by the individual performance of the patients. Previously, Chapter 4.2 identified the extent to which TTIP increases the annual income of EU and US families. The analysis of whether this significantly promotes the self-medication of patients follows in connection with the social success factors.

The consideration of the predicted negative trade diversion effects of the IFO Institute shows similar results for the future sales markets of the BRIC countries, South Africa, South Korea, Mexico, Indonesia and Turkey, as they have already been identified for the automotive industry[331]. When converting the figures to a ten-year period, only Turkey (-0.25%), South Africa (-0.317%) and Mexico (-0.724%) show a significant decline in GDP[332].

Marketing is of particular importance for the pharmaceutical industry compared to other sectors in which the competitive instrument can be abstracted to the mere effect of promoting sales. For prescription drugs, it constitutes the removal of barriers to entry, and it is crucial for the competition with and against generic manufacturers. In a figurative sense, the group of doctors and representatives of hospitals can be interpreted as a barrier to entry into the prescription market, since, in addition to the patient, they are the most important decision-makers in the selection of prescription medicines or generics. Due to the above-described economization of health systems, prescription behavior is influenced by budget limits and, if necessary, the threat of deductibles.

In addition, doctors are the informed reference group for the EU market, as, unlike in the US, marketing for prescription drugs is prohibited in the EU[333]. It is therefore not surprising that many manufacturers spend 50 to 60% of their total marketing costs on the field.[334]

330 BPI (2014), page 24.
331 BPI (2014), page 45 – 46.
332 IFO-Institute (2013), pages 159 - 161.
333 Fischer/ Breitenbach (2007), page 228.
334 Hahn (2006), page 26 – 27.

Generic manufacturers begin to point out the new availability of active substances in advance of a patent exit through marketing and sales activities, unless they are legally prevented from doing so by means of marketing and sales activities. The German pharmaceutical market from 2004 illustrates the necessity or, depending on the point of view, the damage of marketing. After the opening of the substance market, up to 30 new suppliers with medicines identical from the doctor's point of view entered the market. The consequence for the manufacturer of a high-turnover original product was a decline in sales of 22 to 60% in the first half of the year[335]. This effect is due to the large price discrepancy with the original product, as research and development (R&D), testing and approval procedures for the generic manufacturer are eliminated[336]. Furthermore, for the sale of generic stake marketing is a classic instrument of brand loyalty.

The global pharmaceutical industry is expected to lose between USD 12 billion and USD 14 billion for the years 2015 to 2020 due to expiring patents[337]. For completion purposes, it should be noted that the strict separation between original and generic manufacturers is often not possible, since the expansion or reduction of the product range to include both original licensed products and generic products is carried out depending on the strategic positioning[338]. In addition to the example of the Bayer Group, which has already been mentioned, reference can be made to the pharmaceutical manufacturer Boehringer, especially for generics. Following a series of regulatory successes with patent-protected innovative medicines, the full sale of the generics business in the Group was under review[339].

The direct link between marketing and TTIP concerns the time when generic manufacturers are officially allowed to place their medicines on the market.

After the economic consequences of a patent phasing-out have previously been demonstrated, the chapter on the legal success factors is more closely defined, in addition to the actual patent protection, also including a possi-

335 Schöffski/ Fricke/ Guminski (2008), page 216.
336 Schmidt (2000), page 23.
337 Radtke, Reiner. “Umsatzeinbussen der Pharmaindustrie aufgrund auslaufender Arzneitmittelpatente bis 2024”. *Statista.* June 19, 2019. https://de.statista.com/statistik/daten/studie/246868/umfrage/umsatzeinbussen-der-pharmaindustrie-aufgrund-auslaufender-arzneimittelpatente/
338 Hahn (2006), page 26.
339 Handelsblatt, January 16.- 18., 2015, page 21.

ble extension of patent linkage, which protects the patent proprietor from early marketing.

5.2.1.3 Social Factors

In terms of social success factors, current social expectations and the increase in health awareness are crucial for the pharmaceutical industry, in conjunction with a changing age structure. In principle, it is necessary to distinguish between the expectations of a broad public and the expectations of patients, since only the latter is directly affected in the form of a disease. However, in this area, due to wide-ranging overlaps, it is not possible to clearly separate the first and second environment[340].

Public debates about the cost of health systems make patients more price-sensitive, which is reflected, among other things, in the belief that a positive correlation between the price and quality of the drug in favor of a greater personal propensity to save is abandoned. On the basis of price sensitization, the perception of new information opportunities and the increasing use of a say in the prescription of medicinal products follows[341]. The EU's negotiating position indirectly meets patients' information needs, as TTIP seeks to harmonize terminology. The primary objective is to improve the exchange of information between regulatory authorities and companies[342]. Due to the strong involvement of the pharmaceutical industry in social institutional structures and stakeholders, the dissemination of information between groups and organizations can bring about a patient who is of equal quality[343]. For this reason, and for reasons listed in the following paragraph, the marketing activities of the manufacturers focus more on patients in addition to the doctors[344].

The increased health awareness of society leads to an increase in self-diagnosis and self-medication of patients with over-the-counter drugs.

This product class includes cough, cold, allergy, pain, gastrointestinal, vitamins and dermatological products. Manufacturers in the category compete mainly through low prices, high sales volumes and marketing[345].

340 Crisand (1996), page 49.
341 Schmidt (2000), page 27.
342 EU Position on Pharmaceutical Products (2014), page 3.
343 Schmidt (2000), pages 32 – 33.
344 Hahn (2006), page 28.
345 Schmidt (2000), pages 22 – 27.

Manufacturers are responding to the increasing importance of the OTC market as a secondary market for pharmaceuticals by marketing with the attempt to create a brand and maintain it. Early market positioning on the secondary market is intended to gain competitive advantages over generics, especially when a patent expires[346]. Activities of the Bayer Group during recent years demonstrate the increased importance of over-the-counter medicines for strategic positioning. With the introduction of new active ingredients, the group has become the fastest growing manufacturer in the pharmaceutical industry within the first nine months of 2014, but at the same time the pharmaceutical manufacturer Merck has bought divisions via over-the-counter drugs and thus consolidated its position on the second market as the world's second largest supplier[347].

After the previous chapter linked the possible income increases through TTIP with effects on demand and the pharmaceutical industry, the topic must now be rounded off. In principle, it is clear that the agreement can sustainably increase the demand for over-the-counter medicines. The decisive factors are health awareness and self-confidence of patients in terms of self-medication in combination with the economic performance, marketing measures and the significant effects of the secondary market on the strategic positioning of research manufacturers. However, the differentiation according to the sales markets is again indispensable in the determination. For example, the likelihood of using additional income for over-the-counter medicines is considered to be under-proportionate for the EU, the US, and more generally in markets with an already high-income middle class, as previous disposable incomes have already been used for the sensitive issue of health[348]. The marginal use of income within developing or emerging countries is to be considered contradictory. In the case of the ASEAN countries, which, according to CEPR forecasts, would also benefit from a comprehensive agreement, appreciable demand effects are therefore possible.

The increase in health awareness must be closely linked to the age structure of the population, as patients age due to pharmaceutical progress and

346 Fischer/ Breitenbach (2007), page 228.

347 Handelsblatt, December 3, 2014, page 19.

348 See Chapter 5.2.6; Handelsblatt Nr.160. “Verbraucher streben mehr und mehr in den Arzneimittel-Zweitmarkt”. August 21, 2014, page 14.

prolong the process through active intervention[349]. As of 2013, around 13% of the total population was over 65 in the US and around 16% in the EU[350]. For 2030, the share is estimated at 20-30%. For manufacturers, the change in the age structure means a reallocation in the product portfolio. Infectious diseases are becoming less important for the EU and US markets, but sales of medicines for ageing diseases will increase sharply. Furthermore, so-called lifestyle medicines will be of general interest in the markets of industrialized countries. These serve less to eliminate a disease, but rather to increase the quality of life, prophylaxis and correct any deviation from the ideal social image. In order to suit this change, managers with experience in the consumer sector work increasingly in the pharmaceutical industry[351].

The trend towards health apps fits into the development of social success factors. The applications for the smartphone combine the general life-style trend with the benefit for the pharmaceutical industry of presenting itself as a suitable management partner, depending on the clinical picture[352]. The issue of general data protection, which is relevant in this context, is not covered by TTIP, only the handling of directly trade-related data is part of the negotiations[353].

5.2.1.4 Technological Factors

The prescription drug business is characterized by low manufacturing costs, easy-to-copy active ingredients and a subordinate role of brands. This is countered by an essential competence in R&D[354]. For manufacturers, therefore, the technological success factors are important regarding the R&D of new active ingredients, progress in information technology (IT) and the development of new business areas through innovative active ingredients.

349 Scherenberg, Viviane. "Erfolgreiche Gesundheits-Apps von Krankenkassen im Test". *Deutscher Aerztinnenbund e.V. (German Medical Women's Association).* November 19, 2019. https://www.aerztinnenbund.de/Erfolgreiche.2113.0.2.html

350 Urmersbach, Bruno. "USA: Altersstruktur von 2008 bis 2018". *Statista,* September 10, 2019. https://de.statista.com/statistik/daten/studie/165801/umfrage/altersstruktur-der-usa/

351 Fischer/ Breitenbach (2007), pages 225 – 228.

352 World Bank. "Age distribution in the United States from 2007 to 2017." Chart. April 24, 2019. Statista. Accessed November 19, 2019. https://www.statista.com/statistics/270000/age-distribution-in-the-united-states/

353 BMWi Brochure (2014), page 31.

354 Handelsblatt, October 28, 2014, page 5.

The assessment of the Handelsblatt, as set out above, and the conclusions made in this dissertation chapter require inserts and expansion, as technological success factors also include the period that borders on the development of new active ingredients and business areas. In this case, flexibility and the achievement of low production costs should be mentioned. When the health authorities advertise limited quantities of medicinal products for their own procurement, this requires the ability of the manufacturer and its production sites to react flexibly quickly. In the case of the commitment, additional capacities are required which must not jeopardize efficient production in the reverse event. Flexibility is also needed due to the desire of manufacturers to place medicinal products on the market with the date of authorization and the uncertainty surrounding them. Manufacturing costs, although low, are of considerable importance in the pharmaceutical industry, since, unlike in the automotive industry, not all production of a medicinal product is carried out within the group and, consequently, competition with external competitors is permanently dynamic[355].

Due to the short insert and the characteristics of the prescription drug business described above, it is not the only but a big opportunity for manufacturers to gain lasting competitive advantages by developing new substances and to protect them over a certain period of time from generic manufacturers as well as to extract monopoly or polypole profits. A further aspect of the levying of corresponding profits is the link between new and innovative medicinal products and the previously listed pricing framework. Health insurance companies and similar organizations reward the efforts of research manufacturers through annual adjustments to drug expenditure[356].

Progress in IT is an understatement of the need for R&D of new active ingredients. Due to technological progress and its consequential effect on research times and product innovation rates, IT has become an independent success factor, which is to be considered ambivalent in terms of the creation and duration of competitive advantages. With the help of computer-controlled modeling programs, combinatorial chemistry and automated analysis, manufacturers of original preparations accelerate the research process.

The unusual alliance between Sanofi and Evotec, which focuses on the analysis of a total of 1.7 million substances, would be unthinkable without

355 Kets. "Pharma und TTIP" in Markets, 2/2014, page 14.
356 Commons Network (2014), page 8.

modern IT[357]. At the same time, generic manufacturers are quicker to break down and imitate medicines into their constituents using the same technique[358]. Interestingly, technological progress reduces market barriers to entry for third-party companies by simplifying them. IT service providers such as IBM or Oracle, who are now making IT investments for pharmaceutical research and participate in knowledge, are to be listed in this context[359].

The fact that the development of new business areas and pharmaceuticals is not to be attributed to the economic but to the technological success factors is due, among other things, to the process of achieving the goals of the technological success factors. The business areas that will determine the pharmaceutical industry in the future are genetic engineering, medical technology, nanotechnology and biosimilars, which are either highly dependent on the progress of IT or the technology itself is the structure and dynamics of the pharma industry.

The use of genetic engineering offers the option of producing medicines of different characteristics, which take into account the individual needs of individual patients. However, the research and development of this area without modern IT is very complex[360]. At the end of 2012, the European Commission approved the first gene therapy medicine in the Western world[361].

Furthermore, future advances in IT implicitly include the observance of nanotechnology for the development of high-performance computers and so-called biochips, which carry out a very high number of biological tests within a few seconds and test potential drug candidates for compatibility[362]. Finally, the production of generics based on biosimilars must be addressed. These are biological active substances entering the market after the end of a patent for a biopharmaceutical. The biological variance of the molecules compared to the original preparation has been problematic so far. This results in high additional costs for the generic manufacturer during approval, which in turn leads to a lower price drop for the patient[363].

357 Handelsblatt, December 3, 2014, page 18.
358 Schmoly (2005), page 66.
359 Hahn (2006), page 17.
360 Schmoly (2005), page 66.
361 BPI (2014), page 30.
362 Fischer/ Breitenbach (2007), page 222.
363 BPI (2014), page 31.

Although only biosimilars are affected by the new business areas just mentioned, this has an enormous leverage effect for the pharmaceutical industry. The aim of closer cooperation between the regulatory authorities EMA and FDA may subsequently lead to a reduction in additional expenditure for generic drug manufacturers. The EU position paper explicitly emphasizes the option of global standard setting and the increase in authorized biosimilars. The potential economic leverage effect is illustrated by the example of Germany, in which the biopharmaceuticals that expired in 2014 have generated sales of around 370 million euros (€). For 2015, sales had already increased to €1 billion. In view of the imminent end of many patent-protected biopharmaceuticals, the extent to which the approximations pursued will lead to a reduction in the duration of the test will be decisive for the sales of the two pharmaceutical groups.

5.2.1.5 Environmental Factors

Ecological success factors play a minor role in the pharmaceutical industry. Generally speaking, compliance with standards to prevent environmental degradation, the protection of the environment from research and production risks as well as the handling of waste must be mentioned in this context[364]. As stated earlier in the analysis for the automotive industry, TTIP does not include the reduction, recognition or harmonization of EU and US environmental standards. It is not clear at this stage whether manufacturers and pharmaceutical manufacturers in particular will gain influence over future legislation by using ISDS clauses.

5.2.1.6 Legal Factors

Legal success factors in the pharmaceutical industry can be mainly attributed to the regulations on trademark protection, patent protection and licenses. The concept of GMP enshrines a set of rules that form the framework for the production of medicinal products and are enshrined both nationally and internationally. At present, the characteristics of the EU and US GMP rules are very different, which consequently leads to considerable differences, priorities and additional expenditure in the operation of both markets, and with the non-tariff barriers such as those found predominantly in the automotive industry.

364 Crisand (1996), page 48.

The intention of TTIP was the alignment of rules with the aim to avoid duplication of control over compliance[365]. Alignment would affect both US and EU manufacturers, as well as companies from third countries (when exporting to the US or the EU), which would theoretically mean a global standard. As in the automotive industry, intra-company trade is strong in the pharmaceutical industry, which would open up cost-saving potential for EU and US manufacturers[366]. It remains to be seen to what extent, in practice, uniform GMP rules are based on the large sales markets. The reason for the critical assessment is the inherently sensitive issue of health, its monitoring and the different assessments of national authorities[367].

In the study of the developments of the pharmaceutical industry to date within large free trade zones, the high importance of brand names and the associated trademark rights were demonstrated by the example of MERCOSUR. For the present, brand names for the distribution of medicines remain very important. This applies to all product groups but is particularly noteworthy for over-the-counter medicines. In the absence of a separate or detailed negotiating position for the IPR sector by the EU Commission or the US Government, the subsequent intellectual property rights are covered by the reference to CETA and the European Negotiating mandate. The latter includes the ambition of TTIP to express the high value that the parties attach to IPR[368]. So far, there is no evidence that trademark rights are being renegotiated by TTIP.

For the protection of newly developed active ingredients, manufacturing processes and new uses, manufacturers use patents and rights that are indirectly related to the original patent. Due to the interaction of the political, economic and technological success factors listed above, patents of strategic importance are available to research manufacturers, so that the patent application is filed immediately after the finding of an active substance[369].

The potential effects of the agreement will therefore be examined with regard to the approximation of EU and US patent grant procedures and the indirect extension of the duration of further intellectual property rights.

365 EU Position on Pharmaceutical Products (2014), page 2.

366 IFO-Institute (2013). "Pharmaceutical Products are assigned to Trade in Chemicals", page 37.

367 See Chapter 5.2.6 „Reinforced Pharmaceutical Alliances in the US and EU"

368 Council of the European Union 11103/13 DCL 1 (2014), p. 14.

369 Fischer/ Breitenbach (2007), pages 173 – 188.

Although supra-regional and international patent applications are possible, they must not be equated with a world patent. The scope of patent protection is in principle territorially limited. In practice, this situation leads to research manufacturers registering patents in the EU, the US and other important sales markets. In addition, manufacturers of generic medicines also comply with the limits of patent protection. For example, generics intended for the German market are developed in the US, as an infringement of national patent protection during development cannot be claimed there[370].

In addition to the fact that all manufacturers of the pharmaceutical industry are directly affected by the limits of patent protection, the example illustrates the design of the legal protection. Critics of the agreement fear that due to TTIP, there may be an approximation or lowering of European evidence of the benefits of an active substance, as US regulations are considered to be lower in this regard[371]. If these assumptions are justified, there are theoretical restrictions of competition for generic manufacturers, as the number of patents would increase. In the previous draft of CETA, there was no agreement between the negotiators on the patent application. Due to the lack of agreement in this area and the patent application strategies already in place, the option of lowering the conditions is not included in the following scenarios. A detailed description of the procedure of research manufacturers in the patent application can be found in Chapter 5.2.4.

In addition to the actual patent term, which is a maximum of 20 years in the EU and the US, in the order CETA, TTIP and the worldwide setting of a standard for IPR, the rights must be observed, which will continue to provide a protection mechanism for the research manufacturer even after the expiry of the original patent. Supplementary protection certificates, patent linking and handling of unpublished or confidential data are to be listed.

Supplementary protection certificates are of considerable importance in the EU for research manufacturers. Due to long R&D periods, active substances are effectively protected by a patent for only eight to ten years[372]. If it is not a so-called blockbuster drug (turnover of more than USD 1 billion), manufacturers will have problems paying for costs during the remainder

370 Fischer/ Breitenbach (2007), pages 211 – 212.

371 Commons Network (2014), page 6.

372 Schmoly (2005), p. 67; other authors list a longer time for R&D, see Bhardwaj/ Padamavati (2013), p. 316 - 322.

of the patent. The aim of a certificate is to extend the patent term by a maximum of five years. The justification is the elapsed time between the notification and the authorization of the medicinal product[373]. Regulations of a similar effect have so far also been implemented in the US[374]. In the previous CETA draft, the EU and Canada have agreed, under the concept of sui generis protection, on an appeal equivalent to that of the supplemental certificate, with the maximum extension for the Canadian region of two years and five years for the EU[375].

However, this remedy was limited to one active substance in relation to the patent application strategies already indicated and later to be carried out further, which may include multiple applications for an active substance. In this case, the selection of the active substance is the responsibility of the applicant[376]. Within the framework of the content of TTIP, the regulation is interesting for manufacturers with regard to two future fields of action. On the one hand, it is necessary to include a standard setting and thus to adopt the scheme in future FTAs or as a contribution to future negotiations on IPR within the WTO, and on the other hand, supplementary protection certificates at national level must be taken into account. Although the US and the EU already have a similar form, the additional implementation at the level of international treaties can lead to a national consolidation. The background to the consideration is the previously presented increasing politicization, economization and increasing burden on health systems, including for drug expenditure. The scale and the steady progression of the problem illustrates the demographic trends predicted for the EU. In addition to the figures already presented for 2030, the trend continues unabated in the following years. By 2060, more than 148 million EU citizens will be over 60 years old.

As a result, projected health spending as a percentage of EU GDP is up by around 2.1% compared to 2013[377]. National restrictions on the scope of future adjustments should therefore be considered further. In this context, it is true that the EU institutions and the Member States themselves are bound by the agreements concluded by the Union. The provisions on the

373 Fischer/ Breitenbach (2007), page 182.
374 The Chartered Institute of Patent Attorneys. "Patents, Trademarks, Designs, Copyright". December 16, 2014. https://www.cipa.org.uk/
375 CETA Draft (2014), pages 344 – 346.
376 Canadian Centre for Policy Alternatives (2014), pages 58 – 59.
377 EU Commission SWD (2014) 216 final/2 (2014), page 3.

common commercial policy are the exclusive competence of the EU. In addition to the core area of trade policy, the exchange of goods, trade aspects of intellectual property are also subsumed[378]. It remains to be seen to what extent this comprehensive approach of CETA and TTIP, as already presented for the automotive industry, will lead to an overstepping of competence stake in the EU.

Patent linkage is the link between the term of the patent and the date of authorization for the marketing of generic medicines. Accordingly, the granting of the authorization before the expiry of the patent is a violation of the legal protection of the original product. In recent years, patent linkage schemes have increasingly been disseminated through bilateral agreements, primarily with developing countries where generic drug manufacturers are established. The model for the majority of patent linkage regulations is the original US system, which on the one hand is intended to provide an additional incentive for research manufacturers, on the other hand, it includes motivation for generic manufacturers. If a generic manufacturer is able to demonstrably invalidate a patent, it is granted the authorization exclusivity of one hundred and eighty days. Whether the scheme actually provides an incentive for the generic manufacturer is certainly dependent on the individual case, since the dispute involves time and cost calculations.

Unlike in the US, patent linkage is prohibited within the EU, with the exception of a few member states, for ideological reasons. A delay in the entry of generic medicines are therefore supposed to be prevented[379].

The extent to which the EU can and wants to implement its position on patent linkage in TTIP is questionable[380]. The CETA draft contains the regulation, which only covers Canadian patent law.

One reason for the EU's contradictory behavior, in addition to the divergent interests of individual member states, could again be the global standard setting. A distinction must be made in the future sales markets, which do not yet have a patent linkage, and countries such as Mexico or China, where different forms of the system are currently available. If the patent linkage rules are classified according to the level of protection afforded to the research manufacturer, China should be highlighted. For example, in some areas, in addition to the quality of the regulation, it is also crucial who sets standards.

378 Mayer (2014), pages 2 – 3.
379 Bhardwaj/ Padamavati (2013), pages 316 - 322.
380 Canadian Centre for Policy Alternatives (2014), page 60.

The time-limited exclusivity of data generated during the clinical trial period and demonstrating the benefits of the medicinal product is the main protection mechanism for research manufacturers in terms of the duration of protection. Like the original product, the generic one must demonstrate a benefit in order to obtain approval from the relevant authorities. The classification of the data as exclusive prevents the use of the study results for third parties beyond the patent period. The maximum period of protection in the EU is 11 years, and in the US the maximum extension is limited to eight years[381]. As a result, the protection of the US system is shorter than the protection afforded within the EU without patent linkage. It will be important for generic drug manufacturers whether to see how far TTIP could influence the alignment of the time duration, as the US has so far been favored in the choice of location on the basis of the mechanism presented[382]. Similarly, in addition to the standard setting for future markets (in Mexico and Brazil, the regulation is completely absent), this safeguard mechanism must also be based on the consideration already made under the Supplementary Protection Certificate, which is based on the future changeability of the regulation at national level. During CETA negotiations, the Canadian negotiators rejected the EU Commission's initial proposal and agreed on a term of protection of approximately eight years[383].

Patent law and the protection mechanism that goes beyond it is a legal success factor for the pharmaceutical manufacturer, whether research or generic, only if there are also innovative active substances, processes and uses that are worthy of protection on the market.

If this is not the case or is insufficient, licenses become a legal success factor. Licenses are used in their "external impact" to overcome revenue gaps and/ or accelerate the expansion of the product portfolio[384]. For the R&D department, the purchase of external licenses is an increased justification and can lead to the focus and limitation of the research breadth of the individual manufacturers. In the future, licenses will play an important role in the early positioning of R&D (rapid assessment of the level of development of a third-party product) and in the recording of trends[385]. So far, it cannot be assumed that the legal framework of licenses granted by companies to each other would be changed by TTIP.

381 Pharma-Brief (2009), page 2–3.
382 Bhardwaj/ Padamavati (2013), pages 316 - 322.
383 Canadian Centre for Policy Alternatives (2014), page 59.
384 Baecker (2007), page 60 – 61.
385 Fischer/ Breitenbach (2007), page 231.

In order to complete the patent law and IPR sub-section, it must be put in the context of an investment protection chapter. With regard to the future development of IPR, critics of CETA fear that ISDS clauses will allow new interventions for the entire pharmaceutical industry[386]. As previously stated for the automotive industry, a clear legal assessment is currently not possible for the pharmaceutical industry in regard to this matter. It should be added that there is no relevance to the current level of information on the potential quality of investment protection, according to BPI.

5.2.2 Analysis of Interdependencies between Success Factors

Starting with the political factors, interdependencies extend to the technological section, starting from the politicization and economization of health systems. Reference has been made previously to the relationship between innovative medicinal products and the scope of reimbursement. Furthermore, there is this interdependence between the multi-prescription of prescription drugs by the group of doctors, who in turn are confronted with state interventions and the manufacturers' efforts to pay for high R&D costs. The R&D sub-sector is also affected by this voltage ratio. For example, the politically motivated tightening of the authorization requirements for new active substances requires the extension of the duration of research. In addition to this obvious correlation, the use of new IT should be emphasized in this context, since their future task also includes the detailed proof of the benefits of new active substances and thus the fulfilment of authorization requirements[387].

The issue of authorization and technological interdependence is also present in the field of biosimilars. If TTIP brought EU and US regulatory requirements into line and, as a result, an increase in the marketing of medicines based on them, the imitation product would relieve the burden on health systems. A further interdependence exists between technological and social success factors wherever, with the help of technologies, patient data is collected, linked, evaluated and used in genetic engineering with the aim of combating individual disease control[388].

---

386 Canadian Centre for Policy Alternatives (2014), page 61.

387 Sequencing is important in the research of new active substances with mainframe computers. See Frankfurter Allgemeine Zeitung, Nr. 161, July 15, 2014, page 27.

388 PWC (2012), page 3.

Mutual interdependence between the political and social success factors exists where increasing expenditure on medicines is the trend of a society increasingly self-medicating with over-the-counter medicines, as expenditure on this group of medicinal products is not covered by health insurance. Overall, changing social expectations are shifting demand. This means that the separation of markets must be more stringent compared to traditional market breakdowns in the automotive industry.

On the one hand, there is a need for differentiation into original prescription drugs and generics, and on the other hand into the market for over-the-counter medicines, with the preferences or the possibilities of influencing patients on the markets varying. With regard to the classified markets, it was previously established, on the basis of the literature and current purchasing strategies of the Bayer Group, that the pure distinction between research producers, generic manufacturers and producers of over-the-counter products is not possible. This is the result of the growing importance of licenses designed to bridge earning gaps, expand portfolios and, in particular, to perceive shifts in demand/ trends. Consequently, licenses in the pharmaceutical industry are the result of the interdependence of social and legal success factors. Furthermore, licenses have an effect on the extent to which the research manufacturers operate R&D through their "internal effect", i.e. follow-up effects on future research breadth and market sharing[389]. Referring to the whole area of IPR, which concerns the duration of patent protection, extensions of monopoly or polypole position have an impact on the extent of private and public expenditure.

For example, the IPR implemented in CETA would theoretically result in an annual additional burden on the Canadian state of USD 850 million[390]. In view of the increased economic burden, reference must once again be made to the possible national consolidation of the IPR by TTIP, which from the point of view of the research manufacturers is synonymous with long-term planning security.

5.2.3 Scenario Analysis

The definition of scenario analysis and the general approach to creating the scenarios follows the pattern used in Chapter 5.1.3. Due to the divergent

389 Fischer/ Breitenbach (2007), page 231.
390 Canadian Centre for Policy Alternatives (2014), page 57.

specifications and expressions of the success factors, the pharmaceutical industry is divided into alternative scenarios in a different way. Two scenarios will also be drawn up, depending on the extent of the agreement reached. As previously applied, the first scenario forms the basic scenario in which the future development of all success factors is described. The second complementary scenario includes the option of an agreement without a comprehensive IPR. The creation of a third situation, in which the other important success factor - the respective health system - develops contrary to the first scenario, is dispensed with due to a lack of plausibility.

5.2.3.1 Basic Scenario with TRIPS

Success in the prescription drug segment will continue to be determined by the respective health systems after TTIP comes into force. Although the systems have different state-related characteristics, their future development is largely determined by the same factors. Thus, the issues of health and the supply of medicines continue to be perceived as a universal claim of society, thus maintaining the high degree of economization and politicization. Starting with the reference to economization, TTIP makes the general contribution that it acts as an agreement for the EU and US economic area as a small stimulus package, by setting in motion the general reduction in trade costs of the prescription cycle or the demand cycle already described for the basic scenario of the automotive industry. More important than the increase in household disposable income is the increase in employment and the inherent increase in contributions in the area of prescription medicines.

Judging by the size of the US and EU labor market, which will continue to employ six hundred to seven hundred million people in the future and the effect of an increase of two million in the workforce, with a distribution over several years, the effect in this respect is negligible[391].

In view of the negligible impact of the agreement on the level of employment/ contributions and the low cost-side effect that will be achieved for manufacturers by reducing low transatlantic tariffs and by adjusting only selectively in authorization procedures, GMP schemes, biosimilars and generics, health systems will be relatively affected in the years to come by demographic change of societies, the causal burden on drug expenditure and the shift in disease patterns to diseases of civilization as well as multiple

391 Friedrich-Ebert Stiftung (2014), page 3.

diseases. The demands of decision-makers arising from these determinants will maintain the politicization of systems for prescription drugs and make government intervention appear increasingly necessary in the short term.

In light of the development just described, the strategic importance of the TRIPS enshrined in TTIP for the research manufacturers is therefore increasing not only in competition with generic manufacturers, but also for long-term strategic planning against state intervention. Thus, due to the national commitment to the international agreement, the institutions within the EU and the US are only able to force their entry into the market for prescription drugs for generic manufacturers and to counteract thc rights/ costs beyond the original patent term through the various TRIPS. Similarly, an investment protection chapter contained in the agreement will be in the indirect context of competition between research and non-research producers and state intervention.

For the research manufacturers, the ever-increasing burden on health systems in the long term, in terms of marketing towards doctors and health insurance companies, means the increasing orientation of the price setting to the benefits of the medicinal product within the associated therapeutic class and at the general social view, whereby the connection in the future also covers the drugs that still have patent protection.

The interdependence between the price of a prescription drug and its benefits also, according to the agreement, dictates the dependence of research manufacturers on innovative active substances and technological success factors. In view of the low relief effect for health insurance funds, the institutions will continue to insist on detailed proof in the future.

Technological success factors therefore have the main responsibility for the development and detection of innovative active ingredients. The secondary responsibility will lie in ensuring flexibility, low manufacturing costs and high-quality medicines, with a focus on the internal competitive situation of production sites and public procurement. The projected loss of sales by 2020 due to the expiry of patents and the structure of pharmaceutical companies, which requires the continuous supply of three blockbuster drugs per year for its own maintenance, will further determine the need for successful R&D[392]. In order to deal with the challenges, the research manufacturers will establish themselves through targeted company-specific measures in individual areas.

392 Fischer/ Breitenbach (2007), page 211.

Although the pharmaceutical industry will continue to be one of the most research-intensive industries after the conclusion of the agreement, the research and activity fields of the individual manufacturers will continue to differ. This will in principle be done depending on the projections for innovative active substances, the duration of patent terms and the internal orientation by license taking or licensing. In the future, the business segments genetic engineering, medical technology, nanotechnology and biosimilars will also determine the market or at least promote its development. Especially in the industrialized countries, there is demand for medicines that are tailored to the individual patient and work against diseases of civilization and age. The individualization of the patient and the determination of the respective lifestyle are primarily promoted through the use of health, nutrition and sports apps as well as smartwatches[393]. In this context, there is also the increasing importance of all secondary patient data that accrue in the treatment. In particular, the data will be linked to the nature and genetic definition of the individual patient.

On the competition side, the research producers will compete with other research or generic competitors according to the characteristics or business areas listed above, with third-party providers having essential competences in the field of information technology and the management of databases. Furthermore, the non-tariff adjustments achieved by TTIP in the authorization requirements and GMP standards for medicinal products have no significant impact on manufacturers. This is due to the degree of integration already existing within the pharmaceutical industry[394]. However, the observation must not disguise the fact that, in the long term, at least the EU market will be characterized by increasing generic competition[395].

Contrary to the development outlined for prescription medicines, TTIP has an effect on the demand for Over-the-counter medicines. However, this effect will be weak due to the already existing social and spending behavior within the EU, the US and other industrialized countries. For developing and emerging countries, on the other hand, the impact of the agreement's general spillover effects is particularly noticeable in countries where a high-income middle class is developing. Excluding a significant

393 Spiegel Online. "Apple-Uhr soll die Sonne nutzen". February 3, 2014. https://www.spiegel.de/netzwelt/gadgets/iwatch-apple-uhr-soll-die-gesundheit-foerdern-und-die-sonne-nutzen-a-950781.html

394 See Chapter 5.2.6 "Reinforced Pharmaceutical Alliances in the US and EU"

395 BPI (2014), page 49.

negative trade diversion effect, the BRIC countries, Turkey, South Korea and Indonesia should be highlighted as important future markets.

With regard to these markets, the TRIPS agreed in TTIP assumes a worldwide standard setting, which is of strategic importance for the pharmaceutical industry. In addition to the aforementioned protection against short-term government intervention, which is particularly relevant in developed countries with high health expenditures, supplementary protection certificates, patent linking, and exclusivity of test date are important for the emerging-market health systems under development. The protection mechanisms are differentiated according to the country after the first introduction or standardization and simplify the long-term planning of the manufacturers. It is true that manufacturers benefit from established brand names regardless of the market saturation phase. However, these will become more important in the context of the abovementioned safeguards with regard to the structure of the relevant market and will enable transnational pharmaceutical groups to gain market shares on third markets.

The environmental success factors that exist for the pharmaceutical industry develop independently of TTIP and remain at a high level.

5.2.3.2 An Agreement without Intellectual Property Rights (IPR)

At the start of the TTIP negotiations, it was not clear whether it should be a "mixed" agreement or not, i.e. whether the national parliaments of the EU member states should be involved or not. As a result, the problematic area of IPR is excluded from the ratification process[396]. Based on the economization and politicization of health systems as shown in the basic scenario, policymakers are increasingly being prompted to intervene in the short term and to change the framework conditions of the systems. As health spending continues to rise and the not insignificant share of pharmaceutical spending, interventions will no longer be limited to budget restrictions and the like but rather will aim to reduce the duration of protection of TRIPS generic medicine manufacturers to have faster access to the market for prescription medicines and to relieve health systems in this way. In the same way, the authorization requirements for the generic are reduced by the need to provide only the structural proof of the copied active substance, but not its detailed proof of usefulness.

396 Fischer-Lescano/ Horst (2014) page 5, 9 – 10.

For the research manufacturers, unless it is a blockbuster medicine, the indirect consequence is that it is problematic to amortize costs incurred within a shortened monopoly/ polypole period. In the immediate reaction, manufacturers reduce the breadth of R&D to active ingredients that are highly likely to be promising. Overall, the specialization of research manufacturers and the attractiveness of researching rare diseases is decreasing. Generic competition in the EU and US markets is increasing. The absence of TRIPS in TTIP leaves out an international standard setting in the WTO negotiations. Thus, transnational corporations continue to depend on the different framework conditions of the markets, which makes a holistic strategic orientation more difficult.

Future sales markets, such as India, which have a strong pharmaceutical industry in the generics sector, are gaining as an example from the non-introduction of patent linking[397].

5.2.4 Current Strategies of the Pharmaceutical Industry

The overall strategy of the pharmaceutical industry is characterized by the constant adaptation to the PESTEL factors. For example, in the case of political success factors, transnational corporations are prepared to meet different admission requirements, GMP standards and the framework conditions for pricing. In line with the ability to adapt to the respective markets, the strategy is characterized by presence in the growth markets through own production sites or sales organizations[398]. However, the definition differs to parts from the growth market to the definition used by the automotive industry. The pharmaceutical industry is currently pursuing the main goal of serving markets that are characterized by a rapidly growing middle class[399].

The technological success factors are characterized by the fact that the research producers continue to carry out R&D to a high degree, with increasing restructuring and differentiation. In the recent past, for example, some large pharmaceutical companies have made cost reductions due to continued failure to develop new active ingredients. There is also selective cooperation between competitors to bring new active substances to the

397 Bhardwaj/ Padamavati (2013), pages 316 - 322.
398 Interview 4 (see Appendix A)
399 PWC (2012), page 19.

market by pooling databases and competencies[400]. The overall objective is to develop medicines that work against diseases that are not yet treatable or rare[401]. Manufacturers meet the aforementioned requirements for the production of medicinal products with a qualitative and flexible process through lean production and the retention of appropriate capacities.

The further holistic presentation of the current strategy is only possible for the aspect of patent application strategies. The reason for this is a very differentiated approach by the researching pharmaceutical companies. For example, reference has already been made elsewhere in this dissertation to the current different activities and the implied orientation of Sanofi and Evotec, Bayer AG and Boehringer. The fact that these companies are not isolated cases is also demonstrated by the actions of other research-based pharmaceutical companies in recent years[402].

The process of filing a patent is characterized by strategic considerations. For example, patents are partially filed in an "Evergreening Strategy" only in order to create a confusing patent situation for the generic manufacturer and thus to extend the actual term of protection. A distinction must be made between the 'secondary patents', which center on the application for an improved active substance, which also amounts to an extension of the term of protection. Finally, the approaches of "Divisional Applications" and "Defensive Patents" are to be mentioned. In the first form, the patent applicant separates sub-areas from the original patent application and registers them independently. If the procedure is successful, a network of intellectual property rights will be created. Blocking patents are relevant to the competition of research manufacturers among themselves and block the use of a particular technology, even though it is not used by the patent applicant herself/ himself[403].

5.2.5 Strategic Change

The approach to determining strategic changes is similar to the approach chosen for the automotive industry. There is only a difference in the valuation. In addition to the scenarios, the PESTEL analysis is included. This is

400 PWC (2012), pages 24 – 28.

401 Handelsblatt. "Schleichender Favoritenwechsel in der Pharmabranche", Nr. 160, page 14. August 21, 2014.

402 PWC (2012), page 20 – 21.

403 Voit (2010), pages 41 – 46.

followed by a comparison with the current strategy and the extent to which a strategic change resulting from the agreement is due to the agreement.

Already in the PESTEL analysis, it becomes clear that in the product group of prescription drugs the strategy is strongly determined by the stock and the expression of the health systems. Accordingly, the dependency runs strongly through the scenarios created. Irrespective of the different forms of the systems, the long-term economic burden, which is only slightly relieved by TTIP, is increasing in the long term.

Government interventions in health systems are also conspicuous, depending on the economic situation or political motivation. On the contrary, depending on the scope of the agreement, the future binding effect that the agreement emanates and limits the scope for intervention. In the case of technological success factors, the scenarios have similarities to a sustained general research intensity, whereby, in addition to the development of future business areas, the benefit evidence of new active ingredients is superficial and in turn has an influence on the setting of prices. Furthermore, despite the different forms of the scenarios, the increasing differentiation of R&D activities is evident. Strictly linked to R&D, IPR is of considerable importance in terms of national reference, but also in the inclusion of global standard setting. Over-the-counter medicines develop independently of health systems across scenarios and are determined by an increasing self-medication rate and patients' disposable income, making the market more important for all manufacturers.

On the basis of the EU position paper, the pharmaceutical industry is found to experience no strategic change from the reduction of transatlantic tariffs, the partial alignment of authorization requirements and GMP standards, as well as enhanced cooperation in other areas. For example, the measures sought by the negotiators will achieve cost-side effects and faster processes for manufacturers and regulatory authorities, but this will not occur to such an extent that the strategy is reoriented[404]. TRIPS must be considered to be more complex, provided that they are included in the agreement. Since neither the conditions of the patent applications were part of the negotiations between the EU and Canada nor since the current state of negotiations gives rise to a contrary view, no changes will follow from the main element of the patent protection. Consequently, the manufacturing producers will continue to attempt to extend the de facto protection of the active substances by means of a confusing design of the situation or

404 Interview 4 (see Appendix A)

the refusal of access to technological processes through the notification strategies outlined. The situation is different with the intellectual property rights associated with the patent and which have an effect beyond the patent term.

Supplementary protection certificates, patent linkage and the temporal exclusivity of data must be differentiated according to their temporal mode of action.

States which take over those protection rights directly or indirectly through the model effect and are faced with a long-term increasing economic burden on their health systems are, by the international law, in the possibility of an extensive intervention or conversion of the health system. In this respect, the research manufacturers benefit, as the additional anchoring of intellectual property rights protects against a significant strategic change. In the short term, the effect is more effective if only the exemplary effect of the agreement is considered without the economization of the systems. In particular, the focus should be on the future markets of India and China, whose governments intervene and promote generic competition despite the existence of intellectual property rights. It is also worth pointing out the indirect effect of deterrence, since pharmaceutical companies such as Roche now differentiate pricing policy in advance[405]. If the current negotiators conclude agreements in the future with both countries or with countries that are characterized by a similar approach, strategic changes are conceivable in the markets.

For manufacturers of over-the-counter medicines, there will be a need for strategic changes depending on their previous positioning in the previously mentioned future markets, as positive spill-over effects will increase disposable income. The strategic change includes in particular the conscious use and expansion of brand names.

The extent to which ISDS clauses would lead to strategic changes in areas such as patent application and granting can be illustrated by the following example: The case of multinational drug firm Eli Lilly against the Canadian Government demonstrates that countries, in this case Canada, are free "under NAFTA and World Trade Organization agreements, to design a patent system that suits...needs and.... industries"[406]. It should also be noted that

405 PWC (2012), page 21.

406 Gold Richard. "NAFTA patent ruling a big victory for Canadian innovation". *The Globe and Mail.* April 6, 2017. https://www.theglobeandmail.com/report-on-busines

the potential ISDS clauses that could be contained in TTIP may not be identical to those of the NAFTA agreement.

5.2.6 Reinforced Pharmaceutical Alliances in the US and EU

In this context, it is striking that the concentration of pharmaceutical companies on research into new active ingredients and on the growing middle class in China and India has increased since the beginning of the 8th round of TTIP negotiations leading to more and more acquisitions and joint ventures. In this context, the focus is on market leadership in the US and EU in individual core segments:

- In 2014, Pfizer, as the industry leader, began to take over the UK's Astra – Zeneca.
- The industry second Novartis bought the cancer drug segment from the British Glaxo Smithkine (GSK) for $14.5 billion. In return, GSK acquired the vaccine division for $7 billion.
- The US healthcare group Johnson &Johnson took over a number of US biotech companies such as Gilead, Bio Idec and Celgene.
- In the first half of 2014, the US company Gilead Sciences was able to double its sales by one stroke compared to 2013 with the Hepatitis medicine Sovaldi[407].
- The US diagnostics company Abbott split its pharmaceutical division under the name Abbvie.

The traditional pharmaceutical business is once again becoming attractive through new research products, also from the point of view of the capital market. It has recently become apparent that diversification has ultimately brought less added value to the pharmaceutical giants in recent years.

- Pharmaceutical giants Pfizer, Glaxo Smithkline, Merck & Co. and Eli Lilly
- reported a decline in sales in the first half of 2014 as a result of patent processes and increasing price pressure.

---

s/rob-commentary/nafta-patent-ruling-a-big-victory-for-canadian-innovation/article34617647/

407 Handelsblatt. "Schleichender Favoritenwechsel in der Pharmabranche", Nr. 160, page 14. August 21, 2014.

- The ten largest pharmaceutical manufacturers lost further market share in 2014 while still receiving 52% of all drug expenditure, which, however, at the end of 2014, it was only 43%.
- Bayer, the world's largest pharmaceutical company in the 1970s, also had to overcome a drought period for 10 years, before starting a new phase of growth since the beginning of 2015. In the medium term, the group thus has the opportunity to move up from 13th place among the ten leading pharmaceutical producers[408].
- Abbvie, a pharmaceutical company spun off from Abbott, has reduced its dependence on the arthritis drug "Humira" by acquiring the Irish group Shire.

Humira is the highest-selling drug in the entire pharmaceutical industry, bringing Abbvie to nearly $10.7 billion in 2013, more than half of the group's revenue. In 2016, the drug lost its patent protection in the US, which led to significant sales losses and created opportunities for generic producers.

- Mylan Inc., which specializes in generics, is likely to have a lot of interest in "Humira." The U.S. pharmaceutical company bought part of ABBOTT's foreign business, including operations in Europe, for USD 5.3 billion. As part of the deal, Mylan plans to open its legal headquarters in the Netherlands to save taxes. Because some pharmaceutical giants are turning their backs on the US, the US government will close the tax loopholes through tax harmonization soon after the TTIP agreement with the EU comes into force.
- The French pharmaceutical company Sanofi was able to acquire Genzyme in 2013 with significant production capacities in the US. Based on comparable exchange rates, sales at Sanofi improved by 4.9% to EUR 33.8 billion in 2014 due to Genzyme[409].
- In the U.S., Genzyme has been approved for four newly researched influenza pathogens and two active ingredients for rare diseases.

408 Frankfurter Allgemeine Zeitung. “Fusionieren durch TTIP in der Pharmabranche“, Nr. 161, July 15, 2014, page 27.

409 Frankfurter Allgemeine Zeitung. “Sanofi will neuen Chef bis Ende Ende März 2015 ernennen.” Nr. 31, page 18. February 6, 2015.

- Finally, the US medical technology group DANAHER was able to acquire the Swiss dental implant manufacturer Nobel Biocave (18% market share) for 1.8 billion euros[410].

Over the past 30 years, DANAHER has developed into a medical technology giant with a turnover of almost $20 billion and 66,000 employees through the acquisition of more than 400 companies. DANAHER also has a dental division that generates approximately $2.2 billion sales. Together with Nobel Biocare, the US company has annual sales of almost $3 billion in the sector and is therefore expected to be the world market leader.

These "company weddings" in 2013/ 2014 once again impressively document the positioning of the pharmaceutical industry in the EU and US markets as the TTIP negotiations grew at a pace. Both markets are characterized by similarly strict licensing and testing procedures, as well as by a growing generic sector. For the future, manufacturers hope that a EU-US Free Trade Agreement will successfully be concluded, as they would greatly benefit from it. It would give a considerable boost to the integration of various standards in the health-care markets. Naturally, it is precisely this area that would gain enormous dynamism through cost savings and the purchasing power of a large middle class, as is already evident in the run-up to the TTIP entry into force[411]. Also, worth highlighting is the commitment of Microsoft founder Bill Gates, who joined the Tübingen-based company Gurevac with 46 million euros. Bill Gates trusts the biotech company to develop vaccines that can revolutionize medical history. Gurevac and other biotech companies can also compete in the fight against incurable diseases such as cancer and Alzheimer's. In this context, the Munich-based company Micronet was taken over by the US pharmaceutical and biotech group Amgen[412].

Such investment by US corporations in Europe is a good sign of the two markets' convergence before an agreement such as TTIP. They are a pillar of growth in Europe and therefore also for the prosperity and jobs of the

---

410 Handelsblatt. „Milliarden- Übernahme in der Medizintechnik". Nr. 178, page 24. September 16, 2014.

411 „Pharma und TTIP" in Markets, Magazin für Märkte und Chancen, Ausgabe 2/ April 2014, page 14.

412 Handelsblatt. „Deutsche Perlen". Nr. 48, page 1. March 10, 2015.

old continent, but also a sign that, even before the fall of trade barriers, they have a mainstay in Europe as a trade advantage[413].

413 "Transatlantische Fusionen: Die neue Wertschätzung", in, Handelsblatt, Nr.67, page 27. April 8, 2015.

Chapter 6: ISDS[414] with Qualitative Reorientation

Unlike the first five TTIP negotiation rounds under Commissioner Karel de Gucht, Trade Commissioner Cecilia Malmström and his successor as European Commissioner for Trade have ensured great transparency towards civil society in Europe. After each round of negotiations, the drafts of the EU/ US negotiations were made available online on the EU Commission website. Many thousands of pages, e.g. on the important preliminary results on ISDS and arbitration in the respective negotiation round, could thus be available to stakeholders and multipliers. Admittedly, the previous lack of transparency in the first phase of the negotiations had led to critics such as "Food Watch" or "Greenpeace", who had demonstrated on September 28, 2015 in front of the Allianz Forum in Berlin with "Stop TTIP" slogans and demonstrated again together with the DGB on October 10, 2015 in Berlin, Germany.

6.1 Style and Spirit of TTIP Negotiations

In contrast to the "warm-up phase" in the first four rounds of negotiations, which were dominated by competition from the negotiating partners, the energy of the following negotiation rounds had developed more so in a spirit of cooperation.

It was no longer the much-vaunted fear of lowering standards and protection against regulatory reductions on the EU side, but the will on both sides to bring the highest possible standards to one denominator (e.g. U.S. fear in the medical and pharmaceutical sectors with the very strict testing procedures or the fear on the EU side of losing food safety standards.)

In this respect, the protest in Europe has had a very helpful effect on the climate of the negotiating partners. Both sides are under pressure from the public, the health industry, associations and NGOs, but also under pressure

414 Investor-state dispute settlement (ISDS) is an instrument of international law. ISDS allows a foreign investor to initiate a dispute settlement procedure against a state, in which it has invested, if it considers that its rights guaranteed by international public law are violated.

from parliamentarians and governments, who do not want to appear under the influence of lobbyists or having to fear the removal by citizens during upcoming re-elections[415].

6.2 Regulatory Chapter in TTIP

Assuming that both sides recognize pesticide value limits, an institute later finds that pesticide residues are too high, the question of accountability to the legislator would arise.

According to Denis Redonnet, Director of WTO Legal and Trade in Goods, TTIP has therefore become a kind of "turbocharger" for governmental authorities on both sides, which means that the negotiation process now leads to greater transparency, which in turn leads to greater coherence[416]. Redonnet spoke of a "culture of regulatory cooperation rather than competition". More than any other free trade agreement, the focus of TTIP is on breaking down the "behind the border" barriers to reduce costs.

The "toolbox" of the negotiations includes:

- mutual WTO recognition or harmonization of standards in the case of new products due to the latest developments, e.g. in the field of electromobility or even hydrogen propulsion
- consequently, not so much focus on the internal market, but regulatory compatibility and cost reduction
- rather than regulatory dumping, systematically increasing regulations to ensure that a majority is obtained in the Council of Ministers of the EU and in the EU Parliament. The focus is on consumer sustainability and the protection of health.
- Opening up transatlantic trade is seen as a good thing by both negotiating partners. TTIP makes a lot of sense for both sides

415 Allianz Forum in Berlin, Germany with 350 participants from business and stakeholders on the topic: "A TTIP point for Europe in the world?" Jacques Delors Institute. October 28, 2015.

416 Statement at the Allianz-Forum in Berlin, Germany on the occasion of the TTIP conference of the Jacques Delors Institute by moderator Pascal Lamy, former EU Trade Commissioner. October 28, 2015.

- After the 10th negotiation round, there was a better negotiation energy achieved by much more transparency[417].
- In the United States, citizens are nowadays taking food and health protection very seriously. In addition, there is more "public sensibility" compared to two years ago for agricultural products, industrial goods and pharmaceuticals/ chemicals. This has been repeated in numerous US media outlets during the TTIP conference, for example in the Washington Times and the New York Times ((compare Monsanto scandal).

Therefore, more regulatory coherence instead of competitive thinking could be found after the 10th TTIP negotiation round overall between the EU and the US leading to a new "upstream" mechanism, i.e. embedding in structural and existing standards, e.g. on WTO basis, towards regulatory coherence.

Negotiations were no longer conducted in the old style as in the past, but in the form of mandates, which both negotiating partners could implement as "regulatory clusters". TTIP is a much more difficult agreement in comparison to other free trade agreements, as standards of both advanced economies are often very different.

Both regulatory authorities in the EU and US are very active and creative, which will lead to significant cost reductions as a result of the agreement.

Standards are not lowered, contrary to what Food Watch and Greenpeace repeatedly claim, but are raised to ever higher levels of protection. Regulators are not hindered by laws to negotiate higher standards.

With TTIP, there will also be results that are bilateral or follow international WTO standard setting, i.e. recognition of WTO-based standards (e.g. for cars and pharmaceuticals).

This differentiated approach to standard setting/ adoption or harmonization will serve as a model for all other free trade agreements, according to Pascal Lamy, Deputy WTO Director on October 28, 2015 at the Allianz Forum in Berlin, Germany.

It is clear that competition in regulations is increasing worldwide, according to Pascal Lamy, former EU Commissioner for Trade.

417 Statement by Peter Chase, Vice-President German-American Business Chamber at Allianz Forum in Berlin, Germany, October 28, 2015.

6.3 ISDS and the International Commercial Court

On the topic "Foreign investment in TTIP and beyond: what is the right balance in the protection of investors and of states?" at the TTIP conference of the Jacques Delors Institute at the Allianz Forum in Berlin, Germany, the following panel discussants participated: Anna Joubén-Bret, International Investment Lawyer, Avocat la Cour, Paris; Markus Krajewski, Chair of Public and International Law with a research focus on WTO law and international civilian protection at the University of Erlangen-Nuremberg, and Christoph Benedict, Legal Director, Alstom Power (Chief Syndicate).

All participants were in favor of an international arbitration tribunal in the US and the EU. ISDS has been around for 30 years and it has the flaws which is why complaints are on the rise, for example, double-digit investment cases against Spain since 2011. In the opinion of all panelists, there are therefore good reasons to reform ISDS, not least because of 3725 bilateral ISDS agreements with different standards.

Above all, there was consensus that procedures must be swift, fair and equitable. If courts do not decide more quickly, investments will soon be dead, according to the unanimous opinion of the panelists.

The case of the automotive supplier MITEC in Eisenach, Germany, with a four-year litigation before a national German court, clearly shows that the lawsuit against Ford in the US may still take years in national courts.

German Federal Economics Minister Sigmar Gabriel and Matthias Fekl, French Trade Minister, who attended the Allianz Forum on October 28, 2015, stressed that we should never forget that investors only invest abroad in a protected manner. TTIP offers the opportunity to create new innovative investor protection.

Both ministers reported on their proposal for a modern jurisdiction, supported by 6 other trade ministers of EU Member States and as a result, presented by Cecilia Malmström as a proposal for further trade negotiations with the US side. Gabriel reported the US side seemed to be signaling "a green light" and that the International Trade Court is likely to be included in the trade agreement[418].

It will be composed of 15 judges, 5 from the EU, 5 from the US and 5 from third countries. Six judges are to be appointed to an appellate body modelled according to the WTO Arbitration Board.

418 European Parliament Resolution. TTIP 2014/ 2228 (INI) on ISDSS, page 5 and page 17. July 8, 2015.

The previous practice in private arbitration courts with highly endowed lawyers who change to the role of judges would thus be abolished. It is intended to eliminate the possibility of corporations suing states in parallel before the Investment Court and the national courts, as the Vattenfall Group, for example, is currently attempting with the Federal Government over the nuclear phase-out.

According to the ideas of the EU Commission (DG Trade), the losing party should bear the costs of the proceedings.

Hearings and statements in investor protection proceedings are also supposed to be published in the future.

The 2nd pillar in Malmström's proposal is a set of provisions in the agreement on the protection of existing legislation. This is an important chain of arguments for NGOs such as Greenpeace and Foodwatch.

States should still have the right to legislate and regulate to protect their populations or the environment, even if this has a negative impact on investors' expectations, according to Malmström's proposal.

Classic cases before the investor protection court are, for example, the withdrawal of licenses or expropriations by nationalization.

The two ministers and panelists agreed on October 28, 2015 that a new "gold standard" would be introduced through an International Trade Court. With a new trade court, the EU and the US could influence poorer systems internationally, such as agreements with China, Turkey or Middle Eastern states dominated by corrupt administrations[419]. The International Trade Court could be located in Geneva, for instance[420].

6.4 Time Delay in TTIP negotiations

At the end of the TTIP conference, German Federal Economics Minister Gabriel and France's Trade Minister Fekl addressed the long-running negotiation process:

Both reaffirmed the increasing competition of technical standards worldwide. 90% of the world's population is neither American nor European. Therefore, there would be no alternative to TTIP. The agreement could become the "mother of all agreements" by setting standards. A failed TTIP

419 Handelsblatt. „Gerichtshof soll es richten", Nr. 187. September 29, 2015, page 10.

420 European Commission. „TTIP mit modernen Investitionsgerichten". *EU-News, Nr. 15.* September 24, 2015, page 4.

could leave behind a divided EU with enormous collateral damage, because the EU might then have to turn to negotiating other agreements, for example with China.

Even though both negotiating TTIP partners made progress in the areas of ISDS, agricultural markets and public procurement service markets during the 11th round in Miami, in the end TTIP could not be ratified due to overall disagreements regarding specific chapters. Demystifying and disarming previous assumptions of some NGOs opposed to TTIP was also part of the negotiations being held up and delayed. Both ministers reiterated that without an international trade court with an appellate body, there would be no TTIP agreement. Proceedings before the Trade Court would be governed by the principles of the UN Commission on International Trade Law (UNCITRAL)[421]. This would preclude the possibility that decisions, as in the case of private arbitration tribunals, might be taken on a hotel corridor, for instance.

This new system in the TTIP agreement would preserve the right of governments on both sides of the Atlantic to regulate and ensure that investment disputes are settled "with full respect for the rule of law"[422]. The procedures become transparent, the hearings public and the statements would be available online. In addition, parties with an interest in the dispute would be given the opportunity to join the proceedings. Dubious lawsuits would immediately be dismissed, and international and national law would clearly be distinguished from each other[423].

In parallel with the TTIP negotiations, Malmström stated on September 16, 2015 on the occasion of the presentation of the proposal on ISDS, the Commission, together with other countries, would also work towards the establishment of an International Arbitration Court within the framework of further free trade agreements in order to increase efficiency, uniformity and legitimacy.

---

421 „UNCITRAL [*United Nations Commission on International Trade Law*]-Transparency Rules" in Section 3 (Court System), Article 1 (Scope and Definitions), TTIP, Trade and Investment and E-commerce, EU-Commission-Draft-Text, P8-TA-PROV (2015) 0252, p. 11.

422 Cecilia Malmström, EU Trade Commissioner. "Factsheet on Regulatory Coherence". *EU Press Release.*Brussels, September 16, 2015. https://trade.ec.europa.eu/doclib/docs/2015/january/tradoc_153002.1%20RegCo.pdf

423 *TTIP-Trade in Services, Investment and e-Commerce-Chapter II.* Investment, Draft, Section 3 (Court System), September 16, 2015, page 11.

Chapter 7: Assessment of the EU NGO Hearings: TTIP Angst and Fears in Germany, Austria and the UK

At the end of the 10th round of negotiations, the two chief negotiators, EU Trade Commissioner Cecilia Malmström and US Trade Representative Michael Froman, presented the results of the negotiations July 13-17, 2015. During the press conference, both chief negotiators made it clear that the assumptions repeatedly put forward by stakeholders and NGOs in the run-up to the 10th round of negotiations were incorrect.

Malmström and Froman made it clear that

- Custom duties will be reduced
- the standards and regulations in the automotive sector, as well as mechanical and plant engineering, will be brought together in the form of mutual recognition based on the 1998 UNECE Agreement (UN Economic Commission for Europe). (This applies in cases where the negotiating partners could not agree on the equivalence of EU and US standards).
- post-research and development harmonization should be achieved in new technologies, such as in the e-mobility sector with autonomous driving (in this case, the standards or new regulations should be coordinated and harmonized at the planning stage[424])
- mutual recognition of lists of products with regional character and geographical indications is accepted (e.g. Thüringer Rostbratwurst, French Camembert)[425]
- the protection of public services such as health care, education and services of general interest (e.g. urban water supply) remains guaranteed
- the protection of culture and cultural institutions, as well as the subsidized film production, would be maintained
- compliance with the EU's strict chemical safety standards (EU-Reach list) remains in place

---

424 EU Commission. "Conclusion of the 10th TTIP Negotiation Round". *Press Release DG Trade.* July 17, 2015.

425 EU Commission. "Annex I: List of Geographical Indications". *Intellectual Property (IP) and Geographical Indications (GI).* March 21, 2016. https://trade.ec.europa.eu/doclib/docs/2016/march/tradoc_154386.GIPaperAnnex1%20FINAL_REV.pdf

- respect for environmental protection at EU, national, state and local level remains assured
- the promotion of small and medium-sized enterprises is an important task of the agreement
- consensus had been reached on the establishment of transparent arbitral tribunals in the form of a public International Trade Court
- public procurement in both the EU and the US should apply equally in both markets
- the agricultural sector needs to develop more consumer and environmentally friendly production methods

Despite these clear statements of both chief negotiators, the TTIP stakeholder round was held in Brussels on July 15, 2015, two days before the end of the 10th round of negotiations. During this round, the NGOs raised almost identical issues, which they demanded that the negotiators resolve[426].

The focus of the stakeholders was on:

- removal of technical barriers to trade and regulatory coherence in specific sectors, energy and raw materials
- protection of products with regional character
- regulation of agricultural markets in sustainability, environmental and consumer orientation
- rules for sustainable development
- promotion and support for SMEs
- Investment protection and mutual access to public procurement.

The demands of the stakeholder round were thus partly in line with the negotiators' decisions. This was quite controversial in the first nine rounds, especially in Germany, with a subdued Austria, France and the United Kingdom. However, resistance to TTIP was most sustained in Germany, while it flattened out in Austria, France and the United Kingdom at the beginning of 2015. Therefore, the resistance to TTIP in Germany will be examined in more detail below.

426 EU Commission. "TTIP-Stakeholder Events Round 10, Brussels". *Directorate-General for Trade.* Brussels, July 15, 2015.

7.1 The "German Angst" and TTIP Fears

At the end of the 12th round of negotiations held in Brussels February 22 – 26, 2016, Ignacio Garcia Bercero, Chief EU Negotiator for TTIP, in the presence of Daniel Mullaney, Chief US Negotiator for TTIP, gave a remarkable and forward-looking summary to the assembled international press[427]. His remarks emphasized the broad agreement between the US and EU negotiating delegations on TTIP issues still to be addressed by the end of 2016[428], such as

- Investment Protection[429]
- Regulatory cooperation
- and sustainable development.

In his summary, trade facilitation, market access offers for public procurement and "State-to-State Dispute Settlement" in the form of a new dimension of the arbitration court system ("new Investment Court System") were also mentioned as a trailblazer for all future trade agreements[430]. According to Bercero, the 12th round marked the beginning of a new era of EU-US convergence in the field of trade with regard to the Investment Court System (ICCS)[431]. Bercero presented the introduction of a bilateral investment court and an appeal mechanism with judges in the public commercial court, including an appeal body with state regulatory law, but also procedural transparency and judicial independence[432]. Finally, Bercero highlighted the close cooperation between the US and the EU on all kinds of regulations[433].

427 EU Commission. „Conclusion of the 12th TTIP-Negotiation-Round". *Statement by EU-Chief-Negotiator Ignacio Garcia Bercero, DG Trade.* February 26, 2016.

428 United States Trade Representative. "TTIP-Round in Brussels". *US Press-Statement.* February 26, 2016.

429 EU-Nachrichten. "Ehrliche Diskussion über Regeln zum Investorenschutz", Nr. 01, January 22, 2015.

430 EU Commission. "Investment Protection and Investor-to-State-Dispute Settlement in EU-agreements". March 2014.

431 EU-Commission. „Investment Protection and Investor to-State Dispute Settlement in EU-Agreements". *Factsheet.* November 2013.

432 EU-Commission. *(Trade)-Statement,* page 3. February 26, 2016.

433 Frankfurter Allgemeine Zeitung. „Industrie ermahnt Politik zu mehr Engagement für TTIP ", Nr. 17, page 18. January 21, 2015.

Nine relevant areas were defined as final content of the TTIP agreement for regulatory cooperation[434]:

- Automotive sector,
- Pharmaceutical market,
- Chemicals,
- Cosmetics,
- Pesticides,
- Medical devices,
- ICT information and communication technology,
- Engineering,
- Energy[435].

Once again, this selection demonstrates the environmental and consumer protection orientation of both negotiating partners[436]: Barcero stressed, with the agreement of Dan Mullaney, that lowering of standards is out of the question, rather the increase of the quality of standards is always aimed for in all sectors[437].

The implementation of the new "Investment Court System (ICS)"[438] in the TTIP Agreement is of essential importance with a strategic directional focus as a "new generation agreement"[439]. The new quality of investment protection will thus become the guiding principle for all future trade agreements, especially with China and Latin America[440]. So far, the EU has concluded free trade agreements with more than 50 trading partners, including the July 2011 agreement with South Korea as well as the CETA agreement

434 EU Commission. "TTIP and Regulation: An Overview". *DG Trade, Sectoral Provisions*, page 2, Nr. 3.2, pages 12-18.

435 These nine areas had already been identified in the EU guidelines for negotiations on TTIP, October 9, 2014.

436 German Federal Ministry of Economics and Technology. "Federal Ministry for Business emphasizes progress in TTIP negotiations". *Press Release.* March 11, 2016.

437 EU-Commission. "Report of the eleventh Round of Negotiations", Miami, pages 10-16. October 19-23, 2015.

438 Schmucker, Claudia. "TTIP im Kontext anderer Freihandelsabkommen" in: *Aus Politik und*
Zeitgeschichte, Berlin, 64. Jg. 50-51/ 2014, page 17. December 8, 2014.

439 Basedow, Robert. "Licht in den Schutz der Investoren". *Frankfurter Allgemeine Zeitung,* Nr. 224, page 20. September 26, 2014.

440 "Results of the 8th negotiation Round (Regulatory Cooperation) February 2-6, 2015", page 5, in: *EU–US–TTIP-Negotiations.* February 10, 2015.

of September 2014 with Canada[441]. In addition to TTIP, there are eleven EU trade agreements in the negotiation stage with Japan, India, the four ASEAN countries Singapore, Malaysia, Vietnam and Thailand, as well as with the five MERCOSUR countries of South America, such as Argentina, Brazil, Paraguay, Uruguay and Venezuela[442]. This demonstrates that the EU has been pursuing a very active trade policy for years[443]. "Global Europe: Competing in the World" has been the motto of the European Union's trade strategy since 2006, with the aim of improving the EU's competitiveness. Since 2010, the expanded EU trade strategy has been under the motto "Trade, Growth and Competing"[444].

For quite some time now, both the US and EU have been negotiating so-called "MEGA-REGIONALS", i.e. entire world regions with a large share of world trade and global investments, such as the US, EU, Japan and China, but also the "Tiger States" in Asia. In particular, these mega-regional agreements also included the TPP Agreement, in which twelve Asia-Pacific states were supposed to participate (US, Australia, Brunei, Chile, Japan, Malaysia, New Zealand, Peru, Singapore, Vietnam, Canada and Mexico) before the Trump Administration decided to withdraw. Before the withdrawal, TPP was seen as a steppingstone to a free trade agreement with all 21 member states of the Asia-Pacific Economic Community (APEC). Central initiators of the TPP were the NAFTA states US, Canada and Mexico as well as Japan[445]. On the other hand, the US had long been uninterested in global "mega-regionals" following the NAFTA agreement. After NAFTA came into force in 1994, only bilateral agreements with Peru, Colombia and Panama were ratified. It was only under President Obama that trade relations with Asia were strengthened and participation in negotiations on TPP began in March 2010. In addition, President Obama showed a strong interest in deepening trade relations with Europe. Indeed, TPP and TTIP

441 Interview with US-Ambassador John B. Emerson in Germany: „Mehr Möglichkeiten für Investoren und Exporteure weltweit ", in: *Markets-Magazin für Märkte und Chancen*, February 2015 (hrsg. Germany Trade & Invest).

442 "EU und MERCOSUR vertiefen Handelsgespräche" in: DIHK-Bericht aus Brüssel, Nr. 13, page 5. April 11, 2016.

443 EU Commission. "The EU's Bilateral Trade and Investment Agreements - Where are We?" *EU News*. December 3, 2013.

444 EU Commission. "Handelspolitik als Kernbestandteil der EU-Strategie Europa 2020". *Trade Document Library*. October 7, 2014. https://trade.ec.europa.eu/doclib/docs/2010/november/tradoc_146935.pdf

445 Schmucker, Claudia, a.a.O., page 19.

are agreements of global dimension: TTIP is the largest bilateral economic area, with the EU and the US, and accounts for almost 45 percent of world GDP and 44 percent of world trade in goods and services, according to WTO data[446]. According to WTO figures, TPP could account for almost 40 percent of global GDP and 26 percent of global trade[447]. In the globalization of world trade, both agreements are outstanding "trade plus agreements", setting new standards for investment protection, market access, competition, sustainable economic activity, the environment and social affairs. Both mega-regionals TTIP and TPP would therefore have a decisive impact on world trade. TTIP is therefore particularly important for Europe, the smallest continent. In order to be able to shape the rules in the international trading system, the EU in particular needs a trade partnership with the US. Only in this way, it can help shape its values and standards internationally. Europe is more dependent on TTIP than the US.

Not only for this reason, TTIP has become the acid test for democracy, good government and acceptance by the population. In order to compete internationally with economic blocs, the EU, which is responsible for trade for 28 member states, had to set out on its way to TTIP negotiations. Parts of the population, especially in Germany, Austria, and to a lesser extent in the United Kingdom and France, are afraid of the opening of markets. Numerous NGOs and stakeholders believe that there is no need for growth, that Europe can live well from the single common internal market and that more competition threatens the domestic economy. In the following chapter "The German Angst", these fears will therefore be discussed in more detail.

7.2 Environmental, Consumer and Food Protection as Core Concerns

The unease about trade liberalization is increasingly arising as a result of the setting of norms and standards for environmental, consumer and health protection in international free trade agreements in general. Environmental policy, consumer and health protection are key concerns of citizens, the general public and the media, particularly in the EU Member States. Abolishing tariffs and removing trade barriers are even mostly met with a positive response.

446 *WTO-Overview of Developments in the International Trading Environment.* Annual-Report by the Director - General, WT / TPR /OV 16, page 53. January 31, 2014.

447 World Trade Organization, 2012, page 55.

Environmental and consumer protection associations like to use polarizing clichés in ignorance of the actual facts, such as the alleged inferiority of food safety and consumer protection in the US, even though there is a differentiated level of food safety and much stronger consumer protection than, for example, in the German federal states. Although the German automotive industry alone, as the country's largest employer, estimates the annual customs duties incurred in export business with the US at more than one billion euros, and the abolition of customs duties via TTIP is likely to induce more sales and more jobs in Germany[448], TTIP is seen by many consumers in Germany as a "deal for corporations", as "a major contradiction to democracy, environmental protection and fair trade"[449]. In addition, NGOs such as Foodwatch, Campact and Greenpeace claim that large US corporations are threatening workers' rights, environmental standards, water supply and municipal housing construction, and even German fixed book prices, stage and adult education centers - in other words, many things that are dear to German consumers[450]. What is completely concealed is that in mutual free trade not only corporations but above all SMEs will benefit, right up to participation in "public procurement", i.e. also in the tendering and awarding of contracts by public authorities in the US[451]. The clichéd image of the US as a "cultureless, corporate-dominated society" used by some NGOs and parts of the tabloid press culminated, after an unprecedented campaign accompanied by a dose of anti-Americanism, in a large-scale TTIP demonstration in front of the Brandenburg Gate up to the Victory Column in Berlin on October 10, 2015 with half a million people[452]. The large-scale demonstration was organized by the German Trade Union Confederation (DGB), Campact, Foodwatch, Greenpeace, "Friends of the Earth" and farmers' associations[453].

---

448 Verband der Automobilindustrie: "Deutsche Automobilindustrie sagt ja zu TTIP", *Pressemeldung.* January 28, 2015. Acccessed April 27, 2015. https://www.vda.de/de/presse/Pressemeldungen.html

449 Mang, Christian, Campact, and Falke, Andreas: "TTIP Kontrovers", in: *Aus Politik und Zeitgeschichte,* 64. Jg. 50-51 / 2014, page 26.

450 Süddeutsche Zeitung. "Die große Ausnahme: Welche Kultur muss man schätzen", Nr. 204, page 6. December 22, 2015.

451 EU Commission: "EU-US-TTIP: Hier sind die Fakten", pages 2-5. February 18, 2014.

452 Handelsblatt. "Kein frischer Wind vom Pazifik: USA-Freihandelspakt versöhnt Gewerkschaften nicht mit TTIP", Nr. 193, page 9. October 7, 2015.

453 Handelsblatt, Nr. 178, page 19. September 9, 2015.

Figure 2: TTIP Demonstration in Berlin, Germany starting at the world famous "Tiergarten" Park all the way to the Victory Column in front of the Brandenburg Gate landmark

Source: Frankfurter Allgemeine Zeitung, October 10, 2015

7.3 Regulatory Cooperation Body (RCB) for Transparency and Prioritization in the Dialogue with Stakeholders as a TTIP Component

In addition to the reduction of tariffs, an important objective of the TTIP agreement is to remove non-tariff barriers. These result in an average cost effect equivalent to a duty rate of 20 percent[454]. The Association of German Chambers of Industry and Commerce (DIHK) had already welcomed this enormous savings effect at the beginning of the TTIP negotiations back in 2014[455].

---

454 Council of the European Union. "Market access / Trade in goods" in: *Guidelines for the EU / US negotiations on TTIP,* No 11103/13 UE/EU Restricted, page 5. October 9, 2014.

455 Beschluss "Transatlantische Handels- und Investitionspartnerschaft (TTIP)" des DIHK-Vorstandes, page 1. June 4, 2014.

On the other hand, NGOs such as Campact, Foodwatch, Greenpeace and others, criticize that this new quality of dismantling regulations has created a gateway for products from the US, which could put ecological products and added value in Europe under pressure from increased competition. The non-governmental organizations mentioned above reacted particularly sensitively to TTIP negotiations on regulations relating, for example, to food authorization or the use of hazardous substances. Increasingly, NGOs were attracting media attention, particularly through the publication of Tilo Bode's book "The TTIP Lie", mainly as a result of the differing approaches in the EU and the US to the potential risks to consumers[456]. While in the European internal single market, under the premise of the principle of supply, a health hazard must be excluded by the manufacturer, in the US, a product can obtain market approval until a specific health impairment is proven. In that case, the liability lies with the manufacturer, who must pay considerable sums of compensation in the event of damage[457].

In the 7th round of TTIP negotiations from September 29 until October 3, 2014, negotiators on both sides agreed on a compromise regulation for products and procedures that are hazardous to health[458]. Nevertheless, Foodwatch chief Tilo Bode was not interested in the drafts of the EU Commission, which can be viewed by everyone on the Internet, and maintained his false assertions of the health risks posed by TTIP in his book "The TTIP Lie", also published in 2014. The Association of German Chambers of Industry and Commerce also documented in its report from Brussels on February 16, 2015 the "Regulatory Cooperation" US-EU in TTIP, according to which the "Regulatory Cooperation Body (RCB)" will continue to ensure transparency and prioritization after the agreement comes into force[459]. The RCB will be composed of high-level representatives of the regulators on both sides. It is supposed to meet at least once a year with stakeholder trade unions, consumer protection and environmental associations for an

---

456 Tilo Bode: "Die TTIP-Lüge". Hanser Verlag, München, 2014.

457 Clapham, Ronald: "Die Internationale Ordnung in wirtschaftlicher, sozialer und ökologischer Sicht", in:
Zukunft der Sozialen Marktwirtschaft, Verlag Lucius & Lucius, Stuttgart 2006, Bd. 8, page 13.

458 Component Regulation: "Sanitary and Phytosanitary Measures, Chapter: Chemicals, Pharma, Medical Products, Cosmetics, Pesticides", in: EU-COMM Report on 7th TTIP Round, pages 3 – 7. October 29, 2015.

459 DIHK-Bericht aus Brüssel zur "Regulatorischen Kooperation in TTIP", page 5. February 16, 2015.

open exchange. The RCB is supposed to coordinate regulatory cooperation but cannot legislate itself. The minutes of all meetings are publicly accessible. The US side has already made it clear in the stakeholder debriefing at the 8th round of negotiations that the EU side wants a platform for regular regulatory exchange. The EU Commission posted the "Initial proposal for legal text" on its homepage on February 10 after the 8th round from February 2 - 6, 2015[460]. Once TTIP comes into force, this will ensure that stakeholders, NGOs and trade unions are always consulted, and their concerns weighed up when new products of a hazardous nature are approved.

7.4 The Great Fear: Lowering Standards

The protests in Europe and Germany against TTIP make it clear that in international free trade there are not only winners but also losers. Winners, because the removal of barriers in the form of customs duties and bureaucratic jungle leads to cost reductions for producers and service providers as well as to easier market access outside regional markets. As a result, companies benefit from more markets that, like the national domestic market, have a positive impact on growth through increased sales. Consumers benefit from falling prices as a result of increasing supply chains in more countries and also from more employment in the respective domestic market. This can also be seen, for example, in the negotiated free trade agreements with Canada (CETA)[461] and with Vietnam[462].

There are also losers in any free trade agreement, especially those sectors that have benefited from EU-wide or US-wide import protection and are not very competitive. These include the agricultural and food sectors, but

460 Artikel 9 - "Information and Regulatory Exchanges", Artikel 14 – "Establishment of the Regulatory Cooperation Body", in: *Initial Provisions for Chapter Regulatory Cooperation in TTIP*, EU-US-TTIP- Negotiations, pages 7-9. February 10. February 2015.

461 EU Commission. "EU-Canada-Summit (Ottawa) Consolidated CETA-Text". *Article 11: Good Entered after Repair or Alteration, Article 5: Reduction and Elimination of Customs Duties on Imports.* October 18, 2013. http://europa.eu/rapid/pressrellease -MEMO -13-911_de.htm

462 DIHK-Bericht aus Brüssel. "Fortschritte Freihandelsabkommen EU - Vietnam", Nr. 4, page 6. February 2, 2015.

also industrial products such as photovoltaic and textile products which cannot compete with wages in Europe, e.g. those in Vietnam[463].

By contrast, sectors such as automotive, chemicals, pharmaceuticals and mechanical engineering are among the winners of the free trade agreement, as was already demonstrated at the beginning by the case study on the automotive and pharmaceutical industries. The food sector and consumer protection were particularly controversial among stakeholders (associations and NGOs) right from the start until the 12th round of TTIP negotiations[464]. The Green parliamentary group in the German Bundestag, for example, viewed CETA as a gateway for genetic engineering[465] in the EU-Canada free trade agreement that had already been negotiated and assumed that there would be no labelling requirement for the approval of genetically modified organisms in CETA. The German Farmers' Association demanded that there should be no market opening for hormone-treated meat in TTIP[466]. On the other hand, the EU Commission stressed that food with genetically modified ingredients must be labelled accordingly.

Finally, Foodwatch as an NGO brought the "chlorine chicken" into play and stylized it as a symbol against the TTIP agreement par excellence[467]. The media rushed to this information to fuel the debate against TTIP[468]. EU Trade Commissioner Karel De Gucht made a sincere effort to intervene against the highly emotional debate in Germany and assured the German public that there will be no imports of hormone-treated meat or chlorine chicken from Canada or the US[469].

---

463 The White House. "Remarks by the President in the State of the Union Address". February 12, 2013. Accessed September 25, 2014. www.whitehouse.gov/the-press-office/2013/02/12

464 Sturgeon, Jamie: "Early winners and losers in historic EU trade pact". *Global News.* October 18, 2013. Accessed October 11, 2019. http://globalnews.ca/news/910793/early-Winners-and-Losers-in-historic-eu-trade-pact/

465 Frankfurter Allgemeine Zeitung. "Grüne: CETA ist Einfallstor für Gentechnik", Nr. 9, page 17. January 12, 2015.

466 De Ville Ferdi / Siles-Brügge Gabriel: "TTIP-the Truth about TTIP", *Polity Press*, UK, 2016, pages 118/ 119.

467 Frankfurter Allgemeine Zeitung. "Rot-Rot-Grün-Koalition würde am Chlorhühnchen scheitern", Nr. 224, page 3. September 26, 2014.

468 Ernst Klaus: "Viele Fragen sind ungeklärt", in: *Das Parlament* Nr. 40, page 7. September 29, 2014.

469 Frankfurter Allgemeine Zeitung. "Eine Einfuhr von Chlorhühnchen ist ausgeschlossen", Nr. 223, page 17. September 25, 2014.

In a heated debate in the German Bundestag, the Left Party and the Greens rejected the Free Trade Agreement with Canada (CETA) and the US (TTIP) in response to an inquiry from the Left on September 25, 2014[470]. The two opposition fractions felt strengthened in the Bundestag debate by stakeholder associations such as brewers, artists, craftsmen, representatives of the public water industry, book retailers, consumer and farmers' associations[471]. The German Federal Minister of Economics, Sigmar Gabriel, had great difficulty in making arguments in favor of TTIP in the Bundestag debate on September 25, 2014. Following this emotionally charged debate in the Bundestag, German Federal Minister of Economics Gabriel and EU Trade Commissioner Cecilia Malmström hosted a major press conference in Berlin on November 10, 2014 and defended both CETA and TTIP agreements with great vigor[472]. Both endeavored to stress that future negotiations should be "made as transparent as possible"[473]. Peter Steinbrück, MdB, former German Federal Minister of Finance, also supported his party colleague Sigmar Gabriel against the scaremongering of stakeholders and consumer advocates in an article for TTIP in a major national German newspaper[474]. He posed the important "crucial question": "If the US and the EU cannot agree - who will decide policy in the future? In an interview with a major South German national newspaper, EU Commissioner Cecilia Malmström also made it clear that there would be no cutbacks or compromises on consumer protection and food standards in TTIP and CETA: "The Commission can guarantee that we will not negotiate lower standards[475]. With TTIP, we have the opportunity to set international standards[476]. If the Americans want to trade with us, they must

470 Frankfurter Allgemeine Zeitung. "Rot-Rot-Grün-Koalition würde am Chlorhühnchen scheitern", Nr. 224, page 3. September 26, 2014.

471 Müller Klaus, Vorstand des deutschen Bundesverbandes der Verbraucherzentrale: "Das Huhn ist nicht das Problem", in: *Süddeutsche Zeitung*, Nr. 260, page 8. November 12, 2014.

472 Frankfurter Allgemeine Zeitung. "Gabriel hält am Freihandel mit Amerika fest", Nr. 262, page 18. November 11, 2014.

473 Handelsblatt, Nr. 216, page 8. November 10, 2014.

474 Süddeutsche Zeitung. "Angst hilft nicht weiter", page 20. October 27, 201.

475 EU-TTIP-Dokument: "Faktensheet gegen Annahme und Mythen durch EU-Kommissarin Cecilia
Malmström". December 12, 2014.

476 Malmström Cecilia: "Harte Verhandlungen bin ich gewöhnt", Interview zu TTIP und CETA, in:
Süddeutsche Zeitung Nr. 261, page 21. November 13, 2014.

abide by European rules"[477]. EU chief negotiator Ignacio Garcia-Bercero also expressed himself clearly about TTIP in an interview in the daily newspaper of the same name due to the massive protests in Germany. He had negotiated the trade agreement with South Korea for the EU in 2011 and made it clear in the interview that since then, the EU's exports to the Asian industrialized country have increased by a third. According to Bercero, there is therefore no reason to deviate from the high environmental and food standards in relation to the US in TTIP[478].

In an interview with the editorial board of Handelsblatt on April 14, 2016, Chrystia Freeland, Canadian Minister of Commerce, stressed that the agreement on investment security in the CETA agreement guarantees national governments extensive rights to regulate environmental protection and labor law[479]. According to Freeland, Canada has also followed the EU proposal for an investment court with an appellate body and has implemented this in CETA.

7.5 Small and Medium-Sized Enterprises (SMEs) and TTIP

On both sides of the Atlantic, there was a clear political will to maintain the level of consumer protection achieved in 2015 and even more so in the first quarter of 2016.

In the US, TTIP was not a major problem in large political circles. Overall, TTIP was affirmed in the US. In contrast, there was clear protest from NGOs and trade unions regarding the TPP Agreement. Protests against TPP therefore increased the willingness of the US negotiating delegation to agree on a high level of protection, as did the European delegation[480]. Since the beginning of 2015, both delegations had increasingly emphasized the extensive exceptions, which mainly concern the cultural sector and regulation

477 Politik und Weltwirtschaft. "Auf Augenhöhe mit dem Chlorhühnchen", Wirtschaftswoche, Nr. 22, page 20. May 26, 2014.

478 Süddeutsche Zeitung, "Ringen um TTIP - das Versprechen", Nr. 242, page 18. October 21, 2015.

479 Handelsblatt. "Kanada: Freihandel funktioniert nur mit Transparenz: Handelsministerin sieht den CETA-Gerichtshof als neuen Internationalen Standard", Nr. 73, page 14. April 15/16/17, 2016.

480 Beringer, Sarah: "The TTIP from a German Perspective: Economic Interests and Poitical Discource", in Roy, Joaquin: A New Atlantic Communitiy: The European Union, the US and Latin America, Miami-Florida European Union Center / Jean Monnet Chair, 2015, page 66.

at local level[481]. The TTIP Agreement therefore does not restrict the scope for action at the regional and local level[482]. On the contrary, TTIP offers the opportunity to export the high level of regulatory protection to third countries. Third countries may wish to join this transatlantic economic area in the foreseeable future due to the level of TTIP protection, or they may want to adapt their production process for the time being. Instead, a "raise to the bottom" could become a "raise to the top"[483].

In the run-up to the 12th round of negotiations, crisis talk also started in German medium-sized companies, although EU Commissioner Cecilia Malmström, in a contribution by the largest German daily newspaper, recommended the use of the TTIP agreement especially for small and medium-sized enterprises (SMEs). According to Malmström, it costs entrepreneurs - especially from small and medium-sized enterprises - a lot of time and money to comply with US rules and regulations in addition to the European ones. This is often just a bureaucratic double requirement[484].

Indeed, market access, including tariff reductions, increased investment protection and harmonization of future regulations, is intended to avoid duplication of testing and certification procedures as well as to reduce costs. This is particularly important for SMEs. These are rules that have not yet been covered by the WTO either. This includes protection of intellectual property, trade, sustainable development, tariff reduction and trade facilitation, increased competition, access to raw materials and energy[485]. Although EU and US delegations (Froman and Malmström as well as Bercero and Mullaney respectively) negotiated a special chapter for SMEs

---

481 Larivé, Maxime. "TTIP: A Mega-Free Trade Agreement Lost in Translation?", in Roy, Joaquin: A New Atlantic Communitiy: The European Union, the US and Latin America, Miami-Florida European Union Center / Jean Monnet Chair, 2015, page 84.

482 Barrett, Beverly. "Trade in Higher Education Services in the TTIP-Negotiations and Beyond", in: Roy Joaquin, A new Atlantic Community: The European Union, the US and Latin America, Miami-Florida European Union Center/ Jean Monnet Chair, 2015, page 41.

483 Rjeck, Gunter: "Offene Märkte - die TTIP-Partnerschaft", *KAS-Auslandsinformationen*, 5/2015, page 53.

484 Malmström, Cecilia: "TTIP ist für die Menschen in Europa etwas Gutes!", in: *Frankfurter Allgemeine*
Zeitung, Nr. 279, page 10. December 1, 2014.

485 EU-Consilium. "TTIP-Negotiating Mandate Made Public", *De Gucht Delighted*, October 9, 2014. Accessed October 11, 2014. http://data-consilium-europa.eu/doc/document/ST-11103-2013-DCL-1/en/pdf

as part of TTIP on several occasions, there was resistance to TTIP in Germany even from SMEs[486].

At the beginning of March 2016, representatives of the business initiative "SMEs against TTIP" feared disadvantages after the entry into force of TTIP, especially in the case of the approval and operation of equipment and products. Conformity assessment and product approval systems in Europe and the US differ fundamentally. As a result, the TTIP Agreement could lead to a unilateral trade advantage for American companies, according to the business initiative "SMEs against TTIP". On the other hand, according to the EU Commission SME helpdesk implemented after the 8th round of negotiations, TTIP could facilitate or reduce a number of burdensome procedures, such as duplicate controls on EU exports to the US, certificates of compliance/ conformity with regard to US customs procedures, the procurement of which may otherwise take months to obtain, as well as difficulties with regard to the rules of origin of products and tariff classifications of exported goods[487].

Electrified by so much skepticism and pessimism - spreading against TTIP - after a long period of silence, the major German business associations finally rallied in Berlin on November 7, 2014 making a positive statement in regard to TTIP on the occasion of EU Commissioner Cecilia Malmström's visit to German Federal Minister of Economics Sigmar Gabriel[488]. In doing so, however, BDI, BDA, DIHK and ZDH insisted on maintaining the investment protection of old provenance, taking into account previous private arbitration courts[489]. It was precisely this type of ISDS that Malmström and Gabriel no longer wanted to accept at this meeting of the EU Commission, BMWi and leading business associations[490]. They had already agreed on the establishment of an international commercial court.

---

486 DIHK-Wochenspiegel. "Mittelständische Unternehmen gegen TTIP", page 6. March 2, 2016.

487 European Commission. "Help for SMEs". *SME Trade Defence Helpdesk*. February 15, 2019. https://ec.europa.eu/trade/policy/accessing-markets/trade-defence/actions-against-imports-into-the-eu/help-for-smes/

488 European Union. "ISDS und internationaler Handelsgerichtshof". TTIP, *Chapter 7.3*. https://eur-lex.europa.eu/legal-content/DE/TXT/PDF/?uri=CELEX:52014IE5356&from=EN

489 Frankfurter Allgemeine Zeitung. "Deutsche Automanager loben TTIP", page 19. January 29, 2015.

490 Frankfurter Allgemeine Zeitung. "Die Wirtschaft greift Gabriel an", Nr. 260, page 17. November 8, 2014.

7.6 Support for SMEs in the TTIP Agreement by President Obama, European Union and Chancellor Angela Merkel at the Hanover Industrial Fair 2016

The appreciation of small and medium-sized enterprises (SMEs) in the TTIP Agreement was particularly appreciated on the occasion of the Hanover Congress 2016 and the visit by President Obama, accompanied by EU Commissioner Cecilia Malmström and German Chancellor Angela Merkel. All three top representatives of the US, the EU and Germany underlined the participation and importance of SMEs in the European-American trade exchange of the future[491]. The world-famous Hanover Industrial Fair in 2016 was dominated by TTIP and SME. On April 25, 2016, the German Federal Ministry of Economics & Energy and the US Department of Commerce specifically organized a large panel entitled "TTIP - Great Opportunities for Small Enterprises" with major participation by SMEs. The panel included US Secretary of Commerce Penny Pritzker and German Federal Economics Minister Sigmar Gabriel, as well as two German and two US companies each[492]. Nevertheless, on the occasion of President Obama's visit to Hanover, there was another large demonstration against TTIP with 35,000 participants, organized by Compact, Foodwatch and Greenpeace.

Some 3,500 entrepreneurs, on the other hand, applauded President Obama's and Chancellor Merkel's demands for faster conclusion of TTIP negotiations at the opening of the Hannover Messe[493].

Indeed, Obama's visit to the Hannover Fair brought the decisive breakthrough in terms of acceptance of the TTIP agreement by SMEs which had been skeptical for a long time. On the occasion of Obama's visit to Hanover, Ralph Wiechers, Chief Economist of the German Engineering Federation (VDMA), presented the facts of the key industry, which is dominated by SMEs, in advance. In 2015, exports by the German SME-oriented mechanical engineering industry to the US increased by 11.2 percent to 16.8 billion euros. Wiechers saw the opening of the Hanover Fair by President Obama as the representative of the partner country US as "a great opportunity to

491 DIHK-Bericht aus Brüssel. "TTIP wird Schwerpunkt der Hannover Messe 2016", Nr. 13, page 3. April 11, 2016.

492 TTIP-Diskussion: "Maschinenbauer hoffen auf Obama", in: *Handelsblatt,* March 2, 2016. Accessed April 24, 2017. http://www.handelsblatt.com//unternehmen/industrie/ttip-diskussion-maschinenbauer-hoffen

493 Frankfurter Allgemeine Zeitung. „Yes – we want TTIP ", Nr. 95, page 21. April 23, 2017.

expand the economic relations between the transatlantic trading partners even further"[494]. The visit of the US President parallel to the 13th round of TTIP negotiations in Hanover thus brought about a clear change of opinion in attitude to TTIP in the German SME scene. The mechanical engineering sector, which is largely dominated by medium-sized companies, provides around 1 million jobs in Germany with a nominal production volume of 199 billion euros per year[495]. In connection with TTIP, both the workers' side of SMEs and the trade unions have repeatedly criticized that workers' rights in the US would not meet world standards (e.g. social dumping, "non-tariff barriers"). Bernd Lange, Member of the European Parliament and Chairman of the European Parliaments-Committee on International Trade, responded as "Member of the Socialist party of the European Parliament" in an interview with EurActiv on March 1, 2016 to a question from journalist Nicole Sagener on the "worker protection deficits" in the US: "Workers' rights are mutually respected in TTIP. It should be noted that in some US states, workers' rights have improved".

7.7 TTIP Partner Countries U.S. and Germany at the Hannover Expo 2016

The 13th TTIP round of negotiations between the US and the European Union from April 25 – 29, 2016 in New York took place simultaneously with the Hannover Messe 2016, the largest industrial fair in Europe. In 2016, the Hanover Fair stood under the sign of the partnership between Germany and the US as well as under the motto "Industry 4.0". Due to the visit of US President Barack Obama, Hannover 2016 also turned out to be a small TTIP summit, as US President Obama met with German Chancellor Angela Merkel, UK Prime Minister David Cameron, Italy Prime Minister Matteo Renzi and French President Francois Hollande as well as TTIP chief negotiator Michel Froman and EU Trade Commissioner Cecilia Malström.

With pathos and pedagogical passion, President Obama exhorted the Europeans in front of 6000 managers not to succumb to crisis pessimism (Syria - refugee and IS terrorism in Paris and Brussels) and to counter

494 Handelsblatt, Nr. 79, page 16. April 25, 2016.

495 Interview with Bernd Lange, MdEP, Chairman of the European Parliaments-Committee on International Trade, in: *EurActiv-Germany Report*, pages 2-4. March 1, 2016.

the anti-European mood in the EU member states. US President Obama expressed concern about cohesion and fears of the EU breaking up. He appealed to the self-confidence of Europeans and, in his speech in front of 6000 managers in the Hanover Fair Hall, reaffirmed that the US wants a strong Europe. He also referred this wish to the economy of both countries and regretted that the free trade project TTIP is met with so much mistrust, especially in Germany as an industrialized country. The US President reiterated the wish that the EU and the US, with their free markets, together with their already highly developed interdependencies, especially in the automotive and pharmaceutical sectors, seek a common future in an open world. "The ideals of Europe enlighten the world," and "Remember who you are," he added[496].

In a "US-German Business Summit" during the Hanover Fair, chief negotiators Malmström and Froman saw major hurdles against TTIP, especially in Germany. The majority of the EU is pro-TTIP, according to Cecilia Malmström during the panel discussion. According to Malmström, Germans are particularly skeptical, because they have raised the TTIP issue using false examples. The EU Commissioner for Trade mentioned, for example, the threat to public cultural institutions often attributed to the TTIP Agreement, or the lack of soil protection allegedly present in TTIP, or the already "legendary chlorine chicken".

Michael Froman and Cecilia Malmström promoted TTIP as chief negotiators during the Hannover Congress in further discussion forums with managers and trade unions stating that the negotiations regarding customs duties and tariffs had almost been concluded. Ulrich Grillo, President of the Federation of German Industries (BDI) almost imploringly added that there was no reason to oppose TTIP and, above all, reaffirmed the benefits for workers of TTIP leading to more trade. According to Froman, SMEs in particular would have the greatest advantages with their employees if standards were mutually recognized[497]. One billion dollars more export creates 5000 to 7000 jobs, according to Froman. During the Hannover Fair panel discussions with employer and employee representatives, Malström and Froman repeated the statements made by President Obama and Chancellor Merkel that TTIP will not lower any existing standards. On the

496 Klaus-Dieter Frankenberger „Obama: Europas Ideale erleuchten die Welt ", in: *Frankfurter Allgemeine Zeitung,* Nr. 97, page 1. April 26, 2016.

497 Frankfurter Allgemeine Zeitung. „Arbeitnehmer profitieren am meisten von TTIP ", Nr. 97, page 15. April 26, 2016.

contrary, it would be necessary to at least maintain or increase labor law, social and environmental protection standards. TTIP is intended to be a groundbreaking agreement with a great role model for other parts of the world, according to Malmström[498].

Ulrich Grillo, President of the Federation of German Industries (BDI), expressed his conviction at the forum with Froman and Malmström at the Hanover Fair that without TTIP the transpacific principles will prevail worldwide instead of the transatlantic ones. These would then be below transatlantic standards. Speaking on behalf of the entire German industry, Grillo emphasized emphatically: "We will not help shape the future of world trade with a TTIP-light"[499]. He thus agreed with the American President of Industry Thomas Donohue, who during the Hanover Forum demanded "We do not want anything other than a comprehensive agreement". The TTIP Agreement will boost the world's biggest innovation driver, but only if German industry also actively promotes the agreement among the population, according to German Chancellor Angela Merkel at the dinner reception with Obama and German industry representatives on April 25, 2016 during the Hanover Fair.

As a summary of President Obama's Hanover meeting with the German Chancellor, the chief negotiators Malmström and Froman as well as the four European Heads of Government, the following can be stated:

- Never before has the European Commission negotiated a trade agreement as transparently as in TTIP with the US partners.
- German industry in particular, which is strong in Europe, should therefore benefit enormously from the TTIP agreement, if TTIP reduces customs duties, abolishes absurd duplicate approval procedures or makes mutual recognition possible for certifications.
- The costs saved by businesses as a result will benefit Europeans and Americans alike. This is because opening up markets, especially for SMEs, benefits not only businesses but also consumers. Prices are coming under pressure due to increased competition on both sides of the Atlantic.

498 European Commission. „TTIP-State of Play". *Summary state of play of specific negotiating areas*", pages 3–10. April 27, 2016. Accessed Mai 1, 2016. http://trade.ec.europa.eu/doclib/doc5/2016/april/tradoc-154477.pdf

499 Frankfurter Allgemeine Zeitung. „Arbeitnehmer profitieren am meisten von TTIP ", Nr. 97, page 15. April 26, 2016.

- The EU Commission's proposal to implement an investment court instead of private courts in the agreement has the potential to settle the controversy in Europe for disputes between states and companies, as it is already contained in the CETA agreement. The vast majority of TTIP opponents with fundamental opposition in Germany are likely to be satisfied with this and reconciled with TTIP, including in the Netherlands, where a referendum against TTIP was being organized[500].

President Obama's visit, the talks with the TTIP chief negotiators and the four European heads of government during the Hanover Fair have brought the negotiating partners closer together, especially in Germany with the many NGOs opposing TTIP.

7.8 13th Round of Negotiations in New York 2016

During the 13th round of TTIP negotiations, the three pillars of market access, regulatory cooperation and regulations with their respective chapters were negotiated. This involved technical cooperation and consolidation of the chapters that had already been negotiated several times.

All 24 chapters of TTIP were discussed, with the "consolidated texts" and the contentious issues of the texts in square brackets. On April 29, 2016, at the end of the negotiations, NGO stakeholders had the opportunity to learn and discuss details on the status of the negotiations from TTIP negotiators Ignacio Garcia Bercero and Dan Mullaney. The focus was on the following topics: industrial goods, agricultural products, food, services, public procurement and regulations on sustainability, customs duties and trade facilitation[501]. During previous negotiation rounds, 97% of the tariffs had already been negotiated and only 3% were in dispute, especially in the agricultural sector, such as meat with a high potential for dispute. This outcome was also published by EU Commissioner Malmström on April 27, 2016 in her new interim report on the overall negotiations "TTIP State of

500 Frankfurter Allgemeine Zeitung. „Und was wird aus dem Parmesankäse? ", Nr. 98, page 17. April 27, 2016.

501 European Comission, Directorate-General of Trade: *13th Negotiation Round in New York*, April 25-29, 2016. Accessed May 2, 2016. http://trade.ec.europa.eu/doclib/events/index.cfm-id-1479

Play"[502]. Based on this, the two TTIP negotiators did not make any progress in their negotiations on the meat sector in agricultural matters and on "public procurement" in the 13th round in New York. This demonstrates how hardened the positions were on these two chapters. Therefore, Commissioner Malmström's "Interim Report" of April 27, 2016 shed light on the still contentious issues of the 24 chapters of the agreement. According to the "Interim Report", in most of the 24 chapters, first and also second offers were often exchanged on the following topics: tariff rates, the opening of services markets, public procurement, safeguard clauses for regional products such as Black Forest ham or Thuringian bratwurst and the reduction of regulatory barriers.

The removal of regulatory barriers was one of the key elements of TTIP at the time of the publication of the Malmström Report for the European Union. According to Malmström, the aim is to harmonize for example, the duplicate testing procedures and inspections carried out by the regulatory authorities for certain products in the pharmaceutical sector or in the automotive sector for newly emerging products such as in electric mobility. This should help companies to introduce high standards in both markets with "care labels" simultaneously, i.e. "horizontal regulatory coherence" and the abolition of "Technical barriers to trade" (TBT)[503].

The EU's negotiations were also about conceding that the rules of the other side may be different, but that the objective, such as occupational safety, can be achieved just as well (sectoral cooperation)[504]. In particular, the pharmaceutical industry, the automotive sector, the telecommunications industry and the chemical sector have long been hoping for this[505]. The chapters "Small and Medium-sized Enterprises", "Sustainable development", "Energy and raw materials", "Intellectual property rights", "State to state dispute settlement" and "Competition" had also not yet received final

502 European Commission. „TTIP-State of Play ". *Summary state of play of specific negotiating areas*", pages 3–10. April 27, 2016. Accessed Mai 1, 2016. http://trade.ec.europa.eu/doclib/doc5/2016/april/tradoc-154477.pdf

503 European Commission. „TTIP-State of Play ". *Summary state of play of specific negotiating areas*: Regulatory Cooperation, page 5. April 27, 2016. Accessed Mai 1, 2016. http://trade.ec.europa.eu/doclib/doc5/2016/april/tradoc-154477.pdf

504 European Commission. „TTIP-State of Play ". *Summary state of play of specific negotiating areas*: Sectoral Cooperation, page 6. April 27, 2016. Accessed Mai 1, 2016. http://trade.ec.europa.eu/doclib/doc5/2016/april/tradoc-154477.pdf

505 Kafsack Hendrik und Weingartner Max: "Jetzt oder nie", in: *Yes- we want TTIP, FAZ*. Nr. 95, page 21. April 23, 2016.

approval from the US side at the end of the 13th round of negotiations in New York[506].

7.8.1 Public Procurement

According to Malmström's interim report, the chapters on market access were the most precarious at the end of the 13th round of negotiations, particularly in the areas of public procurement and the agricultural sector[507].

Paragraph 24 of the "Guidelines for TTIP Negotiations between the US and the EU" of June 17, 2013, i.e. the essential negotiating points provided for therein, states: "The agreement will be highly ambitious and its scope will, if possible, go beyond the outcome of the negotiations, the revised agreement and government procurement. The TTIP Agreement will aim to provide improved reciprocal access to procurement markets at all administrative levels (national, regional and local) and in the utilities sector, covering the relevant work of undertakings operating in this sector and ensuring treatment no less favorable than that accorded to suppliers established in their own territory"[508].

According to Cecilia Malmström, the negotiating partners EU/ US are a long way from that: "Unlike in other fields, we have only received an initial offer here, which is far from our expectations"[509].

The US Department of Trade and the federal states of the US make access to public contracts more difficult, among other things, because in many cases they require the use of local products ("Buy America"). However, the EU negotiation delegation would like EU suppliers to be considered not only on a national level but also on a regional level for tenders in the same way as US suppliers, i.e. exactly in accordance with the EU - US guidelines on TTIP.

---

506 European Commission. „TTIP-State of Play ". *Summary state of play of specific negotiating areas*: Regulatory Cooperation, pages 6-7. April 27, 2016. Accessed Mai 1, 2016. http://trade.ec.europa.eu/doclib/doc5/2016/april/tradoc-154477.pdf

507 Leitlinien für die Verhandlungen über TTIP zwischen EU – USA Nr. 11103/13 RESTREINT UE/EU
RESTRICTED, Rat der Europäischen Union, page 10, Ziff. 24 (Public Procurement), June 17, 2014.

508 Center for European Policy Studies. "TTIP and Public Procurement". *Policy Brief*, Nr. 339, page 2-3. March 2016.

509 European Commission. „TTIP-State of Play ". *Summary state of play of specific negotiating areas*: Regulatory Cooperation, page 6. April 27, 2016. Accessed Mai 1, 2016. http://trade.ec.europa.eu/doclib/doc5/2016/april/tradoc-154477.pdf

So far, according to Cecilia Malmström, the US delegation has granted access to orders with a volume of 320 billion euros in the TTIP negotiations. However, the EU delegation demands access to 1320 billion euros[510].

7.8.2 Agricultural Sector

Another point of contention in several negotiations was the agricultural sector even before the 13th round. With regard to the progress of negotiations, Malmström's report from April 27, 2016 merely states: "Consolidation underway".

Until April 27, 2016, this chapter dealt with food security, animal and plant health[511]. According to Cecilia Malmström, negotiations naturally involve compromises, but in this particular chapter a give and take cannot occur in exchange for access to public contracts in the US. Europeans are not willing to make concessions on trade in sensitive agricultural products in return for better access to procurement, according to Malmström[512]. Especially in the agricultural sector, according to Malmström, there are products on both sides where Europeans have reservations about broad market opening[513].

On January 6, 2015, the EU delegation had already submitted a list of 1450 protected regional specialties from 28 Member States to the US delegation, including 79 from Germany alone (such as Bavarian beer, Greek feta cheese or Italian Parmesan cheese)[514].

At the beginning of January 2015, the EU Commission had made it clear to the US negotiating partners that the protection of intellectual property and of trademarks such as indications of origin was one of the EU's priori-

---

510 Frankfurter Allgemeine Zeitung. “Bis Jahresende 2016 soll das Freihandelsabkommen TTIP stehen”, Nr. 98, page 17. April 27, 2016.

511 European Commission. „TTIP-State of Play “. *Summary state of play of specific negotiating areas*: Regulatory Cooperation, page 6. April 27, 2016. Accessed Mai 1, 2016. http://trade.ec.europa.eu/doclib/doc5/2016/april/tradoc-154477.pdf

512 Frankfurter Allgemeine Zeitung. “Bis Jahresende 2016 soll das Freihandelsabkommen TTIP stehen”, Nr. 98, page 17. April 27, 2016.

513 Cecilia Malmström. “Negotiating TTIP”. *Blog Post.* May 2, 2014. Accessed May 1, 2016. http://ec.europa.eu/commission/2014-2019/malmstroem/blog/negotiating

514 European Commission. “Agricultural and Rural Development”. December 19, 2019. https://ec.europa.eu/agriculture/quality/door/list.html

ties[515]. The EU protects high-quality agricultural and food products using three quality labels as intellectual property.

The EU has enforced this increased protection, for example, in trade agreements with Canada (CETA), Korea and Singapore. After all, the CETA agreement stipulates 150 out of 1400 regional products and thus protects them. The EU has also established a separate agreement with China to protect designations of origin.

On March 21, 2016, the European Commission published a "Draft text" document on agriculture and products with geographical designations[516]. The draft contains a selection from the list of regional protected products based on intellectual property with the respective name of origin[517]. These account for about 25-30 % of agricultural export products. In return, the EU side agreed to recognize US protected regional products[518], including a significant number of wines and spirits with 145 designations of protected food and beverages[519].

In total, trade between the EU and the US amounted to 616 trillion euros in 2015, of which agricultural products trade had a volume of 31 trillion euros. The EU achieved a trade surplus of 123 trillion, of which 7 trillion in agricultural products[520].

Since the US is the EU's number one export partner (2015-2019), an ambitious TTIP agreement could open up the prospect of a growing export market for agricultural products, wines and spirits, including geographically protected products.

---

515 Representative Office of the European Commission in Berlin, Germany. "EU-Nachrichten", Nr. 1. January 22, 2015. https://ec.europa.eu/germany/news_de

516 Representative Office of the European Commission in Berlin, Germany. „Regionale Spezialitäten und die TTIP-Verhandlungen ", January 1, 2015. http://ec.europa.eu/deutschland/press/pr_Release/12980_de.htm

517 European Commission. "eAmbrosia – the EU geographical indications register". February 14, 2020. https://ec.europa.eu/info/food-farming-fisheries/food-safety-and-quality/certification/quality-labels/geographical-indications-register/

518 European Commission. "List of Geographical Indications". *Annex I.* March 21, 2016. https://trade.ec.europa.eu/doclib/docs/2016/march/tradoc_154386.GIPaperAnnexI%20FINAL_REV.pdf

519 European Commission. "Agriculture and Geographical Indications in TTIP ". March 21, 2016. http://trade.ec.europa.eu/doclib/press/index.cfm?id=1477&title=The-Commission-publishes-further-TTIP-documents-in-ongoing-transparency-commitment

520 European Commission. "Draft text of EU agricultural proposal". March 21, 2016. https://trade.ec.europa.eu/doclib/docs/2016/march/tradoc_154371.pdf

At the time of the 13th round of negotiations (April 25-29, 2016), there was no agreement in sight on the agricultural sector, nor on investor protection, the proposed Commercial Court, the regulations in the aforementioned nine sectors (market access) and in the area of public procurement[521].

Following President Barack Obama's visit, confidential TTIP negotiation minutes were published on Facebook by the environmental protection organization Greenpeace and made available for everyone to read in a large glass case at the Brandenburg Gate in Berlin, Germany[522]. According to Greenpeace, the US side would supposedly do everything in its power to enforce the free import of hormone-treated meat and genetically modified plants into the EU, nor would the US shy away from linking this to the opening of the American automobile markets, which is important for Europeans[523]. Cecilia Malmström commented on this whistleblower indiscretion in her blog post "Negotiating TTIP" on May 2, 2016 with the same words she had already published in the EU interim report on TTIP of April 27, 2016: „It is only normal, that both parties in a negotiation want to achieve as many of their own objectives as possible. That does not mean, that the parties will meet halfway. In areas, where we are too far apart in a negotiation, we simply will not agree. In that sense, many of today's alarmist headlines are a storm in a teacup".

In her blog of April 27, 2016 "TTIP - the State of Play", Cecilia Malmström announced with a view to the 14th round and the "endgame" at the end of 2016: "Our goal for further TTIP negotiations is clear: to make progress as quickly as possible and conclude the negotiations in 2016. There is no doubt that the negotiations will conclude by the end of 2016... There is still a lot of work to be done and I would like to underline the following in advance: Substance is more important than speed. In the end, TTIP needs a solid and balanced agreement that promotes business relations

521 European Commission. „TTIP-State of Play ". *Summary state of play of specific negotiating areas*: Regulatory Cooperation, page 617. April 27, 2016. Accessed Mai 1, 2016. http://trade.ec.europa.eu/doclib/doc5/2016/april/tradoc-154477.pdf

522 Frankfurter Allgemeine Zeitung. "Oberwasser für TTIP-Gegner", Nr. 103, page 1. March 3, 2016.

523 European Commission. "Disputes Persist in Latest TTIP-Talks ", page 1. April 28, 2016. Accessed May 1, 2016. http://ec.europa.eu/commission/2014-2019/malmstrom/blog/negotiating-ttip_en

on both sides of the Atlantic and opens up more opportunities for our consumers as well as strengthening Europe's position on the global stage"[524].

Figure 3: Increase in EU Agriculture Product Exports to the U.S.

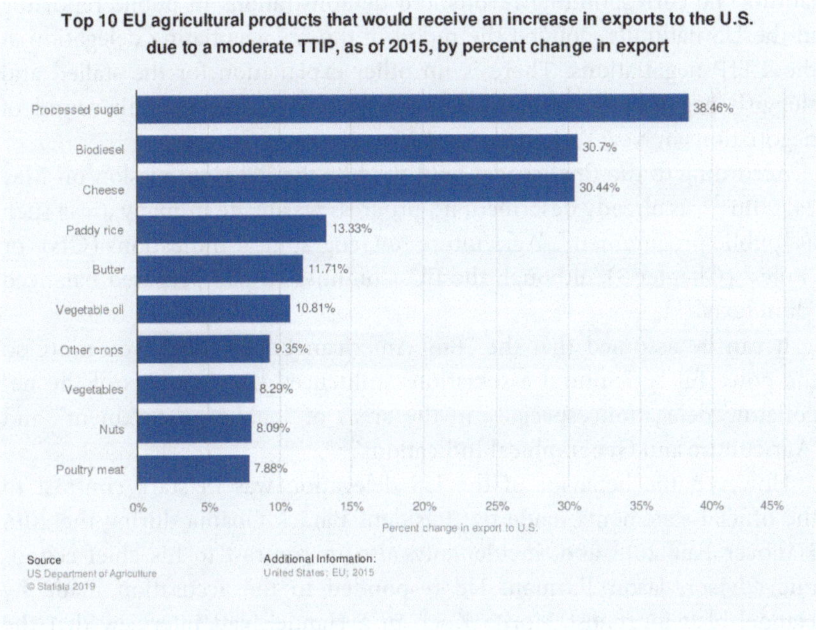

This statistic shows the top ten EU agricultural product exports that would be positively impacted by the implementation of a TTIP that removed all tariffs and trade-rate quotas, by projected percentage change in export value. As of 2015, exports of EU biodiesel to the U.S. would increase by over 30 percent if a TTIP were implemented that removed all tariffs and trade-rate quotas.[525]

524 European Commission. „TTIP-State of Play ". *Summary state of play of specific negotiating areas*: Regulatory Cooperation, page 2. April 27, 2016. Accessed Mai 1, 2016. http://trade.ec.europa.eu/doclib/doc5/2016/april/tradoc-154477.pdf

525 US Department of Agriculture. (November 30, 2015). Top 10 EU agricultural products that would receive an increase in exports to the U.S. due to a moderate TTIP, as of 2015, by percent change in export [Graph]. In *Statista*. Retrieved April 18, 2020, from https://www.statista.com/statistics/546680/top-10-eu-agricultural-product-exports-to-us-positively-impacted-by-ttip-2015/

7.8.3 The U.S. side's Dwindling Negotiating Woes

In the wake of the TTP negotiations with Asian partners, skepticism and fear of any kind of free trade agreement began to rise among the US population. The corresponding revolts and demonstrations in public reporting in the US naturally clouded the mood of the US negotiating delegation at the TTIP negotiations. There is no other explanation for the stalled and sluggish negotiations with the EU delegations during the 13th round of negotiations in New York from April 25 to 29, 2016.

According to the final report published by the EU Commission on May 24, 2016[526], as already described, no progress was made in many areas such as "public procurement", "Agriculture to Geographical Indications (GIs)" or "Rules" (Chapter 3), although the EU Commission had prepared balanced “draft texts”[527].

It can be assumed that the "Buy American Lobby" and even more so the powerful agricultural associations influenced the members of the negotiating delegation especially in the areas of “public procurement” and “Agriculture and Geographical Indications”[528].

However, the behavior of the US delegation was in stark contrast to the official statements made by President Barack Obama during the 2016 Hanover Fair 2016 and, incidentally, also in contrast to his chief economic advisor, Jason Furman. He responded to the accusation made by Handelsblatt journalist Moritz Koch in a Handelsblatt interview that the US secret documents about the TTIP negotiations, which were put online by Greenpeace, revealed a kind of blackmail that was used to loosen consumer protection and open the European market for gene food, as follows: "This debate is completely misleading. The US has very strong consumer protection, the EU has very strong consumer protection. TTIP would not undermine these standards. This is important to us and it is important to Europeans. We find ourselves at a point where we cannot afford to miss opportunities. Trade agreements initially increase what economists

526 European Commission. “Report of the 13thRound of Negotiations for TTIP” (New York, 25. – 29. April 2016), Ziff. 3.5 und Ziff. 1.1. May 3, 2016. http://trade.ec.europa.eu//doclib/docs/2016/May/tradoc-154581.pdf

527 European Commission. “EU-Proposal for an Annex of Medicinal Products”. May 4, 2016. http://trade.ec.europa.eu/doclib/docs/2016/may/tradoc154582.pdf

528 Lange, Bernd: “TTIP hat Potenzial, aber ...”, *in: Handelsblatt* Nr. 86, page 48. May 4, 2016. (Bernd Lange is Chair of International Trade – Committee and TTIP Rapporteur in the European Parliament)

call static efficiency. People produce more of what they can already do. More importantly, however, free trade helps to stimulate innovation and productivity growth by encouraging specialization, expanding markets and developing competitive pressures"[529]. This statement clearly highlights the discrepancy between the US negotiating delegation, the US President and his chief economist after the 13th round of negotiations on TTIP.

Figure 4: Effects of TTIP on U.S. Trade

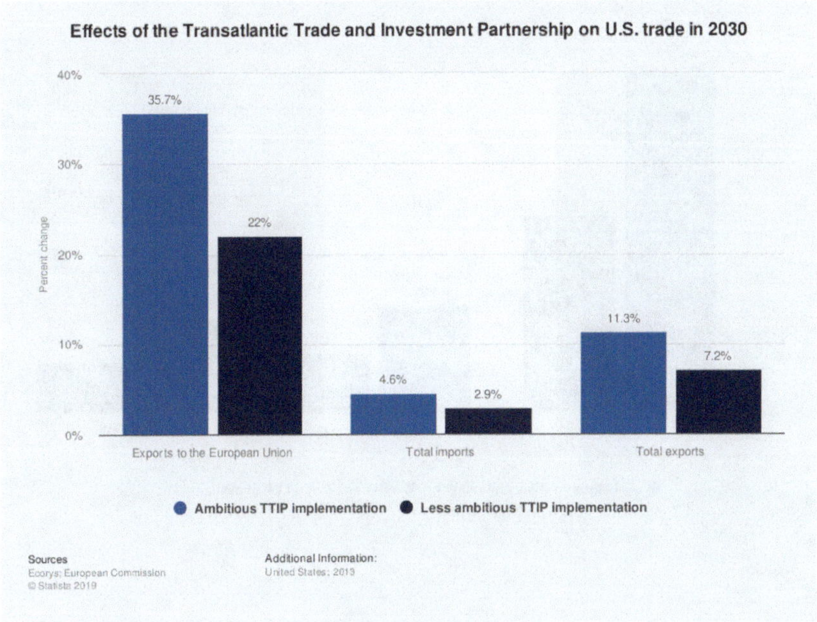

This statistic shows the projections of the macroeconomic effects of the Transatlantic Trade and Investment Partnership (TTIP) on United States trade in 2030. As a result of an ambitious TTIP implementation this model predicts a 35.7 percent increase in U.S. exports to the EU over baseline in 2030.[530]

529 Handelsblatt. "Obamas Chefökonom ist besorgt über die deutsche Investitionsschwäche, Griechenland und den drohenden Brexit ", Nr. 91, page 13. May 12, 2016.

530 Ecorys, und European Commission. "Effects of the Transatlantic Trade and Investment Partnership on U.S. trade in 2030." Chart. May 13, 2016. *Statista.* Accessed April

This statistic shows the projections of the macroeconomic effects of the Transatlantic Trade and Investment Partnership (TTIP) on European Union trade in 2030. As a result of an ambitious TTIP implementation this model predicts a 27 percent increase in EU exports to the U.S. over baseline in 2030.[531]

Figure 5: Effects of TTIP on EU Trade

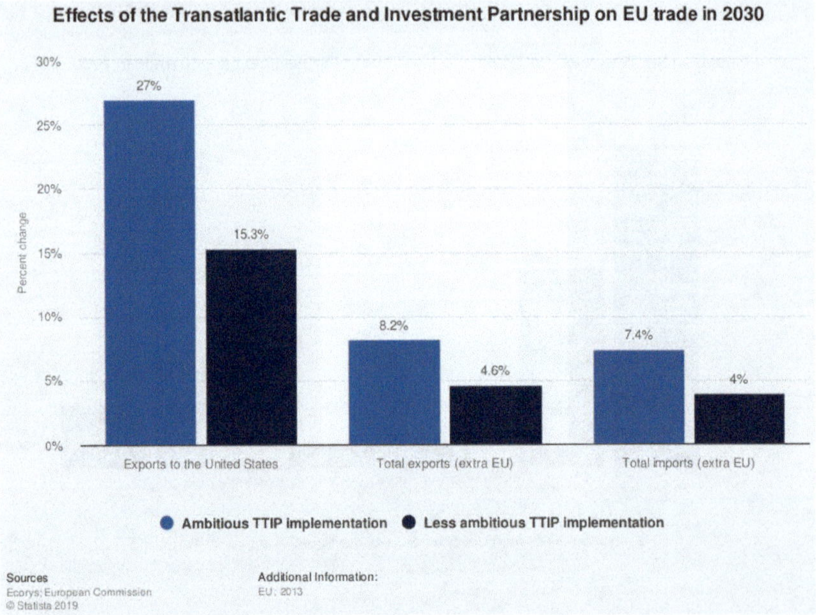

7.8.4 Revival of TTIP Skepticism following the Publication of the US-TTIP Secret Documents by Greenpeace in Germany and Europe

In the midst of the TTIP negotiations, self-doubt in Europe, and especially in Germany, has been beginning to grow since mid-2016 to date about

07, 2020. https://www.statista.com/statistics/547742/trade-effects-of-ttip-on-us-2030/

531 Ecorys, und European Commission. "Effects of the Transatlantic Trade and Investment Partnership on EU trade in 2030." Chart. May 13, 2016. *Statista*. Accessed April 07, 2020. https://www.statista.com/statistics/548282/trade-effects-of-ttip-on-eu-2030/

the EU's cohesion, and even resistance as a result of the prolonged zero interest rate policy in the euro zone. The 28 member states of the EU standing together and helping each other out after the great financial crisis of 2008, the strengthening of banking supervision, the installed planks of the EU member states against frivolous sequential trading via hedge funds, against closed-end real estate funds, against cum-ex tax fraud by financial institutions, the drying up of tax havens, combined with the curbing of tax evasion, and last but not least the bank bailouts including the recapitalization of the banking sector - all these positive achievements of the European community of states seemed to have been forgotten. Last but not least, the repeated restructuring successes of the enormous Greek debt burden were signs of solidarity and participation in problem solving by the Member States.

Euroscepticism, which is being nurtured repeatedly by right-wing populists in Germany, the United Kingdom, France and Austria in particular, calling for the end of the euro zone, and the threat of centrifugal nationalist forces in the United Kingdom to leave the EU, gave fuel and impetus to dangerous national solo attempts by critics of Europe from France to Poland[532], of all times, at the 100th anniversary of the Battle of Verdun[533]. World War I arose from that spirit of nationalism that ruined Europe in a world war. Nationalism, however, means war, sooner or later: This is the lesson that Europeans have learned after two horrific massacres of peoples[534]. In 2016, after 100 years of Verdun, they threaten to forget this lesson again[535].

The refugee crisis in 2015 with the massive influx of one million migrants from Syria via the Balkan route to Austria and Germany led to the suspension of the Schengen Treaty and the introduction of national border controls in a number of EU Member States. The terrorist attacks on a discotheque in Paris and at Brussels airport as well as the related political management failure in Europe to distribute the flow of refugees fairly among the Member States strengthened centrifugal forces and self-sufficiency efforts in Europe. This did not remain without consequences for the

---

532 Ferguson, Niall: „Der Niedergang des Westens ", Ullstein Verlag, Berlin, 2014, pages 17 – 25.

533 Zolling, Peter: „Quo vadis, Europa? ", in: *Handelsblatt*, Nr. 85, page 13. May 3, 2016.

534 Wetzel, Hubert: „Verdun - Europas Geister", in: *Süddeutsche Zeitung*, Nr. 121, page 4. May 28/ 29, 2016.

535 Krumeich, Gerd: „Verdun 2016". Klartext-Verlag, Essen 2016, page 224.

spirit of a transatlantic free trade area, for shaping the future of cooperation between democratic systems in the US and the EU in contrast to closed autocratic societies in North Africa, Asia, Russia and Latin America. The US on the other side of the Atlantic may not be threatened with disintegration as the EU, but the decay of political culture. The destructive successes of the radical candidate Donald Trump in the US election campaign for the presidency bear witness to deep divisions in US society. This division is supported by social media with antisocial platforms that have barbarized and hysterized public debates in the US. Incidentally, the social virtual platforms also contribute massively to the brutalization of political culture in Europe. Via these platforms, it is easy for NGOs such as Attac or Compact to quickly acquire 250,000 signatures against TTIP, as was the case in May 2015. Print media reports on the verbal juries and thus increase the public's awareness of the negative influence of social media platforms. This, in turn, has a paralyzing effect on the elected representatives in regional, national and supranational parliaments, such as the European Parliament, institutions that are increasingly being presented as untrustworthy or as "carriers of the establishment". This decline of democratic convictions and neglect of respect for the diversity of opinions sometimes turns freedom of expression into its opposite, with unforeseeable consequences for the shaping possibilities of the elites elected by the people in pluralistic decision-making processes of parliaments with complicated institutions and bodies, which is what characterizes the US and the EU[536].

These negative debates on both sides of the Atlantic at the end of the 13th round of negotiations at the end of April 2016 had consequences for the TTIP Agreement, which is used by large parts of NGOs to strike free trade and fuel self-sufficiency efforts - right in the middle of the delicate phase following the 13th round.

The interpretation of the 248 pages "Our protective measures in the EU are to be dismantled", published by Greenpeace on the internet and displayed in the glass showcase at the Brandenburg Gate in Berlin with detailed positions of the US delegation, was thus such a targeted measure to use the so-called "TTIP secret papers" to affect free trade, arouse distrust and destroy confidence in world trade. US Trade Representative Michael Froman stated that the "TTIP Leaks" texts interpreted by Greenpeace were

536 Ferguson, Niall: „Der Niedergang des Westens ", Ullstein Verlag, Berlin, 2014, pages 24-25.

misleading at best, but at worst simply wrong[537]. According to Froman, TTIP will preserve the standards and not undermine them[538]. In a Handelsblatt interview, Froman responded to the question of whether tens of thousands of anti-TTIP demonstrators on the streets of Germany and anti-globalization activists such as Donald Trump and Bernie Sanders could bring down the Transatlantic Free Trade Agreement: "For many years, world trade has grown twice as fast as global economic output. Trade was the engine of the global economy. Lately, we have been observing a significant cooling down. The decline in growth in world trade may be a sign that protectionist forces are on the rise. It is particularly important at this time to break down trade barriers in order to put the global economy back on a growth path. The protests on both sides of the Atlantic should not be overestimated. If we look at the polls in the US, we see that a majority of citizens are still in favor of open borders. This is especially true for to younger people. Many Americans are understandably concerned about the changes in their workplace, about the stagnation of their wages. However, this is mainly due to technological trends. You cannot vote on technology, but you can vote on free trade. Agreements such as TTIP therefore become a valve for popular anger"[539]. Despite all the criticism by NGOs and autarkists of free trade in the US and the EU, Michael Froman pointed out: "Trade agreements set the rules for the global economy. They open borders and raise standards. This creates a level playing field for everyone. In addition, it should not be forgotten that jobs in the export industry have, on average, 18 percent higher wages than in the rest of the economy. So, if we increase exports, we will also increase income and reduce inequality. It is therefore now a matter of strengthening the transatlantic relationship at a time when there is a great deal of geopolitical disorder elsewhere in the world. It is in our interest that Europe remains a strong partner. We know that at the moment many centrifugal forces are pulling at the unity of Europe: the refugee crisis, Brexit, the continuing concerns about Greece, and the rise of right-wing populist parties in many countries. Our hope is that TTIP will act as a positive force and that Europe can demonstrate that it can stand together and make important progress for its citizens even in difficult times.

537 Handelsblatt. "Neuer Ärger um Freihandelsvertrag", Nr. 85, pages 6-7. May 3, 2016.
538 Handelsblatt. "Neuer Ärger um Freihandelsvertrag", Nr. 85, page 7. May 3, 2016.
539 Froman, Michael: „Eine einmalige Chance ", in: *Handelsblatt,* Nr. 78, page 10. April 22/ 23/ 24, 2016.

Together with the US, the EU can play a leading role in the world and promote its values"[540].

These are clear words of solidarity with the EU and the TTIP Agreement, which, during uncertain times in 2016, give courage and show perspectives, even if both negotiating parties are still far apart.

This statistic shows the projections of the macroeconomic effects of the Transatlantic Trade and Investment Partnership (TTIP) on the United States economy in 2030. As a result of an ambitious TTIP implementation, this model predicts a 0.4 percent growth in U.S. GDP over baseline in 2030.[541]

Figure 6: Macroeconomic Effects of TTIP on the U.S. Economy

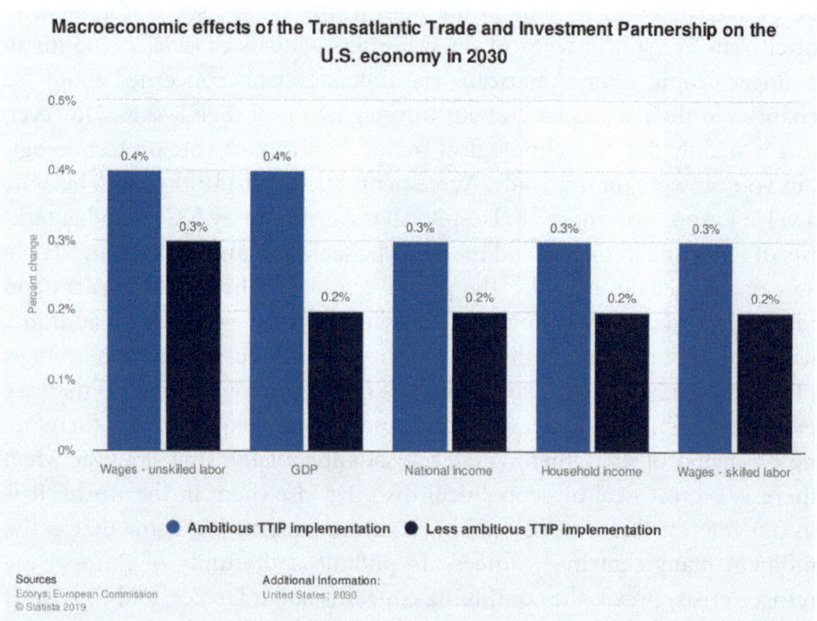

540 Froman, Michael: „Eine einmalige Chance", in: *Handelsblatt*, Nr. 78, page 11. April 22/ 23/ 24, 2016.

541 Ecorys, und European Commission. "Macroeconomic effects of the Transatlantic Trade and Investment Partnership on the U.S. economy in 2030." Chart. May 13, 2016. *Statista*. Accessed April 07, 2020. https://www.statista.com/statistics/547508/macroeconomic-effects-of-ttip-on-us-2030/

This statistic shows the projections of the macroeconomic effects of the Transatlantic Trade and Investment Partnership (TTIP) on the European Union economy in 2030. As a result of an ambitious TTIP implementation this model predicts an additional 0.5 percent growth in EU GDP over baseline in 2030.[542]

Figure 7: Macroeconomic Effects of TTIP on the EU Economy

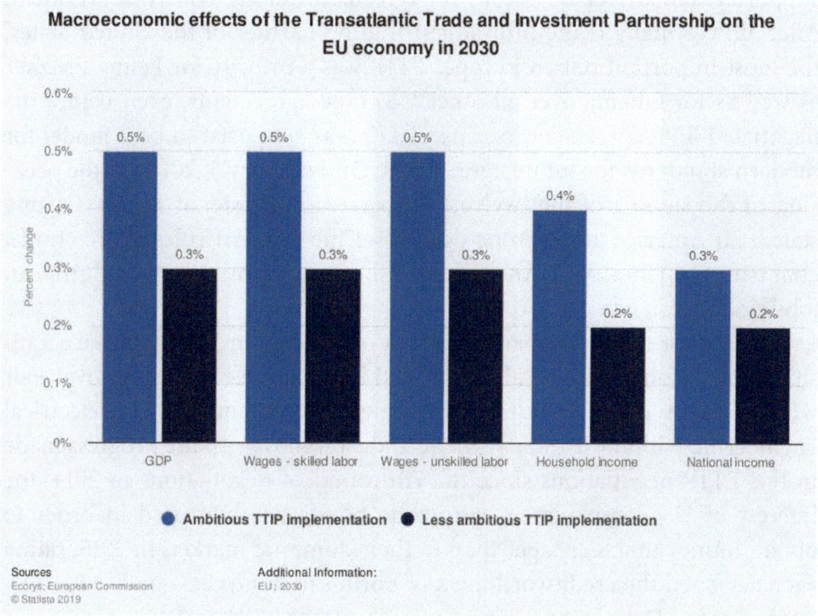

7.8.5 U.S. Economy's Shift towards a Europe of Skepticism

For the first time, the US was a partner of the Hannover Congress from April 25 to April 29, 2016. Not only top politicians and TTIP trade representatives Cecilia Malmström and Michael Froman took advantage of the opportunities for appearances during the fair with President Obama, but

542 Ecorys, und European Commission. "Macroeconomic effects of the Transatlantic Trade and Investment Partnership on the EU economy in 2030." Chart. May 13, 2016. *Statista.* Accessed April 07, 2020. https://www.statista.com/statistics/547612/macroeconomic-effects-of-ttip-on-eu-2030/

also numerous US companies. In this context, Penny Pritzker, US Secretary of Commerce, Harvard and Stanford graduate, who led 270 US companies and business development organizations at the Hannover Messe, deserves special mention. The US Secretary of Commerce is also one of US President Obama's closest advisors and is considered the architect of the "Five-Point Plan" with strategic goals for the years 2014 - 2018, with trade and investment at the forefront[543]. Furthermore, she is also considered a strong supporter and driver of the TTIP Agreement, along with the President. After all, Germany is the fifth largest trading partner of the United States, the most important one in Europe. TTIP was a priority for Penny Pritzker as well as for Obama over all other US trade agreements, even before the negotiated TPP agreement, because TTIP was supposed to be a model for modern standards for future agreements. On February 5, 2016, on the occasion of the signing of the twelve TPP countries, President Barack Obama stated: "If America and Europe do not set the modern rules in free trade, countries like China will. And that would threaten American and European jobs"[544].

The interest of US companies did not only begin in 2015 with the acquisitions of US pharmaceutical groups and in the course of the Hanover Fair with its focus on IT, mechanical engineering, automotive and electrical engineering within the framework of "Industry 4.0". With the progress made in the TTIP negotiations since the 7th round of negotiations in 2014, the interest of US companies in euro-zone bonds has increased in order to obtain money much cheaper than in their domestic market. In 2015, rating agencies rated the creditworthiness of European bonds as "good" with only 0.8 percent of Daimler or 0.7 percent of Deutsche Telekom[545].

In addition to the American and European companies already mentioned in the chapter "Pharmaceutical Group Mergers", takeovers in the pharmaceutical industry continued after a short break in mid-2016: On April 28, 2016, EU and U.S. companies announced acquisitions and offers totaling approximately USD 40 billion. The motives behind these deals are similar: Manufacturers are on the lookout for new, high-growth active ingredients and are reacting to the growing price pressures in the industry

543 Frankfurter Allgemeine Zeitung. „Amerika gibt den Takt vor ", *Special Edition,* Nr. 93, page 1. April 21, 2016.

544 Frankfurter Allgemeine Zeitung. „Amerika gibt den Takt vor ", *Special Edition,* Nr. 93, page 1. April 21, 2016.

545 Handelsblatt. „US-Firmen lieben den Euro ", Nr. 58, page 12. March 23, 2016.

with takeovers. For example, the acquisition of the US company Medivation by the pharmaceutical group Sanofi with 9.3 billion dollars or the takeover of the stem cell specialist Stemcentrx by the US pharmaceutical manufacturer Abbvie with 5.8 billion dollars is imminent[546]. With these acquisitions, Sanofi and Abbvie intend to expand their cancer research. Worldwide, the pharmaceutical industry has now invested more than 100 billion dollars in cancer research funding.

Besides Sanofi, the British pharmaceutical group Astra-Zeneca has also shown interest in the Californian Medivation company. Medivation only has one remedy drug for prostate cancer on the market, two active ingredients are still in the research phase.

7.8.6 Support for the Reindustrialization of US Operations by EU Companies

Moreover, EU, and especially German, companies also play a major role in the reindustrialization of US companies in the run-up to the TTIP Agreement.

For example, in northwest Ohio, jeeps are built by the U.S.-EU automotive company Fiat-Chrysler: The Wrangler and the Grand Cherokee with a total of 460,000 units in 2015. The high productivity of the plant is due in part to the Augsburg, Germany based robot manufacturer KUKA. 250 robots weld, form and assemble the Jeep bodies with 345 workers in three shifts as a joint venture project[547]. In this context, KUKA is also cooperating with the US software company Microsoft. KUKA generates almost one third of its sales in the automotive and aerospace industries in the US.

Not only robot manufacturer KUKA, but also companies such as machine and system builders are investing in automation and digitization in accordance with the 2016 motto "Industry 4.0". Since 2015, the US has once again been the most important export market for German mechanical engineering companies, ahead of China. This also applies to the German electrical industry. The hunger for EU and German capital goods in the

546 Handelsblatt. „Milliarden für neue Medizin ", Nr. 93, page 27. April 29, 2016.
547 Handelsblatt. „Comeback der USA made in Germany ", Nr. 77, page 20. April 21, 2016.

US has been sparked by the rise of the fracking industry to oil and gas production[548].

The same applies to the automotive industry in its US involvement. The heavyweights for EU car manufactures can be found in California due to the IT expertise of US companies such as Google, Microsoft, Facebook and Apple. Interesting joint ventures with a high culture of innovation emerged in 2015 and 2016.

The integration of the virtual world, the networking of man and machine, as well as the analysis of huge amounts of data (cloud computing) help in the implementation of electromobility and battery research for Tesla, or in the development of autonomous driving in Silicon Valley with group joint ventures such as Daimler and Google, or BMW and Apple, groups that see themselves as partners, not competitors, in the run-up to TTIP. The search engine company Google is working flat out on the technology of autonomous driving. However, Google will not become a car manufacturer, but rather an intelligent companion to the necessary digitalization for traffic of the future. After all, Google ranks 9th in the top ten companies with the largest research expenditures[549]. BMW CEO Harald Krüger remarked at a press conference on September 15, 2015 at the International Motor Show (IAA) in Frankfurt, Germany after returning from Apple's test site in Silicon Valley: "Our business purpose is to develop and manufacture cars. At the same time, we appreciate the achievements of Apple and Google, because they have brought the topics of autonomous driving and digitalization in the vehicle into the spotlight so prominently"[550]. Thanks to Apple and Google, the BMW Seven-Series has been equipped with the assistance systems that enable autonomous driving since 2017. In addition, it was launched as a plug-in hybrid with only 49 grams of CO2 consumption. On June 30, 2016, the BMW I8 Spyder with electric drive and modern technology for automated driving was presented at the Electronica trade fair in Las Vegas. Together with Intel and Mobil-Eye, it

548 Handelsblatt. „Comeback der USA made in Germany ", Nr. 77, page 20. April 21, 2016.

549 Innovations-Manager Magazine. „Stärke beweisen: Warum Innovationskraft im Kerngeschäft wichtig ist ", Nr. 35, page 23. June 2015.

550 Frankfurter Allgemeine Zeitung. „Schrecksekunde für BMW", Nr. 215, page 22. September 16, 2015.

was possible to let the prototype drive autonomously with completely new sensor technology in combination with a camera radar system[551].

However, the two German premium car manufacturers are not afraid of the much-cited dominance of American IT and software giants. On the contrary, in the cooperative spirit of the forthcoming TTIP agreement, innovative strength and inventive talent in the U.S. IT industry enable unprecedented opportunities in urgently needed open markets without tariffs, administrative charges and duplicate rules between the automotive industry and the digitalized "smart factory"[552]. This is because Americans and Europeans have also been working together for some time in the electrical engineering sector, for example at the Swedish-Swiss ABB Group (a competitor of Siemens), which has a third of its sales in the US. Despite the growing influence of information technology and software, both sides of the Atlantic have been wrestling ongoing ancient problems, which TTIP aims to solve: Different measures of length as meters and centimeters on one side, yards and inches on the other. This still causes many misunderstandings and is still a big and annoying topic. US and EU companies therefore have high expectations of any type of upcoming EU-US free trade agreement regarding the removal of still existing non-tariff barriers to market access. Only in this way can the "integrated industry" between the U.S. and the EU, the outstanding added value of the networked economy in the digital future between the two trading partners, come to fruition: The U.S. with its leading IT Internet competence, with its "Silicon Valley Culture"[553], the EU and especially Germany with systems engineering in machinery, automotive manufacturing, new drive technologies, sensor and control technology combined with the know-how in industrial processes, especially in the case of the middle class[554].

A Transatlantic Free Trade Agreement would thus act as a catalyst in this interconnected economy on both sides of the Atlantic, accelerating an

---

551 Fröhlich, Klaus. BMW-Entwicklungsvorstand: „Da geht es um Milliarden: Autonomes Fahren als Markt der Zukunft",in: *Handelsblatt*, Nr.126, pages 14-15. July 4, 2016.

552 Handelsblatt. „Comeback der USA made in Germany ", Nr. 77, page 20. April 21, 2016.

553 This term was coined by Michael Ziesemer, President of the German Electrical and Electronic Manufacturers' Association. (ZVEI) at the Hannover Congress during one of the many panel discussions.

554 Ziesemer, Michael: "Bei der Industrie 4.0 kann es keine nationalen Sonderwege geben", in: *Handelsblatt,* Nr.79, page 56. April 25, 2016.

economic process on the threshold of a new US-EU industrial era. It will change production and also revolutionize industrial value creation as a whole. As early as 2015, we experienced the disruptive power of digitization in the US and in the EU. We have been seeing how established business models are being challenged, for example in the field of car sharing, in the taxi industry and in guest room rental: Airbnb, Uber and Drive now, to name only a few, are on the verge of a new kind of mobility. As early as 2016, there has already been talk that in the future, automobile companies will no longer generate their revenues in pure automobile production alone, but above all in the service businesses around it, such as car sharing. The behavior of the younger generation contributes to this: It is no longer necessary to buy your own car, but to rent one instead, in order to avoid the eternal search for a parking space and fines for illegal parking, especially in the cities. Data and customer requests are increasingly creating new business models according to the Silicon Valley mantra: "Move fast and break things "[555].For these new business models of the future, companies and customers need harmonization of technical standards and product requirements based on international standardization organizations. This should and could be resolved by a TTIP Agreement.

7.8.7 China - One of the Most Important trading partners of the EU and the U.S. in Waiting Position

As the two negotiating delegations of the TTIP Agreement have been losing momentum, the Chinese government is increasingly calling for a free trade agreement with the EU. But there are reservations on both the EU and US sides: In addition to the solar technology industry in Europe and the US, steel producers of the two-wheeled industry, ceramics manufacturers and chemical fiber producers, the entire automobile and truck production on both sides of the Atlantic also warns against Chinese low-cost imports. Particularly in the case of the solar industry, which was provided with export subsidies by the Chinese government, this led to the extinction of an industry that was flourishing in Germany, especially in the new federal states in the east. Only a few solar module producers are still on the market.

555 Auerbach, Brad (April 18, 2017). "Review: Move Fast and Break Things: How Facebook, Google, and Amazon Cornered Culture". *Forbes*. Retrieved September 17, 2019. https://www.forbes.com/sites/bradauerbach/2017/04/18/move-fast-and-break-things-how-facebook-google-and-amazon-cornered-culture-book-review/#2afb2f8d422f

In 2013/14, the EU and the US had to step up anti-dumping proceedings against China and impose high tariffs on Chinese solar modules.

The fear and concern about Chinese overcapacities are demonstrated by a survey conducted in Germany by the Trade Association for Metals and the Handelsblatt among 134 German industrial companies from 13 sectors, including many medium-sized enterprises and companies in the basic materials industry[556]. This survey clouds the image of German Chinese trade relations[557]. The trading partner in the Far East is becoming a threat to important industries. The growing concerns of the German economy became the subject of the German-Chinese government consultations on June 12, 2016 in Beijing. During these negotiations, the Chinese government pressed for the status of a "market economy" to be granted to China[558]. However, the German delegation rejected this request, partly because the European Parliament had already previously adopted a resolution against the award of the title "market economy" to China[559].

During the negotiations in Beijing, German Federal Minister of Economics Sigmar Gabriel raised the imaginative measures taken by the Chinese government to protect the Chinese economy: Export tax rebates for copper products, subsidies worth billions for aluminum and steel producers, cross-sectoral energy subsidies - European companies list all these measures when they emphatically draw the attention of the EU Commission and national governments to misdemeanors of Chinese trade policy. Indeed, the Chinese government supports its companies with subsidies and does not get involved in discussions about them. It argues steel exports to Europe have increased solely because of higher international demand and the increased competitiveness of the Chinese steel industry. The German Federation of Employers' Associations of the Metal and Electrical Industry, on the other hand, points to the enormous overcapacity in the Chinese steel industry, which the government in Beijing artificially keeps alive. Therefore, China cannot be recognized as a "market economy", the criticism says[560]. The metal industry was supported in this criticism by other industries. Franziska Erdle, Chief Executive Officer of the German Metal

556 Handelsblatt. "Handelsmacht aus Fernost", Nr. 99. May 25, 2016.

557 Handelsblatt. „Gefährliche Partner ", Nr. 99, pages 1,4 and 5. May 25, 2016.

558 Chinese Ambassador to Germany: „Wir sind längst eine Marktwirtschaft", in: *Handelsblatt*, Nr. 99, page 5. May 25, 2016.

559 European Parliament Resolution on the Market Economy Status of China, Nr. 2016 / 2667 (RSP). May 10, 2016.

560 Handelsblatt. „Gefährliche Partner ", Nr. 99, page 5. May 25, 2016.

Association, warned the European Commission's Directorate-General for Trade and the German Federal government: Market economy status would upgrade China's trade status and weaken the EU and US trading partners. After the status of a "market economy", they could only defend themselves to a limited extent against unfair trade practices by the Chinese. EU anti-dumping proceedings would only be permitted to a very limited extent. EU anti-dumping procedures would be restricted. The companies affected by unfair trade practices would be virtually defenseless against the flood of goods from China. Jo Leinen, Member of the European Parliament, Chairman of the European Parliament's China delegation, underlines the concerns of business associations: As long as all the conditions for fair trade are not met, the EU must be able to resort to effective safeguard measures with punitive tariffs"[561].

As previously mentioned, the European Parliament adopted a corresponding resolution on May 10, 2016 against the recognition of China as a market economy[562]. This also makes it clear what President Barack Obama meant in his speech on April 26, 2016 delivered to business representatives from the US and the EU during the Hanover Fair 2016: "Unless the US and the EU lay down the rules in TTIP for free trade, countries like China will do so"[563].

In the event of the failure of TTIP, the EU and the US would have to expect the massive undermining of free trade rules in free competition by China, resulting in high job losses and the disappearance of companies from the market[564].

7.8.8 BREXIT Impact on TTIP

7.8.8.1 The Future of EU Relations with the UK after Brexit

On March 29, 2017, the government under Prime Minister Theresa May of the United Kingdom formally notified the EU of its intention to withdraw

561 Erdle, Franziska, in: *Handelsblatt,* Nr. 99, page 5. May 25, 2016.

562 European Parliament Resolution on the Market Economy Status of China, Nr. 2016 / 2667 (RSP). May 10, 2016.

563 Frankfurter Allgemeine Zeitung. „Produktion der Zukunft ", Nr. 93 a.a.O., page VI.

564 Handelsblatt. „Gefährliche Partner ", Nr. 99, pag 5. May 25, 2016.

from the EU under Article 50 of the EU Treaty[565]. This had been preceded by a referendum on June 23, 2016 with 46.5 million eligible voters, who were called upon by the government under David Cameron to vote on remaining in the EU. In the run-up to the decision, the "Remainers" and the "Brexiters", i.e. supporters for staying in the EU and opponents for leaving, were almost equal. With a relatively high voter turnout of 72.2 percent, 51.9 percent of voters ultimately voted for the UK to leave the EU and 48.1 percent to remain in the EU. The UK's population was deeply divided. This resulted in very turbulent times. David Cameron ended up resigning and his successor Theresa May had to spend a lot of time in the British House of Commons, accompanied by extremely turbulent parliamentary debates, in order to clarify the question whether a majority would be possible for a contractually regulated withdrawal or for an unregulated, i.e. "Hard Brexit". After numerous extensions of the due decision in parliament, Theresa May resigned and handed over lead to Boris Johnson, who, as the Tory Party's exit campaigner, finally called for new elections in October 2019, leading to a clear majority against the defeated Socialist Party led by Corbyn. Finally, Boris Johnson, who, supported by Nigel Farange, led a tough EU exit campaign, submitted a motion for a regulated exit agreement with the EU in accordance with Article 50 of the EU Treaty (TEU) in Brussels on January 31, 2020[566]. It is still not entirely clear whether David Cameron's original demand to stop the strong immigration from the internal market of the EU could have been recognized by the EU for a period to be negotiated and determined with the EU. This was about the fourth fundamental freedom of the EU Lisbon Treaty, the free movement of people. Especially from Poland and Romania, more and more people had entered the British labor market starting in 2015, but mainly also taking advantage of the state support benefits in the event of unemployment[567]. The UK government un-

565 European Commission. *Brexit negotiations.* January 31, 2020. https://ec.europa.eu/commission/brexit-negotiations_en

566 European Commission. "Negotiating documents on Article 50 negotiations with the United Kingdom". *Documents published as part of the European Commission's approach to transparency on Article 50 negotiations with the United Kingdom.* January 31, 2020. https://ec.europa.eu/commission/brexit-negotiations/negotiating-documents-article-50-negotiations-united-kingdom_en

567 Oster, Manuel and Georg Schlichting. "Der Brexit: Hintergrund, Entwicklung und erwartete Auswirkungen", in: *Wissenschaftliche Schriften des Fachbereiches Wirtschaftswissenschaften,* Nr. 25/ 2017 der Hochschule Koblenz. http://hdl.handle.net/10419/175425

der David Cameron felt it was losing control over immigration, including refugees from the Arab region and Africa.

7.8.8.2 The UK's Soft Exit from the EU

The British parliament's decision to leave the EU with an orderly withdrawal, a "Hard Brexit" with unforeseeable consequences for the UK and the EU was avoided. According to Art. 50 (2) TEU, there are two years after the UK's withdrawal from the EU on January 1, 2020 to conclude an exit agreement and, at the same time, a free trade agreement with the EU[568]. During this period, the still UK remains in the EU. After this period, EU membership expires unless the European Council, by unanimous decision, extends the deadline in order to obtain additional negotiating space[569].

Negotiations on future relations between the EU and the UK began in Brussels on March 2-5, 2020. As the EU negotiator, the EU Commission leads the negotiations under the leadership of Michel Barnier's task force in close coordination with the Council and the European Parliament[570]. Future relations are to be regulated, among other things, by a trade agreement on the movement of goods. There will be further agreements in areas such as digital commerce, copyright, public procurement (tenders/ submission), freedom of movement, transport and energy[571].

For the UK, the most favorable version of the exit would be an agreement with the EU and the countries of the European Economic Area (EEA), which includes the common internal market and the countries of Norway, Iceland and Lichtenstein. These countries do not have full membership in the EU but benefit from approximately 80 percent of the European internal market rules under EEA regulations. These include, in particular,

568 European Commission. *Negotiation mandate.* January 31, 2020. https://ec.europa.eu/commission/brexit-negotiations/guide-negotiations_en

569 Oster, Manuel and Georg Schlichting. “Der Brexit: Hintergrund, Entwicklung und erwartete Auswirkungen”, in: *Wissenschaftliche Schriften des Fachbereiches Wirtschaftswissenschaften,* Nr. 25/ 2017 der Hochschule Koblenz, page 4. http://hdl.handle.net/10419/175425

570 European Commission. *Task Force for Relations with the United Kingdom.* February 9, 2020. https://ec.europa.eu/info/departments/task-force-relations-united-kingdom_en

571 European Commission. *The European Union and the United Kingdom – forging a new partnership.* March 6, 2020.

the four European fundamental freedoms[572]. In particular, the EEA rules allow concessions in trade between the EU and the above-mentioned countries in the EEA such as Norway, Iceland and Liechtenstein, but not with Switzerland. In the case of UK membership, there could be a "deep and comprehensive free trade agreement between the EU and the UK, as with Canada (CETA 2017) and South Korea (2011)", for example[573]. In the case of a DCFTA agreement ("deep and comprehensive free trade agreement"), the financial losses would be relatively cheap: 3 billion euros, that is 0.11 percent of the GDP, or 41 euros per capita in the UK, plus additional net payments from thc 27 EU members to the EU budget. For Germany, as the largest net contributor to the EU, the additional contribution to the EU budget would increase by 2.5 billion euros. In case of a "deep agreement", the higher German net amount would be included in the total burden of 6 billion euros per year for the EU and UK[574]. The UK is the second largest economy in the EU and is responsible for 18 percent of the European GDP. Per capita income is almost 40 percent above the EU average[575]. A membership in the EEA would therefore be the best solution for the UK and the EU, especially for the economies of both countries. A 2016 study by the Bertelsmann Foundation demonstrates that leaving the EU will have negative effects on the economic development of the UK, but only more moderately negative effects for the EU[576]. In the case of a deep free trade agreement, the study estimates certain costs, for example for exporters due to the proof of origin of goods, which must be certified by the Chambers of Commerce and Industry for a fee. If the UK evades the jurisdiction of the

572 Felbermayr, Gabriel. "Weicher Brexit: EWR-Szenario", in: *Wirtschafliche Aspekte des Brexit.* Ifo-Schnelldienst 11/2017, 70. Jg., Ifo-Institut Muenchen, page 37. June 8, 2017.

573 Felbermayr, Gabriel. "Weicher Brexit: EWR-Szenario", in: *Wirtschafliche Aspekte des Brexit.* Ifo-Schnelldienst 11/2017, 70. Jg., Ifo-Institut Muenchen, page 39. June 8, 2017.

574 European Union. "EU-Haushaltsgipfel: Von der Leyen draengt auf raschen Beschluss zu mehrjaehrigem Finanzrahmen", in: *EU News,* Nr. 4/2020, page 3. February 27.2.2020.

575 Felbermayr, Gabriel. "Weicher Brexit: EWR-Szenario", in: *Wirtschafliche Aspekte des Brexit.* Ifo-Schnelldienst 11/2017, 70. Jg., Ifo-Institut Muenchen, page 36. June 8, 2017.

576 Bertelsmann Stiftung. *Brexit – Moegliche wirtschaftliche Folgen eines britischen EU-Austritts,* page 5. August 16, 2016. https://www.bertelsmann-stiftung.de/de/publikationen/publikation/did/policy-brief-201505-br-brexit-moegliche-wirtschaftlihe-folgen-eines-britischen-eu-austrit-1/

European Court of Justice, the mutual recognition of product approvals, professional qualifications and other things are hardly conceivable[577]. After all, in the case of a UK EEA membership, customs duties are not levied on goods. Only imports of goods would have to be paid by the UK in the form of excise duties, which are not payable within the EU for full members[578].

7.8.8.3 Trade Facilitation for the UK in the EEA

The advantages of the European Economic Area regulations compared to the harmonization of a free trade area are clear. They certainly contribute to an intensification of trade through the facilitations outlined above. With an entry of the UK into the EEA, the EU and the UK could signal to businesses on the continent that a central objective of the Brexit negotiations, the preservation of existing value chains and, above all, supply chain management in the automotive industry must remain[579].

A departure of the UK from this principle of a division of labor-sharing production, which is so important for investors from Japan, the US and EU, would inevitably lead to the crash of the most important industrial sector for the UK, coupled with high unemployment. As a result, automobile companies would be forced to close their plants in the UK and produce in the EU internal market. This would have been the course of action for corporations in the case of a Hard Brexit, which could, however, be avoided by the British government and the British parliament.

A "Soft Brexit" would, as explained, be the best of all solutions for both trading partners, for the UK and the EU, with the accession of the UK to the EEA including a free trade agreement. It is also important, because the UK could continue to enjoy the privileges of free movement of capital. Together with the "European Financial Passport", this "fundamental freedom" of the EU internal market is of particular importance for the strong British econ-

577 Felbermayr, Gabriel. "Weicher Brexit: EWR-Szenario", in: *Wirtschafliche Aspekte des Brexit.* Ifo-Schnelldienst 11/2017, 70. Jg., Ifo-Institut Muenchen, page 37. June 8, 2017.

578 Felbermayr, Gabriel. "Weicher Brexit: EWR-Szenario", in: *Wirtschafliche Aspekte des Brexit.* Ifo-Schnelldienst 11/2017, 70. Jg., Ifo-Institut Muenchen, page 37. June 8, 2017.

579 Felbermayr, Gabriel. "Weicher Brexit: EWR-Szenario", in: *Wirtschafliche Aspekte des Brexit.* Ifo-Schnelldienst 11/2017, 70. Jg., Ifo-Institut Muenchen, page 37. June 8, 2017.

omy[580]. Another advantage would be the freedom of people and services within the EEA. It ensures that EU citizens with regular employment contracts remain in the UK, which would benefit the strong British service economy[581]. This is because the UK's strength in services lies primarily in comparative advantages rather than in preferential access to EU markets. Interestingly, the trade-creating effects are stronger for EU providers in the financial sector than for those from the UK[582].

The decline of the once proud steel industry in the UK and the chance of reindustrialization for the country in the EEA makes the proposals presented here the most reasonable solution, which could be implemented by competent parties from politics, business and science for a "Soft" exit. Dominic Raab, acting UK Foreign Secretary, noted in his commentary on the UK's withdrawal request on January 31, 2020: "We could become even better friends. For us, the exit is not an end, but rather a courageous new beginning, the beginning of a new chapter. As of today, January 31, 2020, we have the freedom to create a new relationship with our European partners, a relationship based on strong friendship, shared values and mutual interests. This opens up the possibility of looking forward. We have seen how expanding trade can boost the economy, create jobs, reduce the cost of living and increase consumer choice"[583].

In particular, the negotiations and their conclusion may, among other things, aim to reunite the divided UK and reconcile it with the European integration process. It is also important to revitalize the reindustrialization of the central and northern parts of the UK, especially for "broken cities", such as Sheffeld (UK) with its once proud steel industry, by using robotics,

580 Oster, Manuel and Georg Schlichting. "Der Brexit: Hintergrund, Entwicklung und erwartete Auswirkungen", in: *Wissenschaftliche Schriften des Fachbereiches Wirtschaftswissenschaften*, Nr. 25/ 2017 der Hochschule Koblenz, page 10. http://hdl.handle.net/10419/175425

581 Oster, Manuel and Georg Schlichting. "Der Brexit: Hintergrund, Entwicklung und erwartete Auswirkungen", in: *Wissenschaftliche Schriften des Fachbereiches Wirtschaftswissenschaften*, Nr. 25/ 2017 der Hochschule Koblenz, page 10. http://hdl.handle.net/10419/175425

582 Felbermayr, Gabriel. "Weicher Brexit: EWR-Szenario", in: *Wirtschafliche Aspekte des Brexit.* Ifo-Schnelldienst 11/2017, 70. Jg., Ifo-Institut Muenchen, page 38. June 8, 2017.

583 Raab, Dominic. "Wir koennen noch bessere Freunde sein", *Frankfurter Allgemeine Zeitung*, Nr. 26, page 8. January 31, 2020.

for example, like in the "Rust Belt" of the US[584]. Paul Collier, University of Oxford, has criticized the lack of innovation, spirit of cooperation and lack of strategic networking between the formerly competitive shipyards and the EU mainland in his study "The Future of Capitalism"[585]. To this end, the UK needs the EU with its funding programs such as Horizon 2021-27, as well as the European Regional Development Fund (ERDF). These have been shown to advance the necessary clustering, combined with efficient know-how and knowledge transfer, for the valorization of run-down medium-sized and small towns. The networking of research and development of universities with the regional economic and service environment has, for example, decisively developed the new federal states in Germany (former Eastern Germany), the Baltic States, Poland, the Czech Republic and Slovakia in the direction of reindustrialization and increasing prosperity, as former communist countries which used to be part of the "Iron Curtain". The insularity position of the UK must not be allowed to lead to isolation and thus decline as a result of the country's withdrawal from the EU. Accession to the EEA and the participation in the EU-Horizon as well as in the Erasmus youth exchange program would be decisive steps to escape the threat of isolationism and to move in line with the EU-US Free Trade Agreement.

584 Collier, Paul. "The Globalization Revolution and the Demise of Provincial Cities". *The Future of Capitalism*, pages 128-132. New York: Harper-Collins Publishers, 2018.

585 Collier, Paul. "The Geographic Divide: Booming Metropolis, broken Cities". *The Future of Capitalism*, page 125. New York: Harper-Collins Publishers, 2018.

In the EU proposal document on "EU-US regulatory cooperation" of February 10, 2015, (updated on March 21, 2016), chapter 3.2.7 also deals with "Strengthening of financial market stability between the US and the EU"[586]. This is a forward-looking strategic importance in a trade agreement between the US dollar zone and the EU euro zone. In its resolution on TTIP of July 8, 2015, the European Parliament also reaffirmed that rules between the US and the EU on major economic and financial issues should set an example for third countries and play a stabilizing role in preventing further fragmentation[587]. The question of financial market stability seemed so important to the EU Commission after all that it had already specified the rough proposal in detail well in advance of the 12th round of TTIP negotiations in a separate document dated January 27, 2014 and published it on January 8, 2015, i.e. almost one year later. However, the EU then created another new revised document containing the financial services offer of the European Union made in the context of Transatlantic Trade and Investment Partnership negotiations. “It was tabled for discussion with the US in the negotiating round of July 11-15, 2016 and made public on July 14, 2016. It contains Annex I, II and III”[588].

It was above all the effects of the financial crisis in 2008 that prompted the European Commission to take this step. In doing so, it refers to the international coordination of the G-20 countries after the 2008 crisis. According to the EU, a TTIP Agreement could make an important contribution to financial stability "by ensuring that generally applicable international rules are applied in a consistent manner to the two largest financial services markets in the world, which form the core of the global

586 European Commission. “Regulatory cooperation in TTIP”, pages 19 and 20. February 10, 2015. Updated March 21, 2016. https://trade.ec.europa.eu/doclib/docs/2016/march/tradoc_154379.pdf

587 European Parliament Resolution on TTIP, page 2. July 8, 2015. Accessed May 11, 2016. http://www.europarl.europa.eu/sides/getDoc.do?pubRaf =//EP//TEXT+

588 European Commission. „Cooperation on financial services regulation“. July 14, 2016. https://trade.ec.europa.eu/doclib/docs/2016/july/tradoc_154794.pdf

financial system[589]. The EU position paper goes on to say: "For example, we are currently introducing rules to regulate trading in derivatives, which was one of the causes of the financial crisis"[590]. It is true that both sides have adopted strict prudential rules on financial market regulation after 2008. However, these rules would have been more effective if they had been better coordinated between the US and the EU. The cooperation was useful, but not as efficient as it should have been (e.g. the much stricter Volcker-rule versus the more liberal EU banking union with the bank rescue umbrella bailout)[591]. For example, the Polish Foreign Minister Dr. Witold Waszczykowski stated in his article on TTIP in the prominent series of the Frankfurter Allgemeine Zeitung, "Is Europe falling apart?" on April 4, 2016: "The recent financial crisis has clearly shown that the Economic and Monetary Union project is far from perfect. The transformation of the Eurozone will continue. We do not oppose ideas that seek to strengthen the eurozone in terms of its financial stability and resilience to external economic shocks"[592]. Such a "shock" unexpectedly occurred with the "Brexit" referendum in the United Kingdom (UK) on June 24, 2016 on the financial markets. There were turbulences and price falls on the stock exchanges and in foreign exchange currency trading, but also the withdrawal of the automotive industry from the British Isles to mainland Europe. Many questions about financial market control arose anew after the British referendum:

- Will the London banking center for trading European bonds, currencies and derivatives lose its location when the country is no longer a member of the EU?
- Will the European Central Bank (ECB) still tolerate euro clearing transactions and central securities depositories outside the EU?
- Will the core businesses be relocated from London to the continent, e.g. to Frankfurt or Paris?

---

589 European Commission. „Cooperation on financial services regulation“, page 1. July 14, 2016. https://trade.ec.europa.eu/doclib/docs/2016/july/tradoc_154794.pdf

590 European Commission. “TTIP: EU-Vorschlag zur Regulierungszusammenarbeit”, page 19. March 21, 2016. http://trade.ec.europa.eu/doclib/docs/2015/march/tradoc_153236.pdf

591 European Commission. “TTIP – EU proposal for Chapter: Regulatory Cooperation”, page 4. March 21, 2016. http://trade.ec.europa.eu/doclib/docs/2016/march/tradoc_154377.pdf

592 Frankfurter Allgemeine Zeitung. „Mit der Hand auf dem Herzen“, Nr.78, page 6. April 4, 2016.

- Is the United Kingdom losing up to 20,000 jobs from London to Frankfurt according to estimates by the Frankfurt School of Finance?
- In view of the activities of the major financial institutions in the European Single Market, how can financial market stability still be ensured if European coordination of supervision and regulation is made more difficult by a British exit?
- From this perspective, can the European Banking Authority (EBA) still remain in London and the United Kingdom remain a member of the European Systemic Risk Council (ESRB)[593]?

Andreas Dombret, Member of the Executive Board of the German Bundesbank and responsible for banking supervision, notes in his statement on Brexit that, in view of the close links between British and European banks, financial supervision and financial market stability can only be pursued at EU level. The single rulebook ensures that there is a harmonized European regulatory framework for banks on both sides of the English Channel. A return to more national regulation due to Britain's EU therefore requires new mechanisms and regulations to ensure international supervision and regulation of larger banks[594].

In addition to the problem with the UK, which has always been a difficult partner since the northern enlargement of the EU due to its constant additional requests towards the European Union, its boycott of the euro zone and its lack of solidarity in the refugee crisis in 2015, there is still the fragile state of the euro zone itself. Joseph Stiglitz, winner of the Nobel Prize for Economics, Chief Economist at the World Bank and author of numerous (scholarly) publications, contributes to this subject in one of his books. He refers to the "limits of monetary policy" of the European Central Bank (ECB) and puts forward the thesis: "Europe has lost a decade". His main argument for analyzing the EU monetary union: The fiscal pact is part of the problem. The eurozone countries have performed much worse than the non-eurozone countries since the 2008 financial crisis. In addition, they have performed worse than the US, although the financial crisis was triggered there[595]. As a solution, Stiglitz suggests that the imbalances within the euro zone should be tackled quickly. In his opinion, combining austeri-

593 Dombret, Andreas: „Bankenrisiko Brexit", in: *Frankfurter Allgemeine Zeitung*, Nr.126, page 20. June 2, 2016.

594 Dombret, Andreas: „Bankenrisiko Brexit", in: *Frankfurter Allgemeine Zeitung*, Nr.126, page 20. June 2, 2016.

595 Stiglitz, Joseph: *Rewriting the Rules of American Economy*, New York, 2015.

ty policy with the euro is not enough. What is missing is the horizontal and vertical fiscal equalization, which has been functioning excellently in the Federal Republic of Germany since its foundation in 1949. This means that Germany, with its high export surpluses, prevents the competitiveness of the other members of the currency zone[596]. However, before the introduction of the euro, competition existed through the balancing of exchange rates. In the euro zone, however, the exchange rate is fixed. According to Stiglitz, the euro should unite Europe, but it has divided Europe. The best way to get out of this would be much stronger cooperation[597].

In view of the friction in the European currency zone, the EU proposal to include "Cooperation on financial services regulation" in the TTIP Agreement is excellent[598]. A transfer of know-how among the monetary regulators and financial supervisors on both sides of the Atlantic is necessary given the fragile economic and monetary situation in the EU. The EU proposal states: „The EU and the US have sought to implement these principles of high international standards for global regulation consistently, significant differences have arisen in the process of implementation in a number of areas. Some of these differences are due to differences in EU- and US-market structures and are unavoidable. Others cannot be fully justified on prudential grounds"[599].

Furthermore, the European Commission proposal states that inconsistencies in the financial market system are not only significant barriers to trade and investment, but also undermine the global financial stability that the EU and the US are so keen to achieve. In too many instances, standards have been implemented in a way that ultimately does not allow the regulatory system, i.e. the responsible financial supervisory regulators, to cooperate in this confusion. This situation contributes fundamentally to over-regulation, to the duplication of rules and ultimately confusion.

The fragmentation of regulation in the EU and the US is creating resistance in the financial markets and complicating the urgently needed

596 Collier, Paul. *The Future of Capitalism*", Penguin Random House UK, 2018, pages 149-153 (Development Banks).

597 Stiglitz, Joseph: "Europa hat ein Jahrzehnt verloren", in: *Handelsblatt,* Nr. 77, page 30. April 21, 2016.

598 Hänsel, Lars and Lairo Jeanene: "Politische Faktoren der Verhandlungen über eine Transatlantische Handels- und Investitionspartnerschaft in den USA ", in: *KAS-Auslandsinformationen* 9/2014, page 20.

599 European Comission. „Cooperation on financial services regulation ", page 4. July 14, 2016. https://trade.ec.europa.eu/doclib/docs/2016/july/tradoc_154794.pdf

economic policy decisions on both sides[600]. A financial market regulatory dialogue on a common set of rules has already taken place between the EU and the US. Both parties were also in discussion during detailed meetings to discuss the necessary rules in derivatives markets or the necessary auditing processes. This dialogue has also achieved some successes in recent years[601]. However, the period following the major financial market crisis in 2008, with hectic regulation on both sides of the Atlantic, is far from having achieved the necessary quality of efficient, regulatory cooperation that should be urgently designed[602]. Above all, the focus should now be shifted from the level of the international regulatory aspect to the implementation on the regional financial markets in order to make the differences between the different structures and the various legislative processes as constant as possible. The European Commission also believes that the discrepancy between actual market structures and the legislative framework in the EU and the US is too wide[603]. This would increase the risk of uncertainty in the markets and increase the consequences of action in response to the challenges in the form of cross-border and well-reflected regulations, joint regular consultations and coordination procedures[604]. The European Commission therefore considers financial market regulation too important on both sides, to react under pressure from the markets only in ad hoc, informal meetings at the very last minute, as has always been the case in the past, instead of preparing in a peaceful and preventive manner as well as discussing and deciding on final issues[605].

---

600 European Comission. „Cooperation on financial services regulation ", page 2. July 14, 2016. https://trade.ec.europa.eu/doclib/docs/2016/july/tradoc_154794.pdf

601 Schmucker, Claudia: „TTIP im Kontext anderer Freihandelsabkommen", in: *Transatlantische Beziehungen, aus Politik und Zeitgeschehen*, 64. Jg. 50–51/2014, page 20. December 8, 2014.

602 European Comission. „Cooperation on financial services regulation ", page 2. July 14, 2016. https://trade.ec.europa.eu/doclib/docs/2016/july/tradoc_154794.pdf

603 Juncker, Jean-Claude: "Reformen in Europa jetzt!", in: *Handelsblatt*, Nr. 242, page 96. December 16/ 17, 2017.

604 Grillo, Ulrich. "Die Kapitalmarktunion und der Binnenmarkt fuer Finanzdienstleistungen" in *Europa im Schicksalsjahr 2016*. Herder Verlag, Freiburg, pages 77-79.

605 European Commission. „Cooperation on financial services regulation", page 3. July 14, 2016. https://trade.ec.europa.eu/doclib/docs/2016/july/tradoc_154794.pdf

8.1 Adaptation of Regulations: Example of the EU-US Automotive Sector

As outlined in the automotive and pharmaceutical sectors previously discussed, EU-US regulatory cooperation is focused on industries where more than 30 million people are already employed in the EU, such as pharmaceuticals, medical devices as well as the automotive sector[606]. The remaining of the seven sectors negotiated are: chemicals, cosmetics, mechanical engineering, textiles and pharmaceuticals[607]. It must be said in advance, as has already been mentioned repeatedly, that on both sides of the Atlantic, the highest quality standards in the world already apply anyway, alongside Japan and South Korea. In TTIP, the world's highest level of know-how and experience in manufacturing would eliminate unnecessary duplication of effort in inspections, certifications, testing and approval regulations. This would free up existing resources and manpower for "more rewarding tasks in industry, commerce and administration"[608]. There is no doubt that the automotive sector is the engine of innovation and value creation for the overall economy in the EU and in the US. Therefore, close regulatory cooperation on both sides of the Atlantic would also lead to a greater influence at international level in the following areas:

- <u>Equivalence</u> with the aim of mutual recognition of admission procedures, testing and administrative rules,
- <u>Harmonization</u> based on cooperation at the level of the UNECE Memorandum of Understanding of 1998[609], especially in the fields of new technologies such as e-mobility and autonomous driving (automated driving),

606 European Commission. „TTIP – EU proposal for Chapter: Regulatory Cooperation", page 4. March 21, 2016. http://trade.ec.europa.eu/doclib/docs/2016/march/tradoc_154377.pdf

607 European Commission. „TTIP – EU proposal for Chapter: Regulatory Cooperation", page 15. March 21, 2016. http://trade.ec.europa.eu/doclib/docs/2016/march/tradoc_154377.pdf

608 European Commission. „TTIP – EU proposal for Chapter: Regulatory Cooperation", page 5. March 21, 2016. http://trade.ec.europa.eu/doclib/docs/2016/march/tradoc_154377.pdf

609 United Nations Economic Commission for Europe (UNECE). "Memorandum of Understanding: Governing Collaboration". Accessed March 3, 2020. http://www.unece.org/oes/mou/mou_unifem.html

- Research in the field of common interest, or partnership programs (Twinning Programs)[610].

For, despite all the nationalist tendencies of political currents in the US election campaign year 2016 and the Brexit supporters in the United Kingdom in 2016 ("We want to regain control"), cooperation in international organizations is also becoming increasingly close in the area of regulation. Therefore, close regulatory cooperation between the EU and the US within the framework of TTIP could provide a strong impetus to the development, updating and implementation of international regulations and standards. Regulations agreed between the US and the EU have significantly more chances of being adopted by third countries[611].

According to the EU Commission, closer cooperation between the EU and the US will contribute to the exemplary effect and thus to the removal of trade barriers worldwide. Regulatory cooperation helps to establish international regulations with the highest possible level of protection and to uphold values of the rule of law with open markets[612].

Europe has been very successful in automobile production, especially with premium vehicles from BMW, Audi, Daimler and Porsche, as shown by the clear presence of these vehicles on US roads. Exports to the US have often failed in the past because the US does not apply international standards (ISO or IEC standards) and due to conformity assessments in the US involving higher costs for European manufacturers[613].

TTIP offers the opportunity for closer cooperation between the relevant regulatory bodies in the EU and the US with the aim of making trade much easier:

---

610 European Commission. „EU-position on motor vehicles", in: *Memorandum Directorate-General for Trade,* pages 1-3. May 14, 2014. Accessed April 15, 2015. http://trade.ec.europa.eu/doclib/press/index.cfm?id=1076

611 European Commission. „TTIP – EU proposal for Chapter: Regulatory Cooperation", page 4. March 21, 2016. http://trade.ec.europa.eu/doclib/docs/2016/march/tradoc_154377.pdf

612 European Commission. "Report of the Eleventh Round of Negotiations for the Transatlantic Trade and Investment Partnership". Miami, page 14. October 19-23, 2015. https://trade.ec.europa.eu/doclib/docs/2015/november/tradoc_153935.pdf

613 European Commission. „EU-position on motor vehicles", in: *Memorandum Directorate-General for Trade,* page 2. May 14, 2014. Accessed April 15, 2015. http://trade.ec.europa.eu/doclib/press/index.cfm?id=1076

- In the future, regulations should be more closely aligned
- the respective bodies responsible for setting standards should develop common standards wherever possible going forward,
- conformity assessment procedures should be designed to avoid duplication of testing or certification procedures should be streamlined.

Mutual Recognition of Safety Standards for Passenger Cars

TTIP also aims to improve the compatibility of legislation for vehicles without compromising standards in the EU and the US. The aim of TTIP is for regulators on both sides of the Atlantic to mutually recognize regulatory systems that are largely consistent in terms of safety[614].

With regard to other existing regulations, a medium-term program for the development of global security regulations at UNECE level is supposed to be established. This applies in particular with regard to automated driving[615]. Cooperation in the field of new technologies (keyword "Industry 4.0") should lead to the development of common rules.

614 European Commission. „EU-position on motor vehicles“, in: *Memorandum Directorate-General for Trade,* page 2. May 14, 2014. Accessed April 15, 2015. http://trade.ec.europa.eu/doclib/press/index.cfm?id=1076

615 European Commission. „TTIP – EU proposal for Chapter: Regulatory Cooperation“, page 18. March 21, 2016. http://trade.ec.europa.eu/doclib/docs/2016/march/tradoc_154377.pdf

Figure 8: EU Car Manufacturing in the United States[616]

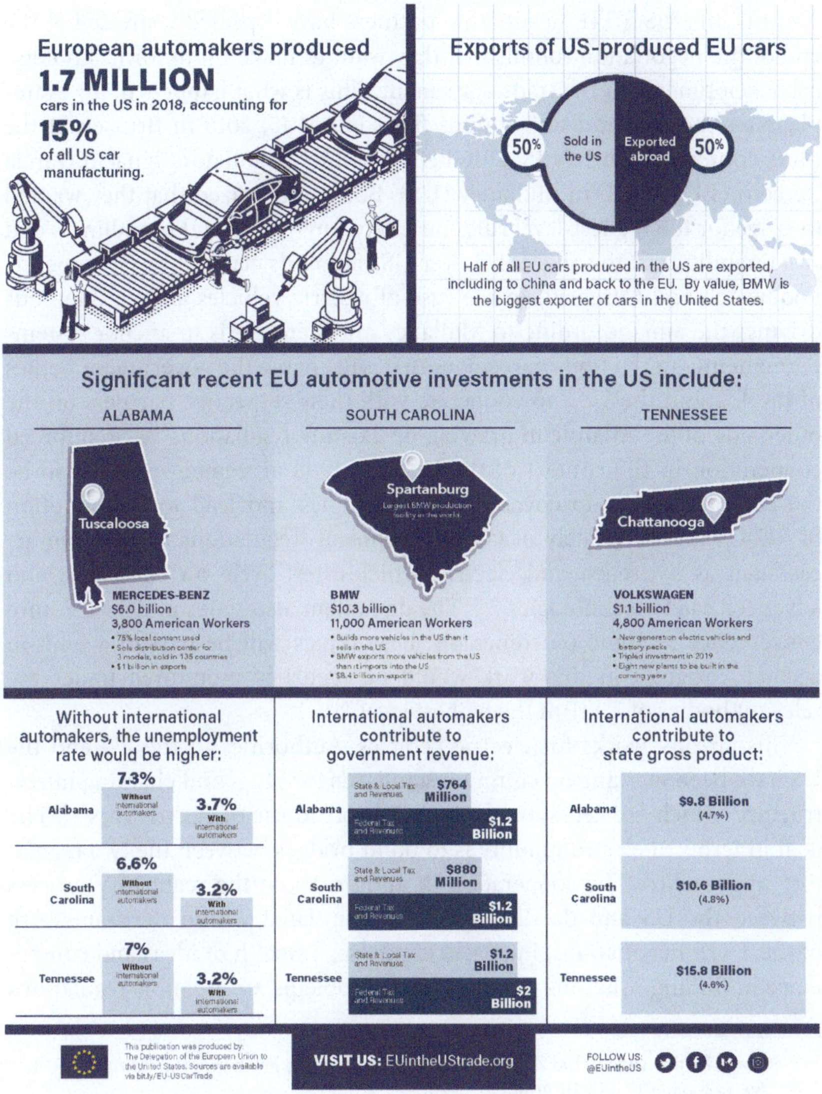

616 Delegation of the European Union to the United States, Washington, DC. February 27, 2020. http://www.euintheustrade.org/wp-content/uploads/2020/03/64346-EU-Car-Infographic_R42.pdf

8.1.1 Electromobility

The EU and US TTIP negotiating partners have repeatedly stressed at the end of the negotiation rounds that they want to make room for technological developments in the trade agreement. This is what happened, for example, after the 13th and 14th rounds from July 11-15, 2016 in Brussels at the press conference on July 15, 2016 between chief negotiators Ignacio Garcia Bercero (EU) and Dan Mullaney (US). Both emphasized that they wanted to strive for the highest-level rules on safety, environmental friendliness and sustainability, not the allegedly lower US standards claimed by Greenpeace, Foodwatch and Campact. In the case of electric vehicles and autonomous driving, the aim, according to Mullaney and Bercero, is to anchor systems permanently in the trade agreement that will enable the government bodies of the EU and the USA to cooperate with their respective partners on the other side of the Atlantic in drawing up existing regulations[617]. "Reinforced cooperation in the context of the UNECE 1998 agreement would also be the central element to cover new technologies and lead to the adoption of EU-US and ultimately of Global Technical Regulations (GTR's), in areas such as hydrogen and electric vehicles, test-cycle on emissions, and advanced safety technologies"[618]. The document also states under "4. Future convergence": "Some outcomes on these topics will be part of a built-in agenda. Progress in this work would be regularly monitored under the relevant bodies of TTIP at the highest level"[619].

This already works for electric vehicles. Authorities in the EU and the US have been working on common standards for plugs and charging infrastructure, which are necessary for the widespread use of electric cars[620]. The goal in terms of electromobility is to build bridges between the two regulatory approaches. The cooperation of authorities in the regulatory process between the US and the EU, which was initiated within the framework of the TTIP negotiations, increases expertise, a wealth of ideas and competence in finding solutions to outstanding problems. Compatible regulations

617 Frankfurter Allgemeine Zeitung. „Das Zerren um das Freihandelsabkommen TTIP", Nr. 164, page 20. July 16, 2016.

618 European Commission. „EU-position on motor vehicles", in: *Memorandum Directorate-General for Trade*, page 3. May 14, 2014. Accessed April 15, 2015.

619 European Commission. „EU-position on motor vehicles", in: *Memorandum Directorate-General for Trade*, page 3. May 14, 2014. Accessed April 15, 2015.

620 European Commission. "TTIP und Regulierung: Ein Ueberblick", page 10. http://trade.ec.europa.eu/doclib/docs/2015/march/tradoc_153236.pdf

are emerging in favor of greater efficiency and competence. Ultimately, such solidarity leads to the reduction of trade barriers "behind the border", to higher regulatory quality and effective implementation. At this stage of cooperation, from development to industrial production, it is important for negotiators and their negotiating delegations to apply technology assessment, including the social and environmental impact on international trade and consumers, of the harmonized legislation to be proposed on both sides of the Atlantic[621].

8.1.2 Joint Regulatory Cooperation Body

One of the greatest achievements of international regulatory cooperation is the WTO Agreement on Technical Barriers to Trade (TBT of 1980). Different standards and conformity assessments are considered to be one of the most important obstacles for companies in the EU that want to export to the US and vice versa[622]. The WTO TBT Agreement affects laws, regulations, standards and norms, such as labelling on product characteristics, their methods of verification of compliance with the requirements for products. Standards and norms designate specific technical solution processes, which are defined, for example, by joint bodies of representatives of the EU and US regulatory bodies[623].

The procedures for verifying whether a product contains a technical regulation or a standard/ norm are referred to as "conformity assessment procedures"[624]. The US and EU negotiators were planning on incorporate these WTO provisions into the TTIP Agreement, as they have proved worthy in other bilateral agreements[625].

Under WTO rules, none of the forthcoming measures resulting from the TTIP Agreement may be discriminatory or even restrict trade, without

621 European Commission. "TTIP und Regulierung: Ein Ueberblick", page 10. http://trade.ec.europa.eu/doclib/docs/2015/march/tradoc_153236.pdf

622 European Commission. "TTIP und Regulierung: Ein Ueberblick", page 10. http://trade.ec.europa.eu/doclib/docs/2015/march/tradoc_153236.pdf

623 European Commission. „EU-position on motor vehicles", in: *Memorandum Directorate-General for Trade,* page 2. May 14, 2014. Accessed April 15, 2015.

624 European Commission. "TTIP und Regulierung: Ein Ueberblick", page 12. http://trade.ec.europa.eu/doclib/docs/2015/march/tradoc_153236.pdf

625 European Commission. "Technical Barriers to Trade (TBT)". *Textual Proposal,* page 1, Article 2. January 7, 2015. https://trade.ec.europa.eu/doclib/docs/2015/january/tradoc_153025.pdf

endangering safety, health, consumer and environmental protection[626]. In the TTIP Agreement, both delegations want to go beyond the provisions of the TBT Agreement of the WTO regulations wherever possible. The aim should be to achieve a high standard of safety for the products represented in EU-US trade, to avoid unnecessary barriers to trade, to stimulate the labor market and generate added value[627]. In this context, the EU and the US are supposed to

- Draw up technical regulations and standards by having a joint presence in international bodies
- foster closer cooperation in international bodies which set standards and norms
- cooperate closely on conformity assessment procedures in the mutual acceptance of test laboratory results.

626 European Commission. "TTIP und Regulierung: Ein Ueberblick", page 13. http://trade.ec.europa.eu/doclib/docs/2015/march/tradoc_153236.pdf

627 European Commission. "TTIP and Regulation: An Overview", page 13. February 10, 2015. https://trade.ec.europa.eu/doclib/docs/2015/february/tradoc_153121.pdf

Figure 9: EU Automotive Industry in the United States[628]

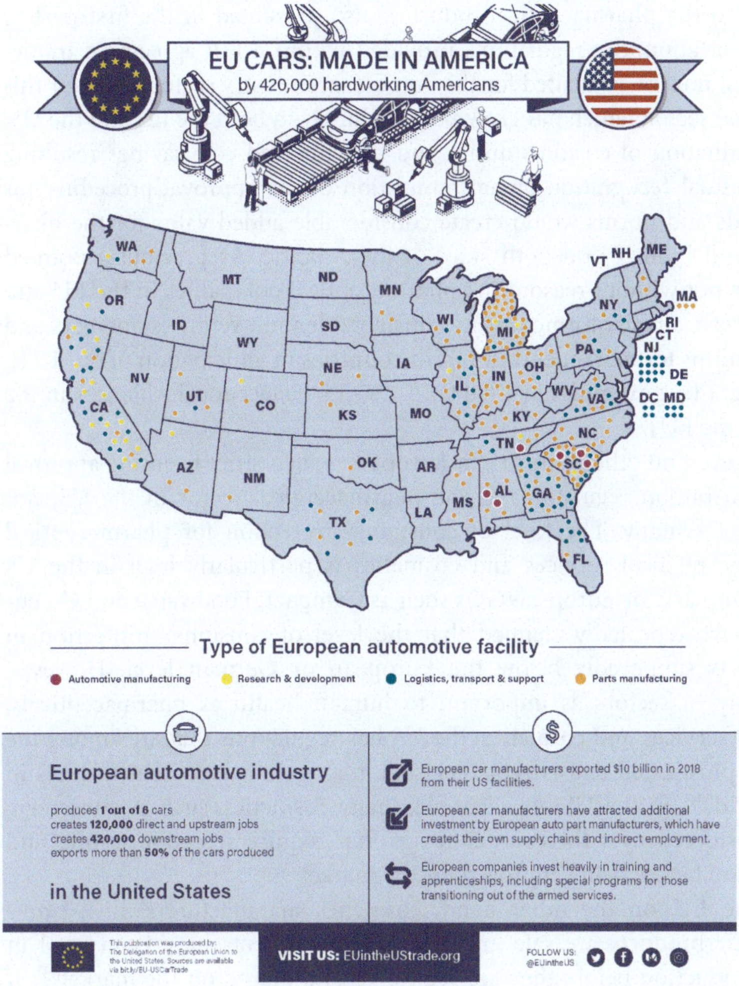

628 Delegation of the European Union to the United States, Washington, DC. February 27, 2020. http://www.euintheustrade.org/wp-content/uploads/2020/03/64346-EU-Car-Infographic_R42.pdf

8.2 Adaptation of Regulations: Pharmaceutical Sector Case Study

Similar to the pharmaceutical industry, also presented in the first part of this dissertation, the regulations provided within TTIP agreement framework will now be presented for this important industry sector. Even for this industrial sector, which has grown astonishingly in both the EU and the US, the elimination of customs duties and the expected cost savings resulting from mutual recognition or harmonization of the approval procedure for standards and norms would create considerable added value for the pharmaceutical industry on both sides of the Atlantic. As previously pointed out, it is not without reason that pharmaceutical companies in the EU and the US have already formed many considerable joint ventures, mergers and corporations for market entry in third countries in anticipation of the TTIP agreement (see examples in Chapter 5.2.6 - Pharmaceutical Alliances in the US and the EU).

Moreover, no other industry in Europe has such strict licensing approval and distribution regulations as the pharmaceutical sector in the US, not even in Germany. The level of consumer protection for pharmaceutical products, medical services and cosmetics is particularly high in the US and exemplary for Europe. NGOs such as Campact, Foodwatch and Greenpeace have repeatedly claimed that the level of consumer protection in the US is supposedly below the European or German level. However, especially in sectors as important to human health as pharmaceuticals, medical services and cosmetics, the US has regulations that are among the most sophisticated and effective legislation as well as enforcement tools in the world[629]. In the US, for example, many cosmetics, such as sunscreen, are considered over-the-counter drugs that require scientific testing and evaluation before being approved for the market[630].

In the EU, on the other hand, cosmetics manufacturers must prove that their products are safe and that safe ingredients have been used in their production before they are registered and placed on the market[631]. If sunscreens contain UV filters, they must also be scientifically tested and evaluated in the EU, just like in the US.

629 European Commission. "TTIP and Regulation: An Overview", page 8. February 10, 2015. https://trade.ec.europa.eu/doclib/docs/2015/february/tradoc_153121.pdf

630 European Commission. "TTIP and Regulation: An Overview", page 8. February 10, 2015. https://trade.ec.europa.eu/doclib/docs/2015/february/tradoc_153121.pdf

631 European Commission. "TTIP and Regulation: An Overview", page 9. February 10, 2015. https://trade.ec.europa.eu/doclib/docs/2015/february/tradoc_153121.pdf

TTIP aims to promote the exchange of scientific assessments of existing and novel UV filters between regulators on both sides, thereby accelerating the approval of products already approved for one market for the other one. This would benefit consumers from a wider range of innovative and safe products[632].

Regulatory cooperation between the EU and the US in the fields of pharmaceuticals and medicine has already led to close confidence-building in the registration and authorization of pharmaceutical products for human use through existing agreements at a high bilateral level in the framework of the "International Conference on Harmonization and Technical Requirements" (ICH)[633].

Therefore, TTIP would strengthen the existing collaborative process in the pharmaceutical sector through the following measures:

a) Establishment of bilateral agreements to facilitate the process of authorization of pharmaceutical products and to optimize agency resources (i.e. with respect for good practice in inspections and exchange of confidential information)

(b) to reinforce additional harmonization of technical requirements in new areas or in areas where improvements in harmonization are needed at identified bilateral or international level (for example, generics, pediatrics, homeopathy, incurable diseases)

(c) strengthening community approaches to scientific advice and quality evaluation in design applications.

The actions in focus should enable greater efficiency and lead to greater concentration on the use of regulatory resources. They should also help to avoid unnecessary duplication and trigger the best possible regulatory exercise, to the benefit of patient safety, better innovation and greater cost efficiency.

632 European Commission. "TTIP and Regulation: An Overview", page 16. February 10, 2015. https://trade.ec.europa.eu/doclib/docs/2015/february/tradoc_153121.pdf

633 European Commission. „EU position on pharmaceutical products", in: *The Transatlantic Trade and Investment Partnership (TTIP) Regulatory Issues,* page 1. May 14, 2014. http://trade.ec.europa.eu/doclib/docs/2014/may/tradoc_152471.pdf

The measures are compatible with the EU medical regulatory framework and with the EU's move towards mutual recognition of GMP[634] inspections, which are already included in agreements with third countries[635].

Regulatory cooperation in the pharmaceutical and medical sector can contribute to the deepening of various areas:

- Audits in Quality Management Systems (e.g. ISO Certification)

These are regular inspections of producers. The purpose is to check whether they meet the requirements for the production of safe products. Mutual recognition of inspections on both sides of the Atlantic would save time and money for both government agencies and the pharmaceutical industry.

- Labelling Systems for Traceability

Labelling systems facilitate the traceability of pharmaceutical and medical devices for the benefit of patients and consumers, for example, via UDI (Unique Device Identifiers) labelling. It standardizes product detection in critical cases and can therefore prove to be effective[636].

- Authorization of the Market Access Procedure for New Pharmaceutical Products

Forms used by companies to request authorization for market access for new products. A common application form would make it much easier for the pharmaceutical industry to apply for such a permit simultaneously in the EU and in the US. In the event of a product recall, identification is of great importance[637].

Even before TTIP or any other agreement coming into force, the US and the EU have been working on compatible labelling systems for pharmaceutical and medical products. This measure stimulates trade and facilitates traceability on both sides of the Atlantic.

634 GMP = Good Manufacturing Practices

635 European Commission. „EU position on pharmaceutical products“, in: *The Transatlantic Trade and Investment Partnership (TTIP) Regulatory Issues,* page 1. May 14, 2014. http://trade.ec.europa.eu/doclib/docs/2014/may/tradoc_152471.pdf

636 European Commission. "TTIP and Regulation: An Overview", page 17. February 10, 2015. https://trade.ec.europa.eu/doclib/docs/2015/february/tradoc_153121.pdf

637 European Commission. "TTIP and Regulation: An Overview", page 17. February 10, 2015. https://trade.ec.europa.eu/doclib/docs/2015/february/tradoc_153121.pdf

8.3 CETA - Achieving the TTIP Objectives before a TTIP Agreement

Opponents as well as supporters of the EU's CETA agreement with Canada have repeatedly claimed that CETA is the blueprint for TTIP[638]. Opponents of trade paid particular attention to CETA, because it has been viewed as a blueprint for the economically even more important TTIP[639]. Negotiations between the EU and Canada in the form of CETA[640] had begun in June 2009. The agreement was signed at the EU-Canada summit in Brussels on October 17 and 18, 2016. Previously, the EU Commission had submitted the final negotiated agreement with 1600 pages to the Council of the European Union on July 5, 2016. The CETA trade agreement has been translated into the 24 official EU languages. The EU Commission initially took the view that only the EU Council and the European Parliament should approve the agreement (exclusive EU competence for trade agreements). However, this legal interpretation of the EU Commission was controversial, after the German Federal Government had forwarded an expert opinion from the European law expert Prof. Dr. Franz C. Meyer, according to which CETA is a "mixed agreement"[641]. This made it clear that the national parliaments of the 28 Member States had to ratify as well, as parts of the agreement affect the competence of the EU Member States. Nevertheless, the agreement is to enter into force provisionally for those parts of CETA that do not fall within the competence of the member states[642].In the meantime, the agreement has been ratified by all 28 parliaments of the EU member states and entered into force.

Organizations within the EU and Canada save tariff duties through the provisional application of CETA, while consumers benefit from falling prices and a wider choice of Canadian products. Companies in Canada and in the EU benefit from the mutual recognition of technical standards. At the same time, EU standards remain at the same level as before the agree-

638 For example, MDR-Info Interview with Bärbel Höhn, Member of the Green Party in the German Bundestag, Member of the Board of Trustees, German Federal Foundation for the Environment, January 7, 2014.

639 Braune, G. „Freibrief für Freihandel mit Kanada", in: *Handelsblatt*, Nr. 183, page 8. September 23, 2014.

640 CETA = Comprehensive Economic and Trade Agreement

641 DIHK-Bericht. „CETA soll ein gemischtes Abkommen werden", Brussels, Nr. 25, page 6. July 11, 2016.

642 EU-Nachrichten. „Nationale Parlamente werden in die Entscheidung eingebunden", Nr. 12, page 4. July 7, 2016.

ment. In addition, CETA created a court system for trade and investment disputes with independent judges, public proceedings and appeals, which is exemplary for the entire world trade system[643]. "The EU-Canada trade agreement is our best and most advanced trade agreement to date, and I would like it to enter into force as soon as possible", stated former EU Commission President Jean Claude Juncker on July 5, 2016 on the occasion of the forwarding of the finalized CETA agreement to the Council of the European Union[644].

Key Provisions in the CETA Agreement

Upon provisional application from October 18, 2016, 99% of duties have been removed. According to the EU Commission, the bilateral trade volume could increase by just under a quarter, i.e. by around 25 billion euros. The EU Commission estimates the potential growth of the EU gross domestic product of up to 11.6 billion euros annually. The EU expects the TTIP agreement to have a far greater effect[645]. Furthermore, the CETA Agreement fully respects Europe's high standards in areas such as food safety, environmental protection and workers' rights. Business opportunities have been opening up for EU and Canadian companies not only in the production of cars, machinery and electrical appliances, but also in services such as maritime transport, telecommunications, engineering or environmental and auditing services. This facilitates the mutual recognition of professional qualifications, giving representatives of the above-mentioned services new opportunities to work on the other side of the Atlantic. European brand names with regional references contained in TTIP are also protected in the CETA agreement for more than 140 food and beverage products. For the Thuringian Rust Bratwurst sausage, for example, or "Budvar beer" as the Czech national drink or the French "Chassis de Dijon", trademark protection against plagiarism and brand piracy now exists in the EU and Canada[646].

643 European Commission. "CETA – an EU free trade deal fit for the 21st century". *Memo,* Strasbourg, July 5, 2016. http://europa.eu/rapid/press-release_MEMO-16-2372_en.htm

644 EU-Nachrichten. „Freihandelsabkommen CETA mit Kanada", Nr. 12/7, page 4. July 2016.

645 Handelsblatt. "Freibrief für Freihandel mit Kanada", Nr. 183. September 23, .2014 and Frankfurter Allgemeine Zeitung, Nr. 89, page 22. April 16, 2016.

646 EU-Nachrichten. „Freihandelsabkommen CETA mit Kanada ", Nr. 12, page 4. July 7, 2016.

However, CETA is the first trade agreement to apply the new UN rules on transparency in state-investor disputes with the UNCITRAL transparency rules. Thus, the provisions on investor protection are at the heart of the CETA Agreement[647]. Only certain issues can be brought before an arbitral tribunal. Only complaints relating to non-discriminatory treatment and investment protection can be brought before an arbitral tribunal under CETA[648]. In CETA, the Investor-State Dispute Settlement (ISDS) is strictly limited to breaches of only a few investment provisions, which lay down principles such as non-discrimination, expropriation for the sole benefit of the general public against appropriate compensation and fair and equitable treatment. Furthermore, an investor must have suffered damage as a result of the above-mentioned infringements[649]. The ISDS scheme cannot be invoked by an investor intending to sue for a breach of another part of the agreement, for example in order to obtain market access in this way.

The CETA agreement also prohibits parallel proceedings: Investors may not simultaneously appeal to national courts and make use of the investor-state dispute settlement mechanism[650]. CETA also contains provisions to prevent fraudulent or manipulative claims. For example, it is forbidden to make an investment or corporate restructuring with the aim of filing a lawsuit (as Philip Morris tried to do in order to sue the Australian government, which had enacted drastic, national laws on tobacco use)[651].

It is clearly stated in CETA that the ISDS rule cannot lead to the repeal of laws or measures adopted by national parliaments of an EU Member State or in Canada. In addition, the ISDS scheme does not allow the imposition

647 European Commission, DG Trade, Article 8.2.9 – Article 8.3.6 in *CETA, Chapter 8.* August 24, 2018. *https://ec.europa.eu/trade/policy/in-focus/ceta/ceta-chapter-by-chapter/*

648 European Commission, DG Trade, Article 13.20 "Dispute Settlement", page 105 and Article 8.29, page 63 in *CETA chapter by chapter.* August 24, 2018. *https://ec.europa.eu/trade/policy/in-focus/ceta/ceta-chapter-by-chapter/*

649 European Commission, DG Trade, Section D, Article 8.9 "Investment protection", page 46 in *CETA chapter by chapter.* August 24, 2018. *https://ec.europa.eu/trade/policy/in-focus/ceta/ceta-chapter-by-chapter/*

650 European Commission, DG Trade, Section D, Article 8.9 "Investment protection", page 47 in *CETA chapter by chapter.* August 24, 2018. *https://ec.europa.eu/trade/policy/in-focus/ceta/ceta-chapter-by-chapter/*

651 European Commission, DG Trade, Section D, Article 8.9 "Investment protection", page 48 in *CETA chapter by chapter.* August 24, 2018. *https://ec.europa.eu/trade/policy/in-focus/ceta/ceta-chapter-by-chapter/*

of fines, as is possible under national law. CETA provides for a system for the swift dismissal of unfounded or abusive claims[652].

The agreement also provides for the establishment of an appellate mechanism[653]. With the modern dispute settlement procedure and the creation of a public investment court with worldwide jurisdiction and transparent rules, the private arbitration tribunals feared by NGOs and the former German Minister of Economics Sigmar Gabriel are off the table in CETA[654].

It is also noteworthy that CETA will open up the Canadian public procurement market, to which SMEs in the EU will also have access[655].

With the modern investor-state dispute settlement system, combined with an international commercial court and appeals body, the European side has developed a pioneering agreement with CETA, thanks to the Canadian concession, which will of course serve as a model for all future trade agreements, especially for TTIP or any other EU-US trade agreement. The former German and French economics ministers Gabriel and Macron have thus also considered their repeated requests for an international trade court in CETA and TTIP to have been fulfilled. This was an essential condition for the acceptance of both trade agreements, especially in the context of the German trade unions' conflicting views on private arbitration courts.

From this point of view, the modern CETA agreement was, of course, the guiding principle and orientation for the TTIP agreement.

---

652 European Commission, DG Trade, Section D, Article 8.9 "Investment protection", page 49 in *CETA chapter by chapter.* August 24, 2018. *https://ec.europa.eu/trade/policy/in-focus/ceta/ceta-chapter-by-chapter/*

653 European Commission, DG Trade, Article 8.2.9 and 8.31, page 63, in *CETA chapter by chapter.* August 24, 2018. *https://ec.europa.eu/trade/policy/in-focus/ceta/ceta-chapter-by-chapter/*

654 Straser, Maritta, Campact-Activist: „US-Firmen können über kanadische Niederlassungen EU-Staaten vor privaten Schiedsgerichten verklagen, sobald sie durch Umwelt- oder Sozialstandards ihre Gewinne geschmälert sehen ", in: *Freibrief für Freihandel mit Kanada*, Handelsblatt, Nr. 183. September 23, 2014. https://www.genios.de/presse-archiv/artikel/HB/20140923/freibrief-fuer-freihandel-mit-kanad/F577387B-6585-484E-BEA1-99592EB4ACA7.html

655 Frankfurter Allgemeine Zeitung. „CETA wird insbesondere auch kleinen Firmen zugute kommen", page 8. July 6, 2016.

8.4 Resistance of Trade Unions in Germany against CETA and TTIP

As explained above, former German Federal Minister Sigmar Gabriel in Germany and former Minister Emmanuel Macron in France, as Economy Ministers responsible for Trade, had always insisted on an International Trade Court during the TTIP and CETA negotiations. In the final negotiations and transmission to the Council of the European Union, the International Commercial Court has thus actually become an integral part of the CETA agreement instead of private arbitration courts. In 2016, the trade unions in Germany had also always emphasized that they would support CETA and TTIP if the International Trade Court is included with an appeals body. European standards must not be weakened in either agreement, nor must ILO workers' rights, consumer and environmental protection. However, all this is ensured in CETA, as already explained[656].

Nevertheless, the trade unions in Germany and France did not stand by their promises and unexpectedly announced a major demonstration against CETA together with 50 NGO organizations with a total of 250,000 participants on September 17, 2016 in Berlin, Germany[657]. No wonder that former German Federal Minister of Economics Gabriel, who wanted CETA to be implemented, declared TTIP to have "failed" as the head of the German Social Democratic Party with his affinity to the trade unions[658]. With this claim, he tried to distract from CETA and to make the unions change their minds in favor of CETA[659]. With the major demonstration on September 17, 2016, Germany was in the spotlight once again as the main opponent in the EU of 28 Member States after the big demonstration on October 10, 2015 the year before with 1 million participants. This opposition in a country in the middle of Europe where one in three jobs and two thirds of exports are generated due to the EU internal market. TTIP and CETA should therefore

656 On the sidelines of the G-20 Summit in Hangzhou, China, from September 3-4, 2016, European Commission President Juncker spoke with Canada's Prime Minister Justin Trudeau about CETA, which Juncker described as "the best and most advanced agreement the EU has ever negotiated". In *EU-Aktuell Newsletter.* September 9, 2016.

657 Handelsblatt. „Die Gewerkschaften machen gegen das Handelsabkommen CETA mobil ", Nr. 163, page 6. August 24, 2016.

658 German Federal Economics Minister Sigmar Gabriel's speech during the occasion of the "Open Day" of the German Federal Government within the framework of a Press conference on Sunday, August 28, 2016, in Berlin, Germany.

659 Frankfurter Allgemeine. „Gabriel verärgert mit TTIP-Skepsis Brüssel und Berlin", Nr. 202, page 15. August 30, 2016.

be particularly close to Germany's interest as the largest exporting nation in Europe.

The EU Commission and Michael Froman, US chief negotiator for TTIP in 2016, reacted with unusual indignation emphasizing that the negotiations were still on the right track and that they saw the end of 2016 as a real opportunity to finalize the agreement[660].

During the EU summit at the end of the Dutch Presidency on June 22, 2016, Jean-Claude Juncker, President of the European Commission, had raised the question of whether all EU partners were in agreement with the objective of concluding negotiations by the end of 2016. The 28 heads of government voted unanimously in favor of the deal conclusion by the end of 2016. Juncker invited the trade ministers to Bratislava from September 22-23, 2016 on the occasion of the Slovak Presidency of the Council, where EU Commissioner Cecilia Malmström took stock of the negotiations so far. The gaps were still evident in the area of public procurement due to the "Buy America" rule, as well as in the area of agricultural tariffs, investment protection and the public-law commercial court with an appellate body instead of private courts. On the other hand, good progress had been made in protecting "regional products"[661].

The criticism on the part of the business associations of the federal government in Germany and in particular of Federal Minister Sigmar Gabriel for his assertion that TTIP had failed was fierce against the background of the oppressive extent of the resistance of the trade unions and non-governmental organizations (NGOs). Ulrich Grillo, President of the Federation of German Industry, accused Gabriel of "shirking his responsibilities for TTIP"[662]. Eric Schweitzer, President of the Association of German Chambers of Industry and Commerce (DIHK) was stated: "Especially now, we must not slack in our efforts to seriously continue the negotiations. Negotiations with such a confident partner as the US are indeed a challenge. Against the background of increasing protectionism worldwide, but also of unwavered exports, it would be an important signal to conclude an agreement based on common values and interests"[663].

---

660 Frankfurter Allgemeine Zeitung. „EU und Amerika halten an TTIP-Zeitplan fest", Nr. 164, page 4. July 16, 2016.

661 Katsack, Hendrik: „Durchbruch im Streit um Investorenschutz", in: *Frankfurter Allgemeine Zeitung.* May 3, 2016.

662 Handelsblatt. „Koalitionskrach um Freihandel", Nr. 154, page 8. August 11, 2016.

663 Frankfurter Allgemeine Zeitung. „Vieles offen, wenig klar", *TTIP,* Nr. 186, page 21. August 11, 2016.

In a pugnacious guest commentary in the Handelsblatt, the president of German industry expressed "deep disappointment" at the German government's lack of public relations work and advocacy on free trade agreements in general and on CETA and TTIP in particular: "This is about stating clearly why TTIP and CETA are useful and necessary... The government must take a much clearer stand for free trade. Germany, its companies and its workers benefit enormously from free trade as well as from trade and investment agreements. The understanding of why we trade and how prosperity is created is dwindling immensely. There are many good reasons to support agreements such as TTIP and CETA"[664].

Matthias Wissmann, President of the Association of the Automotive Industry in Germany, also made that clear in a well-received article in the Frankfurter Allgemeine Zeitung titled "A TTIP stop does not solve questions about the future ":"Those who just hold up the stop sign are partly responsible for the consequences that a failure of the negotiations could entail. The consequences will far exceed the cost of the current custom duties. For Europe, the scope for trade policy would become narrower. The chance of being actively involved in shaping globalization would be reduced. With TTIP and CETA similar mistakes as with Brexit must not be made: "In one case, completely exaggerated hopes were aroused only to be bitterly disappointed; in the other case, fears were deliberately stirred up instead of citing facts and pointing out opportunities". His closing sentence ends with a clear cue to politicians in a trade-politically significant position: "Brexit and TTIP reflect two sides of one realization: Anyone who flees from complex questions about the future to only simple answers flees from political responsibility in "representative democracy"[665].

According to Germany's economic research institutes, which were asked to comment on CETA and TTIP in a survey organized by the Ifo Institute in Munich in cooperation with the Frankfurter Allgemeine Zeitung, 72 percent of the 124 participating professors also supported CETA and 66 percent supported the TTIP free trade agreement. More than half of the economics professors fear negative impact on the German economy over the medium term as well as a lasting weakening of political weight and in-

664 Grillo, Ulrich: „Vereinfacher und Angstmacher geben den Ton an", in *Handelsblatt* Nr. 144, page 5. July 25, 2016.

665 Wissmann, Matthias: „Ein TTIP-Stopp löst keine Zukunftsfragen", in: *Frankfurter Allgemeine Zeitung*, Nr. 196, page 20. August 23, 2016.

fluence of the EU in the event of a failure of CETA and TTIP[666]. Germany thrives on international trade, which is why a failure of TTIP and CETA would do great harm to the country. A conclusion of both agreements would promote growth in Germany, according to eighty percent of respondents[667].

A German association called "More Democracy" filed a complaint against the CETA Agreement with the Federal Constitutional Court in Karlsruhe, Germany, much to the distain of trade business associations, the federal government and the chambers of industry and commerce. Ralf-Uwe Beck, spokesman for the federal board of directors of the association, had 60 boxes of signature authorizations transported to the Federal Constitutional Court in Karlsruhe by truck in order to provide public support for the filed lawsuit. "The constitutional judges should examine whether CETA as a whole and a provisional application after approval by the Council of the EU and the European Parliament is compatible with the German Basic Law", Ralf-Uwe Beck justified his signature campaign[668]. The associations "More Democracy", "Foodwatch" and "Compact" had entered into an "action alliance" in the context of the complaint before the German Federal Constitutional Court. They clash with the "expert committees" for determining standards and approval procedures, for example in the pharmaceutical and automotive sectors, and with the "lack of Bundestag involvement"[669]. In doing so, the plaintiffs overlook the fact that for standard and certification processes "experts", i.e. technicians, engineers from certification institutions in Canada and Europe - e.g. from the German TÜV (vehicle inspection) - must participate rather than parliamentarians or representatives of associations. All 28 member states, i.e. governments elected by the people, gave the EU Commission, responsible for foreign trade, a mandate for the CETA and TTIP negotiations at the beginning of the negotiations. Therefore, the agreement can enter into force provisionally, after approval by the democratically legitimate Council of the European Union and the European

666 Frankfurter Allgemeine Zeitung. „Professoren für transatlantische Handelsabkommen", Nr. 173, page 15. July 2, 2015.

667 Handelsblatt. „Freihandelspakt TTIP: Wirtschaft Kontra Gabriel", Nr. 167, page 9. August 30, 2016.

668 Thüringer Allgemeine. „125.000 Menschen unterstützen Verfassungsbeschwere gegen CETA", page 2. August 31, 2016.

669 Frankfurter Allgemeine Zeitung. „Scharfe Kritik an Gabriel wegen Äußerungen zu TTIP", Nr. 204, page 2. September 1, 2016.

Parliament[670]. It goes without saying that the 28 national parliaments are involved in the ratification process in the case of a "mixed agreement" such as CETA and submit their opinions or requests for amendments, including the German Bundestag.

In fact, the responsible economic committee of the German Bundestag discussed CETA in a public session on September 5, 2016. Experts from the Federation of German Industries (BDI), the Association of German Chambers of Industry and Commerce (DIHK) as supporters of the agreement and the Federation for Environmental Protection and Nature Conservation (BUND) as opponents were also present. While BDI and DIHK praised CETA as a very modern trade agreement, BUND criticized the "separate rights of action with which they can sue governments by passing European and national legal proceedings"[671]. The opposition parties represented in the German Bundestag, the "Left" Party and the "Green" Party, requested that CETA not be provisionally entered into force after approval by the EU Council and the European Parliament. The large majority of CDU and SPD acknowledged the agreement as very successful and approved CETA by a majority in the economic committee. The committee's recommendation for approval is decisive for the Bundestag plenary.

8.5 NAFTA, TTP and TTIP: Skepticism about Free Trade reaches the US

The example of Sigmar Gabriel as German Minister for Economic Affairs and advocate of TTIP and his sudden change to the camp of the opponents shows once again the dependence of members of government in Europe and the US on the "zeitgeist", on the mood of the population. The mood has turned on both sides of the Atlantic, it has become protectionist. The latent anti-stance against free trade as "a project of the elites for the elites"[672] not only in the EU, above all in Germany, but also in the US election campaign

670 Das Parliament. „TTIP paradox: Trotz der offensichtlichen Vorteile hat sich bei den Deutschen ein tiefes Misstrauen festgesetzt", Nr. 35/36, page 13. August 29, 2016.

671 Frankfurter Allgemeine Zeitung. „Über CETA wird nur ein bisschen gestritten", Nr. 207, page 21. September 5, 2016.

672 Münchrath, Jens: „Die Antiglobalisierung ", in: *Handelsblatt,* Nr. 168, page 14. August 31, 2016.

for the White House between Donald Trump (Republican) and Hillary Clinton (Democrat) was given wings[673].

Donald Trump, in particular, quickly understood that free trade was anything but popular among the population, and adapted to the mood, although the Republican party in the Senate and House of Representatives in particular had supported free trade for decades. Even the authorization of President Obama, combined with the granting of the TTIP negotiating mandate, would not have been conceivable without Republicans. Also, Hillary Clinton, as the actual supporter of free trade, had no other choice but to reject proposed trade agreements, similar to Bernie Sanders, her opponent in the bidding process for the highest office in the US. Trump: "We want control back. Free trade agreements are "the number one enemy of the state"[674]. In view of negative experiences with the NAFTA agreement, which was concluded in 1993 under President Bill Clinton, Trump blamed the stagnating average income of the US middle class on the expansion of free trade. Trump also attributed the growing gap between rich and poor in the US to NAFTA. Two thirds of US citizens are convinced that the country is moving in the wrong direction with its policy of trade liberalization[675].

More than half of US citizens believe that market opening increases the pressure on domestic wages and that competitive pressures shift more and more jobs abroad[676].

With the liberation of global capital through various trade and investment protection agreements, the battle for the economic pie is increasingly transnational," notes Jeff Faux, the founder of Economic Policy (EPI) in Washington[677]. This tendency towards skepticism about free trade in the

673 Ziegler, Jean. *Warum wir die kannibalische Weltordnung stürzen müssen: Das Versagen der Eliten*, page 181. Penguin Verlag Zürich 2016.

674 Kafsack, Hendrik: „Handelsunfähig ", in: *Frankfurter Allgemeine Zeitung*, Nr. 171, page 15. July 25, 2016. https://www.faz.net/aktuell/wirtschaft/ttip-und-freihandel/ttip-ceta-freihandels-befuehrwoerter-muessen-strategie-aendern-14355632.html

675 Frankenberger, Klaus-Dieter: „Pendelschlag", in: *Frankfurter Allgemeine Zeitung*, Nr. 190, page 15. August 16, 2016.

676 Kafsack, Hendrik: „Handelsunfähig ", in: *Frankfurter Allgemeine Zeitung*, Nr. 171, page 15. July 25, 2016. https://www.faz.net/aktuell/wirtschaft/ttip-und-freihandel/ttip-ceta-freihandels-befuehrwoerter-muessen-strategie-aendern-14355632.htm

677 Faux, Jeff: „Das abgekartete Spiel fliegt auf ", in: *Handelsblatt* Nr. 160, page 64. August 19. /20. /21., 2016 (Guest Commentary).

US did not develop overnight.[678] Loss of confidence in fair economic policy is deeply rooted due to the banking crash of 2008/2009 and the resulting pattern for the current free trade skepticism: "Large structures liquidate the small ones. Events such as the global financial crisis, the disappearance of banks and credit unions as well as the destruction of capital driven by sheer greed have given citizens the feeling that they are living in an age in which "one certainty after another is sweeping away"[679].

It is widely known that, according to the British economist David Ricardo, all market systems create economic classes[680]. Thus, it is becoming increasingly clear to the average US citizen that even the expansion of trade agreements rarely serves them.

Jeff Faux of the EPI in Washington therefore argues that a mobile group of international investors and billions of working people should no longer be allowed to face each other head-on and think in "outdated competitive patterns". Rather, in his opinion, the world needs a new model of economic integration in which "the supposed enemy of American workers are no longer Mexican or Chinese workers"[681], as Trump had repeatedly instilled in his listeners during his campaign speeches. "Even if trade liberalization leads to higher overall output production, large population groups could still end up worse off'[682].

8.6 Free Trade versus Protectionism, Liberal World Order versus Nation-State Isolation: Rethinking Globalization

In Europe, the argumentation of TTIP and CETA opponents against free trade is generally similar among NGOs such as Campac, Attac, Greenpeace and Foodwatch: Grillo ("cinque stelle", Italian political party – Five Star

678 Stiglitz, Joseph. "Globalization of Trade". *The Price of Inequality: How Today's Divided Society Endangers Our Future.* New York: W.W. Norton & Company, 2012, pages 100-105.

679 Ingendaay, Paul: „Filmreife Ermächtigung", in: *Frankfurter Allgemeine Zeitung,* Nr. 204, page 9. September 1, 2016.

680 Ricardo, David. *Über die Grundsätze der Politischen Ökonomie und der Besteuerung,* Metropolis-Verlag, Marburg 2006, Chapter 20/21, pages 231-245.

681 Faux, Jeff: „Das abgekartete Spiel fliegt auf ", in: *Handelsblatt* Nr. 160, page 64. August 19. /20. /21., 2016 (Guest Commentary).

682 Stiglitz, Joseph. "Globalization of Trade". *The Price of Inequality: How Today's Divided Society Endangers Our Future.* New York: W.W. Norton & Company, 2012, page 101.

Movement), Le Pen, Kaczynski, Wilders, Strache, Johnson - they all denounce free trade as a disaster for citizens, the middle class and the working population[683]. Above all, the relocation of jobs to low-wage countries and the substitution of jobs by automation, combined with the "outrageous greed" of several "global players" to escape the social costs of government through tax evasion, is received with rage and horror by citizens of all stripes and destroys confidence in the democratic constitutional state, which is watching these activities powerlessly, as in Ireland, for example[684]. A blatant example of such audacity has occurred as follows: There, Milton Friedmann's fiction of a utopian island state that obeys only globalization and tolerates no "bureaucratic authorities" became reality. Apple paid a tiny 0.005 percent tax on profits in 2014 to the Republic of Ireland[685]. Compared to EUR 13 billion, i.e. only EUR 15 000 per EUR 1 million of corporation tax paid by the group. EU Commissioner Margreth Vestager added that Apple as a company "is escaping its social responsibility"[686]. The Commissioner called on the Executive Committee to return this amount to the Republic of Ireland. After all, this blatant example of tax evasion was an incentive for the 28 European finance ministers of the EU to quickly close the tax evasion loopholes for corporations[687]. Apple paid the outstanding taxes on profits into a blocked account that is not accessible to anyone until the pending lawsuit before the European Court of Justice (ECJ) has clarified the legal position for repayment to one or more EU member states[688]. After all, the EU Commission has been drawing up a "blacklist of uncooperative tax havens" on the urgent problem of tax justice[689]. The list was adopted by the EU Council of Finance Ministers in 2017. The EU Commission also presented the corporate tax base to the Council and Parliament in 2017

683 Frankenberger, Klaus-Dieter: „Pendelschlag", in: *Frankfurter Allgemeine Zeitung*, Nr. 190, page 15. August 16, 2016.

684 Bender, Justus: „Freie Bürger, zarte Seelen", in: *Frankfurter Allgemeine Zeitung*, Nr. 186, page 19. August 11, 2016.

685 Riecke, Torsten: „Apple macht noch keinen Staat", in *Handelsblatt*, Nr. 177, page 28. September 13, 2016.

686 Handelsblatt. „EU-Finanzministertreffen und der Kampf um Apples Steuermilliarden", Nr. 176, page 8. September 12, 2016.

687 Ingendaay, Paul: „Filmreife Ermächtigung", in: *Frankfurter Allgemeine Zeitung*, Nr. 204, page 9. September 1, 2016.

688 Handelsblatt. „EU-Finanzministertreffen und der Kampf um Apples Steuermilliarden", Nr. 176, page 28. September 12, 2016.

689 Handelsblatt. „EU-Finanzministertreffen und der Kampf um Apples Steuermilliarden", Nr. 176, page 28. September 12, 2016.

on the "Common Consolidated Corporate TaxBase" (CCCTB). There is no doubt that corporations, as actors in free trade, cannot and must not evade taxation in their head office and sub-seat host countries. After all, tax justice is one of the key points in regaining the confidence of citizens in free trade. Ultimately, the UK Bexit referendum was also "driven by a sentiment not only against Brussels, but also against globalization and corporate tax evasion[690].

8.7 The EU in Discovery Crisis: Ways Out of the Free Trade Acceptance Trap

In addition to dissolving of tax havens and correcting the course of a misguided tax policy within the EU, dumping prices, especially in the steel and textile sectors, are high on the international agenda. As previously pointed out, China does not pursue a "fair trade" policy and subsidizes over capacities with high financial input, flooding the international markets at rock-bottom prices, particularly in the Mercosur and Pacific Alliance countries of Central and Latin America. Within the GATT framework, there are opportunities to introduce quotas, which cannot be exceeded, similar to those introduced when the European Coal and Steel Community (ECSC) was founded in 1963. In addition to fiscal justice and anti-dumping measures by the EU, the Member States of the EU and the US are called upon to reduce the sharp income gap by correcting the balance with the help of social policy. Just and equitable welfare systems are the right answers to the challenges posed by free trade, not the populist calls to raise borders and operate autonomously. Free trade, in particular, has brought a great deal of growth, more added value and growing employment to Europe, with its own large internal market of 500 million consumers. At the same time, according to Guntram Wolff, Director of the Brussels-based think tank Bruegel, free trade also means tough competition: Wages have been rising less sharply or stagnating for part of the population, while others

690 Wolff, Guntram: „Es profitieren alle Länder“, in: *Handelsblatt*, Nr. 125, page 7. July 1/2/3, 2016.

have even been losing their jobs[691]. In addition, a speed of change has been emerging that overwhelms some people[692].

The bottom line, however, is that free trade is positive for the economy and society, according to Bruegel Director Wolff. This is often taken for granted by citizens, while the disadvantages are particularly addressed in the media, especially in the US and the EU[693].

A debate on the reform of the international economic order within the framework of GATT and WTO is therefore overdue. Globalization must indeed be "re-thought"[694], as demanded by Handelsblatt authors Torsten Riecke and Jens Münchrath, and incidentally also by Jeremy Riffkin with his thesis for more "participatory economy"[695] (collaborative economy) in his book "The 3rd Industrial Reform". Nobel Prize winner Joseph Stiglitz is also among the admonishers and calls for repairs to the international economic order[696]. Last but not least, President Clemens Fuest of the Munich Ifo Institute for Economic Research and Marcel Fratzscher, Director of the German Institute for Economic Research (DIW), Berlin[697].

Free trade, open borders, international division of labor, multilateral treaties and standards have long been accepted by most countries as a golden path to prosperity and peace[698]. As previously pointed out, this consensus has been shattered in large parts of the population in the EU and in the US, partly because the income of many workers have been stagnating, jobs have been migrated abroad, the proportion of foreigners in the populations of the US and the EU has been rising noticeably, financial crisis have been occurring in cities in the Ruhr area in Germany, for example,

691 Wolff, Guntram: „Es profitieren alle Länder", in: *Handelsblatt*, Nr. 125, page 7. July 1/2/3, 2016.

692 Hagelueken, Alexander. "Der Abstieg der Mittelschicht", in: *Das gespaltene Land: Wie Ungleichheit unsere Gesellschaft zerstoert und was die Politik aendern muss*, Knaur Verlag: Muenchen, 2017, pages 112-119.

693 Wolff, Guntram: „Es profitieren alle Länder", in: *Handelsblatt*, Nr. 125, page 7. July 1/2/3, 2016.

694 Riecke, Torsten and Münchrath, Jens: „Volle Kraft zurück: Globalisierung neu denken", in: *Handelsblatt*, Nr. 160, pages 40-41. August 19/20/21, 2016.

695 Riffkin, Jeremy: *Die 3. Industrielle Revolution*, Campus Verlag: Frankfurt/M. 2013, pages 145-146.

696 Stiglitz, Joseph: „Reform oder Scheidung", in: *Handelsblatt*, Nr. 177, page 48. September 13, 2016.

697 Fratzscher, Marcel: „Globalisierung als Sündenbock in: „Globalisierung neu denken", *Handelsblatt*, Nr. 160, page 43. August 19/20/21, 2016.

698 Juncker Jean-Claude: „Rede zur Lage der Union 2016: Hin zu einem besseren Europa", *European Commmission*, page 15.

but also in England, in the US, southern Italy, Romania, Spain and Greece. In addition, open borders have been enabling terrorist attacks in Brussels, Paris, Würzburg, Ansbach and Madrid. Resistance to the global economic and social order is further increased by the dramatic events of the flood of migrants from Syria to the EU in 2015 and from Latin America to the US during recent years.

In contrast to the US, after the great financial crisis in 2008/ 2009, within the EU, it has not been possible to completely overcome the economic stagnation, the dramatic development on the labor market with youth unemployment of 40 to 50 percent in Spain, Portugal, Greece and southern Italy, especially in southern Europe. The decline in the investment ratio in relation to gross domestic product was particularly dramatic in the southern euro zone: It fell from 21.7 percent in 2007 to 14 percent in 2014.

In the United Kingdom, this decline was similarly marked from 15.9 percent in 2007 to 11 percent in 2012, only to rise again slightly to 13 percent by 2014. This investment ratio, even in Germany, at just 17.5 percent below the average normal 19-21 percent, is blamed for the moderate to poor economic situation and high unemployment rate in the EU[699]. In addition, the impact of austerity programs on economic growth and employment has been largely underestimated. Since 2013, the International Monetary Fund and the OECD have increasingly drawn attention to this danger in the media. The investments in innovation and research provided for in the ERDF, i.e. the European Regional Development Fund 2014 - 2020 and the EU-HORIZON Program 2014 - 2020 for research and development, as well as the boost provided by cluster management in the EU programs, have also made only slow progress in the EU economies, as is clearly shown by the low level of funds drawn down by the end of 2016 of 30 to 40 percent[700].

After all, according to Joseph Stieglitz, Nobel Prize winner and professor of economics at Columbia University, one of the roots of the EU's loss of acceptance among its citizens lies in the euro currency, which has been flawed from the outset and, in his view, lost the exchange rate as its most important adjustment mechanism when it was introduced. Because countries like

699 Kern, Christian, Bundeskanzler der Republik Österreich: „Europa muss wieder gerecht werden", in: Serie: „Zerfällt Europa?", Nr. 15, *Frankfurter Allgemeine Zeitung*, Nr. 213, page 6. September 12, 2016.

700 According to information provided via telephone September 15, 2016 by the Thuringia Aufbaubank as ERDF-Manager for the EU funding period in Thuringia 2014-2020.

Spain, Portugal and Greece have accumulated budget deficits as a result of the banking crisis and bank bailouts, their ability to reduce debt and invest in the future has been severely limited. In fact, these countries would have to be temporarily freed from the fixed exchange rate in the euro zone in order to be able to steer economic development towards growth by means of floating exchange rate adjustments[701]. Because Germany rejects averaging the interest burden on government bonds with the help of Eurobonds, but due to the euro currency clearly benefits of the balance of trade in the single European market, the economically weaker countries have little chance of becoming competitive with their products[702]. After all, in a euro currency zone and in the European Single Market, Germany's enormous trade surpluses at fixed exchange rates are the losses of the economically weaker EU member states on the shadow side of the EU.

All this contributes to a paradoxical constellation in that Germany nolens volens contributes to a disruption of the European structure through these contradictions in the monetary union and its economic dominance in the internal market[703]. But the disintegration of the euro zone would also be a death sentence for the EU. Guy Verhofstadt: "The Euro represents three quarters of the EU GDP. If the Euro falls, the Union will also fall. In short, it is the future of Europe itself that is at stake here."[704]

At the end of 2016, the EU was thus, at least in part, in an "existential crisis", as the President of the EU Commission put it to the European Parliament in his speech "The State of the European Union" in Strasbourg on September 14, 2016 [705]. He stated that never before had he seen so much division and so little public spirit within the European Union[706]. However, in his speech to the European Parliament, Jean-Claude Juncker presented

701 Stiglitz, Joseph: „Reform oder Scheidung", in: *Handelsblatt*, Nr. 177, page 48. September 13, 2016.

702 According to the German Federal Statistical Office, the foreign trade surplus for Germany in 2015 was 247.88 billion euros with a record export volume worth 1195.935 billion euros (imports: 948,053 billion euros). See here: Fischer World Almanac 2017, Fischer-Verlag Frankfurt/M., p. 620.

703 Diner, Dan, Hebrew University of Jerusalem: „Sind wir wieder im 19. Jahrhundert? ", Opening Speech of „M 100-Sanssouci-Colloquium" on the topic "War and Peace" in Potsdam, *Frankfurter Allgemeine Zeitung*, Nr. 216, page 11. September 15, 2016.

704 Guy Verhofstadt. *Fuer Europa! Ein Manifest.* Hanser Verlag: Muenchen, 2012, page 13.

705 Frankfurter Allgemeine Zeitung. „Existentielle Krise, aber nicht bedroht", Nr. 216, page 2. September 15, 2016.

706 Handelsblatt. „Wider den Europa-Frust: EU-Kommissionschef Juncker verteidigt die europäische Idee", Nr. 179, page 12. September 15, 2016.

a number of possible solutions to the MEPs, which could make this not optimally positioned Europe fit for the future again and make it a serious player in world politics[707]. In the following, the planned measures of the European Commission and further options will be presented by renowned representatives from science and industry. After all, even a well-negotiated free trade agreement with the US is worth little if its partner is weakening Europe and cannot breathe life into it for its own benefit in future.

8.8 Prospects for Solutions regarding Greater Integration and the EU's Capacity for Action as a Trading Partner with Global Players

Jean-Claude Juncker's speech "on the State of the European Union" on September 14, 2016 can be viewed as "historic". The President of the European Commission addressed numerous points of interest to EU citizens. He initiated a change of course in order to make the EU once again a project of enlightenment, to make it relevant to the people. His proposals, which the European Commission also wants to implement step by step with the help of the Council of the EU and the European Parliament, were designed to put the Union on a new path to drive more innovation, value creation and stimulate employment. The following EU projects were supposed to be either set in motion or existing programs and measures were supposed to be stepped up in response to the crisis:

- Extension of the European Investment Fund until 2020 combined with an increase to EUR 630 billion, twice as much as previously planned
- Comprehensive expansion of WLAN Internet access and 5G network by 2025 to create around 2 million jobs[708]
- Creation of an Africa fund with 44 billion euros (investment plan for Africa) to transform the migration option into a prospect of staying in their countries, especially for young people (complementing EU development aid with the 79 ACP countries: Africa-Caribbean-Pacific)
- This fund is of great importance considering that Africa and the Arab countries located there have the lowest gross domestic product per capita

707 European Parliament. "From jobs to migration: the European Commission's 10 priorities". *News.* September 4, 2015.

708 Jean-Claude Juncker. "State of the Union 2016". *Speech,* page 13. September 14, 2016. https://op.europa.eu/en/publication-detail/-/publication/c9ff4ff6-9a81-11e6-9bca-01aa75ed71a1/language-en/format-PDF/source-30945725

in the world[709]. Also, in the Muslim-influenced belt of North and East Africa, from Morocco to Somalia, 400 million people are projected to attempt to migrate to the EU in the next 20 years, due to the enormous birth surplus, the lack of prospects there and the lowest level of education worldwide, according to the PISA International Study 2015

- More unity and common ground instead of wrangling over competences and rivalries in the EU of 28 Member States in order to be taken seriously as a future trading partner of the United States. "Only then will Europe be more than the sum of its parts"[710].
- Above all, the preservation of peace in Europe, which has already been lasting for 75 years, for wars and conflicts are poison for world trade and development through trade, combined with a flourishing job market world.
- Peace has included values such as freedom, democracy and the rule of law and the four fundamental freedoms of the European Single Market since 1992 (free movement of goods and services, free movement of people and free movement of capital).
- Trade with its neighbors outside Europe is and must remain essential for the EU. EU trade agreements have already been concluded with 140 countries around the world, because free trade also means more jobs through more orders from third countries. "Every billion euros earned in exports creates 14000 new jobs across the EU. More than 30 million jobs, or one in seven jobs in the EU, now depend on exports to third countries" (as of 2016)[711].
- Therefore, the EU-Canada Free Trade Agreement (CETA), the best and most progressive agreement the EU has negotiated since its inception in 1957, cannot be overstated in its role as a model for the world (such as provision of public services, labor rights, environmental protection,

709 Sigmar, Gabriel. „Für eine internationale Teilhabe-Gesellschaft“, Gastbeitrag in: *Handelsblatt,* Nr. 160, page 49. August 19/20/21, 2016.

710 Jean-Claude Juncker. “State of the Union 2016”. *Speech,* page 8. September 14, 2016. https://op.europa.eu/en/publication-detail/-/publication/c9ff4ff6-9a81-11e6-9bca-01aa75ed71a1/language-en/format-PDF/source-30945725

711 Jean-Claude Juncker. “State of the Union 2016”. *Speech,* page 10. September 14, 2016. https://op.europa.eu/en/publication-detail/-/publication/c9ff4ff6-9a81-11e6-9bca-01aa75ed71a1/language-en/format-PDF/source-30945725

improved investment jurisdiction mechanisms with the highest possible degree of independence)[712]

- Strictly prohibiting tax evasion and enforcement of tax justice, as well as protection against market abuse by cartels; taxes must be paid where profits are generated, regardless of how large or small the companies are. Europe must insist on this tax fairness, because it "is the social side of competition law"[713]
- Development of European data protection on the basis of the "European Data Protection Regulation" adopted by the European Council and European Parliament in May 2016 - a very strict European law that applies to all companies in the 28 member states, "wherever they are based and whenever data is processed"[714].
- The digital European single market also includes the development of wireless Internet access in the most important public places of European cities and municipalities, as is exemplary in Estonia, as well as a law for a "European Travel Information System" so that "we know who is travelling to Europe before he or she arrives"[715].
- Establishment of a capital market union, after the banking union and financial market stabilization, as the second pillar of corporate financing alongside bank loans. The turmoil surrounding the lack of equity capital base of credit institutions in the years before and after the 2008/2009 banking crisis urgently requires a resilient financial system with easier and more diversified access to finance, including micro-credits and start-up financing. In many cases, business start-ups did not receive seed capital from credit institutions in the early-stage phase and often also not in the growth phase of the founding companies. In addition to business

712 European Commission. „Brücken statt Mauern – Malmström und Freeland betonen Bedeutung von CETA ". September 19, 2016. https://ec.europa.eu/germany/news/„brücken-statt-mauern"---malmström-und-freeland-betonen-bedeutung-von-ceta-und-wollen-auf_de

713 Jean-Claude Juncker. "State of the Union 2016". *Speech,* page 11. September 14, 2016. https://op.europa.eu/en/publication-detail/-/publication/c9ff4ff6-9a81-11e6-9bca-01aa75ed71a1/language-en/format-PDF/source-30945725

714 Negt, Oskar: "The tax state is dying, large companies are proud of paying no more taxes or very little. Although they make intensive use of the infrastructure, the education system and transport routes, they pay less and less for the community", in: *Gesellschafts-Entwurf-Europa*, Steidl-Verlag Göttingen, 2012, p. 66.

715 Jean-Claude Juncker. "State of the Union 2016". *Speech,* page 18. September 14, 2016. https://op.europa.eu/en/publication-detail/-/publication/c9ff4ff6-9a81-11e6-9bca-01aa75ed71a1/language-en/format-PDF/source-30945725

angels, the Capital Market Union is intended to mobilize EUR 100 billion in funding to provide venture capital and market-based financing, and to support start-ups in addition to the EUR 500 billion from the EFSI by 2020 (EUR 630 billion by 2022) to facilitate their launch[716]. This could provide the foundation for implementing innovations to create new businesses for the next generation. It must be clearly seen that many companies in Europe will disappear from the scene, because they can no longer find a successor.

- The mobilization of additional investment sums with the help of the Capital Market Union, as announced by the President of the EU Commission, is of high priority in order to develop a genuine start-up culture, including a 2nd and 3rd chance, like in the US. It is not appropriate, for example, that in the event of a first insolvency, start-up entrepreneurs in Germany cannot obtain bank loans on the capital market for six years and, after the creditors' repayment period has expired after six years, they still remain on the so-called "Schufalist" of credit institutions for three years with a bad credit report rating. This means that they are blocked for a second start-up attempt for almost a decade of their lives and are artificially kept out of the market because the credit institutions do not grant them any credit for nine years. Steve Jobs, the founder of Apple, and Marc Zuckerberg, the founder of Facebook, had both filed for bankrupt after their first start-up attempt. Today they are billionaires after the second start-up attempt. In Germany, such a thing would never have been possible after a first insolvency[717].
- In 2017, the EU Erasmus program was thirty years old. Since its inception, five million students in Europe, more than 380,000 teachers and 100,000 other young people have been networked within the European Voluntary Service. Thus, Erasmus brings together 220,000 young people and youth workers in Europe every year. This EU initiative is a unique success story and must be extended to vocational training[718]. These ex-

---

716 Jean-Claude Juncker. "State of the Union 2016". *Speech,* page 15. September 14, 2016. https://op.europa.eu/en/publication-detail/-/publication/c9ff4ff6-9a81-11e6-9bca-01aa75ed71a1/language-en/format-PDF/source-30945725

717 Porschen, Hubertus: „Wo sind die Gründer?“, in: *Frankfurter Allgemeine Zeitung,* Nr. 222, page 15. September 22, 2016. (Hubertus Porschen Hubertus is Federal Chairman of the Association of Young Entrepreneurs in Germany)

718 Jean-Claude Juncker. "State of the Union 2016". *Speech,* page 16. September 14, 2016. https://op.europa.eu/en/publication-detail/-/publication/c9ff4ff6-9a81-11e6-9bca-01aa75ed71a1/language-en/format-PDF/source-30945725

changes and connections help young people to understand each other better, build Europe from the bottom up and promote mobility in the single market[719].

- A new "European Solidarity Corps"[720] was created for 100,000 young Europeans who can voluntarily provide assistance where it is most needed in crisis situations, such as the refugee crisis or earthquakes such as the one in August 2016 in the Abruzzo region of Italy[721].
- Social cohesion in Europe must be strengthened in order to cushion the job losses partly caused by free trade or jobs relocated to third countries. This postulate is closely linked to the above-mentioned EU investment plan (EFSI program) for jobs, added value, welfare and social justice (convergence in the euro area with anchoring of social rights to reflect the changing world of work with 116 billion new investments in 26 member states within the first year)[722].
- Contrary to widespread skepticism and anti-government sentiments by NGOs such as "More Democracy", Attac, Campact, Foodwatch, Greenpeace and others, one of the EU's main priorities is free trade and "a reasonable and balanced free trade agreement between the EU and the United States of America "[723] (ratification of CETA, continuation of work towards concluding the TTIP Agreement, continuing ongoing bilateral negotiations with Japan and opening negotiations with Australia, Chile and New Zealand, as well as ratification of the EU-Singapore FTA[724]. In

719 Navracsics, Tibor, EU Commissioner for Education, Culture, Youth and Sports. „Europa – eine Bedrohung für die nationale Identität?", in: *Frankfurter Allgemeine Zeitung*, Nr. 216, page 4. September 15, 2016.

720 Jean-Claude Juncker. "State of the Union 2016". *Speech,* page 17. September 14, 2016. https://op.europa.eu/en/publication-detail/-/publication/c9ff4ff6-9a81-11e6-9bca-01aa75ed71a1/language-en/format-PDF/source-30945725

721 European Youth Portal. *European Solidarity Corps.* March 29, 2020. https://europa.eu/youth/solidarity_en

722 Jean-Claude Juncker. "State of the Union 2016". *Speech,* page 34. September 14, 2016. https://op.europa.eu/en/publication-detail/-/publication/c9ff4ff6-9a81-11e6-9bca-01aa75ed71a1/language-en/format-PDF/source-30945725

723 Jean-Claude Juncker. "State of the Union 2016". *Speech,* page 29. September 14, 2016. https://op.europa.eu/en/publication-detail/-/publication/c9ff4ff6-9a81-11e6-9bca-01aa75ed71a1/language-en/format-PDF/source-30945725

724 Jean-Claude Juncker. "State of the Union 2016". *Speech,* page 30. September 14, 2016. https://op.europa.eu/en/publication-detail/-/publication/c9ff4ff6-9a81-11e6-9bca-01aa75ed71a1/language-en/format-PDF/source-30945725

a press release[725], the German Federal Government also underlined the importance of TTIP and CETA for Europe in terms of product diversity, the removal of trade barriers and customs duties, and the increase in jobs[726].

- Establishment of the European Border and Coast Guard by enhancing FRONTEX operations to protect Europe's external land and sea borders using the European Border Management Agency's operational forces. This should allow for more careful control of border crossings into the EU to prevent "barbaric crimes of 2015 and 2016" in Brussels, Paris, Würzburg and Ansbach from being repeated by unidentified terrorists from the Middle East in the stream of migrants and refugees[727]. More security success will help to win back the acceptance of free trade as an important element of welfare and a source of job security, as well as reducing the fear of globalization. This naturally includes a reform of the EU's existing migration policy with the responsibility of the country of arrival, usually Greece, Italy, Bulgaria and Germany (Dublin Regulation), as well as a harmonization of asylum conditions (reform of EU asylum law) ensuring generosity towards particularly vulnerable groups (e.g. the Roma), refugees, asylum seekers (e.g. Yazidi, Christians, Copts, Kurds in the Middle East) and strict action against abuse, for example through immigration into the social systems of the EU member states (use of social assistance and child benefit, which can be used to finance the cost of living without work for migrants with many children)[728].
- Europe needs "more weight on the international stage" by strengthening the EU's foreign policy and defense policy[729]. Europe's citizens were gripped by fear in the wake of the Madrid bombings in 2004 and more

---

725 Bundespresseamt. „Freihandelsabkommen TTIP und CETA: Frei handeln und gewinnen", *Presseerklärung*. September 23, 2016.

726 Fekel, Matthias. „EU und USA haben Besseres verdient", in: *Handelsblatt*, Nr. 185, page 12. September 23/24/25, 2016.

727 Jean-Claude Juncker. "State of the Union 2016". *Speech,* page 41. September 14, 2016. https://op.europa.eu/en/publication-detail/-/publication/c9ff4ff6-9a81-11e6-9bca-01aa75ed71a1/language-en/format-PDF/source-30945725

728 Jean-Claude Juncker. "State of the Union 2016". *Speech,* page 42. September 14, 2016. https://op.europa.eu/en/publication-detail/-/publication/c9ff4ff6-9a81-11e6-9bca-01aa75ed71a1/language-en/format-PDF/source-30945725

729 Frankfurter Allgemeine Zeitung. „Existentiell in der Krise, aber nicht bedroht", Nr. 216, page 2. September 15, 2016.

than 30 other terrorist attacks, including 14 in 2015 alone[730]. More than 600 innocent people died in European cities such as Brussels, Paris, Nice or Ansbach in Bavaria. With the accompanying paralysis of festive culture and freedom of assembly in public places in Europe, there is a growing aversion to everything global, including skepticism about free trade. Therefore, "a Europe that defends itself" and upholds its European values such as "democratic, pluralistic, open and tolerant societies" is of the utmost importance (Area of Freedom, Security and Justice)[731].

- Europe needs the Defense Union. "It can no longer afford to remain in the shadow of other powers militarily or, for example, to leave France alone in the fight against the Bokko Haram in Mali"[732]. With a common headquarter to avoid parallel operations in Africa and the Middle East, to harmonize the compatibility of weapons systems and a "European Defense Fund" in favor of "permanent structured cooperation" in the Europe of 27, this process of a strong Europe should be taken forward[733].

This positive agenda in favor of an effective and determined European Union is a prerequisite for demonstrating strength on the G20 world stage in the face of terrorist acts as well as growing populism, and ultimately also for better communicating the new FTA character as a world trading partner in negotiations, including with China and possibly Russia. In this respect, President Juncker's announcement in his remarkable Strasbourg speech to the European Parliament on "Building a Europe that protects" is an important step towards realistic solution perspectives with concrete initiatives for investments in the labor market, the digital single market, social Europe as well as security and convergence in the European area of freedom, security and justice[734]. At their informal meeting in Bratislava on

730 Declaration of Bratislava on the initiative of the French and German Minister of Defense. "Joining forces and increasing efficiency" in the presence of EU Foreign Affairs Commissioner Federica Mogherini. September 27, 2016.

731 Inglehart, Ronald: „Economic-Security and Value Change", in *American Political Science Review* / 88, 1994, pages 336 - 354.

732 Jean-Claude Juncker. "State of the Union 2016". *Speech,* page 19. September 14, 2016. https://op.europa.eu/en/publication-detail/-/publication/c9ff4ff6-9a81-11e6-9bca-01aa75ed71a1/language-en/format-PDF/source-30945725

733 Jean-Claude Juncker. "State of the Union 2016". *Speech,* page 19. September 14, 2016. https://op.europa.eu/en/publication-detail/-/publication/c9ff4ff6-9a81-11e6-9bca-01aa75ed71a1/language-en/format-PDF/source-30945725

734 Mogherini, Federica. "Die Erinnerung Europas in einer kooperativen Weltordnung", in *Armin Laschet: Europa im Schicksalsjahr 2016,* Herder Verlag: Freiburg, 2016.

September 16, 2016, the 27 Heads of State and Government of the European Union endorsed the roadmap for the 10 political priorities of the Juncker's "State of the Union" address on September 14, 2016 with the "Bratislava Declaration" for the next 12 months[735].

8.9 Failure of the TTIP Negotiations and Interim Standstill after Donald Trump's Inauguration as US President-elect

The large demonstration in Germany on September 17, 2016 by German trade unions and 50 non-governmental organizations (NGOs) with about 250,000 participants against the CETA agreement was demoralizing for the TTIP Negotiators from the US and the EU. In fact, the TTIP Agreement would have had a chance of being finalized by the end of 2016, the end of US President Barak Obama's term of office. The 28 trade ministers of the EU Member States, who held a meeting September 22-23, 2016 on the occasion of the Slovak Presidency of the Council in Bratislava, as described in Chapter 9.4, called for the conclusion of the negotiations at the end of 2016[736].

The main culprit for the failure of the TTIP negotiations shortly before their conclusion, however, lies with the agricultural lobby in the US and the EU, which wanted to see high meat export quotas of 35,000 tons per year enshrined in the TTIP agreement, although, according to WTO rules, agricultural products such as meat, grain and soya have no place in a trade agreement. Under the GATT-WTO system, export subsidies are not allowed[737]. However, when GATT was established on January 1, 1948, the US insisted on a "loophole" for agricultural products in the trade agreement, which has also been exploited on a large scale by the EU for some time[738].

---

735 European Union. "Bratislava Declaration and Roadmap", *European Council.* September 16, 2016. https://www.consilium.europa.eu/en/press/press-releases/2016/09/16/bratislava-declaration-and-roadmap/

736 Frankfurter Allgemeine Zeitung. „EU und Amerika halten am TTP-Zeitplan fest", Nr. 164, page 4. July 16, 2016.

737 Giese, Ernst: *Globalisierung der Wirtschaft,* Verlag Schöningh, Reihe UTB, 3449, Paderborn 2011, pages 28-31.

738 Krugmann, Paul: *Internationale Wirtschaft,* 10. Auflage, Pearson-Verlag; München 2015, Chapter 10.4.2., pages 342 – 344 (GATT-WTO-System without agriculture, but "loophole" for the US)

The German governmental organizations, as representatives of the largest trading nation within the EU with the greatest export-import benefits in international trade, should also have taken a much stronger stand in favor of free trade and TTIP. Instead, the German government, with the Chancellor and her Minister for Economic
Affairs, buckled in the face of demonstration pressures. Federal Minister of Economics Gabriel even spoke of a failure of TTIP at the last stage of negotiations.

On January 20, 2017, Donald Trump was sworn in as 45th President of the US in Congress in Washington D.C. This was preceded by elections on November 8, 2016 to the 115th Congress with a majority of the Democratic Party in the House of Representatives and a majority of Republicans in the Senate. The elections were marked by fierce clashes on TV, radio, print media and social media between Donald Trump and Democratic party top candidate Front-runner Hilary Clinton. Hilary Clinton won the popular vote by a clear majority[739]. However, after a time-consuming counting process, Hilary Clinton finally lost only due to the greater weighting of votes from rural areas over the dominance of urban areas in the outdated US majority voting system that has not been updated for more than two centuries[740].

8.9.1 The "Trump Phenomenon", "Older White Men" and the "Swing States"

As the Republican candidate, Donald Trump achieved the best poll ratings among Republican supporters after a July/August 2015 primary. As a "real estate tycoon" from New York born in 1946, he coined the slogan "Make America great again" and, as an opponent of the "Washington establishment", quickly managed to unite the majority of the Republican Party's delegates behind him[741]. His campaign focused on major events, sending short messages on social media via "Twitter" as well as constant provocations and violations of "political correctness", which in turn generated headlines in

739 Chronik „Wahlkampf und Innenpolitik der USA ", in: Fischer Weltalmanach 2017, Fischer-Verlag, Frankfurt/M. 2016, page 492.

740 Hagelüken, Alexander: „Das gespaltene Land ", Knaur-Verlag, München 2017, pages 155 – 163.

741 Lecture by Prof. Reint E. Gropp, Leibniz Institut for Economic Research in Halle, Germany, on the topic „Europa zwischen Handelskrieg und Verhandlung" at the Amerikahaus, Munich, Germany. June 4, 2019.

the media[742]. In the rural areas of Ohio, Michigan, Pennsylvania, Virginia, North Carolina, South Carolina, Georgia and Florida, which had been neglected by Hilary Clinton during the election campaign and were affected by the structural change of the collapsing steel and furniture industry as well as by unemployment among the "older white men" ("Swing States"), he succeeded in winning particular increases in votes for his election with the help of large demonstrations (52% in the "Swing States" compared to 46% in the US as a whole)[743].

Indeed, the so-called "older white men", i.e. most recently unqualified workers without college degrees, were Trump's main target group in the 2016 congressional elections, who had been suffering from job relocation and from stagnating real wages for several years[744]. Even as acting president, Donald Trump likes to still pose as the protector of these "hard-working citizens" on the basis which constitutes the myth of America's immigrant generations of past eras[745].

8.9.2 August 2019 EU-US Agricultural Negotiations and Agreement

This also applies to farmers of the "swing states" belt, for whose sake he was guaranteed special quotas of 35,000 tons of beef deliveries from the US to the EU within seven years under the US-EU agricultural agreements of August 2, 2019. This corresponds to 80 percent of the total import quota of the EU. The European Council already approved the EU-US agricultural agreement of August 2, 2019 at the end of the legislative period of the EU Parliament. As part of the agricultural agreement, the EU Commission pledged to purchase more soybeans and liquefied natural gas within seven years starting 2020. Members of the EU trade delegation interpreted the agricultural agreement as a concession by the US trade delegation and the President as a signal to continue negotiations on the suspended transatlantic agreement trade talks. This new agreement demonstrates a great deal of support for the agricultural lobby in the US on part of the EU and

742 „Phänomen Trump" in Fischer Weltalmanach 2017, page. 493.

743 Mark, Lilla Mark. "The end of identity ", *New York-Times.* November 18, 2016.

744 Leggewie, Claus: „Trump kann erneut gewinnen ", in: *Handelsblatt,* Nr. 95, page 64. May 18/19, 2019. (Guest commentary as a political scientist at the University of Gießen, Germany and long-term researcher at universities in the US).

745 Handelsblatt. „EU-Widerstand gegen freien Agrarhandel", Nr. 86, page 8. May 6, 2019.

therefore, the issue of agriculture would no longer have to be included in a future transatlantic agreement. This new agreement is remarkable for US farmers, given the trade war between the US and China, because China has greatly reduced its purchases of soybeans and beef from the US[746]. As a result, the president's standing in the popular vote of farmers and the rural population could also increase in the 2020 election. The Trump campaign organization for the 2020 presidential election, plans to repeat its success in the 2016 elections in the 2020 election year, by creating a new constituency in the aforementioned "swing states" based on white Republican Party voters. Therefore, the US-EU agricultural agreement of August 2, 2019 was an important milestone for the President in view of the 2020 rural elections in order to appease farmers, who have been facing enormous sales difficulties for soya and grain as a result of the US trade war with China[747]. But it was also a step to reassure the worried residents of the "Rust Belt", i.e. the states around Chicago, Cleveland and Pittsburgh all the way down the East Coast with "Swing States" such as Georgia and Florida[748]. The mobilization of the fear of white men and women by Trump of no longer being able to represent their own nation alone and, moreover, of falling behind culturally, i.e., of falling into a minority position in the face of "particularly rapidly growing Latinx" or "Hispanics" as of 2040, is the background to his increasing attacks and his efforts to close off the southern border of the US by building a "Big Wall" as well as detention camps for refugees and migrants from all over Latin America[749]. Opinion polls from 2019 show hence the fact that no president of the US is so popular among white voters of the Republican Party, and as unpopular as Trump among the Spanish-speaking population of the US[750].

8.9.3 Growing Protectionism and Counterstrategy of the EU with the Help of Further Free Trade Agreements

Incidentally, the course for the US-EU agricultural agreement of August 2, 2019 was set on the occasion of the agreement between EU Commission

746 Handelsblatt. „Handelskrieg: Schrecken ohne Ende", Nr. 148, pages 8-9. May 18/19, 2019.

747 Zitos, Salena: *The Great Revolt,* Penguin Random House, 2018, page 320.

748 VanceJohn D.: *Hillbilly Elegie,* Verlag Harper & Row, 2016, page 264.

749 Hewitt, Hugh: *The Fourth way: The conservative Playbook for a Lasting GOP-Majority*", Verlag Simon & Schuster, 2017

750 Fischer Weltalmanach 2019, pages 491-492.

Figure 10: Top 20 Agricultural Food Exports from the US to the EU

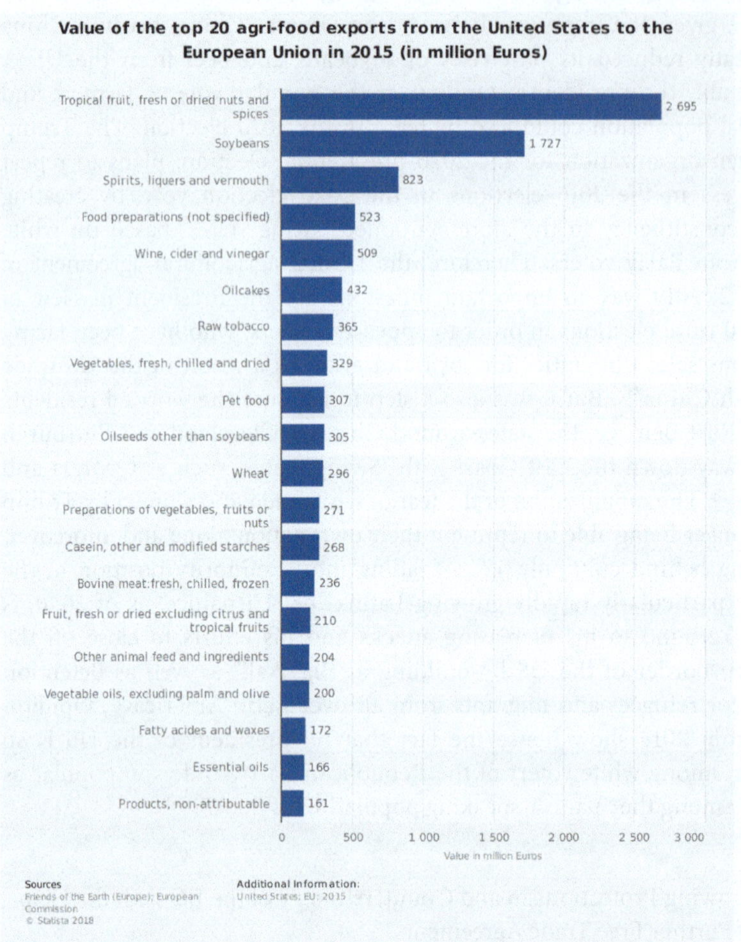

President Jean Claude Junker and Donald Trump on July 25, 2018 in Washington, D.C., according to which the EU committed to purchase large quantities of soy beans, beef and liquid gas.

This statistic shows the top 20 agri-food exports from the United States to the European Union in 2015. Raw tobacco accounted for 365 million Euros in U.S. exports to the EU in 2015.[751]

In return, President Trump promised to postpone the announced 25 percent tariffs on cars and supplier parts from the EU until November 1, 2019. This meeting between the two Presidents on July 25, 2018 must also be viewed positively in view of the agreed declaration to negotiate on the further development of transatlantic relations between the US and the EU in the near future: "We will continue to work constructively with our US partners on the basis of the mandates given to us by the Council of Ministers. We are convinced that a strong and balanced transatlantic relationship based on reciprocity is a win-win situation for both sides. Neither the US nor the EU can have any interest in entering into a trade dispute[752]. We have also noticed that the EU and the US are security partners and that therefore neither American nor European products can pose a security threat to the other side"[753].

At the OECD meeting in Paris on May 22, 2019, Robert Lighthizer, US Trade Representative, met with EU Trade Commissioner Cecilia Malmström to discuss the gradual implementation of the Juncker/ Trump presidential declaration[754].

This statistic shows the top 20 agri-food exports from the European Union to the United States in 2015. Olive oil accounted for 800 million Euros in EU exports to the U.S. in 2015.[755]

751 Friends of the Earth (Europe). "Value of the top 20 agri-food exports from the United States to the European Union in 2015 (in million Euros)." Chart. April 28, 2016. *Statista*. Accessed April 21, 2020. https://www.statista.com/statistics/546313/top-20-agri-food-exports-from-us-to-eu-2015/

752 Handelsblatt. „Auch Europa lässt sich jetzt auf Handelsgespräche ein“, Nr. 75, page 6. April 16, 2019.

753 European Commission. “EU-U.S. Joint Statement of 25 July: European Union imports of U.S. Liquefied Natural Gas (LNG) are on the rise”. *Press Release*, Brussels. August 9, 2018. https://ec.europa.eu/commission/presscorner/detail/en/IP_18_4920

754 “Handel EU–USA: EU demonstriert Härte”, in: *Handelsblatt*, Nr. 99, page 11. May 25, 2019.

755 Friends of the Earth (Europe). "Value of top 20 agri-food exports from the European Union to the United States in 2015 (in million Euros)." Chart. April 28, 2016. *Statista*. Accessed April 21, 2020. https://www.statista.com/statistics/546214/top-20-agri-food-exports-from-eu-to-us-2015/

Figure 11: Top 20 Agriculture Food Exports from EU to U.S.

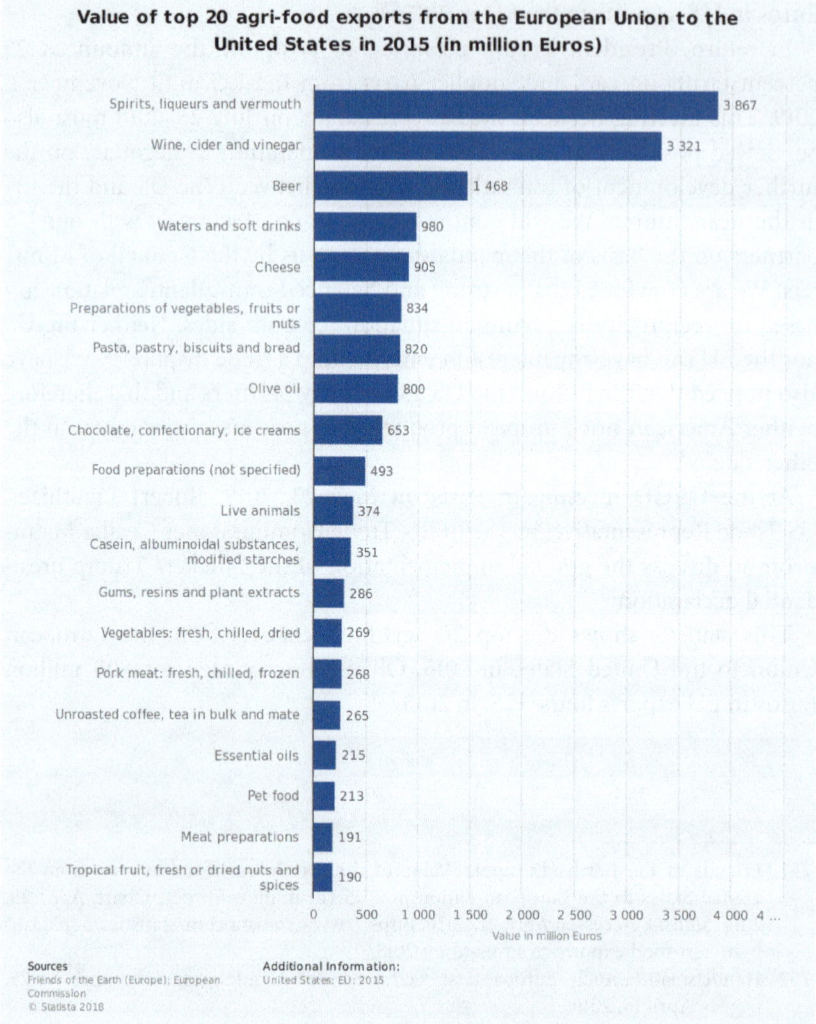

8.9.4 Growing Protectionism and Necessary WTO Reforms

In its 2018 Annual Report on barriers to trade and investment of June 14, 2019, the European Commission placed growing protectionism as a trend in the world at the heart of the report with great concern[756]. It has presented no fewer than 425 active trade obstacles since the 2008 financial crisis. In 2018 alone, 45 new trade and investment barriers were reported by exporters and investors. They range from hygiene rules, prevented access to public tenders, import duties, regulatory requirements to licensing procedures. Most of the newly designed barriers were implemented by China, India, the US and Algeria. They cost companies billions of euros every year. Since the time of the Hanseatic League, however, trade has relied on fairness as well as reciprocity and is therefore not a one-way street. After all, 36 million jobs in the European Union depend on trade - jobs not only for export companies, but also in the entire value chain, with suppliers and service providers. According to Cecilia Malmström, the EU has been exchanging information with exporters and trying to help where it can[757]. In 2018, for example, 35 barriers were removed and in the last five years 123 barriers to trade were removed in tough negotiations in numerous sectors, ranging from agroeconomics, the automotive industry, pharmaceuticals and cosmetics to ICT production. For example, the EU has initiated WTO proceedings against Russian anti-dumping duties on commercial vehicles (motor scooters) imported by Italy and Germany, with the result that Russia has lifted the duties in 2018. These examples demonstrate once again the EU's determination to combat growing protectionism for the benefit of its businesses and consumers. However, this is not often successful. The EU is therefore strongly committed to stricter rules at the international level to combat unfair trade practices and increasing protectionism within the framework of WTO modernization.

On the 25th anniversary of the GATT (Marrakesh Agreement) on April 15, 2019 and the WTO rules derived from the GATT agreement of the 124 member states, it is now time to modernize the world trading system. This includes new appointments to the appellate body of the WTO Dispute Settlement Mechanism, the "arbitration court" of the world trade system. After

756 European Commission. "Trade policy and you". *DG Trade,* 2018. http://ec.europa.eu/trade/trade-policy-and-you

757 Malmström, Cecilia: „Wider den Protektionismus ", in *Handelsblatt*, Nr. 114, page 48. June 17, 2019.

all, the regular re-election of judges at the end of 2019, rendered the appellate body incapable of reaching a decision without appointment replacements and calls into question the binding nature of the WTO regulatory system[758]. Two thirds of non-European exports by European companies are based on WTO rules. The WTO provides basic and globally uniform rules for trade, enables transparency and monitoring of member actions as well as dispute resolution settlement between members. Ultimately, many regulations in the EU's regional and bilateral trade agreements are based on WTO rules.

At the G-20 summit in Osaka, Japan, on June 28-29, 2019, the EU Commission therefore implemented clear provisions in the final document on the reform of the WTO, in particular the controversial dispute settlement issue and the development of rules for digital trade[759]. According to this final report, the EU one wants to maintain free, fair and non-discriminatory trade and keep markets open[760]. The need to reform the WTO is explicitly reaffirmed in this final report as well as the need to improve the dispute settlement system[761].

8.9.5 MERCOSUR and other EU Free Trade Agreements

What will surely be included in the trade history books as a result of the G-20 summit was the ceasefire in the ongoing trade dispute between the US and China. Negotiations are supposed to be resumed as a direct result of the summit and the tariff war has been halted in the meantime. There are supposed to be no further tariffs for the time being. China has pledged to resume buying U.S. agricultural products again[762]. What remains in this conflict, however, is still uncertainty. According to Gabriel Felbermayr, President of of the World Economic Institute in Kiel, Germany,

---

758 DHK Bericht. „25 Jahre Welthandelssystem", Brussels, Nr. 14/2019. April 15, 2019.

759 Felbermayr, Gabriel: „Jahrmarkt bilateraler Tauschgeschäfte", in: *Handelsblatt*, Nr. 123, page 48. July 1, 2019 (Guest commentary on the G-20 summit)

760 Frankfurter Allgemeine Zeitung. „EU setzt Zeichen für den freien Welthandel", *Report*, Nr. 149, page 15. July 1, 2019.

761 Frankfurter Allgemeine Zeitung. „Die wichtigsten Ergebnisse des G-20-Gipfels in Osaka", Nr. 149, page 15. July 1, 2019.

762 Frankfurter Allgemeine Zeitung. „Der Handelskonflikt China–USA kennt nur Verlierer", Nr. 183, page 17. August 9, 2019.

"the struggle for dominance in the world economy is still far from being decided"[763].

On the other hand, the real highlight of the Osaka Summit could be achieved by the European Union with the conclusion of the EU-MERCOSUR Free Trade Agreement including Argentina, Brazil, Paraguay and Uruguay[764]: the largest free trade area in the world in terms of population, creates a free trade area for 780 million people. Value added in the EU was estimated by the World Economic Institute in Kiel, Germany, to increase by around EUR 30 billion[765]. The agreement also committed Brazilian President Bolsonaro to climate protection (reduction of deforestation in the Amazon basin)[766].

With the MERCOSUR Agreement, the EU has forged a genuine alliance for free trade, taking into account the previous free trade agreements with Canada (CETA), in particular with Japan (JEFTA) of February 1, 2019, not to mention the smaller EU free trade agreements with South Korea, Singapore and Vietnam (already negotiated)[767]. Free trade agreements between the EU and Australia, New Zealand and Indonesia are in preparation as well. All these EU-Asian agreements could also be interpreted as a signal to President Trump along the lines of: If the US does not want to accept the rules of the WTO, then the proponents of multilateral free trade conclude as many agreements as possible among themselves. According to Gabriel Febermayr, President of the World Economic Institute in Kiel, German, this could certainly help against the opponents of globalization and populists for autarky efforts in the world[768].

This multitude of agreements shows once more that the EU is fully dependent on trade. The EU exports goods worth nearly two trillion euros a year - more than the US, which exports only about 1.4 trillion euros, and slightly less than China, which exports more than 2.1 trillion[769].

763 Felbermayr, Gabriel. „Handelskonflikte lähmen die Weltwirtschaft", in: *Handelsblatt*, Nr. 140, page 11. July 24, 2019.

764 Handelsblatt. „Handelsmacht Europa ", Nr. 32, page 14. July 1, 2019.

765 Felbermayr, Gabriel: „Jahrmarkt bilateraler Tauschgeschäfte ", in: *Handelsblatt*, Nr. 123, page 48. July 1, 2019 (Guest commentary on the G-20 summit).

766 Frankfurter Allgemeine Zeitung. „Klimawandel und Globalisierung ", Nr. 123, page 8. July 1, 2019.

767 Hüther, Michael in „Die erschöpfte Globalisierung ", Springer-Verlag, Berlin 2018, page. 308

768 Handelsblatt." Die weltgrößte Freihandelszone, Nr. 123, page 8. July 1, 2019.

769 Wolff, Guntram, Director of the Think Tank Bruegel, Brussels. „Welthandel ohne Regeln ", in: Handelsblatt, Nr. 73, page 64. April 14, 2019.

As previously explained, this process of bilateral deals began long before Trump. In the age of the new systemic competition between the US-EU-China and, in the future, India, as well, these world trade markets must be regulated bilaterally with their respective partners. For this reason, the WTO rules on a consensus between the three or four trading powers with the WTO must be designed in such a way as to maintain a certain willingness of the major trading powers to cooperate[770]. After decades of catching up with patent and trademark infringements as well as the absorption of know-how skimming in the US and the EU, China is also on its way to becoming an economic power with inventive talent. In view of the Silk Road projects (one road, one belt), the EU must take note of the fact that China had already filed around 1.2 million patents by the end of 2018 (US 300,000, South Korea: 200,000, Germany 68,000) and therefore now has a great interest in patent and trademark protection as well as compliance[771]. European institutions are becoming increasingly aware that China is on its way to becoming the world's largest economy with corporations such as Alibaba and Huawei (network equipment suppliers) as well as from the much-quoted "know-how theft exploiter" to a value driver and further developer of high-tech products[772]. It is not only since 2018 that city names such as Shenzhen have become common in the US and Europe, where most I-Phones, laptops and DVD players, and soon most electric cars with lithium-ion batteries from the CATTL Group, come from, electric cars for the Chinese market itself, for which European car companies have not yet been able to produce in such large quantities[773]. Europe and the US have long seen China as a Far Eastern sales market[774]. But since 2018/ 2019, China has been heading westward with the new Silk Road project, and the EU must recognize that China's targeted takeover of critical infrastructure, such as the German energy operator 50 Hertz or the innovative robotics manu-

770 Seiffert, Thomas: „Die Pazifische Epoche: Wie Europa gegen die neue Weltmacht Asien bestehen kann", Deutike-Verlag, Wien 2015, pages 192-193 ("Crisis of global governance systems" such as 67, G20, WTO, UN).

771 Hüther Michael: „Die erschöpfte Globalisierung", Springer-Verlag, Berlin 2018, pages 240-241.

772 „Patente: Information zum Patentschutz", Herausgeber Deutsches Patent- und Markenamt, München 2018, pages 26-27.

773 Das Parliament. „Neue Seidenstraße: Globalisierung made in China", Nr. 33-34, page 3. August 12, 2019.

774 Handelsblatt. „Handelsmacht Europa: Spielball der Mächte", Nr. 24, page 12. February 4, 2019.

facturer KUKA Augsburg, could pose a threat[775]. In addition, free trade policy is often linked to foreign trade policy as well as foreign policy. In foreign policy, however, the principle of unanimity prevails within the EU in the European Council, the Achilles' heel against unity in appearance and enforcement against the US, China and other major economic powers[776]. This principle would have to be unanimously transformed into a majority principle[777]. This is currently not to be expected, but neither is a place in the world[778]. By 2050, the share of Europeans in the world's population is projected to fall to four percent, and the share of global economic output over the same period from the current 14 percent is supposed to decrease to only nine percent[779].

The liberal world economic order has come under pressure, especially in the wake of the trade war between the US and China as well as in the wake of populists who propagate autarchy and protectionism. Above all, Europe is being massively challenged by the new Silk Road project. Therefore, the EU needs to be much more committed to leadership on the world stage for open markets, fair competition and free trade. This requires courage, a united approach and active, strong support from the EU Member States. As the largest EU economy, Germany bears a special responsibility in this respect.

8.9.6 USMCA (USA-Mexico-Canada-Agreement) Impact on the Automotive Sector (former NAFTA)

NAFTA is a trade agreement between the US, Mexico and Canada which included standards of the 25-year-old "North American Free Trade Agreement". The Trump administration formally launched a NAFTA renegotiation in May 2017. After two years of negotiations, the successor agreement USMCA was signed on April 18, 2019. According to Jacob Kirkegaard,

775 Handelsblatt. „Handelsmacht Europa: Spielball der Mächte“, Nr. 24, page 13. February 4, 2019.

776 China Contact. „Belt and Road“, 22. Jg. Nr. 7/8/2018, pages 15/16.

777 Handelsblatt. „EU geht gegen Chinas Seidenstraße vor“, Nr. 225, page 10. November 21, 2018.

778 German Trade & Invest (GTAI) „China überall präsent“, (Studie „China in Afrika“) 2018, pages 20-28.

779 Das Parliament. „American Dream in China: 70 Jahre Volksrepublik“, 69. Jg., Nr. 33-34, page 1. August 12, 2019.

Figure 12: Patent Applications 2016

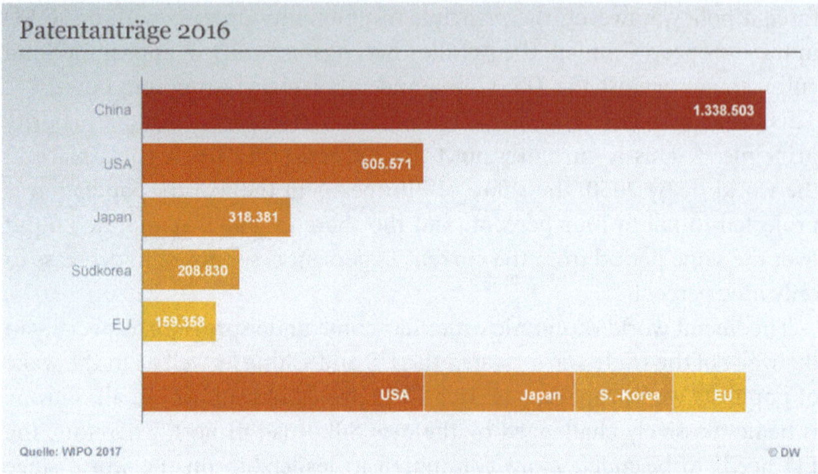

Source: World Intellectual Property Organization 2017 in *Deutsche Welle*

senior fellow at the Peterson Institute for International Economics, "USMCA is 95 percent the existing NAFTA agreement"[780]. President Trump had repeatedly threatened to exist NAFTA. However, existing NAFTA without a new agreement, would have triggered WTO rules with higher tariffs for the three involved nations.

USMCA contains provisions on the protection of intellectual property, such as patent and trademark protection, the Internet, including protection against cybercrime, investment for state-owned enterprises and the currency sector. The agreement is limited to the areas of automotive, the Internet, digitalization, and in the agricultural sector only to poultry, egg, dairy, cheese and wine products. The agreement also contains provisions for the protection of high-priced specialty drugs known as "biologicals".

780 White, Martha. "Trump signs USMCA trade deal to replace 'nightmare NAFTA'". *NBS News*. January 29, 2020. https://www.nbcnews.com/business/economy/trump-signs-usmca-trade-deal-replace-nightmare-nafta-n1125526

Mainly the automotive sector is relevant for this dissertation research. The main provisions are as follows:

- The agreement makes it easier for OEMs (parent companies) producing in the US, such as BMW, Ford, GMC, Toyota, and Volkswagen, to do business in the amount of $34 trillion over a five-year period[781].
- Mexico, which has received an investment of 24.8 trillion from 2009-2018 by the previously mentioned car companies, is estimated to exceed this amount by 9.2 trillion over the next 5 years[782].
- NAFTA included a 62.5 percent production share of vehicles for North America with zero tariff restrictions. The new USMCA raises this percentage to the threshold of 75 percent with no time limit[783]. However, this means fewer car parts for vehicle manufacturers (OEMs) from Mexico, Germany, Japan, South Korea or China. The agreement calls for 70 percent of steel and aluminum originating in North America to be melted and cast on this continent.
- The new agreement stipulates that 40-45 percent of car parts for each duty-free vehicle must come from a so-called high-wage factory. These factories must pay a minimum wage of 16 US dollars per hour on average to each production worker. This is three times higher than the current average wage at any factory in Mexico.
- Public administrations hope that car manufacturers will either buy more parts from Canada or the US and increase wages in Mexico.
- Critics, however, urge caution, because factories could be able to play with the rules by raising salaries of managers (bonuses). This would actually pose a risk for the changes in the USMCA compared to NAFTA.
- Automotive analysts warn that wage increases could reduce costs for American companies, and higher prices for car buyers could slow down the growth of the car market in the US, especially economic growth.

781 Office of the United States Trade Representative. "Estimated Impact of the United States-Mexico-Canada Agreement (USMCA) on the U.S. Automotive Sector". *Executive Office of the President.* April 18, 2019.

782 Center for Automotive Research: "A Summary of the Car-Book of Deals Annual Report". *Historical Trends,* 2009-2018 (2019), https://www.cargroup.org/automakers-announced-4-8-billion-in-north-american-investments-in-2018

783 New York Times. "Trump Just Signed the USMCA: A trade agreement with Mexico and Canada revises Mexico's labor laws and encourages more auto production in North America", January 29, 2020. https://www.nytimes.com/2020/01/29/business/economy/usmca-deal.html

It can be noted positively that the minimum wage requirement for Mexico in several key industries has pushed back the arbitrariness of the NAFTA arbitration system. It has been widely condemned many times by both parties in the US House of Representatives.

The new USMCA includes benefits to ensure better occupational safety, especially in Mexico.

Overall, the USMCA contains improvements compared to NAFTA, especially for the US and also Canada, by keeping an estimated 76,000 jobs in North America. These jobs could have migrated to Mexico as a former low-wage country if NAFTA had continued. Due to the increase in the minimum wage in Mexico, the country seems to be no longer as attractive for car companies as it used to be.

Chapter 9: Signals for Resumption of Transatlantic Trade Agreement Negotiations in 2019 and 2020

In 2017, it was not clear whether, when and how negotiations on a transatlantic free trade agreement between the US and the EU would be resumed. However, the first steps were taken in 2018 as previously described in Chapter 8. As a result of the U.S.-EU meeting in 2018, EU Member States gave the European Commission permission to start formal trade negotiations with the US in April 2019[784] after an "economic analysis by the European Commission" demonstrated "significant gains" from a US-EU agreement[785].

Figure 13: EU-US Trade in Goods[786]

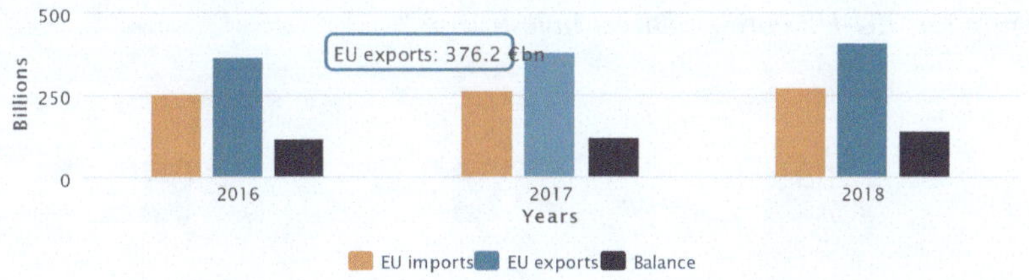

According to this analysis, the EU and the US "have the largest bilateral trade and investment relationship and enjoy the most integrated economic relationship in the world".

784 European Commission. "EU-U.S. Trade: Commission welcomes Council's green light to start negotiations with the United States". *Press release,* Luxembourg. April 15, 2019.

785 European Commission. *Significant economic gains from eliminating EU-US industrial tariffs.* Brussels, February 19, 2019. *https://trade.ec.europa.eu/doclib/docs/2019/february/tradoc_157693.pdf*

786 European Commission. *EU-USA: Trade in goods.* April 17, 2019. https://ec.europa.eu/trade/policy/countries-and-regions/countries/united-states/

Figure 14: EU-US Trade in Services[787]

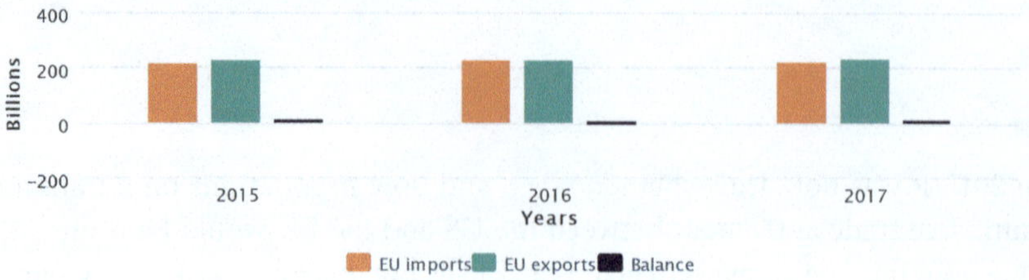

Together, the US and the EU account for almost half of the entire world's GDP[788]. According to the Office of the United States Trade Representative, the "EU countries, together, would rank 1st as an export market for the United States" and the "EU countries together, would rank as the 2nd largest supplier of imports to the United States"[789].

Figure 15: EU-US Foreign Direct Investment[790]

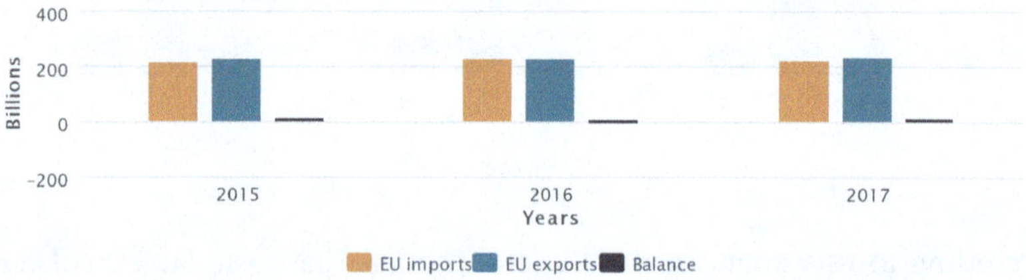

787 European Commission. *EU-USA: Trade in services.* April 17, 2019. https://ec.europa.eu/trade/policy/countries-and-regions/countries/united-states/

788 European Commission. "European Union, Trade in goods with USA". *Directorate-General for Trade.* January 4, 2020. https://webgate.ec.europa.eu/isdb_results/factsheets/country/details_usa_en.pdf

789 Office of the United States Trade Representative. "U.S.-EU Trade Agreement Negotiations". *European Union.* April 10, 2020. https://ustr.gov/countries-regions/europe-middle-east/europe/european-union

790 European Commission. *EU-USA: Foreign direct investment.* April 17, 2019. https://ec.europa.eu/trade/policy/countries-and-regions/countries/united-states/

Figure 16: Volume of U.S. Imports of Trade Goods from the EU[791]

This graph shows the growth in the U.S. import volume of trade goods from the European Union from 1997 to 2019. In 2019, U.S. imports from the EU amounted to approximately 514.89 billion U.S. dollars.

In July 2019, the European Commission issued a progress report on EU-U.S. trade negotiations[792] including an "Update on the EU-US Executive Working Group"[793].

791 US Census Bureau, und US Department of Commerce. "Volume of U.S. imports of trade goods from the European Union from 1997 to 2019 (in billion U.S. dollars)." Chart. February 5, 2020. *Statista.* Accessed April 08, 2020. https://www.statista.com/statistics/187737/volume-of-us-imports-of-trade-goods-from-the-eu-since-1997/

792 European Commission. *EU-U.S. trade talks – one year on: strengthening EU-US relationship – factsheet.* July 25, 2019. http://trade.ec.europa.eu/doclib/press/index.cfm?id=2052

793 European Commission. *Synopsis report.* Brussels, July 9, 2019. http://trade.ec.europa.eu/doclib/docs/2019/july/tradoc_158068.pdf

In November 2019, the EU published a proposal[794] for an agreement with the U.S. "on the mutual acceptance of results of conformity assessment[795].

At the beginning of 2020, there have been several signals indicating that both partners might be willing to resume talks sooner rather than later. On the one hand, there was a clear signal from US President Donald Trump at the World Economic Forum 2020 in Davos. Due to the upcoming US presidential elections in November 2020, he has to take actions in order to be re-elected. Therefore, he indicated that he is planning on concluding trade agreements that are in the interest of the US. Following an agreement with Japan and a partial agreement with China, he apparently has now been seeking trade agreements with the European Union and with the departing United Kingdom.

In a conversation with Ursula von der Leyen, President of the European Commission, in Davos on January 22, 2020, the US President expressed confidence that he could conclude a trade agreement with the EU: "They will make a deal, because they have to"[796]. With this indirect threat, the US President has already alluded to the 25 percent tariffs against European car exports to the US announced for the year 2020. Shortly after, the President of the European Commission stressed the importance of economic and social ties between the EU and the US: "Europe is a reliable partner who asks for fairness in return." She emphasized the EU's great tradition of free trade: "We now have 83 EU trade agreements, and we are at the beginning of negotiations with the United Kingdom from March 2-5, 2020"[797] .

Even before the World Economic Forum in Davos, the new EU Trade Commissioner Phil Hogan met with US Secretary of Commerce Robert Lighthizer and US Secretary of the Treasury Steven Mnuchin. During his visit from January 13-16, 2020, he called for an update of the joint EU-US trade agenda, thus contributing to prosperity on both sides of the Atlantic, but also to future solutions for global challenges during his keynote address

---

794 European Commission. *Explanatory Note.* November 20, 2019. https://trade.ec.europa.eu/doclib/docs/2019/november/tradoc_158449.pdf

795 European Union. *EU Proposal.* October 25, 2019. https://trade.ec.europa.eu/doclib/docs/2019/november/tradoc_158448.pdf

796 Frankfurter Allgemeine Zeitung. "Trump droht – von der Leyen kontert", Nr. 19, page 17. January 23, 2020.

797 European Commission. "Read-out by the Commission of the meeting between Commission President Ursula von der Leyen and U.S. President Donald Trump". *Statement.* January 21, 2020. https://ec.europa.eu/commission/presscorner/detail/en/statement_20_97?mc_cid=77a32be7f7&mc_eid=8bf4e6570b

at the Center for Strategic and International Studies (CSIS) in Washington, D.C.: "If we approach the EU-US trade agenda in the right way and work together, the mutual benefits can be enormous. However, if we fail to do so, the damage will be significant, not only for our two communities of states, but also for the world we have built together"[798].

What is significant about Phil Hogan's visit to the US is the agreement reached between the EU, USA and Japan on the tightening of the existing rules on industrial subsidies within the WTO[799].

All three partners, together with the WTO, will supplement the WTO Agreement on subsidies and compensatory measures with new types of prohibited subsidies[800]. This refers especially to China, which offers steel exports on foreign markets with state subsidies far below the prices, thus not only creating overcapacity with wasted resources from its own location, but also destroying jobs in the US, the EU, Japan and the UK[801]. This agreement should be seen as a good sign for a possible cooperation between EU and US with regard to a transatlantic trade agreement in the spirit of fair competition of market forces[802]. This very current and recent example demonstrates that China does not currently deserve the desired quality label "market economy", as already previously established (dumping of solar panels in the international market and destroying the international solar panel industry especially in California and Germany)[803].

---

798 Hogan, Phil. "Refreshing Transatlantic Trade Relations". *Speech.* January 16, 2020. https://www.csis.org/events/refreshing-transatlantic-trade-relations?mc_cid=9683b54813&mc_eid=8bf4e6570b

799 European Commission. *Joint Statement of the Trilateral Meeting of the Trade Ministers of Japan, the United States and the European Union.* Washington, D.C. January 14, 2020. https://trade.ec.europa.eu/doclib/docs/2020/january/tradoc_158567.pdf

800 European Commission. "Trade/ WTO: EU, U.S. and Japan agree on new ways to strengthen global rules on industrial subsidies". *Press release,* Brussels. January 14, 2020. file:///C:/Users/m.goergmaier/Downloads/Trade_WTO__EU__U.S._and_Japan_agree_on_new_ways_to_strengthen_global_rules_on_industrial_subsidies.pdf

801 European Commission. "Trade/WTO: EU, U.S. and Japan agree on new ways to strengthen global rules on industrial subsidies". *Press Corner,* Brussels. January 14, 2020. https://ec.europa.eu/commission/presscorner/detail/en/ip_20_43

802 European Commission. "How the European Commission investigates subsidized imports". *Factsheet.* October 8, 2014.

803 European Commission. "The European Union's Measures against Dumped and Subsidized Imports of Solar Panels from China". *Factsheet: Solar Panels Update.* February 29, 2016. http://trade.ec.europa.eu/tdi/case_history.cfm?id=2383&init=2383

9.1 Declaration of the Three EU Presidents

In this context, the great response to the joint declaration of the three Presidents of the European Commission, Ursula von der Leyen, the President of the European Council, Charles Michel, and the President of the European Parliament, David Sassoli, on January 31, 2020, deserves to be highlighted on the occasion of the end of the UK's 45-year membership: "In a time of conflict, we have all become aware that the EU is more than a market or an economic power. It stands for values that we all share and that we stand for. In a time of strong power competition and turbulent geopolitics, size does play a role. No country alone can find solutions for the digital future or make itself heard in the ever increasing cries of the world, We can do it, because the EU can bring its considerable economic power into the balance during talks with allies such as the US, Japan, India, Africa and the MERCOSUR states"[804].

9.2 Current Trade Positions between US and EU

Any upcoming transatlantic trade negotiations will not be easy. After all, some outstanding issues that were still in dispute until the 14th round of negotiations were abandoned in December 2016, especially, the agricultural sector, which is under strong lobbying influence in both the EU and the US putting pressure on politicians. It is true that in the agricultural trade talks in August 2019 (as previously explained in Chapter 9.9.2), the EU made considerable concessions in the agreement reached between the former European Commission President Juncker and US President Trump (significant meat quotas, soy bean and liquid gas volumes). In the partial agreement between the US and China, China has also pledged substantial agricultural product quota purchases amounting to 32 billion US dollars. Nevertheless, Europeans are likely to come under US pressure in the agricultural sector trade talks. In consideration of France, however, the EU does not want to accommodate concessions in the agricultural sector. In doing so, it invokes WTO rules, which do not allow the agricultural sector in regional FTAs except for an emergency exemption. Unfortunately, how-

804 Von der Leyen, Ursula, Charles Michel und David Sassoli: "Ein neuer Tagesanbruch fuer Europa", in: *Frankfurter Allgemeine Zeitung*, Nr. 26, page 8. January 31, 2020.

ever, this loophole has almost become the norm[805]. European Commission President von der Leyen made it clear once again in Davos during talks with US President Trump that all EU countries do not want to include the agricultural sector in the transatlantic trade agreement under any circumstances[806].

On the other hand, the EU and the US are expected to agree on common standards and rules for future technologies such as "autonomous driving", robotics and 3D printing. The same applies to energy standards and prophylaxis by improved coordination in monetary and financial matters, to prevent a disaster like that of 2007/ 2008 from occurring in the first place. There could also be even more agreement on divergent safety standards in the pharmaceutical and food sectors, as well as harmonization of certification and licensing approval requirements in the automotive sector: On July 11, 2019, a milestone was reached between the EU and the US regarding the mutual recognition of pharmaceuticals[807].

With regard to a proposed trade agreement between the US and the United Kingdom, it should also be noted in this context that the British government will considerably dampen the hopes of the US government for a comprehensive trade agreement: The British House of Commons has approved a tax change bill proposed by the government under Prime Minister Boris Johnson on April 1, 2020, according to which a tax of 2 percent will be introduced on digital revenues from social media platforms, search engines and online marketplaces, provided that the turnover of the companies exceeds 500 million pounds per year. However, this should be the case for Google, Apple, Microsoft and Amazon[808]. This has been introduced by the British government until an international solution can be found, which will require the WTO, the EU, the US, Japan and many other trading partners.

---

805 Hoppe, Till and Torsten Riecke. "EU-Widerstand gegen freien Agrarhandel". *Handelsblatt,* Nr. 86, page 8. May 6, 2019.

806 Handelsblatt. "Transatlantischer Handelsstreit: Gesucht die neue Sojabohne", in: Nr. 19, page 8. January 28, 2020.

807 European Commission. "EU-US trade talks: milestone reached in mutual recognition of pharmaceuticals". *Press Release.* July 11, 2019. https://ec.europa.eu/commission/presscorner/detail/en/IP_19_4090

808 Frankfurter Allgemeine Zeitung. "Trump droht – von der Leyen kontert", Nr. 19, page 17. January 23, 2020.

9.3 EU Work Program 2020

Legitimate hopes for renegotiations despite the expected difficulties exist not only on the part of the US government, but also officially from the EU side. The "work program" of the new European Commission for 2020 states in several passages that in the overarching goals, derived from the core objectives of the strategic agenda of the European Council for the period 2019-2024, "all measures and initiatives will be strongly oriented towards external action"[809]. In addition to the "Action Plan for the Enforcement of Internal Market Legislation" for better implementation of internal market rules, the European Commission is concerned with fair competition and a level playing field in the global market[810]. A "White Paper on an instrument against foreign subsidies" on possible new instruments sets out how to combat the distorting effects of foreign subsidies in the internal market[811]. The "White Paper" is, as always, an inventory of blatant abuse of competition and paves the way for a legislative proposal to follow immediately in 2020 or 2021 with effective sanctions to be expected[812]. This is undoubtedly an urgent measure directed, above all, against China that also accommodates the US, which has so far not achieved any visible tangible results with constant admonitions from the Chinese negotiating partners[813]. On March 4, 2020, the EU already decided on further measures against steel products from China as an anti-dumping duty on imports of steel wheels from China at a rate of between 50.3 and 66.4 percent put into force by the EU Commission[814]. With this announcement, in the run-up to the

---

809 European Commission. "Arbeitsprogramm der Europaeischen Kommmission fuer 2020: Fahrplan fuer eine Union, die mehr erreichen will", page 5. January 29, 2020. https://ec.europa.eu/germany/news/20200129-arbeitsprogramm

810 European Commission. "Steel industry: Commission takes action to preserve sustainable jobs and growth in Europe". *Press release,* Brussels. March 16, 2016. https://ec.europa.eu/commission/presscorner/detail/en/IP_16_804

811 European Commission. "Case AD652 – Steel road wheels". *Trade Defence Investigations.* April 9, 2020. http://trade.ec.europa.eu/tdi/case_details.cfm?id=2383

812 European Commission. *2020 Commission Work Programme – key documents.* January 29, 2020. https://ec.europa.eu/info/publications/2020-commission-work-programme-key-documents_de

813 European Commission. "History of proceeding". *Trade Defence Investigations.* April 9, 2020. http://trade.ec.europa.eu/tdi/case_history.cfm?id=2383&init=2383

814 European Commission. *Commission imposes more anti-dumping measures on steel products from China.* March 4, 2020. https://ec.europa.eu/commission/presscorner/detail/en/mex_20_388

resumption of transatlantic trade negotiations, the European Commission is thus demonstrating how much it is interested in a partnership with the US in the sense of maintaining a world order with free and fair trade[815]. The 2020 work Programme states: "Europe must become more geopolitical in the way it thinks and acts and must be more united and effective. It must invest in alliances and coalitions to give greater weight to its values and promote and protect its interests through open and fair trade[816]...The EU is convinced that free and open trade can work with a strong WTO capable of action. The European Commission wants to be at the forefront of international efforts and work with partners on a reform of the WTO to create even more fair and enforceable rules with a level playing field for all trading partners".[817]

Amid the world-wide coronavirus pandemic, the EU and 15 World Trade Organization members including China still managed to follow through on this promise[818]. On April 8, 2020, the European Commission "imposed provisional anti-dumping duties on hot-rolled stainless-steel coils and sheets from China, Indonesia and Taiwan...in order to remove economic damage for European producers[819]. Therefore, the EU Commission will likely also launch a comprehensive initiative on WTO reform following the next WTO Ministerial Conference in June 2020[820].

The problems and opportunities identified in the relationship between the transatlantic partners US and EU show once again how difficult it is to

815 European Commission. *Trade Defence Statistics covering 2019.* January 9, 2020. https://trade.ec.europa.eu/doclib/docs/2020/january/tradoc_158564.pdf

816 European Commission. *2020 Commission Work Programme – key documents,* page 7. January 29, 2020. https://ec.europa.eu/info/publications/2020-commission-work-programme-key-documents_de

817 European Commission. *2020 Commission Work Programme – key documents,* page 8. January 29, 2020. https://ec.europa.eu/info/publications/2020-commission-work-programme-key-documents_de

818 European Commission. "EU and 15 World Trade Organization members establish contingency appeal arrangement for trade disputes". *Press corner,* Brussels. March 27, 2020. https://ec.europa.eu/commission/presscorner/detail/en/IP_20_538?mc_cid=418455de9d&mc_eid=8bf4e6570b

819 European Commission. "Commission continues its action in support of fair trading conditions for EU steel producers". *Press corner.* Brussels: Daily News. April 8, 2020. https://ec.europa.eu/commission/presscorner/detail/en/mex_20_631

820 European Commission. "Commission ensures continuation of trade defence procedures despite the limitations imposed by COVID-19 outbreak". *Trade Defence,* Brussels. March 13, 2020. https://trade.ec.europa.eu/doclib/press/index.cfm?id=2120

reach a consensus on bilateral and regional trade agreements, but also the responsibility for maintaining the rules-based world trade order in close co-operation between the EU and US. In the matter of the Transatlantic Trade Partnership, however, there are justified hopes for a resumption of the trade agreement talks in 2020 on the basis of the previous recent talks between the EU and the US and the EU's protection in the fight against China's (constant) overreaching on its trading partners by chronically subsidizing important export goods.

Chapter 10: Consequences of TTIP and Policy Recommendations

As previously established in this book, a Transatlantic Trade and Investment Partnership between the US and the EU would create new opportunities for both sides of the Atlantic Ocean. However, even if the transatlantic agreement never comes to fruition or changes in shape, TTIP aspects contribute to a broader literature applicable in other cases of trade agreements. For instance, many aspects of TTIP can be found in the free Comprehensive Economic Trade Agreement (CETA) between Canada and the EU.

Some European trade opponents view TTIP as a threat, when in reality, a transatlantic agreement would be a huge opportunity to become a part of a global trading force. If the European Union and the United States are left behind in the global trading competition, there could potentially be far more outcomes that are negative in consequences as opposed to the implementation of a transatlantic agreement. Globalization and global trade cannot be halted in the 21st century. Obama stated in his joint press conference with German Chancellor Merkel in Hannover, Germany on April 24, 2016 that there will be Trans-Atlantic trade no matter what (with or without TTIP). The question is under what terms. "...as you see other markets like China... and Asia beginning to develop, and Africa growing fast, we've got to make sure that our businesses can compete here"[821] in the United States as well as in Europe. Instead of opposing TTIP as a whole, it is far more important to seize this opportunity to provide constructive criticism and valuable input for the precise transatlantic agreement terms. Even after TTIP's failure, there could potentially still be another similar trade agreement in the future, because trade will continue in any case. A transatlantic agreement would be a huge opportunity as the largest regional trade deal in history, as the US and the EU combined would account for the

821 The White House, Office of the Press Secretary. "Remarks by President Obama and Chancellor Merkel in Joint Press Conference". Schloss Herrenhausen in Hannover, Germany. April 24, 2016. https://www.whitehouse.gov/the-press-office/2016/04/24/remarks-president-obama-and-chancellor-merkel-joint-press-conference

largest economic relationship in the world[822]. Consequently, a transatlantic agreement is necessary and it if does not happen now within the next couple of years, it will most likely be unavoidable to implement it or a similar agreement in the future anyway. A transatlantic agreement would not only create positive consequences upon implementation, but there will also be opportunities "after" a transatlantic agreement. Because of their mutual occidental origin, as well as their long-term peaceful partnership for 70 years, the European Union and the United States are well suited to move closer together than ever with the TTIP standards, even beyond the character of a pure free trade agreement. As an Atlantic "community of values", TTIP standards should first serve as a "blueprint" for other future trade agreements. Whatever copyright laws and regulations or environmental standards China might be violating now, it would have to adjust to certain standards, if a transatlantic agreement was to be implemented. The creation of such an "Atlantic Union" would move the European Union and the US to number 1 of the world rankings concerning the areas of economic power, entrepreneurship and invention spirit based on the Gross Domestic Product of the EU ($16,21 billion) and the US ($16.72 billion) in 2013 – combined: $32.93 trillion[823]. In the period from 2003 until 2012, China was placed on number 1 with a $12.14 billion export sum, followed by Germany with $11.89 billion and the U.S. with $11.38 billion. Economically an exporter of raw material, Russia reached only $3.43 billion, since proceeds essentially flow to external accounts in the West and generally are not reinvested into the country for modernization but are rather used for consumer goods from the West. For this reason, President Obama referred to Russia as a "Regional Power" during the EU-US Summit on March 26, 2014 in Brussels, Belgium.

Since the BRICS States are growing at a much faster rate than the EU and the U.S., forces have to be joined economically in the form of a trade agreement, but in other areas as well such as investment. The geographic situation of the EU and the U.S. close to each other "only" divided by the Atlantic Ocean, also favors a transatlantic agreement as well as a potential

822 De Lecea, Antonio. "The EU-US trade and investment before and after TTIP: What can Latin America expect from it?" in Joaquín Roy and Roberto Domínguez (editors). *The TTIP: The Transatlantic Trade and Investment Partnership between the European Union and the United States.* Miami-Florida European Union Center/ Jean Monnet Chair, 2014 page 1. https://eucenter.as.miami.edu/_assets/pdf/ttip.pdf

823 Simon, Hermann. "EUROSTAT", *Frankfurter Allgemeine Zeitung,* Nr. 69 (1), March 22, 2014 pp. 8-20.

future Atlantic Union with close neighbors such as Canada and Mexico. The US already is a very important trading partner for the EU and vice versa. After the reduction of some trade barriers, trade volume would consequently increase even more if a transatlantic agreement was to be implemented resulting in export increases as well as creation of numerous new jobs. However, the exact number of these increases will certainly depend on the final contents of the agreement. If a transatlantic agreement only includes elimination of custom duties without standardization of norms and certifications, the beneficial numbers will be a lot less than if everything was to be implemented. According to several different research studies conducted, TTIP would boost GDP in the EU and in the US by providing a wider range of product diversity, lower prices for goods, and more jobs. Especially small and medium-sized enterprises would benefit from TTIP, as they are being prevented from investing "transatlantically" today due to regulatory barriers. One of the challenges between the US and the EU today is the fact that there are "50 million small- and medium-sized businesses, but only 260,000 of them engage in trade across the Atlantic. TTIP can help... improve on that figure, strengthening .... Trans-Atlantic economic bonds"[824]. In addition, a transatlantic agreement would provide ease of mobility for entrepreneurs.

To touch more on TTIP criticisms: "TTIP will not have any negative impact on...sustainable development, because compliance with sustainability criteria like labor protection and environmental protection is a primary goal of the negotiators on both sides"[825]. Contrary to what some (media) critics claim and what the general public often tends to repeat (without necessarily always knowing the actual facts), the goal for the EU and the US is "to agree on high standards and fair transatlantic trade regulations with a global impact"[826]. This includes standards pertaining to food products.

---

824 Medick, Veit. "US Commerce Secretary on TTIP: 'Our Administration Wants a Deal This Year'". Washington, DC: Spiegel International. April 25, 2016. http://www.spiegel.de/international/world/ttip-interview-with-us-commerce-secretary-penny-pritzker-a-1089072.html

825 German Federal Ministry for Economic Affairs and Energy. "Frequently asked questions about the Transatlantic Trade and Investment Partnership". *Press Release.* Accessed May 22, 2016. http://www.bmwi.de/EN/Topics/Foreign-trade/TTIP/faq.html

826 German Federal Foreign Office. "Towards a transatlantic economic agreement – the Transatlantic Trade and Investment Partnership (TTIP)". January 29, 2016. http://www.auswaertiges-amt.de/EN/Aussenpolitik/RegionaleSchwerpunkte/USA/TTIP.ht

Europeans do not want chickens cleaned with chlorine allowed within their markets. However, that omitting this cleaning process can pose a potential salmonella risk as the other side of the story is almost completely omitted by most of the European media sources, which is quite interesting. There seems to be a visible pattern of (European) media bias despite the fact that the European Commission already clarified that the goal is not to lower standards. On the contrary, the main idea is to actually adhere to higher standards from whatever side (US or EU), according to Ignacio Garcia Bercero and Dan Mullaney in the TTIP 11th round stakeholder press conference held in Miami on October 21, 2015. This pattern of general anti-trust is not only directed towards the US from the European population, but also towards each country's own government or the EU institutions as a whole in general. This deep founded distrust tends to be stronger these days than any real tangible criticisms. For example, in the TTIP context, critics sometimes refer to the non-discrimination clause under the WTO, which states "countries cannot normally discriminate between their trading partners". However, "some exceptions are allowed" in the form of a free trade agreement, for instance[827]. Fact is that there is a World Trade Organization Agreement on the Application of Sanitary and Phytosanitary Measures (SPS Agreement) which has been in existence since the Uruguay Round of Multilateral Trade Negotiations in 1995. This agreement refers to food safety as well as animal and plant health regulations in regards to international trade allowing countries to set their own regulation standards based on "scientific justification,...appropriate assessment of risks so long as the approach is consistent, not arbitrary"[828]. Contrary to TTIP critiques, based on the text of this agreement, the EU *can* actually require US producers to mention that their food contains genetically modified organisms (GMOs). Whether the US transatlantic agreement negotiators will accept the EU terms is a different story, but it is technically not only possible, but also highly recommendable to insist on the higher standards in this important case. According to the EU Commission, EU negotiators "must ensure that products imported into the EU meet...high standards"

---

ml?searchArchive=0&searchEngineQueryString=ttip&searchIssued=0&searchIssuedAfter=27.11.2013

827 World Trade Organization. "Principles of the trading system". Accessed May 11, 2016. https://www.wto.org/english/thewto_e/whatis_e/tif_e/fact2_e.htm

828 World Trade Organization "Understanding the WTO Agreement on Sanitary and Phytosanitary Measures". May 1998. https://www.wto.org/english/tratop_e/sps_e/spsund_e.htm

protecting "people's health and safety, and the environment" and that "EU governments fully maintain their right to adopt rules or laws to protect people and the environment"[829]. According to the EU Commission, "TTIP will not change existing food safety rules. The EU will keep its restrictions on hormones or growth promoters in livestock farming just as the US will keep its rules on microbial contaminants...Growing and selling genetically modified organisms is subject to an authorization process in line with EU law. TTIP will not change this law. EU countries must also agree to any growing of GM plants. This will not change through TTIP"[830]. The EU Commission further confirms, "TTIP will not open the EU market to hormone-fed beef. And the EU will continue to regulate these substances in line with legislation already in force"[831]. Even in the unlikely event that genetically manipulated food product standards would be somehow lowered in a transatlantic agreement, and chlorine chickens or GMO products were to be offered within the European Market, it would be legitimate on part of the EU to insist on label requirements for those particular (US) products based on these already existing EU laws in place. Consequently, if consumers do not buy these products, they would automatically be eliminated by the competition. This is the beauty of a free market that this sort of market self-regulation can and will happen to genetically manipulated food for example. There has been a huge trend of US consumers avoiding those kinds of products, which is why organic supermarkets such as Whole Foods, fresh markets etc. have risen in popularity. People are willing to spend more money in order to buy healthier products which has been forcing "regular" supermarkets to now also avoid offering genetically manipulated products, for example Aldi, which has recently committed to eliminating GMO products and has therefore requested from its suppliers to only deliver GMO free products.[832]

829 European Commission. "Inside TTIP: An overview and chapter-by-chapter guide in plain English". Luxembourg: Publications Office of the European Union, 2015, page 6 http://trade.ec.europa.eu/doclib/docs/2015/july/tradoc_153635.pdf

830 European Commission. "Inside TTIP: An overview and chapter-by-chapter guide in plain English". Luxembourg: Publications Office of the European Union, 2015, page 22. http://trade.ec.europa.eu/doclib/docs/2015/july/tradoc_153635.pdf

831 European Commission. "Inside TTIP: An overview and chapter-by-chapter guide in plain English". Luxembourg: Publications Office of the European Union, 2015, page 30. http://trade.ec.europa.eu/doclib/docs/2015/july/tradoc_153635.pdf

832 Peterson, Helen. "Aldi is fixing its biggest weakness, and that should terrify Whole Foods". *Business Insider*. January 23, 2016. http://www.businessinsider.com/aldi-is-fixing-is-biggest-weakness-and-that-should-terrify-whole-foods-2016-1

Historically, the partnership between the US and the EU is not only important economically, but in the view of some realists, a transatlantic agreement is also a strategic partnership like many trade agreements are perceived in general terms. However, events such as the NSA affair have triggered critics in Europe, especially in Germany, to mistrust the US in general including anything related to TTIP. No matter the obvious benefits, most of the media as well as the general public claim to be uninformed and in fact are uninformed, because they either do not make the effort to visit the European Commission website, for example, where all document chapter summaries are in fact visible to anyone including some of the original texts, or they simply still don't know that these documents are available. Due to most media coverages still claiming that TTIP negotiations are secretive, the general public believes it and therefore does not even attempt to access or search for any documents and is in fact not effectively using the resources provided to them. Daily news reports on public TV and in the newspapers every single day, mainly focusing on all the threats that TTIP supposedly brings certainly contributes to these opinions. There seems to be a dangerous pattern creeping up throughout Europe whether it is related to TTIP, the migration crisis, or the EU in general – the trend of the general public and the media is to oppose it all entirely without any compromise. When looking back at the Euro implementation 14 years ago, it was the same trend, the same counter-arguments, the same fears, when in fact, Germany above all, tremendously benefited from the Euro and so did many other European countries. Therefore, the media will continue to play a vital role, because not each individual will take a step back and examine the actual facts on their own before repeating everything they see on daily biased media coverage. The general EU public views TTIP as a threat and most of the media coverage constantly feeds into those fears creating a vicious circle. Relevant EU institutions should therefore continue their effort to make as much factual material as possible not only available, but specifically target the media, NGOs and other stakeholders with this material by hosting information sessions on local levels in every city and town through the appropriate local EU representative or EU Centers targeting schools and universities as well.

A transatlantic agreement is technically flexible in terms of disagreement threats. As key negotiators have pointed out during numerous summit occasions regarding TTIP, if there are disagreements between the EU and the U.S. (for example GMOs, consumer protection laws etc.), key negotiators have already or will potentially decide that those (trade) areas will not be part of TTIP. Therefore, many of the fears expressed by the population as well as by lobbyists are unfounded in the sense that they will not apply. Concerning the alternative outcome that a transatlantic agreement will not take place, the EU and the U.S. will be becoming smaller and smaller in all aspects of rankings when compared to the BRICS States. TTIP "would serve as a powerful demonstration that the West is not doomed to decline. Perhaps most importantly, a transatlantic agreement would underpin the international liberal order at a time of global power shifts. If the EU and the US can agree on critical standards and regulations with each other, they will significantly enhance their ability to make these the international standard, forcing China and other rising powers to buy into Western norms and principles or else risk falling behind[833].

The European Coal and Steel Community was used as a tool for Europe's reconstruction. In addition, the U.S. was present at the European Union's creation and has frequently been using (former) Germany as well as the European Union (at that time the European Economic Community before 1992) as a (economic) shield during the Cold War. Even before then, the U.S. originates from Europe, and due to this long mutually beneficial history, based on shared strong fundamental beliefs in democratic government, human rights and market economies, the relationship between the U.S. and the EU is central and irreplaceable in the world. "Today, security and justice and prosperity for our world depend on America and Europe working in common purpose. That makes our transatlantic ties as vital as they have ever been"[834].

In addition to trade, investment will be key for the future strength of the US/ EU and will be part of the impact of a transatlantic agreement on the global competition. "There are major priority aims in the energy sector (given Europe's dependence on Russian gas), and in securing access to raw materials where combined pressure on other countries may be vital"[835]. Consequently, the transatlantic agreement negotiation committee should

833 Brattberg, Eric. "TTIP is too important to fail". *Europe's World*, January 31, 2016. Accessed May 12, 2016. http://europesworld.org/2016/01/31/ttip-important-fail/#.VzNgSOSvyek

834 White House Office of the Press Secretary. US President Bush, February 19, 2005. https://georgewbush-whitehouse.archives.gov/news/releases/2005/02/text/20050219.html

835 Abbott, Roderick. "A close look at the Transatlantic Trade and Investment Partnership". *Europe's World,* March 28, 2014. Accessed, May 23, 2016. http://europesworld.

recommend appropriate policies that need to be implemented in order to strengthen both, the U.S. and EU economies.

A transatlantic agreement has the potential to advance environmental standards consequently also positively influencing global public health policies. Many scholars view all these areas separately. However, all those areas are interconnected and affect one another. A transatlantic agreement could have a huge economic, social, environmental and public health impact on U.S. and EU consumers and population. In addition to trade, climate and global public health policy will be key for the future strength of the US/EU and will be part of the impact of the transatlantic agreement on the global competition. Consequently, the transatlantic agreement negotiation committee should recommend appropriate policies that need to be implemented in order to strengthen both, the U.S. and EU economies. While economic, climate and global public health policies all affect one another, many scholars have treated them as separate entities, even though they are intertwined and affect each other. Another fascinating fact is that TTIP, similar to the notion of the EU, is "bound together by will....not forced by conquest, war or political pressure".[836]

Besides tariff abolishment and increased legal security, particularly for small and medium-sized enterprises, a transatlantic agreement would improve transfer of technology in the automobile economy and in the information and communication technology (ICT) industry, which will, in turn, lead to cost advantages created by common service management including fixed exchange rates for euro and dollar. TTIP "could boost the U.S. economy by more than $100 billion per year and create close to a million new jobs"[837]. In view of the carbon dioxide (CO2) increase and the dramatically increasing climate change, energy supply with renewable energy sources, combined with a better climate and environmental protection, present a further challenge, which can only be mastered jointly by the U.S. and Europe. On both sides of the Atlantic, economic stimulus of up to €200 billion

---

org/2014/03/28/a-close-look-at-the-transatlantic-trade-and-investment-partnership/#.VzNfzeSvyek

836 Roy, Joaquin and Roberto Domínguez (eds.). *The Transatlantic Trade and Investment Partnership between the European Union and the United States.* Miami-Florida European Union Center/ Jean Monnet Chair, 2014, page 8. https://eucenter.as.miami.edu/_assets/pdf/ttip.pdf

837 Delegation of the European Union to the United States. "More Trade brings more jobs", accessed March 24, 2016. http://www.euintheus.org/press-media/op-ed-by-ambassador-vale-de-almeida-in-the-hill-more-trade-brings-more-jobs/

and 200,000 more jobs are expected in 10 years after the implementation of a EU-US trade agreement. Likewise, public health policy is to be mastered more easily on both sides, in solidarity, in view of aging societies.

For all these reasons, "TTIP is too important to be left to economists"[838] only. It has to be viewed from other angles as well. "TTIP provisions on services, state-owned enterprises, environment, labor and competition policy could set precedents for global standards and future WTO negotiations".[839]

10.1 Common Economic and Fiscal Union in the Dollar-Euro-Area

In the U.S. and in Europe, great importance of production consists of the respective other marketing area (e.g. *Barbie, Apple, Google, Microsoft, and Facebook* in Europe - *BMW, Daimler, Audi, and Porsche* in the U.S.). The 50 largest European subsidiaries of U.S.-parent companies produce approximately €170 billion in revenue, in the US, the 50 largest European holdings even with €330 billion in sales.

---

838 Hamilton, Daniel. 2014. *The Geostrategic Aspects of a Transatlantic Trade and Investment Partnership.* Brookings Institution Press. Center for Transatlantic Relations, John Hopkins University SAIS, page 4. Accessed May 13, 2016. http://transatlantic.saisjhu.edu/publications/books/The%20Geopolitics%20of%20TTIP/Hamilton_TTIP_geopolitics_summary_final.pdf

839 Schott, Jeffrey. *Broad Objectives and Prospects for TTIP.* Peterson Institute for International Economics. May 1, 2014, page 2. http://www.piie.com/publications/papers/schott20140501ppt.pdf

Figure 17: US-EU Trade[840]

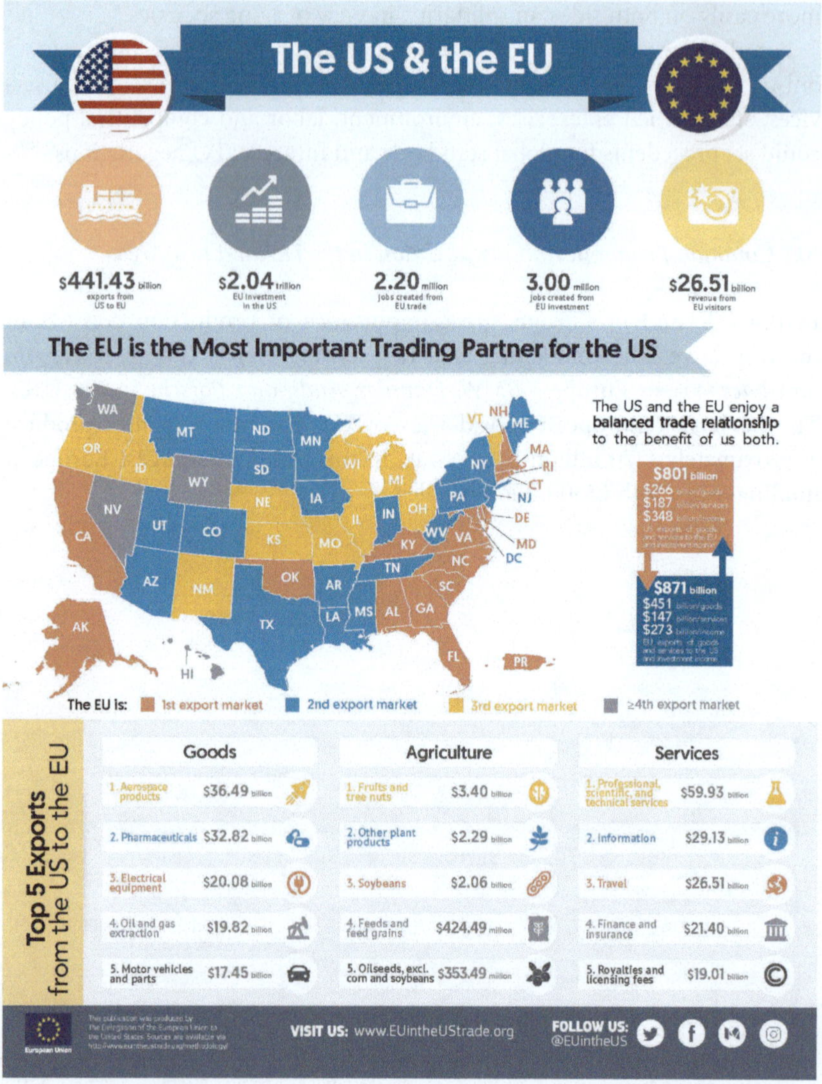

840 Delegation of the European Union to the United States, Washington, DC. February 27, 2020. http://www.euintheustrade.org/wp-content/uploads/2019/07/US-main-infographic_revised_v3.pdf

In the United States and in the EU, there is a high appreciation of universities and research institutions with long traditions of technology and knowledge transfer on both sides (including exchanges of scientists and students). U.S. investors represent one of the most important foreign direct investors who buy out and/ or save European enterprises (e.g. German tableware manufacturer WMF Group was acquired by American investment firm KKR; Advent International bought perfume and cosmetic company Douglas; BMW's investment in Moses Lake and Linde's investment in the U.S. Lincare Group). On both continents, business startups and elevator pitch actions create enterprise outsourcing as well as business network founder scenes in world cities such as Miami, Berlin and Regensburg with foundation chairs for start-ups (Example: U.S. Professor Dowling at University of Regensburg in Germany). The guidance function of the US-market with lower energy prices, and with the re-industrialization initiated by President Barack Obama, sets impulses towards the European Union with strong de-industrialization in the United Kingdom, Spain, Greece, Portugal and Ireland. Vice versa, through acquisitions in the US, the EU is providing impetus to strengthen the re-industrialization there, such as SAP software, through the acquisition of success factors and the retail network provider Ariba or Fresenius – acquisition of the US dialysis technology chain Liberty-Dialysis or Reimann, the acquisition of Starbucks competitor Peet's Coffee & Tea and vitamin manufacturer Schiff through a stake in Reckitt-Benckiser. Europe sets impulses in the U.S. to strengthen re-industrialization by introducing SAP-Software based on success factors. The U.S. is ranked 3rd after China and Japan in the mutual exchange of goods (import/export) for European enterprises; vice versa, Europe is ranked 2nd after China in the mutual exchange of goods for American enterprises. Mutual anti-dumping measures established by the U.S. and Europe already exist, for instance, for solar products implemented in May 2013. A growth spurt in the mutual goods traffic is expected on a long-term basis by the formation of a foreign trade zone between the United States and the European Union. Currently, the exchange of goods is still obstructed by different trade standards. The standardization of trade standards might take up to 10 years of implementation concerning topics such as the 5-7% custom duties, non-tariff barriers, certification requirements, terms of payment, safety standards, technical defaults, subsidies, immigration regulations and many more. However, some of these details could gradually be implemented after the implementation of TTIP or a similar EU-US agreement.

10.2 Agenda Proposal to Shape a Common Climate and Energy Policy

The dramatic increase of CO_2 in the atmosphere from 30,000 to 420,000 ppm from 1965 to 2012 leads to enormous entropy in the atmosphere. According to the laws of thermodynamics, energy is not evaporated on earth, but is converted into heat instead. This heating of the atmosphere strikes back on humanity: an unusually high and increasing number of floods, tornadoes, hurricanes, heat waves over 40°C and an increase in the deserts on earth are the consequences. Entire regions, such as some in Bangladesh, are no longer habitable, as the sea level rises inexorably, caused by the melting of the glaciers and the melting of the Arctic and Antarctic. Europe has taken the initiative to create objectives and strong legal rules for the reduction of CO2 emissions by the year 2020 which include power supply, changes of the drive systems in traffic (smart mobility, smart cities), and development of energy efficiency and fight of climate change. While the U.S. was lacking behind in comparison to the EU under the Bush administration, the Obama administration has significantly managed to advance climate and energy policy within the US. Therefore, there is now an opportunity for a joint climate and energy policy in TTIP based on the following:

- Introduction of limited access in large cities to environmental zones and privilege approach for electric vehicles
- Increased Sustainability Awareness
- Reversal of coastal building developments (nature needs to remain on coasts instead of one hotel/ building next to another)
- Photovoltaic and solar thermal energy in the private and operational building of houses for the cooling and generation of energy
- Conservation and reserve attitude of fossil combustibles for emergencies and future generations (coal, oil rest occurrences, gas)
- More usage of terrestrial heat for heating/ energy supplies of cities
- Increased usage of hybrid and electric cars/ vehicles for enterprises and government organizations as model effect for the population
- Energy supply net development in Europe and the U.S. within country and offshore wind farms
- Common research efforts toward the change of industrial companies with "smart technology" (industry 4.0) in order to kindle prosperity and growth in a structural change

- Climate friendly heating with disperser settlement structures created by wood pellets and wood briquettes instead of gas and oil consumption
- Conversion from statutory orders to climate friendly energy policy

Figure 18: EU-U.S. Energy[841]

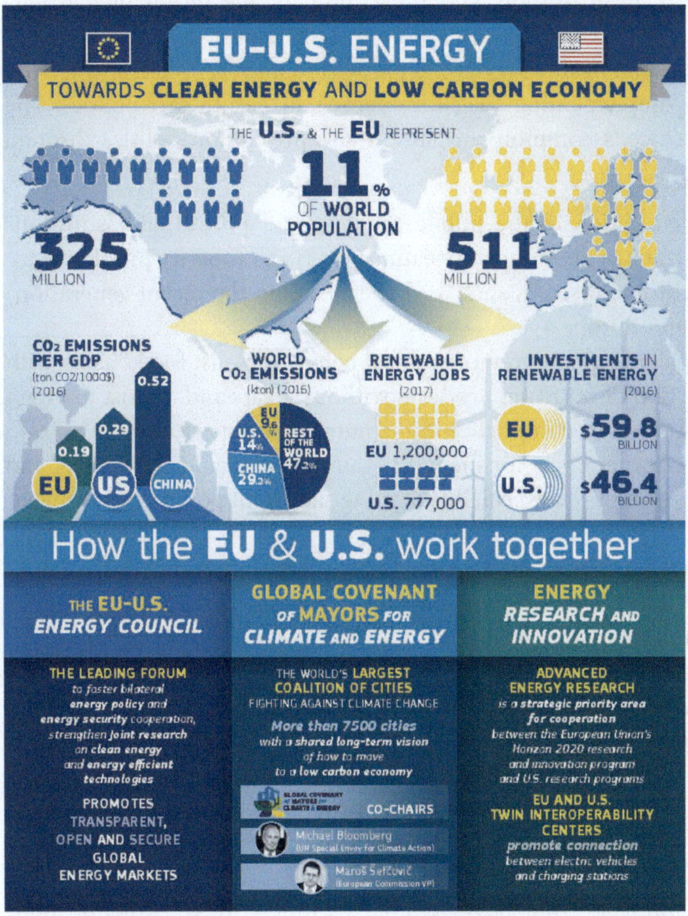

841 Delegation of the European Union. *EU-U.S. Energy.* February 2, 2018. https://eeas.europa.eu/delegations/united-states-america/45766/eu-us-energy_en

10.3 Agenda Proposal for a Common Health/ Disease Prevention Policy

Research and development for pharmaceutical and diagnostics are already closely related between the U.S. and Europe. In both the U.S. and Europe, national public health policy has increasingly become more important in the sense of health-supply and prevention for the recent increasingly aging generation (drugs/ alcohol/ nicotine addiction) in order to avoid cost explosions in health services. Europe and the U.S. can profit from each other by implementing a legal framework for health care politics. The TTIP market needs common precaution and prevention politics through the following:

- Increased education of the public by consumer protection institutions and organizations about healthy eating/ nutrition (obesity problems, increase of chronic diseases such as diabetes within the recent generation) in the US and Europe
- Joint campaigns calling on more ethical behavior of fast food chains with the production of nutrition products without sugars and against too high cholesterol content (compliance in the nutrition industry on both sides)
- Exchange of experiences for the fight against alcohol addiction, drug and tobacco consumption, especially targeting the youth population (prevention)
- Joint campaign measures as coordinated prevention policy to more movement and sports in the young and adult generations on both sides of the Atlantic
- Increasing network of research and development strengthened by technology within the medicine field as well as in the biotechnology field (e.g. minimum invasive medical technology for the reduction of cost-intensive operations/ surgeries and periods spent in hospitals)
- Increasingly strengthened networking structure for startups in medical technology, biotechnology and pharmaceutical sectors between universities and incubators of universities
- Increased motivation for business angels to invest in start-ups on both sides of the Atlantic.

The inclusion of SMEs in the TTIP agreement is exemplary for all other future trade agreements of the EU as well as the US and could become a blueprint in future agreements. This important accent distinguishes TTIP in a special way.

The abolition of customs duties, simplification of market access and simplification or mutual recognition of regulations behind the border as core areas of the TTIP Agreement are also a win-win situation for SMEs in bilateral trade between the US and the EU. After all, with 20 million companies in the EU of the 28 member states, SMEs are the backbone of the economy and account for 98 percent of companies across the EU. SMEs will therefore benefit most from TTIP over the long term.

A significant proportion of SMEs are suppliers in the global automotive sector: In the past, finished cars were sent back and forth across the Atlantic. Today, many parts of a car travel back and forth several times across the Atlantic as part of modern supply chain management and production in stages. The elimination of customs duties, duplicate certifications, fees and time-consuming administrative bureaucracy such as double approval procedures on both sides of the Atlantic will save many costs and a lot of time. After all, SMEs are subject to much greater cost pressure than industrial companies anyway. Finally, the consumer is also benefiting from lower prices and civil society benefits from new jobs as a result of stronger economic performance[842].

For example, two-thirds of the new jobs created in the US in the last 15 years can be attributed to SMEs[843]. Furthermore, the importance of SMEs in transatlantic trade between the US and the EU is demonstrated as follows:

842 Oehme, Sven: "TTIP - ja oder nein?", Fordham Graduate School of Law, President European-American Business Organisation Inc, New York, July 8, 2014. www.eabo.biz

843 EU Commission. "EU - US-Zusammenarbeit", in: *Unternehmen und Industrie-Magazin*, Nr. 15, page 10. February 2013.

- In goods and services, the EU and the US are each other's largest trading partners with more than 650 billion euros in annual trade or 1.8 billion euros per day.
- EU exports of SMEs to the US are three times higher than those to China and seven times as high as the ones to Japan.
- The US-EU transatlantic economy provides 15 million SME jobs.
- Total US investment in the EU is three times higher than in all of Asia.
- EU investment in the US is eight times higher than in India and China combined[844].

Following the entry into force of TTIP, the following impulses for the economy as a whole could be generated in the future by SMEs' involvement in connected US-EU markets on both sides of the Atlantic:

- Optimization of product standards (e.g. ISO certification in Europe and Balanced Scorecard in the US) in the form of web-based entities for SMEs to provide market access on both sides of the Atlantic (e.g. in accordance with the model of the web portal for European and Chinese standards).
- Cooperation in respect of intellectual property rights along the lines of the abovementioned new EU trademark regulation of the EUIPO (EU-Intellectual Property Office) in Alicante, Spain[845]. The Office of the European Union for intellectual property oversees the protection of intellectual property (trademarks and designer rights) for goods in transit. This creates groundbreaking legal certainty and awareness regarding the assertion of trademark rights.
- This new awareness, including trademark protection, can also benefit the entire US trading area after TTIP (extend European Union trademark to transatlantic trademark)
- Crowdfunding for start-ups in financing investments as joint relief.
- SME funding problems in the EU and the US (developing joint inventions, networking research projects, networking elevator pitch and matching events, acquire business angels for venture capital)
- Optimizing cluster formation, e.g. in the automotive, optoelectronics and medical care sectors to use joint R&D funding, use of joint office and service capacities (cluster alliances).

844 EU Commission. "EU - US-Zusammenarbeit", in: *Unternehmen und Industrie-Magazin*, Nr. 15, page 11. February 2013.

845 Verordnung (EU) 2015/2424. February 23, 2016.

- In implementing these examples of enhanced cooperation through the TTIP Agreement, SMEs could be more closely introduced into world trade via the Atlantic Bridge (e.g. SME joint ventures between the EU and the US on involvement in third countries). Value-added management in the automotive, ICT, mechanical engineering and pharmaceutical sectors could be deepened in terms of cost savings, customer service, sales and marketing for mutual benefit
- After all, in the age of digitalization and Industry 4.0, the rising costs of Big-Data-Services and Cloud-Computing could generate enormous cost savings through SME collaborations on both sides of the Atlantic.
- The European and US automotive industry represents more than 12 million jobs and net exports worth more than 50 billion euros. In view of increasing competition with the Far East, both sides of the Atlantic should, after TTIP, take advantage of all the opportunities offered by the enlarged economic area of the US - EU (e.g. in software or B2B service providers). This can lead to better capacity utilization and lower transport costs, and above all to more added value through ICT networking in traditional industries.

Figure 19: EU-U.S. Data Flow[846]

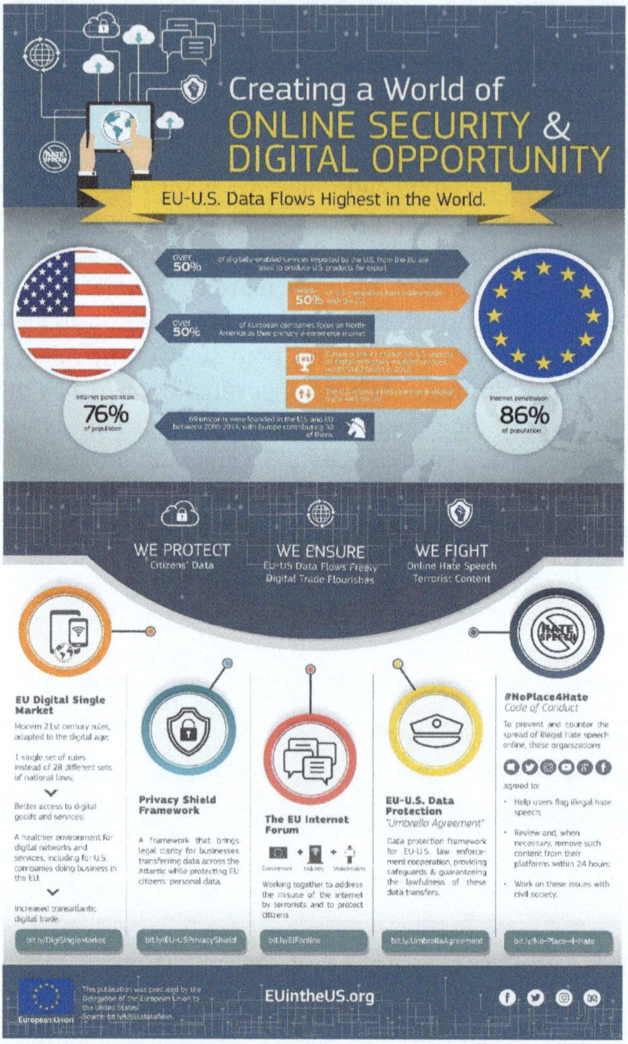

846 Delegation of the European Union. *EU-U.S. Energy.* February 27, 2020. https://eeas.europa.eu/sites/eeas/files/eu_infographic_data_flows_final_for_wall.pdf

Figure 20: U.S. Exports of Goods to EU

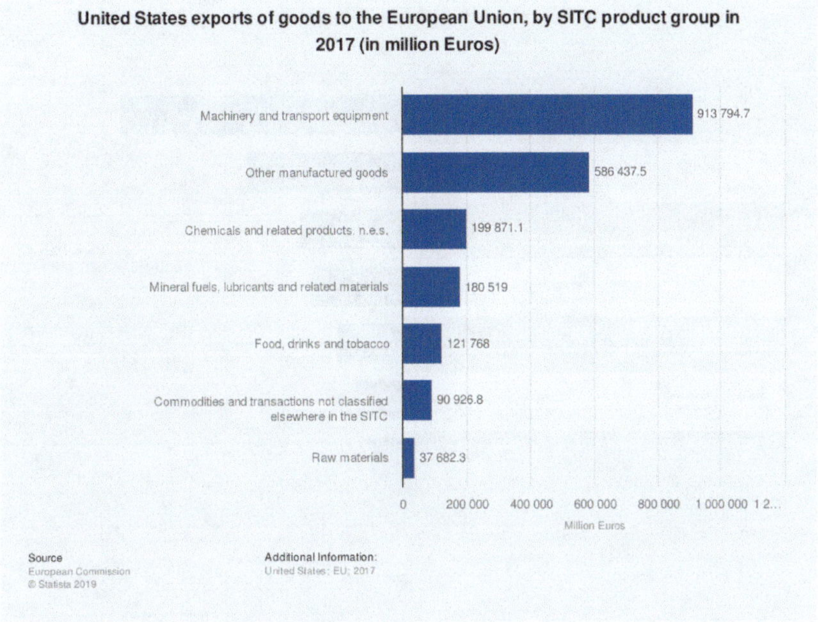

This statistic shows the value of goods exported to the European Union from the United States in 2017, by Standard International Trade Classification (SITC) product group, in million Euros. In 2017, U.S. exports of raw materials to the EU totaled over 37.68 billion Euros.[847]

847 European Commission. "United States exports of goods to the European Union, by SITC product group in 2017 (in million Euros)." Chart. April 17, 2019. Statista. Accessed April 18, 2020. https://www.statista.com/statistics/547324/us-goods-exports-to-eu-by-sitc-product-group-2014/

Figure 21: EU Goods Export to U.S.

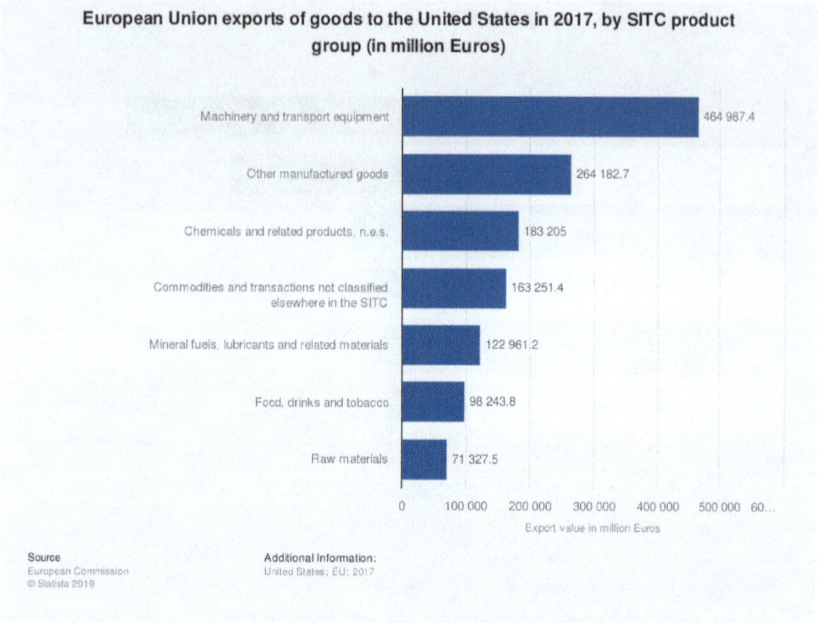

This statistic shows the value of goods exported to the United States from the European Union in 2017, by Standard International Trade Classification (SITC) product group, in million Euros. In 2017, EU exports of raw materials to the U.S. totaled around 71.3 billion Euros.[848]

These solution perspectives for the time "after TTIP" could lead to a true blossoming of the highly developed EU-US ICT economy with the familiar precision of the European economy and, via the TTIP agreement, set the course for market penetration, especially in the Far East.

Financial market supervision and regulation in the EU and the US requires constant cooperation and consultation, including the establishment of a robust set of rules from a single source. For in the globalization of markets, one could not react with fragmented financial market regulation. The EU advocates a rules-based process of forward-looking and crisis-proof

848 European Commission. "European Union exports of goods to the United States in 2017, by SITC product group (in million Euros)." Chart. April 17, 2019. *Statista.* Accessed April 18, 2020. https://www.statista.com/statistics/547288/eu-goods-exports-to-us-by-sitc-product-group-2014/

financial stability on both sides. According to the European Commission, regulatory cooperation should be based on the following four principles:

- joint cooperation to implement common standards for financial market regulation and supervision
- Regular consultations in the future on the preventive perspective between the US and the EU without having to react to surprising turbulence on either side or to negotiate legislation under market pressures
- joint review of existing regulations, also with a view to ensuring that they do not create unnecessary barriers to trade between the two partners, given the changing nature of markets
- a permanent agreement on whether each other's legislation of rule is equivalent in effect and not disruptive.

In the EU's view, this demand for common financial market regulation and supervision is in line with the G-20 agreements and serves to make functioning financial markets both transparent and forward-looking. The G-20 declaration of September 2013 should thus be respected and, for example, even the sometimes dangerous derivatives trading should be made safe and acceptable for customers through prudent and high-quality regulation on both sides.

The claim of regular cooperation between the US and the EU should also work if different rules are counterproductively damaging the markets over time[849]. Then, in the spirit of regulatory cooperation, we should jointly strive for effective, high-quality regulations. For the "benefits" of the transatlantic partnership are obvious:

- Regulatory coherence serves financial stability and reduces irregularities in markets in advance of emerging risks.
- The transatlantic "bridge-regulation" of divergent legislation will strengthen marketplaces in the EU and the US.
- The ability to improve the financial system integrated on both sides protects the operating real economy and, finally,
- integrated financial marketplaces on both sides of the Atlantic have a stronger global ambition and serve as a role model for other marketplaces outside the EU and US in the world[850].

849 European Comission. „Cooperation on financial services regulation ", page 4. July 14, 2016. https://trade.ec.europa.eu/doclib/docs/2016/july/tradoc_154794.pdf

850 European Comission. „Cooperation on financial services regulation ", page 5. July 14, 2016. https://trade.ec.europa.eu/doclib/docs/2016/july/tradoc_154794.pdf

The European Commission's proposals on the regulatory coherence of financial markets between the EU and the US were accepted by the US side in the 14th round of negotiations on TTIP from July 11-15, 2016[851].

Due to globalization with emerging economic great powers in Asia and Latin America, there is a risk that the US and the EU will be squeezed out of competition. However, some Europeans are afraid of a trade agreement with the US due to hormone-treated meat, gene-manipulated food, consumer protection and data protection concerns even though most of these fears are unfounded. The opportunities for an EU-US trade agreement far outweigh the risks.

Negotiations regarding the Euro-Atlantic economic area offer a great opportunity to incorporate key and fateful issues of our time into an agreement between the United States and the European Union. Apart from trade liberalization and monitoring of competition, a common Euro-Atlantic climate and energy policy based on the European model should also be included, as well as a common generational and public health policy for both continents. After all, a European-American climate and energy policy has the power to act as a role model and therefore affect the BRICS states to change their consumption habits in order to avoid CO2 entropy. In comparison to Asia and Latin America, however, the US and Europe have aging societies requiring more health care and investment. By building a network structure, common research and development politics, transfer of technology and enterprise cooperation, smart mobility as well as a solid environmental and public health policy (smart health) should play an important role in an agreement on both sides.

Overall, there are many areas of action that can contribute to a positive turnaround on both sides of the Atlantic, creating a spirit of departure and innovation to reduce energy consumption, make more efficient use of resources and more environmentally friendly, such as healthy lifestyle of the population. An agreement such as TTIP would certainly be able to contribute during the implementation phase to reducing over-regulation in the two democratic constitutional states of the United States and the European Union also for the benefit of all civil societies. Consequently, it does not have to lead to the decline of the West, as the best-selling Ameri-

851 European Commission. „14. TTIP-Verhandlungsrunde beendet". http://trade.ec.europa,eu/doclib/press/index.cfm?id=1230

can scholar Niall Ferguson predicts[852], but a breakthrough for democracies and economies in the US and Europe in favor of a model for the rest of the world. In the meantime, dictatorial regimes in Asia, Latin America, and Africa are opening their markets under the pressure of globalization, moving toward the development of the rule of law and a Western-style civil society. In this process, the West, in the form of the US and the European Union, cannot and must not passively allow the decline to take place within, but must actively shape the global distribution of power as a "global player" through reforms with and "after TTIP".

Helping to shape the global distribution of power as a "global player" through reforms naturally requires reform within the European Union. In the near future (2020-2027), the EU faces major challenges. In order to be able to live and work in freedom and security in an increasingly digitalized world, enormous efforts and a determined course of action are required, above all in regard to network security, the protection of Europe's external borders, in regard to the threat of climate change and in regard to the danger of increasing protectionism:

- In foreign and security policy, the course is set for the FRONTEX Agenda 2020- 2030[853]. By 2030, significant steps in the EU's external border protection management should be implemented[854].
- For years, Europe has been demonstrating the scope for future action in trade policy. The current policy of concluding regional agreements based on WTO rules, such as the with Canada, Japan, Singapore, South Korea, the MERCOSUR countries and Vietnam in the spirit of open markets, is the right way forward. Constantly raising tariffs and erecting new barriers "Behind the border" causes markets to crash into turbulence and the confidence of companies in the markets to collapse.
- Above all, the negotiations on the Transatlantic Agreement, which were not concluded in 2016, must be continued in the spirit of the Declaration

852 Ferguson, Niall. “The Great Degeneration”. *Allen Lane (Penguin Books),* London 2012.

853 European Commission. “Annual State of the EU address by President Juncker at the European Parliament”. *State of the Union 2018. https://ec.europa.eu/commission/priorities/state-union-speeches/state-union-2018_en*

854 Opening Statement in the European Parliament Plenary Session by Ursula von der Leyen, President of the European Commission. “A Union that strives for more: My agenda for Europe”. *Political Guidelines for the next European Commission 2019-2014,* pages 8-14. July 16, 2019. https://ec.europa.eu/commission/sites/beta-political/files/political-guidelines-next-commission_en.pdf

by President Juncker and President Trump of July 25, 2018 on the further development of transatlantic relations between the US and the EU[855]. Especially regarding China's "Belt and Road Initiative", combined with enormous project financing extending as far as the Balkans, the EU and the US must cooperate more closely.

- The monetary and banking union must be further deepened and made weatherproof in the face of looming international crises in the Middle and Far East, Latin America and Africa, with state bankruptcies, such as Argentina, sometimes dangerously approaching. "Bad/ lazy loans" must be reduced, as they encourage the smoldering risk of credit degradation. More ethics and compliance in the securities sector, with its risky sequence methods "a la Russian roulette", is necessary by implementing mandatory regulations for the area of the EU monetary union and the dollar area.
- A Tax bases must be harmonized in the European Single Market to prevent tax evasion, money laundering and horrendous fraud against the general public (e.g. cum-ex transactions with networks in Europe, US and Australia). Taxation of IT companies must take place where value creation occurs[856]. After all, fair taxation strengthens the confidence of EU citizens, as do the stabilization efforts for the future of the EURO.
- The Structural Funds in the 2021-2027 funding period should focus on innovation and digitization of the economy and strengthen SMEs. To this end, high-performance broadband and 5G networks in the territory of the EU Member States are essential.
- Far more equity and venture capital is needed to optimize the dwindling founder scene activity from the start-up to the growth phase. Better access to capital for investors, especially for research-active and innovative younger companies, is crucial for their future.
- Due to the permanent technological revolution, especially in the ICT sector, the strengthening of the existing EU HORIZON PROGRAMME from 2020 - 2027 must be cumulatively combined with regional policy and thus strengthened.
- The newly elected European Parliament must become the laboratory of a kind of new design policy, i.e. more cross-party, substantive majority voting, in order to advance important issues and tasks in the EU, such as

855 See Chapter 8.9.3

856 Europlan Commission: „Draft Ethics Guidelines for Trustworthy AI", *High-Level Expert Group on Artifical Intelligence*, Brussels, 1812.2018, pages 14-23.

the application of majority voting in foreign and security policy as well as in monetary and fiscal policy.

Chapter 12: Conclusion

As this research has demonstrated, many of the TTIP criticisms overall are non-fact based and unjustified. They are rooted in fears and past actually unrelated events such as the Iraq war under the Bush Administration, Guantanamo tortures, and the NSA scandal. These examples demonstrate the constructivism approach that politics and emotions cannot be separated. However, globalization cannot be halted, and it will wait neither for the EU nor for the US. Therefore, policy makers can only target those fears specifically by educating the public further about facts vs. fiction related to TTIP. During the scope of this research, not all aspects of TTIP could be covered and this research serves mainly for summary purposes and to raise understanding about TTIP. However, even by only touching on the main points, the following becomes apparent:

Apart from trade liberalization and control of the adherence to the competition, a common Euro-Atlantic energy policy is to be included in a transatlantic agreement according to the European model, as well as a common public health policy for both continents. A European-American energy policy has the power to act as a role model and therefore affect the BRICS states to change their consumption habits in order to avoid CO2 entropy. In comparison to Asia and Latin America, the U.S. and Europe have aging societies requiring more health supplies and investments. By building a network structure, common research and development policies, transfer of technology and enterprise cooperation, smart mobility as well as a solid environmental and public health policy (smart health) are to play an important role in the agreement on both sides. As outlined in this book, the opportunities of TTIP exceed the risks overall. Not only can the US-EU friendship be emphasized rooted in common values and world leadership by TTIP, but also peace and prosperity can be advanced at the same time with this geostrategic agreement. Essentially, a transatlantic agreement presents an opportunity for the EU and the US to create the highest standards in the world on environment, labor and many other crucial subjects. Negotiations about the Euro-Atlantic transatlantic agreement area offer large opportunities to build key questions concerning the fate and future of our time in terms of the agreement between the U.S. and the European Union.

The peculiarity of TTIP is that the agreement is part of a new generation of international treaties and is negotiated between the world's largest economic blocs. Mere agreements to reduce tariff barriers would not lead to social discourse, nor would it have a significant impact on global trade. The real barriers to trade and market entry barriers are the non-tariff barriers in the 21st century.

After TTIP negotiations failed, some of the drafts/ chapters were still ratified individually after engaging in comprehensive dialogue between the negotiating partners in the context of mutual trade links. However, this only pertained to soybean trade as well as the pharmaceutical industry. As for the remaining TTIP draft chapters, therefore, the question arises as to when will the barriers between the EU and the US be removed? Both markets (EU and US) have long-term saturation tendencies, while third countries become more attractive for world trade and can thus set standards. In the event that the agreement enters into force, subsequent agreements on the de facto reduction of remaining non-tariff barriers will no longer have any significant effects. This is due to a higher degree of integration created by TTIP between the EU and the US. Consequently, the future political motivation to reach agreements that go beyond the regulatory content of a comprehensive transatlantic trade agreement must be considered to be negligible.

Separated from the direct negotiators, the timing of a transatlantic agreement becoming an integral part of global trade links is crucial. In order to establish a global meaningful standard based on the understanding of both negotiating partners, it is necessary to ratify a transatlantic agreement before future bilateral agreements. Examples include the potential expansion of the Trans-Pacific Partnership and future comprehensive agreements that China will have (such as the Regional Comprehensive Economic Partnership). In this way, the maintenance of flows of goods is particularly encouraged by investment. In turn, therefore, ISDS clauses must be considered as to which investments are to be secured[857].

Unless developed countries are able to agree on a level above the previous standard, future negotiations will not make any improvements. Accordingly, this picture also includes the importance for EU and US companies of achieving a qualitative and comprehensive agreement.

857 Grzanna, Marcel. "Wie China den Freihandel verschlief". *Sueddeutsche Zeitung.* August 14, 2014. https://www.sueddeutsche.de/wirtschaft/ttip-abkommen-wie-china-den-freihandel-verschlief-1.2089495

The new scholarly contribution of this book is that it does not, like many other studies, predict trade patterns and employment figures, but explicitly also the measures contained in the agreement to align those non-tariff barriers with the individual success factors of the key industries, automotive and pharmaceutical industries. This shows that the developments of the past within existing free trade areas will be transferable to the general processes within the EU and the US. Excluding a development such as that shown by MERCOSUR, positive welfare effects can be identified for the economic area through cost-related effects. There are also parallels for the individual branches of industry. As in the past, the automotive industry benefits in the scenarios from the removal of tariff and non-tariff barriers sustainably, the pharmaceutical industry above all from regulations in the field of IPR. A general impairment cannot be predicted for both industries.

The strategic changes outlined above show that they are stronger and more concrete for the automotive industry as a whole due to the higher cost-side effect compared to the scenarios that have been created for the pharmaceutical industry. The scope of the cost-side effect must be directly linked to TTIP and distinguishes the agreement from other FTAs. The necessary differentiation is mainly due to the geographical location and importance of the EU and US economies in global trade and the extent of the agreement sought. The potential role model effect with subsequent standardization and the situation with regard to the combination of sourcing and production strategies should be highlighted. For the pharmaceutical industry, both the cost-side effect of a tariff reduction and the selective alignment are too small to produce lasting changes. In addition to R&D, the determinants of the long-term orientation are and will remain the health systems, which will experience an indirect intervention through the IPR enshrined in TTIP.

The strategic changes that the agreement will bring to the automotive and pharmaceutical industries do not change the globalization of the markets. Demand in the respective market, proximity to customers, the use of comparative advantages and, above all, modified intra-company trading will continue to be decisive for both major global industries.

The European Union can only remain a community of values in a turbulent international community of states, if it works harmoniously internally, if it finally applies the "double majority" that has long been agreed upon in the area of financial and tax policy, and if it expands its foreign policy in global competition. The EU must set stronger footprints to the outside world to help shape the international system of tomorrow[858]. It has so far demonstrated brilliantly that, within the framework of the modernization of the international trade order (WTO), it is committed to global standard setting and to help shaping world trade more efficiently. This rule and regulation setting is also needed in international conflict management in order to create a more peaceful world. Due to the corona crisis, cooperation between the EU and the U.S. is more urgent than ever before, especially in regard to public health challenges and climate change issues mentioned in this dissertation that are connected to general causes of pandemic outbreaks (swine flu, BSE, COVID-19) such as wildlife habit destruction[859] as well as animal abuse and mistreatment[860]. In order to tackle these issues connected to trade, it would be so much easier to combat these difficult tasks if the EU and the U.S. could team-up rather than going this route "alone" the hard way.

---

858 European Commission. *How our Europe will gain its strength: op-ed by Ursula von der Leyen, President of the European Commission.* April 4, 2020. https://ec.europa.eu/commission/presscorner/detail/en/ac_20_602

859 Roston, Eric/ Bloomberg. "Want to Stop the Next Pandemic? Start Protecting Wildlife Habitats". *Time.* April 8, 2020. https://time.com/5817363/wildlife-habitats-disease-pandemics/?fbclid=IwAR3rh9wPneEZtgcSTU69J2WS-yTIkRN-7Wt0bwQr_eP-TpEbtcMl9DGnZp4

860 Allen, Elisa. "The best way to prevent future pandemics like coronavirus? Stop eating meat and go vegan". *EuroNews.* April 2, 2020. https://www.euronews.com/2020/04/01/the-best-way-prevent-future-pandemics-like-coronavirus-stop-eating-meat-and-go-vegan-view?fbclid=IwAR3ln2UeL--NiFhzQdR_e0hoRTcw5xloGCth5Q3zo22d6jLX8bpT1OajS8E

Appendix A

A.1 Interviews

- Interview 1: Teleconference with Ms. Günnewig, EU-Affairs Department of Volkswagen AG in Brussels. November 21, 2016.
- Interview 2: Teleconference with Dr. Koers, Head of the Department of Economics and Strategy of the VDA in Berlin. November 25, 2017.
- Interview 3: Teleconference with Mr. Heck, Head of BPI in Brussels. December 17, 2018.
- Interview 4: Teleconference with Mr. Eckelmann, Managing Director of Bayer Weimar GmbH und Co. KG VI. January 9, 2019.

Appendix B

B.1 TTIP Content – An Overview[861]

European Commission

The Transatlantic Trade and Investment Partnership (TTIP)
Towards an EU-US trade deal

Inside TTIP

An overview and chapter-by-chapter guide in plain English

February 2016 edition

Trade

861 European Commission. "Inside TTIP". *TTIP Content – An Overview,* page 9. Luxembourg: Publications Office of the European Union, 2015. http://trade.ec.europa.eu/doclib/docs/2015/july/tradoc_153635.pdf

Appendix C

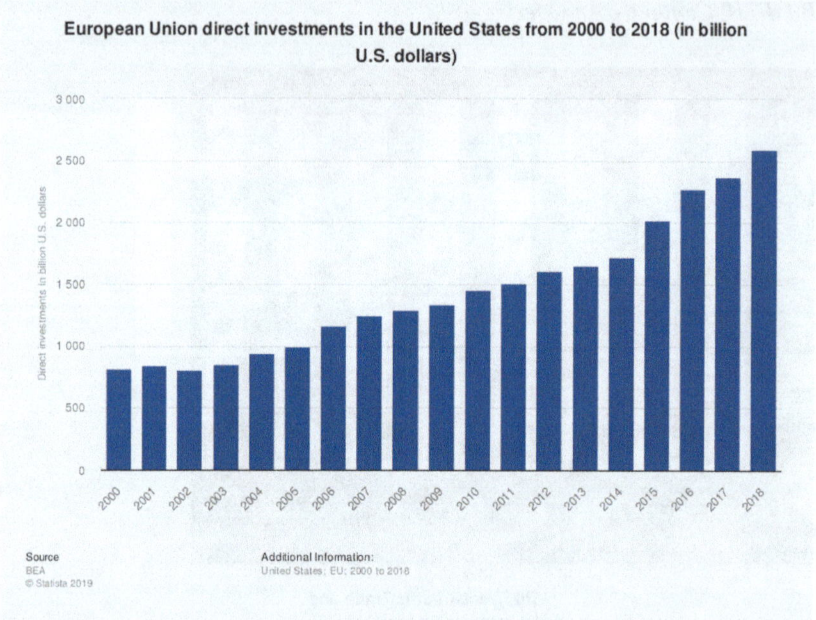

This statistic shows the value of foreign direct investments from the European Union into the United States from 2000 to 2018. European Union direct investments in the U.S. totaled over 2.59 trillion U.S. dollars in 2018.[862]

862 BEA. "European Union direct investments in the United States from 2000 to 2018 (in billion U.S. dollars)." Chart. July 26, 2019. *Statista.* Accessed April 22, 2020. https://www.statista.com/statistics/547083/eu-fdi-in-us/

Appendix D

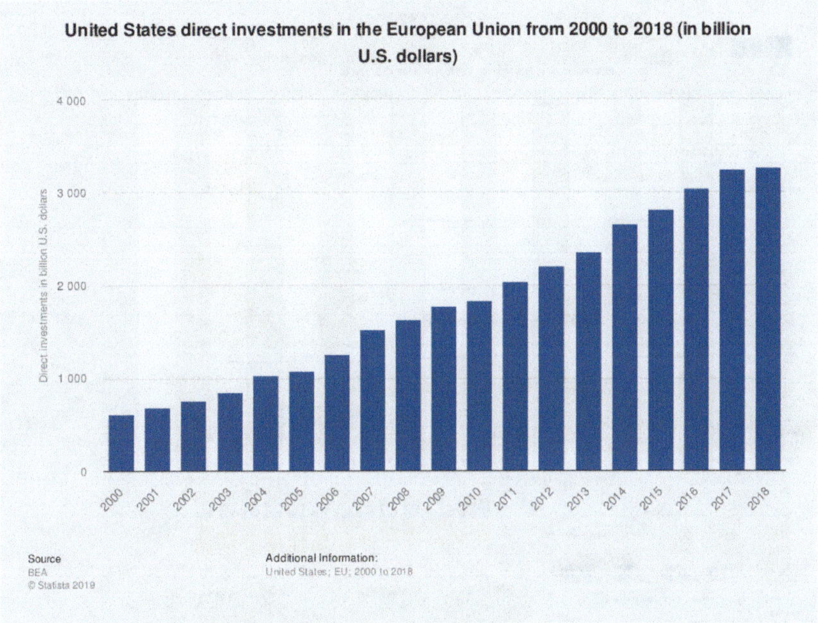

This statistic shows the value of foreign direct investments from the United States into the European Union from 2000 to 2018. United States direct investments in the EU totaled over 3.27 trillion U.S. dollars in 2018.[863]

863 BEA. "United States direct investments in the European Union from 2000 to 2018 (in billion U.S. dollars)." Chart. November 14, 2019. Statista. Accessed April 22, 2020. https://www.statista.com/statistics/547108/us-fdi-in-eu/

Appendix E[864]

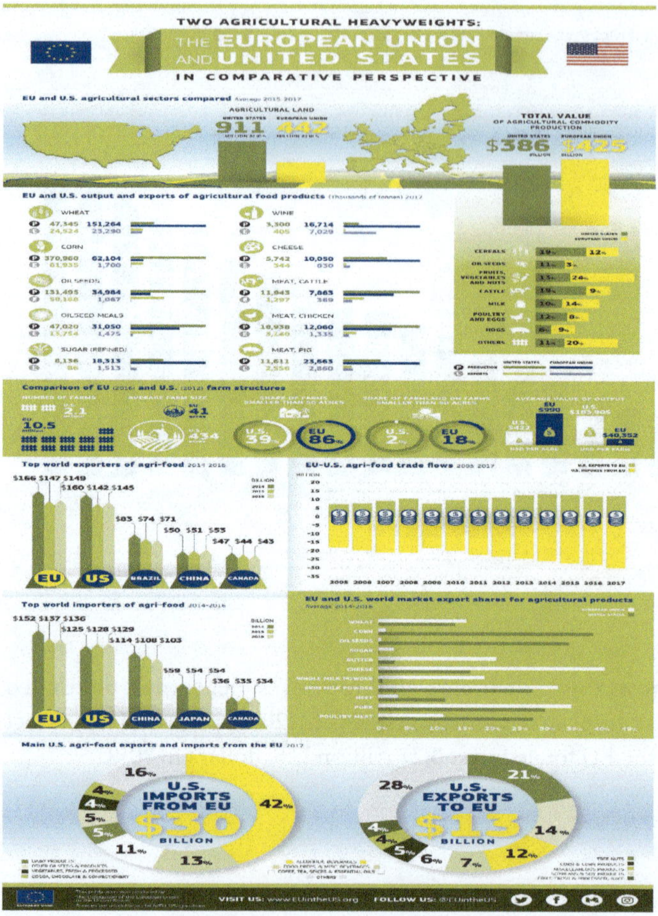

864 Delegation of the European Union to the United States. “Two Agricultural Heavyweights”. November 1, 2019. https://eeas.europa.eu/delegations/united-states-america/56420/two-agricultural-heavyweights_kk

Appendix F[865]

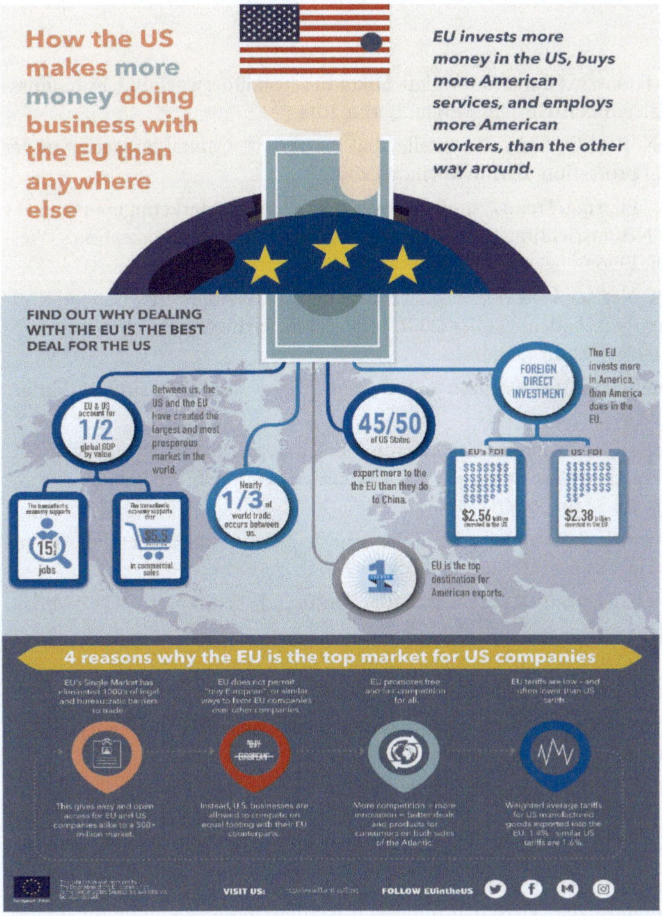

865 Delegation of the European Union to the United States. *EU-U.S. Doing Business.* February 20, 2020. https://eeas.europa.eu/sites/eeas/files/us_downpayment_extended_vertical_0.pdf

Core Sources/ Primary Sources

Monographs

Aust Stefan and Thomas Ammann. Digital Diktatur: Totalüberwachung Datenmissbrauch,Cyberkrieg, Econ-Ullstein-Verlag, Berlin 2014.

Baecker, Philipp N. Real Options and Intellectual Property – Capital budgeting under imperfect patent protection. Berlin: Springer, 2007.

Crisand, Marcel. Pharma-Trends und innovatives Pharma-Marketingmanagement – Strategische Neuausrichtung einer ärztegerichteten Marketingkonzeption. Wiesbaden: Springer, 1996.

Ehrhardt, Marcus. Netzwerkeffekte, Standardisierung und Wettbewerbsstrategie. Universitaet Giessen, Wiesbaden: Gabler, 2001. https://link.springer.com/content/pdf/bfm:978-3-322-91480-4/1.pdfInaugural-

Friedmann Thomas. „Die Welt ist flach ", 1st Edition, Farrar Straus & Giroux - Verlag, New York, 2005.

Frontzkowski, Katja. Die Probleme des kanadischen Außenhandels unter Berücksichtigung der potentiellen Auswirkungen des nordamerikanischen Freihandelsabkommens, Frankfurt am Main, 1994.

Gerken, Lueder. Von Freiheit und Freihandel - Grundzüge einer orderliberalen Außenwirtschaftstheorie. Tübingen: Mohr Siebeck, 1999.

Giese, Ernst: Globalisierung der Wirtschaft, Ferdinand Schöningh /UTP-Verlag, Paderborn, 2011.

Hahn, Olaf. Patient Relationship Management – Ein CRM-Ansatz für die pharmazeutische Industrie. Wiesbaden: Springer, 2006.

Johnson, Scholes, Whittington. Strategisches Management eine Einführung – Analyse, Entscheidung und Umsetzung. Munich: Pearson, 2011. 9th Edition.

Krugman, Obstfeld, Melitz. Internationale Wirtschaft - Theorie und Politik der Außenwirtschaft. Munich: Pearson, 2012. 9th Edition.

Le Monde diplomatique. Atlas der Globalisierung: Welt in Bewegung, Le Monde diplomatique-Verlag, Berlin 2019.

Meyer Bernd: Wie muss die Wirtschaft umgebaut werden? Bundeszentrale für politische Bildung, Bd. 717, Bonn 2008.

Missler-Behr, Magdalena. Methoden der Szenarioanalyse. Wiesbaden: Springer, 1993.

Nolte. Freihandel, Protektion oder Fair-Trade auf den Weltautomobilmärkten? – Analyse von struktureller Entwicklung und Wachstumspotentialen der Pkw – Industrie, insbesondere der Voluminahersteller in der Bundesrepublik Deutschland, Frankfurt am Main, 1991.

Pfändner. Strategische Entscheidungen für den europäischen Binnenmarkt – Am Beispiel der deutschen Automobilindustrie, Frankfurt am Main; New York: P. Lang,1992.

Schmidt, Sascha. Megamerger in der pharmazeutischen Indutrie – Ein Beitrag zur Strategieprozessforschung, Bern: Peter Haupt Verlag, 2000.

Stratmann, Werner: Der Zusammenhang zwischen Wertschöpfungsketten und strategischen Wettbewerbsvorteilen. Fallstudien mit strategischer Analyse am Beispiel der europäischen Automobilwirtschaft, Frankfurt 2010.

Schmoly, Jens. Wandel der Unternehmensorganisation infolge des globalen Wettbewerbs – Dargestellt am Beispiel der chemisch-pharmazeutischen Industrie, Marburg, 2005.

Steinmann, Schreyögg, Koch. Management – Grundlagen der Unternehmensführung, Konzepte, Funktionen, Fallstudien. Wiesbaden: Springer, 1997, 4th Edition.

Stieglitz, Joseph and Bruce Greenwald. Die innovative Gesellschaft, Econ-Verlag, Berlin, Columbia University Press 2015.

Wüste, Peter. Innovations- und Nachhaltigkeitsstrategien in der Automobilindustrie – Der Einfluss des Marktes auf die Entwicklung alternativer Antriebe, Hamburg: Diplomica, 2010.

Books

Bartels, Lorand and Ortino, Federico. Regional Trade Agreements and the WTO legal System, Oxford, 2007.

Bundeszentrale fuer politische Bildung. Fischer Weltalmanach 2018, Fischer Verlag: Frankfurt/M. 2018.

Comanor, William and Schweitzer, Stuart. Pharmaceutical Economics, Padstow: Engelska, 2013.

De Melo, Jaime and Arvind Panagariya. New Dimensions in regional integration, Cambridge University Press, 1993.

Fischer and Breitenbach. Die Pharmaindustrie – Einblick, Durchblick, Perspektiven. Munich: Springer, 2007, 2nd Edition.

Hesser, Feilzer, de Vries. Standardization in Companies and Markets, Helmut-Schmidt-University: Hamburg, 2010.

Kilper, Heiderose and Ludger Pries. Die Globalisierungsspirale in der deutschen Automobilindustrie – Hersteller-Zulieferer-Beziehungen als Herausforderungen für Wirtschaft und Politik, Econstor: Munich and Mering, 1999.

Pries, Ludger and Markus Hertwig. Deutsche Autoproduktion im globalen Wandel – Altindustrie im Rückwärtsgang oder Hightech-Branche mit Zukunft? Berlin: Sigma, 2005.

Radtke, Pilipp and Abele Eberhard: Die smarte Revolution in der Automobilindustrie. Redline-Wirtschaft bei Überreuter, Frankfurt/M. 2014.

Roy, Joaquín. A New Atlantic Community: The European Union, the US and Latin America, European Union Center/ Jean Monnet Chair, University of Miami, Coral Gables, FL, 2015. https://eucenter.as.miami.edu/_assets/pdf/atlantic2015.pdf

Roy, Joaquín and Roberto Dominguez Riviera. The TTIP: The Transatlantic Trade and Investment Partnership between the European Union and the United States, European Union Center/ Jean Monnet Chair, University of Miami, Coral Gables, FL, 2014. https://eucenter.as.miami.edu/_assets/pdf/ttip.pdf

Schöffski/Fricke/Guminski. Pharmabetriebslehre. Berlin: Springer, 2008, 2nd Edition.

Stieglitz, Joseph: Reich und Arm – die wachsende Ungleichheit in unserer Gesellschaft, Munich: Random House, 2017.

Stieglitz, Joseph: Der Preis der Ungleichheit – wie die Spaltung der Gesellschaft unsere Zukunft bedroht, Munich: Pantheon-Random–House, 2014.

Voit, Ralph. Marktzugangsbedingungen und Marktzugangsschranken, Baden-Baden: Nomos, 2010.

Weißer Ulfried: Erfolgsmodell Soziale Marktwirtschaft, Wiesbaden: Springer, 2017.

Research Studies, Legal Reports, Position and Discussion Papers

AHK. "Exporthandbuch NAFTA", 2011.

Bekerman, Sirlin. "Static and dynamic impacts of Mercosur: the case of the pharmaceutical sector", Cepal Review 75, 2001.

Bertelsmann Stiftung. "Die Transatlantische Handels- und Investitionspartnerschaft (THIP)- Wem nutzt ein Transatlantisches Freihandelsabkommen?", 2013 VIII.

BMWi: "Transatlantische Handels- und Investitionspartnerschaft (TTIP) zwischen der EU und den USA; Fakten und Informationen: häufig gestellte Fragen und Antworten", 2014 XI

Buko Pharma-Kampange. "Pharma-Brief Nr. 1", January/ February 2009.

Bundesverband der Pharmazeutischen Industrie e.V. "Pharma-Daten 2014", October 2014.

Bundesverband der Deutschen Industrie e.V. "Positionspapier Schutz europäischer Investitionen im Ausland: Anforderungen an Investitionsabkommen der EU", March 2014. Canadian Centre for Policy Alternatives: "Making sense of the CETA", September 2014, Ottawa.

Center of Economic Policy Research: "Reducing Transatlantic Barriers to Trade and Investment, an Economic Assessment", Final Project Report, March 2013.

Commons Network: "The Transatlantic Trade and Investment Partnership-TTIP: A civil society response to the big pharma wish list". March 24, 2014.

Daemmrich, Arthur: "U.S. Healthcare Reform and the Pharmaceutical Industry". *Working Paper.* September 14, 2011.

Deutsch Thailändische Handelskammer: "ASEAN Roadmap 2015 Geschäftschancen für den deutschen Mittelstand", 2013.

ECORYS: Study by „EU-US High Level Working Group"-Final Report. October 22, 2012.

Ferguson Niall: "Der Niedergang des Westens", Ullstein Vrlag/Propyläen Verlag, Berlin 2013.

Fischer-Lescano, Horst: "Europa- und verfassungsrechtliche Vorgaben für das

Comprehensive Economic and Trade Agreement der EU und Kanada (CETA)", October 2014, Munich.

Fiorentiho, Verdeja, Toqueboeuf: "The Changing Landscape of Regional Trade Agreements: Update 2006", WTO, 2007 IX.

Friedrich-Ebert Stiftung: "TTIP, Freihandel und wirtschaftliche Entwicklung", Dezember 2014.

Hans Böckler Stiftung: "Arbeitspapier Nr. 303 – Das transatlantische Handels- und Investitionsabkommen zwischen der EU und den USA", May 2014.

Hagelüken, Alexander: „Das gespaltene Land: "Wie Ungleichheit unsere Gesellschaft zerstört und was die Politik ändern muss", Munich: Knaur-Verlag, 2017.

Healey, Justin. "Free Trade and Globalisation", Spinney Press, 2014.

Hüther, Michael/ Diermeier, Matthias/ Goecke, Henry: „Die erschöpfte Globalisierung - zwischen transatlantischer Orientierung und chinesischem Weg", Wiesbaden: Springer Verlag, 2018.

Ifo Schnelldienst 6/2013 – 66. Jahrgang – March 27, 2013. https://www.ifo.de/DocDL/SD-6-2013.pdf

Institut für Makroökonomie und Konjunkturforschung: "Außenhandel der EU: Eine regionale und sektorale Analyse", Nr. 83. June 2013.

Institut für Makroökonomie und Konjunkturforschung: "Außenhandel der USA: Eine regionale und sektorale Analyse", Nr. 85. July 2013.

Kommerskollegium National Board of Trade: "Potential Effect of an EU-US Free Trade Agreement"-Sweden in Focus, 2012.

Leibnitz-Institut für Wirtschaftsforschung an der Universität München e.V.: "Dimensionen und Auswirkungen eines Freihandelsabkommens zwischen der EU und den USA", January 2013.

Leibnitz-Institut für Wirtschaftsforschung an der Universität München e.V.: "Dimensionen und Auswirkungen eines Freihandelsabkommens zwischen der EU und den USA: Zusammenfassung", February 2013.

Mayer, Franz. "Stellt das geplante Freihandelsabkommen der EU mit Kanada ein gemischtes Abkommen dar?" – Rechtsgutachten für das BMWi, August 2014.

PWC: "How to stay No. 1! – Impulse für die zentralen Herausforderungen der Automobilindustrie", September 2013.

PWC: "From vision to decision" Pharma 2020, November 2012.

Ricardo, David: "Über die Grundsätze der politischen Ökonomie und der Besteuerung" (Hrsg. Gehrke Christian), Metropolis-Verlag, Marburg 2000.

Rifkin, Jeremy: *Die dritte industrielle Revolution*. Campus Verlag, Frankfurt/M, New York, 2011.

Safranski, Rüdiger: *Wieviel Globalisierung verträgt der Mensch?* Munich: Carl Hanser,, 2013.

Sandschneider, Eberhard: „Der erfolgreiche Abstieg Europas: heute Macht abgeben, um morgen zu gewinnen ", Munich: Carl Hanser, 2011.

Seifert, Thomas: „Die Pazifische Epoche: Wie Europa gegen die neue Weltmacht Asien bestehen kann", Vienna: Deuticke-Verlag im Paul Zsolnay-Verlag, 2015.

Schill, Stephan. "Auswirkungen der Bestimmungen zum Investitionsschutz und zu den Investor-Staat-Schiedsverfahren im Entwurf des Freihandelsabkommens zwischen der EU und Kanada (CETA) auf den Handlungsspielraum des Gesetzgebers" (Kurzgutachten), 2014.

Schröder, Christoph. "Industrielle Arbeitskosten im internationalen Vergleich", 2012.

Snyder, Timothy: „Der Weg in die Unfreiheit (Russland, Europa, Amerika) ". (Prof. of History, Yale University), Munich: C.H. Beck, 2018.

Stratmann, Uwe. "Der Zusammenhang zwischen Wertschöpfungsorganisation und strategischen Wettbewerbsvorteilen - Eine auf Fallstudien basierende strategische Analyse am Beispiel der europäischen Automobilwirtschaft", Mering Rainer Hampp Verlag, 2010.

UNCTAD: "Recent Developments in Investor-State Dispute Settlement", May 2013.

U.S. International Trade Commission: "The impact of trade agreements; Effect of the

Tokyo Round, U.S- Israel FTA, U.S.-Canada FTA, NAFTA and the Uruguay Round on the U.S. economy", 2003.

Vetter, Reinhold: „Nationalismus im Osten Europas", *Zentralen für politische Bildung*,

Bonn, Christoph Links-Verlag, Berlin 2017.

World Bank: "Global economic prospects, Trade, Regionalism and Development"; 2005.

Zakaria, Fareed: „Der Aufstieg der Anderen: das post-amerikanische Zeitalter", Munich:

Siedler/ Random House, 2009.

EU-Documents

Aus Politik und Zeitgeschehen (APuZ), 64. Jg. 1-3/2014 („Welthandel")

Aus Politik und Zeitgeschehen (APuZ), 67. Jg. 18/2017 („USA")

Rat der Europäischen Union 11103/13 DCL1, October 9, 2014.

Delegation of the European Union to the United States. *Trade.* http://www.euintheustrade.org/

European Commission. "Automobilindustrie – Umfassende Entwicklungsanalyse der Autoindustrie in Europa", 2009.

European Commission: "Consolidated CETA Text". September 26, 2014.

European Commission. "Germany". *Vetretung in Deutschland.* Accessed December 9, 2019. https://ec.europa.eu/germany/

European Commission: *Kommission macht Vorschläge zur Reform der WTO.* September 8, 2018. http://ec.europa.eu/index_de.htm

European Commission. "News archive". http://trade.ec.europa.eu/doclib/press/index.cfm?id=1139

European Commission: "Pharmaceutical Industry – A strategic sector for the European economy", SWD (2014) 216 final/2. August 1, 2014.

European Commission. "State of the Union". *Speech by President Juncker.* 2016, 2017, 2018.

European Commission: "The Transatlantic Trade and Investment Partnership Regulatory Issues – EU Position on motor vehicles". May 14, 2014.

European Commission: "The Transatlantic Trade and Investment Partnership Regulatory Issues – EU Position on pharmaceutical products", May 14, 2014.

European Union. *Lisbon Treaty.* Berlin, 2010.

Journal Articles (Peer Reviewed)

Bhardwaj/Padamavati: "The impact of patent-linkage on marketing of Generic Drugs", Journal of Intellectual Property Rights Vol. 18, July 2013, pp 316 – 322.

Langhammer, Rolf. "Effekte der Handelsschaffung und Handelsumlenkung".

Wirtschaftswissenschaftliches Studium. Beck, Munich, Vol. 9, 1980, Issue 2, pages 75-76. http://www.econstor.eu/handle/10419/3691. Accessed December 9, 2019.

Newspapers & Periodicals

Aus Politik und Zeitgeschehen (APuZ), 67. Jg. 37/2017 („Europa")

Aus Politik und Zeitgeschehen (APuZ), 68. Jg. 4-5/2018 („Freihandel")

Bundesministerium für Wirtschaft und Energie (BMWi): "Transatlantische Handels- und Investitionspartnerschaft (TTIP) zwischen der EU und den USA; Fakten und Informationen: häufig gestellte Fragen und Antworten", Berlin 2014.

Das Parlament (2018, 2019)

Frankfurter Allgemeine Zeitung (2015, 2016, 2017, 2018, 2019, 2020)

Handelsblatt G 02531 Nr. 207. October 28, 2014.

Handelsblatt G 02531 Nr. 220. November 14. – 16, 2014.

Handelsblatt G 02531 Nr. 233. December 03, 2014.

Handelsblatt G 02531 Nr. 02. January 05, 2015.

Handelsblatt G 02531 Nr. 08. January 13, 2015.

Handelsblatt G 02531 Nr. 11. January 16. – 18., 2015.

Handelsblatt (2014, 2015, 2016, 2017, 2018, 2019, 2020)

Markets International 2018/ 2019 (Germany Trade & Invest)

NBC News 2020

New York Times 2016

OstContact-Außenwirtschaftsmagazin 2018

Bibliography

Abbott, Roderick. "A close look at the Transatlantic Trade and Investment Partnership". *Europe's World,* March 28, 2014. https://www.friendsofeurope.org/global-europe/a-close-look-at-the-transatlantic-trade-and-investment-partnership

Abbott, Frederick M. "The North American Integration Regime and Its Implications for the World Trading System." In *The EU, the WTO, and the NAFTA*, The EU, the WTO, and the NAFTA, Chapter 6. Oxford University Press, 2001.

Alden, Edward. „With TPP and TTIP, U.S. and EU Reassert Control Over Rules of Global Trade ". *World Politics Review.* December 19, 2013. http://www.worldpoliticsreview.com/articles/13454/with-tpp-and-ttip-u-s-and-eu-reassert-control-over-rules-of-global-trade

Alden, Edward. "How President Putin Has Given a Boost to U.S.-EU Trade Talks". *Council on Foreign Relations.* March 25, 2014. http://blogs.cfr.org/renewing-america/2014/03/25/how-president-putin-has-given-a-boost-to-u-s-eu-trade-talks/

AmCham Germany. *Transatlantic Business Barometer 2020.* https://www.amcham.de/fileadmin/user_upload/Publications/Business-Barometer/2020/Transatlantic_Business_Barometer_2020_ENG_WEB.pdf

Ash, Timothy G. "La Gran Red de Occidente". *El País: Opinión.* July 15, 2013.

http://elpais.com/elpais/2013/07/12/opinion/1373629706_693593.html

Atilgan, Canan et al. "The Eurasion Union". *Konrad-Adenauer Stiftung International Reports,* February 2014, page 8-10. http://www.kas.de/wf/doc/kas_36785-544-2-30.pdf?140207134233

Baldwin, Richard E. *A Domino Theory of Regionalism.* 1993

Baldwin, Richard. "A Domino Theory of Regionalism." *NBER Working Paper Series,* 1993, 4465.

Baldwin, Richard E. *21st Century Regionalism Filling the Gap between 21st Century Trade and 20th Century Trade Rules.* 2010.

Barisch, Katynka and Michael Heise. „Will TTIP Harm The Global Trading System?", *Yale Global Online.* January 9, 2014. http://yaleglobal.yale.edu/content/will-ttip-harm-global-trading-system

Beise, Marc. "Handel für alle – eine transatlantische Freihandelszone", *Süddeutsche Zeitung,* Nr. 136, June 15/ 16, 2013, p. 11-12a.

Berger, Roland. „Europas Werte, Europas Wirtschaft". *Frankfurter Allgemeine Zeitung,* Nr. 167, June 22, 2013, page 7.

Bhagwati, Jagdish. "Regionalism versus Multilateralism." *World Economy* 15, no. 5, 1992: 535-56.

Bhagwati, Jagdish. *Termites in the Trading System: How Preferential Agreements Undermine Free Trade.* Oxford University Press, 2008.

Bhagwati, Jagdish. "Why PTAs Are a Pox on the World Trading System." In *Termites in the Trading System*, Termites in the Trading System, Chapter 3. Oxford University Press, 2008.

Bomberg, Elizabeth, John Peterson, and Richard Corbett. *The European Union: How Does it Work?* NY: Oxford, 2012, 3rd edition.

Boland, Margaret and Lily Moodey. *The "TTIP-Ping" Point? NAFTA's Uncertain Future.* Washington, United States, Washington: The Council on Hemispheric Affairs, 2013.

Brattberg, Eric. "TTIP is too important to fail". *Europe's World*, January 31, 2016. Accessed May 12, 2016. http://europesworld.org/2016/01/31/ttip-important-fail/#.VzNgSOSvyek

Bromund, Theodore et al. "Transatlantic Trade and Investment Partnership (TTIP) : Pitfalls and Promises". *The Heritage Foundation,* Issue Brief # 4100 on Trade, December 5, 2013. http://www.heritage.org/research/reports/2013/12/transatlantic-trade-and-investment-partnership-ttip-pitfalls-and-promises

Bundesministerium fuer Bildung und Forschung (Federal Ministry of Education and Research in Germany). "Industrie 4.0". Accessed December 9, 2019. https://www.bmbf.de/de/zukunftsprojekt-industrie-4-0-848.html

Bundeszentral fuer politische Bildung (Federal Agency for Civic Education in Germany).

« Altersstruktur und Bevoelkerungsentwicklung ». October 18, 2018. http://www.bpb.de/nachschlagen/zahlen-und-fakten/europa/70503/altersstruktur

Cameron, Fraser. *The EU Model of Integration – Relevance Elsewhere ?* University of Miami European Union Center and Jean Monnet Chair, 2005. Accessed May 24, 2016. https://eucenter.as.miami.edu/_assets/pdf/cameroneuma1.pdf

Campbell, Kurt, and Michael O'Hanlon. *Hard Power: The New Politics of National Security.* New York: Basic Books, 2007. <http://public.eblib.com/choice/publicfullrecord.aspx?p=952693>

Center for Transatlantic Relations, The Paul H. Nitze School of Advanced International Studies, The Johns Hopkins University. "TTIP and the Transatlantic Economy". 2014. http://transatlantic.sais-jhu.edu/

Cini, Michelle & Perez-Solórzano Borragán, Nieves. *European Union Politics.* Oxford University Press, 2003.

Congressional Research Service. *Trade Promotion Authority (TPA): Frequently Asked Questions.* June 21, 2019. https://fas.org/sgp/crs/misc/R43491.pdf

Corporate Europe Observatory. *Leaked European Commission PR strategy: "Communicating on TTIP".* November 25, 2013. http://corporateeurope.org/trade/2013/11/leaked-european-commission-pr-strategy-communicating-ttip

Council of the European Union. "Directives for the negotiation on the Transatlantic Trade and Investment Partnership between the European Union and the United States of America". Nr. 11103/13, Brussels, June 17, 2013, pp. 5-14. http://data.consilium.europa.eu/doc/document/ST-11103-2013-DCL-1/en/pdf

Das Parliament. "Das Transatlantik Handels- und Investitions-Partnerschaftsabkommen (TTIP)" in: *TTIP im Kontext anderer Freihandelsabkommen.* 64.Jg. 50-51/2014. December 8, 2014 p. 20-23.

De Gucht, Karel. "Der richtige Anstoß", *Süddeutsche Zeitung*, Nr. 184, August 10 /11, 2013, p. 12-13.

De Gucht, Karel. *The Transatlantic Trade and Investment Partnership: Global Impacts.* Brussels: European Commission, 2013.

De Lecea, Antonio. 2014. "The EU-US trade and investment before and after TTIP: What can Latin America expect from it?" in Joaquín Roy and Roberto Domínguez (editors). *The TTIP: The Transatlantic Trade and Investment Partnership between the European Union and the United States.* Miami-Florida European Union Center/ Jean Monnet Chair, page 1. https://eucenter.as.miami.edu/_assets/pdf/ttip.pdf

De Ville, Ferdi and Gabriel Siles-Bruegge. 2016. *TTIP: The Truth about the Transatlantic Trade and Investment Partnership.* Cambridge/Malden: Polity Press, page 2.

Delegation of the European Union to the United States. *Op-Ed by Ambassador Vale De Almeida in the Hill: "More Trade Brings More Jobs".* December 12, 2013. Accessed March 24, 2016. http://www.euintheus.org/press-media/op-ed-by-ambassador-vale-de-almeida-in-the-hill-more-trade-brings-more-jobs/

Delegation of the European Union to the United States. "The EU is the Most Important Trading Partner for the US". *The US & the EU.* Accessed April 6, 2020. http://www.euintheustrade.org/wp-content/uploads/2019/07/US-main-infographic_revised_v3.pdf

Delegation of the European Union to the United States. "Transatlantic Trade and Investment Partnership (TTIP). Creating Jobs, Boosting Exports, and Investing in the Economy of Tomorrow". *TTIP Fact Sheet.* http://www.consulfrance-miami.org/IMG/pdf/TTIP_Publicatiopn_85x11in_High_res.pdf

Dendrinou, Viktoria. "TTIP Talks Look Unlikely to Conclude during Obama's Final Term." *The Wall Street Journal Eastern Edition*, 2016.

Deutsche Presse Agentur. „Obama will Handel mit Europa erleichtern". *Thüringer Allgemeine,* 14 July 2013, page 2.

Die Zeit. "Was handeln wir uns da ein?" *TTIP. Nr. 27, 2014.* July 10, 2014.

https://www.zeit.de/2014/27/ttip-freihandelsabkommen-us-konzerne

Doyle, M. "The Democratic Peace". *International Security* 19, no. 4 (1995): 180-84.

Dudek, Carolyn M. 2014. "Genetically Modified Foods and Trade Controversy", in Joaquín Roy and Roberto Domínguez (editors). *The TTIP: The Transatlantic Trade and Investment Partnership between the European Union and the United States.* Miami-Florida European Union Center/ Jean Monnet Chair, page. 111. https://eucenter.as.miami.edu/_assets/pdf/ttip.pdf

Economy in Crisis. *Transatlantic Free Trade Area (TAFTA) or Transatlantic Trade and Investment Partnership (TTIP).* Accessed March 25, 2016. http://economyincrisis.org/transatlantic-free-trade-area-tafta-or-transatlantic-trade-and-investment-partnership-ttip

English News CN. *Interview: Dutch expert says TTIP might be game changer for geopolitics.* January 31, 2014. Accessed March 26, 2016. http://news.xinhuanet.com/english/indepth/2014-01/31/c_133087281.htm

EU Delegation to the US. *The Schuman Declaration.* Accessed November 23, 2018. https://europa.eu/european-union/about-eu/symbols/europe-day/schuman-declara tion_en

EurActiv. *French Senators Strongly Attack EU-US Trade Deal.* January 13, 2014.

http://www.euractiv.com/eu-elections-2014/french-senators-violently-attack-news-532 705

EurActiv. *Brussels proposes pooling world development aid funding.* July 17, 2013.

http://www.euractiv.com/development-policy/commission-proposes-pooling-worl-ne ws-529322

EurActiv. *EU plans for own retaliation in aircraft dispute with US.* April 9, 2019. https://www.euractiv.com/section/economy-jobs/news/eu-plans-for-own-retaliation-in-airc raft-dispute-with-us/?utm_source=EURACTIV&utm_campaign=b0481c84c3-EMAI L_CAMPAIGN_2018_05_25_02_56_COPY_01&utm_medium=email&utm_term=0 _c59e2fd7a9-b0481c84c3-114732983

EurActiv. *MEPs demand moving EU elections to May 2014.* November 23, 2013. Retrieved September 2, 2013. http://www.euractiv.com/future-eu/meps-demand-moving-e u-elections-news-516221

EurActiv. *TTIP negotiations threaten European consumer protection.* December 16, 2013. http://www.euractiv.com/trade/mep-ttip-negotiations-threaten-e-interview-532363

Euractiv. *TTIP puts the EU's environmental and social policies on the line.* January 13, 2014. http://www.euractiv.com/trade/ttip-puts-eus-environmental-soci-analysis-532 724

European Commission. "2018 Annual Activity Report". *Directorate-General for Trade. Annual Report on Trade and Obstacles to investment.* June 14, 2019 http://ec.europa.e u/trade/trade-policy-and-you

European Commission. "A balanced EU-US Free Trade Agreement: Freer trade – without sacrificing Europe's standards ". Accessed May 10, 2016. http://ec.europa.eu/ priorities/balanced-eu-us-free-trade-agreement_en

European Commission. "Comprehensive Economic and Trade Agreement (CETA". *EU-Canada Trade Agreement.* Accessed December 9, 2019. https://ec.europa.eu/trad e/policy/in-focus/ceta/

European Commission. "End of Life Vehicles". *Environment.* August 7, 2019. https://ec. europa.eu/environment/waste/elv/index.htm

European Commission. "EU-Mexico Trade Agreement". April 2018. https://ec.europa.e u/trade/policy/in-focus/eu-mexico-trade-agreement/

European Commission. "European Semester 2014: strengthening the recovery". Ec.europa.eu. November 13, 2013. Retrieved November 15, 2013.

European Commission. "EU-US Trade Talks: EU and US announce 4th round of TTIP negotiations in March; Stocktaking meeting in Washington D.C. to precede next set of talks." *Press Release,* January 28, 2014.

European Commission. "EU-US Transatlantic Trade and Investment Partnership: Raw materials and energy". *Initial EU position paper.* November 15, 2014.

http://trade.ec.europa.eu/doclib/docs/2013/july/tradoc_151624.pdf

European Commission. "Expert group to advise European Commission on EU-US trade talks." *Press Release,* January 27, 2014.

European Commission. "Fact Sheet: Why the new EU proposal for an Investment Court System in TTIP is beneficial to both States and investors". *Press Release.* Brussels, November 12, 2015. http://europa.eu/rapid/press-release_MEMO-15-6060_en.htm

European Commission. "Feedback Questionnaires ". *Trade Policy Public Consultations.* Accessed May 1, 2016. http://trade.ec.europa.eu/consultations/index.cfm?cons

European Commission. "Inside TTIP: An overview and chapter-by-chapter guide in plain English". Luxembourg: Publications Office of the European Union, 2015. http://trade.ec.europa.eu/doclib/docs/2015/july/tradoc_153635.pdf

European Commission. "Investment ". *DG Trade.* January 2015. Accessed May 8, 2016. http://trade.ec.europa.eu/doclib/docs/2015/january/tradoc_153018.5%20Investment.pdf

European Commission. "Investment Protection and Investor-to-State Dispute Settlement in EU agreements". DG Trade Fact Sheet. November 26, 2013, p. 2. Accessed May 7, 2016. http://trade.ec.europa.eu/doclib/docs/2013/november/tradoc_151916.pdf

European Commission. "Local offices in EU member countries." *Representations of the European Commission.* Accessed May 9, 2016. http://ec.europa.eu/represent_en.htm

European Commission. "Online public consultation on investment protection and investor-to-state-dispute settlement (ISDS) in the Transatlantic Trade and Investment Partnership Agreement ". *Commission Staff Working Report.* Brussels, January 13, 2015, p. 4. http://trade.ec.europa.eu/doclib/docs/2015/january/tradoc_153044.pdf

European Commission. "Question and Answers on the results of the public consultation on investment protection in EU-US trade talks". *DG Trade Policy,* January 12, 2015. http://trade.ec.europa.eu/doclib/press/index.cfm?id=1233

European Commission President Barroso, Jose Manuel. *Press Release.* Brussels, February 9, 2005.

European Commission. RES Legal Europe. *Regulations on renewable energy generation.* 2012. Retrieved August 1, 2013. http://www.res-legal.eu/home/

European Commission. "The EU-South Korea free trade agreement". *Trade Policy.* Accessed December 9, 2019. https://ec.europa.eu/trade/policy/countries-and-regions/countries/south-korea/

European Commission. "The Transatlantic Trade and Investment Partnership". May 05, 2014. http://ec.europa.eu/trade/policy/in-focus/ttip/

European Daily. *Europe is still pretty close to paradise.* September 19, 2013. Accessed May 25, 2016. http://europeandaily.com/opinion/2012/09/19/europe-still-pretty-close-paradise

European Parliament Research Service Blog. "TTIP & ISDS". *EU-documents.* February 4, 2015. https://epthinktank.eu/2015/02/10/ttip-isds/

European Parliament resolution of July 8, 2015 containing the European Parliament's recommendation to the European Commission on the negotiations for the Transatlantic Trade and Investment Partnership (TTIP). Texts adopted in Strasbourg, 2(d) (xv). http://www.europarl.europa.eu/sides/getDoc.do?pubRef=-//EP//TEXT+TA+P8-TA-2015-0252+0+DOC+XML+V0//EN&language=EN

European Union, 1995-2013. *Further Expansion History 2000-2009*. Accessed April 23, 2019. http://europa.eu/about-eu/eu-history/2000-2009/index_en.htm

European Union. "Contact: Questions about the EU – Telephone, Email, Contact points in your country". Accessed May 5, 2016. http://europa.eu/contact/index_en.htm

European Union. "Legislative package for banking supervision in the Eurozone". September 9, 2013. Retrieved November 21, 2013. http://europa.eu/rapid/press-release_MEMO-13-780_en.htm

European Union Publications Office. "Inside TTIP". *Directorate-General for Trade*. Accessed May 10, 2016, p. 51. http://bookshop.europa.eu/en/inside-ttip-pbNG0215971/?CatalogCategoryID=m0sKABstN9AAAAEjuJAY4e5L

European Union. "TTIP – Trade in Services, Investment and E-Commerce: Chapter II – Investment". European Commission, November 12, 2015. http://trade.ec.europa.eu/doclib/docs/2015/november/tradoc_153955.pdf

Fabbricotti, Alberta, Joost Pauwelyn, and Gabrielle Marceau. "Multilateralizing Regionalism and the Future Architecture of International Trade Law as a System of Law." *American Society of International Law. Proceedings of the Annual Meeting*, 2009, 119-28.

Fawcett, Louise L'Estrange., and Andrew Hurrell. *Regionalism in World Politics: Regional Organization and International Order*. Oxford [England]; New York: Oxford University Press, 1995.

Federation of German Industries (BDI). "BDI-Konferenz zur transatlantischen Handels- und Investitionspartnerschaft (TTIP)". *Conference Statement (BDI Nachrichten)*. November 12, 2013. Accessed May 5, 2016. http://bdi.eu/artikel/news/bdi-konferenz-zur-transatlantischen-handels-und-investitionspartnerschaft-ttip-imagegallery/

Federation of German Industries (BDI). "Massive uncertainty in the economy". November 9, 2016. Accessed April 23, 2019. http://bdi.eu/artikel/news/bdi-konferenz-zur-transatlantischen-handels-und-investitionspartnerschaft-ttip-imagegallery/

Felbermayr, Gabriel. 2013. "TTIP, Macroeconomic Effects", *GED-Studie*. Gütersloh: Bertelsmann-Stiftung, June 17, 2013. Accessed May 26, 2016. http://www.bfna.org/sites/default/files/TTIP-GED%20study%2017June%202013.pdf

Fiorentino, Roberto V., Christelle Toqueboeuf, and Luis Verdeja. *The Changing Landscape of Regional Trade Agreements: 2006 Update*. Geneva, Switzerland: World Trade Organization, 2007.

Florida House of Representatives. House Resolution HR 9093. May 1, 2014.

Francois, Joseph, Miriam Manchin, Hanna Norberg, Olga Pindyuk & Patrick Tomberger, 2013. "Reducing Transatlantic Barriers to Trade and Investment: An Economic Assessment," Institute for International and Developmental Economics Discussion Papers 20130401.

Frankfurter Allgemeine Zeitung. *Auftakt zum "knallgrünen" Europawahlkampf.* Nr. 32, February 7, 2014, page 16.

Frankfurter Allgemeine Zeitung. *Das Vertrauen in die EU waechst.* July 17, 2013. Accessed May 8, 2016. http://www.faz.net/suche/?query=eu+integration&suchbegriffImage.x=0&suchbegriffImage.y=0&resultsPerPage=20

Frankfurter Allgemeine Zeitung. "Die Handelsgespräche mit Amerika". Nr. 38, February 14, 2014, page 13.

Frankfurter Allgemeine Zeitung. "Eurokrise". November 14, 2013. Retrieved November 16, 2013. http://www.faz.net/aktuell/wirtschaft/eurokrise/spanien/eurokrise-auch-spanien-braucht-keine-weitere-hilfe-mehr-12665277.html

Frankfurter Allgemeine Zeitung. EUROSTAT 1/2014, page 8/20, Nr. 69, March 22, 2014, Prof. Dr. Hermann Simon, Marketing-Lehrstuhl Uni Mainz.

Frankfurter Allgemeine Zeitung. "Handelsgespräche mit Amerika stocken". Nr. 38, February 14, 2014, page 13.

Frankfurter Allgemeine Zeitung. "Unternehmen machen den Atlantik zur Brücke". Nr. 139. June 19, 2013, page 16.

Friedman, Thomas L. *The Lexus and the Olive Tree.* First Anchor Books ed. New York: Anchor Books, 2000.

Froman, Michael. "Getting Trade Right". *Democracy Journal of Ideas,* Nr. 38, Fall 2015. https://democracyjournal.org/magazine/38/getting-trade-right-1/

German Federal Foreign Office. "Towards a transatlantic economic agreement – the Transatlantic Trade and Investment Partnership (TTIP)". January 29, 2016. http://www.auswaertiges-amt.de/EN/Aussenpolitik/RegionaleSchwerpunkte/USA/TTIP.html?searchArchive=0&searchEngineQueryString=ttip&searchIssued=0&searchIssuedAfter=27.11.2013

German Federal Ministry for Economic Affairs and Energy. "Frequently asked questions about the Transatlantic Trade and Investment Partnership". Accessed May 11, 2016. http://www.bmwi.de/EN/Topics/Foreign-trade/TTIP/faq.html

German Missions in the United States. *TTIP Could Create almost 2 Million New Jobs in the US and Germany.* Jun 19, 2013. Accessed May 9, 2016. http://www.germany.info/Vertretung/usa/en/pr/PWash/2013/06/19-Bertelsmann.html

German Missions in the United States. *TTIP Offers Prospects for More Growth and Employment.* Jul 8, 2013. Accessed May 31, 2016. http://www.germany.info/Vertretung/usa/en/__pr/P__Wash/2013/07/08-TTIP-Start.html

German Missions in the United States. "Industries of the Future: Economic Growth through Clean Energy and Clean Jobs". May 9, 2011. Accessed May 1, 2016. http://www.germany.info/Vertretung/usa/en/__events/TCB/2011/05/09__Clean_20Industries_20Atlanta__S.html

German Missions in the United States. "*Renewable Energies Already Provide More Than 380,000 Jobs in Germany.*" *April 13, 2012.* Accessed May 1, 2016. http://www.germany.info/Vertretung/usa/en/__pr/GIC/2012/04/13Renewables.html

Goergmaier, Dietmar. "Aufbau der Sozialen Marktwirtschaft in Deutschland – Vorbildwirkung fuer die Umsetzung in der Europaeischen Union". *Die Europaeische Union zwischen Krise und Aufbruch – Wohin driftet Europa?* Staatswissenschaftliches Forum e.V. Tagunsberichte 5/2019.

Goergmaier, Melanie. "The Transatlantic Trade and Investment Partnership (TTIP): Consequences for the European Union and the United States." Jean Monnet/ Robert Schuman Paper Series, European Union Center/ Jean Monnet Chair, Coral Gables, FL, Vol.19, Special, May 2016. https://eucenter.as.miami.edu/_assets/pdf/goergmaier_ttip.pdf

Gilpin, Robert., and Gilpin, Jean M. *The Political Economy of International Relations.*

Princeton, N.J.: Princeton University Press, 1987.

Global Economic Dynamics. "Transatlantic Trade and Investment Partnership (TTIP). Who benefits from a free trade deal?" *Bertelsmann Stiftung.* June 17, 2013. Accessed May 30, 2016. http://www.bfna.org/sites/default/files/TTIP-GED%20study%2017June%202013.pdf

González, Elizabeth. "Chart: Trade Flows in the New TPP-11". Americas Society. Council of the Americas. March 14, 2018. http://www.as-coa.org/articles/chart-trade-flows-new-tpp-11?utm_source=News+%26+Views&utm_campaign=21e63ee131-EMAIL_CAMPAIGN_2018_03_22&utm_medium=email&utm_term=0_ae40703cec-21e63ee131-24291621

Gowa, Joanne. 1995. *Allies, adversaries, and international trade.* Princeton, N.J.: Princeton University Press.

Griswold, Daniel. "Bilateral Deals Are No Threat to Global Trade." *The Financial Times,* 2003.

Grzanna, Marcel. "Wie China den Freihandel verschlief". *Sueddeutsche Zeitung.* August 14, 2014. https://www.sueddeutsche.de/wirtschaft/ttip-abkommen-wie-china-den-freihandel-verschlief-1.2089495

Guérot, Ulrike. „Zur Zukunft der europäischen Demokratie". *Aus Politik und Zeitgeschehen,* 63. Jg. 6-7/ February 4, 2013.

Haas, Ernst B., *ed. (2004) [1958]. The Uniting of Europe: Political, Social, and Economic Forces, 1950–1957 (3rd ed.). Notre Dame, Indiana: University of Notre Dame Press.*

Haas, Ernst B. (1964), *Beyond the Nation-State – Functionalism and International Organization* (Stanford, Cal.: Stanford University Press).

Haas, Ernst B. (1976), "Turbulent fields and the theory of regional integration", *International Organization,* vol. 30, no. 2: 173-212.

Haas Institute, University of California, Berkley. "Trans-Pacific Map". March 9, 2016. http://haasinstitute.berkeley.edu/tpp

Hamilton, Alexander. *Report of the Secretary of the Treasury of the United States, on the Subject of Manufactures: Presented to the House of Representatives, December 5, 1791.* 1793.

Hamilton, Daniel. 2014. *The Geostrategic Aspects of a Transatlantic Trade and Investment Partnership.* Brookings Institution Press. Center for Transatlantic Relations, John Hopkins University SAIS, page 4. Accessed May 13, 2016. http://transatlantic.saisjhu.edu/publications/books/The%20Geopolitics%20of%20TTIP/Hamilton_TTIP_geopolitics_summary_final.pdf

Hamilton, Daniel and Joseph Quinlan. *The 50 U.S. States: European-Related Jobs, Trade and Investment.* John Hopkins University SAIS. https://transatlanticrelations.org/wp-content/uploads/2020/03/Chapter4_TA_economy_2020.pdf?mc_cid=32360aea50&mc_eid=57ee20fb96

Hampton Roads International Security Quarterly. "Final Report of the High-Level Working Group on Jobs and Growth", 2013, 95.

Handelsblatt. “Behind the border”. Nr. 114, June 17, 2019, p. 48.

Handelsblatt. “Diese Konzerne sind Forschungsweltmeister”. October 28, 2014.

https://www.handelsblatt.com/unternehmen/industrie/ausgaben-fuer-entwicklungen-diese-konzerne-sind-forschungsweltmeister/10898476.html?slp=false&p=10&a=false&ticket=ST-22469913-jkcJ6FMoAVD5aJgIgyUS-ap6#image

Handelsblatt. "EU legt Verhandlungspause ein". Nr. 15, January 22, 2014, p. 11.

Henry, Sanford G. “Is Time Running Out for Agreement on TTIP?” *Chatham House: Independent thinking on international affairs.* December 13, 2014. Accessed May 7, 2016. http://www.chathamhouse.org/media/comment/view/196234

International Financial Law Review. "Financial Services under a TTIP." October 2013.

Ishikawa, Jota. “The Ricardo-Viner Trade Model with an Intermediate Good.” *Hitotsubashi Journal of Economics 41,* no. 1, 2000: 65-75.

Japsen, Bruce. “Obamacare Will Bring Drug Industry $35 Billion in Profits”. *Forbes.* May 25, 2013. https://www.forbes.com/sites/brucejapsen/2013/05/25/obamacare-will-bring-drug-industry-35-billion-in-profits/#189aca4134a5

Jervis, Robert. *Perception and Misperception in International Politics.* 2017.

John Hopkins University. “*Cutting Costs and Job Creation through Energy Efficiency: Effective Policies from a US and European Perspective*”. March 29, 2011. Accessed May 1, 2016. http://www.germany.info/Vertretung/usa/en/__events/TCB/2011/03/29__EnergyEffic_40JHU__S.html

Johnson, Scholes, and Whittington: *Strategisches Management eine Einführung – Analyse, Entscheidung und Umsetzung,* 9. Auflage, München, 2011.

Kant, Immanuel, and Ted Humphrey. *Perpetual Peace and Other Essays on Politics, History, and Morals: A Philosophical Essay.* Indianapolis: Hackett Pub. Co, 1983. <http://public.eblib.com/choice/publicfullrecord.aspx?p=775229>

Katzenstein, Peter J. "International Interdependence: Some Long-term Trends and Recent Changes." *International Organization* 29, no. 4 (1975): 1021-034.

Kenen, Peter B. *Managing the World Economy: Fifty Years after Bretton Woods.* Washington, DC: Institute for International Economics, 1994.

Keohane, Robert O. *After Hegemony*. Princeton University Press, 2005. <http://www.myilibrary.com?id=275144>.

Keohane, Robert O. "The Old IPE and the New." *Review of International Political Economy* 16, no. 1 (2009): 34-46.

Keohane, Robert O. and Nye, Joseph S. *Power and Interdependence: World Politics in Transition.* Boston: Little, Brown, 1977.

Kindleberger, Charles. *The World in Depression 1929-1939.* London: Allen Lane, 1973.

Krasner, Stephen D. *International Regimes.* Cornell Studies in Political Economy. Ithaca: Cornell University Press, 1983.

Krueger, Anne O. *Trade Creation and Trade Diversion under NAFTA* (December 1999). NBER Working Paper No. w7429. Available at SSRN: https://ssrn.com/abstract=203157

Layne, Christopher. "Offshore Balancing Revisited." *The Washington Quarterly* 25, no. 2 (2002): 233-48.

Layne, Christopher. *The Peace of Illusions: American Grand Strategy from 1940 to the Present.* Cornell Studies in Security Affairs. Ithaca: Cornell University Press, 2006.

Langhammer Rolf, 2013. "Effekte der Handelsschaffung und Handelsumlenkung". *Open Access Publications from Kiel Institute for the World Economy (IfW).* Beck, Munich, Vol. 9, Iss. 2, pp. 75-76. https://www.econstor.eu/bitstream/10419/3691/1/735671370.pdf

Langhammer, Rolf J. & Piazolo, Daniel & Siebert, Horst, 2002. "Assessing proposals for a transatlantic free trade area," *Open Access Publications from Kiel Institute for the World Economy 2769, Kiel Institute for the World Economy (IfW).*

Lenin, Nikolai. *Imperialism, the Highest Stage of Capitalism.* 2017.

L'Intraprendente. "Ode liberista al TTIP". March 4, 2016. http://www.lintraprendente.it/2015/07/ode-liberista-al-ttip/

Mansfield, Edward D., and Helen V. Milner. "The New Wave of Regionalism." *International Organization* 53, no. 3 (1999): 589-627.

Marx, Karl, Friedrich Engels, and Gareth Stedman Jones. *The Communist Manifesto.* London: Penguin, 2002.

Mearsheimer, John J. *The Tragedy of Great Power Politics.* Updated ed. New York, NY: W.W. Norton, 2014.

Medick, Veit. "US Commerce Secretary on TTIP: 'Our Administration Wants a Deal This Year'". Washington, DC: Spiegel International. April 25, 2016. http://www.spiegel.de/international/world/ttip-interview-with-us-commerce-secretary-penny-pritzker-a-1089072.html

McCormick, John. *European Union Politics.* London/ New York: Palgrave/ Macmillan, 2011.

McGuire, Steven, and Michael Smith. *The European Union and the United States.* New York: Palgrave MacMillan, 2008.

McKeon, Michael. "Latest round of TTIP talks boost momentum". EurActiv, March 10, 2016. http://www.euractiv.com/section/trade-society/opinion/latest-round-of-ttip-talks-a-momentum-boost/

Mena Report. "Belgium, Brazil, United States: TTIP Free Trade between the EU-US Undermines the Global Food Security." London: 2014.

Mena Report. "Belgium: EU and US to Hold Second round of Trade Negotiations (TTIP) in Brussels on 11-15 November." London: 2013.

Mena Report. "Belgium: European Commission Launches Public Online Consultation on Investor Protection in TTIP." London: 2014.

Mena Report. "Belgium: Full Support by All EU Governments": *Statement by EU Trade Commissioner Karel De Gucht on the Transatlantic Trade and Investment Partnership (TTIP)*." London: 2014.

Mena Report. "Belgium, Ireland, United States: US-EU TTIP Agreement to make Education More Commercial Based." London: 2014.

Mena Report. "Belgium, United Kingdom, United States: AGRIBUSINESS is the Biggest Lobbyist in the US-EU (TTIP) Trade Deal." London: 2014.

Mena Report. "Sweden: Ewa Bjorling Extends Invitation to Discuss Transatlantic Trade and Investment Partnership (TTIP)." London: April 29, 2014.

Mena Report. "United Kingdom: Financial Industry Associations urge TTIP Negotiators to include Financial Services Regulatory Coordination in US-EU Trade Agreement." London: July 15, 2014.

Mitrany, David. *The Prospect of Integration: Federation or Functional?* in International Regionalism: Readings, ed. Joseph S. Nye Jr. (Boston: Little, Brown and Company, 1968), p. 52

Monbiot, George. „The lies behind this transatlantic trade deal ". *The Guardian,* December 2, 2013. http://www.theguardian.com/commentisfree/2013/dec/02/transatlantic-free-trade-deal-regulation-by-lawyers-eu-us

Moravcsik, Andrew. "Preferences and Power in the European Community: A Liberal Intergovernmental Approach". *Journal of Common Market Studies,* December 1993.

Morrison & Foerster LLP. "Patent term extensions and regulatory exclusivities for pharmaceuticals in Asia and South America". June 27, 2012. https://www.lexology.com/library/detail.aspx?g=0a295b70-e577-461b-99e5-48e0eeeac512

Negt, Oskar. „Plädoyer für ein gerechtes Gemeinwesen Europa". *Aus Politik und Zeitgeschehen,* 63. Jg. 6-7 /February 4, 2013.

Neuerer, Dietmar. „EU-Handelskommissar provoziert die SPD". *Handelsblatt.* October 10, 2014. https://www.handelsblatt.com/politik/deutschland/handelsabkommen-ceta-und-ttip-eu-handelskommissar-provoziert-die-spd/10823508.html?ticket=ST-22414223-jHdccGU9h4EbXlmMUUAZ-ap6

Nye, Joseph S. *Soft Power: The Means to Success in World Politics.* New York: Public Affairs, 2009. <http://public.eblib.com/choice/publicfullrecord.aspx?p=903654>.

ObamaCare Facts 2019. "Facts on Everything Related to the Affordable Care Act". November 4, 2019. https://obamacarefacts.com/obamacare-facts/

Oettinger, Günther H. „Europas Herausforderung in Wirtschaft-Währung und Energie". *Integration, Vierteljahreszeitschrift des Instituts für Europäische Politik,* 35. Jg. 1/2012, Nomos-Verlag, Baden-Baden.

Office of the United States Trade Representative. "Fact Sheet: United States to Negotiate Transatlantic Trade and Investment Partnership with the European Union". *Executive Office of the President.* February 13, 2013. https://ustr.gov/about-us/policy-offices/press-office/fact-sheets/2013/february/US-EU-TTIP

Office of the United States Trade Representative. "Final Report: High Level Working Group on Jobs and Growth". *Executive Office of the President.* February 11, 2013. https://ustr.gov/sites/default/files/02132013%20FINAL%20HLWG%20REPORT.pdf

Office of the United States Trade Representative. "List of Lead Negotiators for the Transatlantic Trade and Investment Partnership (TTIP)". *Executive Office of the President.* Accessed May 3, 2016. http://www.ustr.gov/sites/default/files/lead%20negotiators%20list%20TTIP.pdf

Office of the United States Trade Representative. "Transatlantic Trade and Investment Partnership". Trade Agreements: Free Trade Agreement. Retrieved May 10, 2014. http://www.ustr.gov/ttip

Office of the United States Trade Representative. "United States Trade Representative Michael Froman". *Executive Office of the President.* Accessed May 2, 2016. http://www.ustr.gov/about-us/biographies-key-officials/united-states-trade-representative-michael-froman

Office of the United States Trade Representative. "U.S. International Trade Commission Releases Report on How T-TIP Will Benefit Small Businesses". Press Release. March 28, 2014. Accessed May 2, 2016. http://www.ustr.gov/about-us/press-office/press-releases/2014/March/USITC-Releases-Report-How-TTIP-Will-Benefit-Small-Business

Office of the United States Trade Representative. "U.S. – Korea Free Trade Agreement". *Free Trade Agreements.* Accessed December 9, 2019.

https://ustr.gov/trade-agreements/free-trade-agreements/korus-fta

Office of the United States Trade Representative. "White House Fact Sheet: Transatlantic Trade and Investment Partnership (T-TIP)". *Executive Office of the President*, June 2013. https://ustr.gov/about-us/policy-offices/press-office/fact-sheets/2013/june/wh-ttip

Olson, Mancur. *The Logic of Collective Action: Public Goods and the Theory of Groups.* Harvard Economic Studies; v. 124. Cambridge, Mass.: Harvard University Press, 1971.

Open Democracy. "Cameron Faces TTIP Showdown over NHS." London, November 18, 2014.

OpenDemocracy. "TTIP and TPP: Harnessing the Anger of the People." London: October 27, 2014.

Otero-Iglesias, Miguel. "The Geopolitics of the TTIP seen from Beijing". *Real Instituto Elcano, Expert Comment 78/2013-11/12/2013.* http://www.realinstitutoelcano.org/wps/portal/rielcano_eng/Content?WCM_GLOBAL_CONTEXT=/elcano/elcano_in/zonas_in/commentary-otero-iglesias-geopolitics-ttip-seen-from-beijing

Oxford Analytica. "International trade partnerships: Deal or no deal?" July 31, 2014. http://bilaterals.org/?international-trade-partnerships

Peterson, Helen. "Aldi is fixing its biggest weakness, and that should terrify Whole Foods". Business Insider. January 23, 2016. http://www.businessinsider.com/aldi-is-fixing-is-biggest-weakness-and-that-should-terrify-whole-foods-2016-1

Pharma-Zeitung. "GBI: Sparmassnahmen in Europa beeinflussen Preisbidlung von Generika". *Markt-Studie.* June 22, 2012. http://www.pharma-zeitung.de/gbi-sparmasznahmen-in-europa-beeinflussen-preisbil.4548.php

Piketty, Thomas, and Arthur Goldhammer. *Capital in the Twenty-First Century*. 2018. <https://doi.org/10.4159/9780674982918>

Polanyi, Karl. *The Great Transformation*. First Beacon Paperback ed. Beacon Paperback No. 45. Boston: Beacon Press, 1957.

PR Newswire. "Statement from United States President Barack Obama, European Council President Herman Van Rompuy and European Commission President Jose Manuel Barroso." New York, 2013.

Ricardo, David. *On the Principles of Political Economy and Taxation*. London: Electric Book, 2001.

Ricardo, David. *The Principles of Political Economy & Taxation*. Everyman's Library. Science, No. 590. Dent: Dutton, 1911.

Rifkin, Jeremy Rifkin. „Der europäische Traum". Campus Verlag, Frankfurt/M, 2004.

Rogowski, Ronald. "Political Cleavages and Changing Exposure to Trade." *The American Political Science Review* 81, no. 4 (1987): 1121-137.

Rosecrance, Richard. "The Resurgence of the west. How a Transatlantic Union can prevent war and restore the United States and Europe". New Haven: Yale University Press, 2013.

Roy, Joaquín and Roberto Domínguez (eds). *Lisbon Fado: The European Union under Reform*. Miami-Florida European Union Center/Jean Monnet Chair, 2009. https://eucenter.as.miami.edu/_assets/pdf/lisbon-fado-textfinal-all.pdf

Roy, Joaquín and Roberto Domínguez (eds.) *The Transatlantic Trade and Investment Partnership between the European Union and the United States*. Miami-Florida European Union Center/ Jean Monnet Chair, 2014. https://eucenter.as.miami.edu/_assets/pdf/ttip.pdf

Roy, Joaquín and Roberto Domínguez (eds.) *Towards the Completion of Europe: Analysis and Perspectives of the New European Union Enlargement*. Miami: European Union Center/Jean Monnet Chair, 2006. https://eucenter.as.miami.edu/_assets/pdf/eu-enlarg-book-text-cover.pdf

Roy, Joaquín in "Transatlantic Relations and Modern Diplomacy". Edited by Sudeshna Roy, Dana Cooper and Brian M. Murphy. *Routledge New Diplomacy Studies*. November 2013.

Ruggie, John Gerard. 1982. "International Regimes, Transactions, and Change: Embedded Liberalism in the Postwar Economic Order". *International Organization*. 36, no. 2: 379-415.

Sandler, Todd. *Collective Action: Theory and Applications*. Ann Arbor: University of Michigan Press, 1992.

Schaake, Marietje. "Blackbox Freihandel", Süddeutsche Zeitung Nr. 286, December 11, 2013, page 19.

Schäuble, Wolfgang. „Neuer Schub für Europa". *Das Parlament*, 62. Jg. Nr. 27/28/2013.

Scherenberg, V. & Kramer, U. (2013): Digitale Prävention - Über Chancen und Risiken von Gesundheits-Apps, in: Dr. med. Mabuse, September/Oktober Ausgabe 205, S. 43-45. https://www.aerztinnenbund.de/Erfolgreiche.2113.0.2.html

Scherenberg, V. & Kramer, U. (2013): Schöne neue Welt: Gesünder mit Health-Apps? Hintergründe, Handlungsbedarf und schlummernde Potenziale, in: Jahrbuch Healthcare Marketing 2013, New Business Verlag, Hamburg, S. 115-119.

Schmidt. *Megamerger in der pharmazeutischen Indutrie – Ein Beitrag zur Strategieprozessforschung,* Zürich, 2000 VII.

Schoeberl, Dennis. "CES-Highlights 2015: Bestes Connected Car-Produkt". *Chip.* January 9, 2015. https://www.chip.de/artikel/CES-Highlights-2015-Bestes-Connected-Car-Produkt_139961693.html

Schott, Jeffrey. *Broad Objectives and Prospects for TTIP.* Peterson Institute for International Economics. May 1, 2014, p. 2. http://www.piie.com/publications/papers/schott20140501ppt.pdf

Serfaty, Simon (ed.) *Visions of the Atlantic Alliance.* Washingto, DC.: CSIS, 2006.

Simon, Hermann. "EUROSTAT", *Frankfurter Allgemeine Zeitung,* Nr. 69 (1), March 22, 2014 pp. 8-20.

Smith, Adam. *An Inquiry into the Nature and Causes of the Wealth of Nations.* London: Electric Book, 2001.

Spielgel. "Apple-Uhr soll die Sonne nutzen". February 3, 2014. https://www.spiegel.de/netzwelt/gadgets/iwatch-apple-uhr-soll-die-gesundheit-foerdern-und-die-sonne-nutzen-a-950781.html

Stiglitz, Joseph E. *Globalization and its discontents.* 2017.

Stiglitz, Joseph E. *The Price of Inequality.* First ed. New York: W.W. Norton &, 2012.

Statista. "Potentielle Umsatzeinbussen der weltweiten Pharmaindustrie aufgrund auslaufender Arzneimittelpatente in den Jahren 2006 bis 2024". Accessed December 9, 2019. https://de.statista.com/statistik/daten/studie/246868/umfrage/umsatzeinbussen-der-pharmaindustrie-aufgrund-auslaufender-arzneimittelpatente/

Statista. "USA: Altersstruktur von 2008 bis 2018". September 10, 2019. https://de.statista.com/statistik/daten/studie/165801/umfrage/altersstruktur-der-usa/

Stratmann. *Der Zusammenhang zwischen Wertschöpfungsorganisation und strategischen Wettbewerbsvorteilen - Eine auf Fallstudien basierende strategische Analyse am Beispiel der europäischen Automobilwirtschaft.* 2010.

Süddeutsche Zeitung. "Befürchtungen von Marietje Schaake, Mitglied des Europäischen Parlaments", in "Blackbox Freihandel", Nr. 286, December 11, 2013, p. 19.

Süddeutsche Zeitung. „Das Grundrecht auf ungestörte Investitionen". Nr. 92, April 22, 2014, page 4.

Süddeutsche Zeitung. "Es gibt keinen Grund, Angst zu haben". Nr. 13, January 17, 2014, p. 7.

The Economist. *Free trade across the Atlantic: Come on, TTIP.* February 16, 2013. http://www.economist.com/news/leaders/21571890-good-idea-state-union-address-business-should-rush-support-come-ttip

The Hill. *TTIP advice to Obama from four former USTRs.* December 20, 2013.

http://thehill.com/blogs/congress-blog/foreign-policy/193682-ttip-advice-to-obama-from-four-former-ustrs

The White House, Office of the Press Secretary. "Remarks by President Obama and Chancellor Merkel in Joint Press Conference". Schloss Herrenhausen in Hannover, Germany. April 24, 2016. https://www.whitehouse.gov/the-press-office/2016/04/24/remarks-president-obama-and-chancellor-merkel-joint-press-conference

The White House. *Statement from United States President Barack Obama, European Council President Herman Van Rompuy and European Commission President Jose Manuel Barroso.* February 13, 2013. https://obamawhitehouse.archives.gov/the-press-office/2013/02/13/statement-united-states-president-barack-obama-european-council-president

United States of America. Department of Commerce. International Trade Administration. "Transatlantic Trade and Investment Partnership (TTIP)". September 27, 2013. http://www.trade.gov/mas/ian/tradeagreements/fta/tg_ian_005287.asp

Vavrik, Peter. "Contribution of the European Parliament to multilevel governance".

European Parliamentary Research Service, PE 599.350 – March 2017.

Vega Canovas, Gustavo. "The Mexico-European Union Free Trade Agreement, NAFTA and TTIP", in Joaquin Roy and Roberto Dominguez: *The TTIP*, 2014, pages 151-171.

Viner, Jacob. "Power Versus Plenty as Objectives of Foreign Policy in the Seventeenth and Eighteenth Centuries." *World Politics* 1, no. 1. October 1948: 1-29.

Wahlers, Gerhard (ed.). *The United States of America and the European Union.* Washington, DC: Center for Transatlantic Relations/Konrad Adenauer Foundation, 2007.

Wendt, Alexander. "Anarchy Is What States Make of It: The Social Construction of Power Politics". *Theories of International Relations, 2008.* 301-335.

Wendt, Alexander. *Social Theory of International Politics.* New York: Cambridge University Press, 2014.

Wesemann, Kristin. "Gemeinsam einsam: Südamerikanische Bündnisse MERCOSUR und UNASUR in der Krise". Berlin: *Auslandsinformation der Konrad-Adenauer-Stiftung,* February 2014. http://www.kas.de/wf/de/33.36787/

Wesemann, Kristin. "South American Alliances Mercosur and Unasur face crisis". *Konrad-Adenauer-Stiftung International Reports.* February 2014. https://www.kas.de/documents/252038/253252/7_dokument_dok_pdf_36787_2.pdf/f6d81e46-4d24-0923-4ba1-788f12ddbdb2?version=1.0&t=1539654628782

White House Fact Sheet: Transatlantic Trade and Investment Partnership (T-TIP), Executive Office of the President. Accessed May 11, 2016. www.ustr.gov/about-us/press-office/fact-sheets/20B/june/wh-ttip

White House Office of the Press Secretary. US President Bush, February 19, 2005.

https://georgewbush-whitehouse.archives.gov/news/releases/2005/02/text/20050219.html

World Trade Organization. *Members and Observers.* Accessed May 1, 2019. https://www.wto.org/english/thewto_e/whatis_e/tif_e/org6_e.htm

World Trade Organization. "Principles of the trading system". Accessed May 11, 2016. https://www.wto.org/english/thewto_e/whatis_e/tif_e/fact2_e.htm

World Trade Organization. "Regional Trade Agreements". *Database.* Accessed December 9, 2019. http://rtais.wto.org/UI/publicsummarytable.aspx

World Trade Organization. “Regional Trade Agreements”. Accessed December 9, 2019.
https://www.wto.org/english/tratop_e/region_e/region_e.htm#facts

World Trade Organization. “Trade-Related Aspects of Intellectual Property Rights”. *Trade Topics.* Accessed December 9, 2019. https://www.wto.org/english/tratop_e/trips_e/trips_e.htm

World Trade Organization. “Understanding the WTO Agreement on Sanitary and Phytosanitary Measures”. May 1998. https://www.wto.org/english/tratop_e/sps_e/spsund_e.htm

Zoellick, Robert. "US Trade Strategy and European Interests." *CESifo Forum* 4, no. 3 (2003): 18-23.

Zuesse, Eric. “Harry Reid Effectively Kills Obama’s TPP and TTIP International Trade Deals”. *OpEdNews,* January 30, 2014. http://www.opednews.com/articles/Harry-Reid-Effectively-Kil-by-Eric-Zuesse-Corporate-Accountability_Corporate-Corruption-Crime_International-Trade-Agreements_President-Barack-Obama-POTUS-140130-857.html

VITA

Melanie Goergmaier was born and raised in Munich, Germany. She received her elementary education at Gröbenbachschule in Gröbenzell and her secondary education at High School Gröbenzell. She holds a Bachelor of Science Degree in Business Administration from Catawba College in North Carolina as well as a Master's Degree in Business Administration from Elon University in North Carolina. As a European Union citizen, she has participated in and/ or taught in numerous global study abroad programs in France, Spain, Australia, Jamaica, Costa Rica, Chile, and Argentina.

Melanie Goergmaier was a Ph.D. Candidate as well as a Graduate Teaching and Research Assistant for the European Union Center at the University of Miami Department in International Studies until she graduated with her Ph.D. from the University of Miami in May 2020. Her specializations are International Relations and International Political Economy with a focus on European Union Studies and Trade Politics. She has been working and teaching in Higher Education in both Europe and the United States since 2007.